REEL WORLD

REEL WORLD

AN ANTHROPOLOGY OF CREATION

ANAND PANDIAN

With a foreword by Walter Murch

DUKE UNIVERSITY PRESS

Durham and London

2015

Printed in the United States of
America on acid-free paper ∞
Designed by Amy Ruth Buchanan
Typeset in Chaparral Pro by
Tseng Information Systems, Inc.

Library of Congress Cataloging-in-Publication Data
Pandian, Anand, author.
Reel world : an anthropology of creation / Anand Pandian ;
with a foreword by Walter Murch.
pages cm
Includes bibliographical references and index.
ISBN 978-0-8223-5957-9 (hardcover : alk. paper)
ISBN 978-0-8223-6000-1 (pbk. : alk. paper)
ISBN 978-0-8223-7516-6 (e-book)
1. Motion picture industry—India—Tamil Nadu.
2. Motion pictures—Production and direction—India—
Tamil Nadu. 3. Motion pictures—Social aspects—
India—Tamil Nadu. I. Title.
PN1993.5.I8P274 2015
791.430954′82—dc23
2015017940

Cover art: Film shoot for *Sarvam* (2009), directed by
Vishnu Vardhan. Photo by the author.

DUKE UNIVERSITY PRESS GRATEFULLY ACKNOWLEDGES THE
SUPPORT OF JOHNS HOPKINS UNIVERSITY, KRIEGER SCHOOL
OF ARTS AND SCIENCES, WHICH PROVIDED FUNDS TOWARD
THE PUBLICATION OF THIS BOOK.

Chapter 8, "Light," was previously published as "In the Light of
Experience: An Indian Cameraman," in *Bioscope* 4 (1): 81–92.
Chapter 11, "Imagination," was previously published as "Imagination:
Cinematic, Anthropological," in *Social Text* 30 (4): 127–41.

FOR SANCHITA

CONTENTS

Walter Murch

Set this giant dream machine in motion! Wrestle with the angel of light, the angel of machines, the angels of space and time!
—Jean Cocteau, director, on the first day of production of *Beauty and the Beast* (1946)

Cocteau's invocation hints not only at the multifaceted nature of cinema, but also at the mysterious forces that seem to govern it. I am sure that the Tamil filmmakers we meet in Anand Pandian's book *Reel World* would immediately approve of Cocteau's prayer, so similar to some of their own, recognizing Cocteau as a brother filmmaker despite his distance from them in time, space, and culture. In fact, his angels of Space, Light, and Time lend their names to three of *Reel World*'s chapter headings.

This mutual recognition between filmmakers seems universal: whenever I have traveled for work or teaching—in Europe, South America, India, Africa, Southeast Asia—I have experienced an immediate familial bond with the local filmmakers, an understanding that we belong to the same tribe, so to speak, and that this tribal alliance trumps the cultural or linguistic differences that would nominally separate us. I certainly found the same thing in the pages of this marvelous book, which brings fourteen Tamil films under the anthropological magnifying glass, placing them in a deep cultural context (and Tamil culture is one of the world's deepest), while also dissecting each of seventeen cinematic arts and crafts, as well as painting vivid portraits of the practitioners.

What emerges repeatedly over the course of the book are different versions of the phrase—spoken in wonder, exhaustion, contemplation—"Just go with it, try anything": an acceptance of the circumstances of the moment, but also a leveraging of those circumstances to make a creative leap beyond the immediate problem or situation. This is not unique to Tamil cinema (although for various reasons it may have found its apotheosis there); the tension between control and spontaneity is deeply woven into the fabric of cinema. It recalls an observation that my mentor Francis Coppola made about directing: "The director is the ringmaster of a circus that is inventing itself."

Francis is the master of this kind of spontaneous invention. One example among thousands: Vito Scotti, the supporting actor playing Nazorine the baker in *The Godfather*, made too many sweeping hand-gestures in the first take of his scene with Marlon Brando, probably out of nervousness. The overuse of hand gestures, shorthand signature for Italians in cinema, was something that Francis was anxious to restrict throughout the film. But this shot was particularly significant because it was the first, on the first day of shooting, and if it wasn't right it would be a bad omen for the rest of the process. Francis later told me, "My heart sank: the first shot, and I was seeing the very thing that I most wanted to avoid." What did he do?

A lesser director would have reminded Scotti not to use his hands so much. But of course this would only make the actor overly self-conscious and probably even more nervous. Instead, Francis said, "Cut. Excellent, excellent. Except that I just realized I made a mistake in the staging. Tom Hagen [Robert Duvall] would have already poured you a welcoming glass of brandy." And here he gestured to Duvall to give Scotti a glass and *fill it right up to the brim*. So, take 2 proceeded with Scotti in position, but gingerly balancing a glassful of brandy in his hand. The gestures were still there, natural in their accents, but reduced to the minimum. And Scotti was less nervous because the director had admitted that *he himself* had been mistaken. The results you can see for yourself in the film.

My own mantra for this paradoxical state is *open closedness*. Or, if you prefer, *closed openness*. Filmmaking requires a resolute faithfulness to the plan you have in mind, otherwise the chaos of the world tears your film to shreds. In that sense, you must close yourself off to outside influences. But you must not be *too* closed, otherwise you will blind yourself to the opportunities that are offered up by the angels of circumstance. Francis did not have the idea of the brandy glass in his mind before shooting the Nazorine scene, but he was alive to its potential, and the glass emerged at the right moment as the solution to an unexpected problem.

A concrete image to go with this is the *parachute*, which functions correctly when it is in the dynamic equilibrium of exactly this state of closed/openness. If it never opens, you are dead. But if it opens too far, you are just as dead.

A side effect of this Zen-like contradictory tension is the presence of the spiritual dimension in filmmaking. Because of its complexity (the precise meshing of those seventeen arts and crafts) and because time is so crucial, it is among the most contingent of human activities. For better or worse, so much depends so frequently on so little: a chance meeting, a glance, a sudden change in the weather, a broken wire, what the cameraman had for breakfast. Consequently, there are few filmmakers who are not superstitious. In Tamil productions, the superstition is more ritualized than, say, in American filmmaking: here you will find garlanded cameras, anointed with sandalwood and saffron, and priestly invocations of a *puja* at the beginning of shooting (and indeed at any momentous turning point during the making or marketing of the film). But Cocteau had his prayer to the angels of cinema, and all of Francis Coppola's films, too, begin with a ritual on the first day of shooting: the crew coming together to hold hands in a circle and calling out a chant given to them by Francis: "Poowahba, poowahba, poowahba"—meaningless syllables, perhaps . . . but perhaps, at a deeper level, not.

Tamil cinema does not have (thankfully, not yet) the corporate rituals of focus groups and market research (which are themselves a kind of superstition). The creative talents and film tribes in *Reel World* are operating largely on their own, like Hollywood in the 1920s, using their personal intuitions about what the culture will respond to, what it longs for, what it requires. And the results are, unsurprisingly, commercially uncertain; there are several poignant images here of desolate theaters with films, whose creation we have followed, playing to unenthusiastic audiences of a dozen people. But on a percentage basis, the results of the rough-and-ready Tamil approach to filmic creation are not far from the results of sophisticated U.S. market research: 131 films were made in Tamil Nadu in 2009, of which 19 recovered their costs, and perhaps 5 turned a substantial profit. A quick calculation says that the remaining 107 films, or 81 percent of the total, lost money, which agrees closely with the conventional Hollywood wisdom that 80 percent of the films made each year lose money. So the precariousness and contingency we see during production seems to extend to all aspects of the industry, no matter what the underlying technology or culture. Apart from a few huge successes, the return on investment for the industry as a whole, worldwide, is meager compared to other major industries.

Which begs the question, asked in a broad cultural context: Why do we keep doing this? Collectively, we are clearly not doing it solely for profit, though inevitably a few lucky individuals do become wealthy.

One of the answers is that the matter is out of our control: we filmmakers appear (to ourselves) to be intermediaries, not authors. We do this because we cannot *not* do it. Nirav, the cinematographer, observes, "I am not a magician. I am the medium. I'm not creating anything." Yuvan, the composer, says: "I'm sort of a messenger. It just flows through me . . . I'm just a mediator." The same idea is expressed many other times throughout *Reel World*: the inspiration (the breath) blows through us, sometimes unbidden. We do not create it, we transmit it from somewhere else into this world. A mysterious creative force appears to be using us (all of us) to further its own ends, and we are devotees of this force—resistance is hopeless.

Of the many unique things about *Reel World*, the most ambitious is Pandian's attempt to capture this moment of creation, in writing, composing, directing—the moment that the spark of inspiration connects the individual artist to the numinous forces around him—Cocteau's angels, so to speak. This is overtly referenced in the chapter on music, where the spark of creativity is simply ascribed to the goddess Saraswati: "Where else does it come from?" asks the sound engineer working for composer Yuvan. From personal experience, I can say these moments (when they do occur) are very quick and must be acknowledged rapidly or else they vanish in a pique. We must always, even in our most mundane moments (paradoxically, frequently the most fertile), be ready to see things, or hear things, out of the corner of our eye/ear, and drop everything to seize the moment. Most of all, we cannot solicit these moments: they will come when they feel we are ready for them (which may not be how we feel). As Picasso said, "Inspiration comes, but she has to find you working."

I still strongly remember one of my own "Saraswati moments"—the stunned shock I experienced when, almost on a whim, I put the sound of a helicopter in synchronization with the rotating ceiling fan in Willard's Saigon hotel room in *Apocalypse Now*. The effect was so powerful, and the power was so unanticipated, that the editing machine I was using seemed to have been transformed. I, who was conscious of what was happening mechanically was nonetheless completely convinced that the sound was being created by the fan itself. "If it convinces me, it will convince an audience," I remember thinking. That fleeting moment was the fertilized egg out of which I could construct, in a montage of superimposed images, sounds, and Jim Morrison's music, the opening eight minutes of the film (which was unscripted): a nightmare of slow-motion helicopters and napalm that swirl and coalesce into this one concrete (and mundane) image/sound, which pulls dreaming Willard back into consciousness (*Saigon. Shit. I'm still only in Saigon.*), and from which he then descends into the darker and more jungly nightmare forecasting his future.

Most often, Saraswati visits us when we are alone; and when that aloneness is paired with the tangential fleetingness of these encounters, it is not surprising that Pandian never witnessed—as he acknowledges— an actual moment of creative insemination. It is conceivable that an ethnographer like himself could have been in the room with me at my "helicopter" moment, but the actual sparking event itself was unanticipated, and over in a few milliseconds. And then the ethnographer's presence itself might have made Saraswati hesitate to appear. These things are delicate.

In compensation, *Reel World* goes into much fascinating detail about the consequent development of the original ideas, in some cases quite soon after the moment of inspiration; and if we use our imaginations we can project backward in time to the moment itself, as astrophysicists do searching for the ineffable moment of the Big Bang.

Another possible clue to the *Why?* question posed earlier occurs when Pandian describes attending a public screening of *Subramaniyapuram*, a Tamil film made in 2008, which quickly became a tremendous popular and critical hit. A scene within the film takes place in 1980 in a cinema theater, centered around the release of an earlier blockbuster Tamil film. The whistling enthusiasm of the audience onscreen was mirrored and amplified in the packed audience around Pandian such that "it was impossible to distinguish the whistling of the loudspeakers from [the whistling audience] around us." There was an unnerving feeling of immediacy around Pandian, the theater packed with bodies that "teetered between jubilation and violence."

I remember a somewhat similar situation upon the release of *The Godfather* in 1972. The Baptism montage—where the baptism of Michael's godson was intercut with the simultaneous revenge-killing of Michael's enemies—was intended by Francis (and by all of us who worked on it) to be a chilling sequence in which we saw Michael cold-bloodedly trading his immortal soul for worldly power, completing his transformation into the Godfather. Many audiences of the time, however, were violently vocal during that scene, expressing their bloodlust for retribution in Michael's name, and ignoring (or so it seemed) the damage being done to Michael's soul. I remember that Francis's experience of watching his film with audiences like this shook him, and somewhat painfully he rearranged his previous expectations of audience response. There is an echo of this in Pandian's account of the audience's response to the "crude beheading" of the villain of *Subramaniyapuram*: "Joy was everywhere, impossible to place."

A bit of mathematics can help us here. The making of a film might require, on average, a total of 150 people working for two years, which would work out to three hundred human-years of work. In a single large theater, however, you might find an audience of six hundred with an average age of twenty-five years, which works out to fifteen thousand years of human experience sitting there in the dark waiting for the film to begin. Fifteen thousand years is twice the length of recorded human history. Fifteen thousand years of hopes, dreams, tragedy, success, pain, pleasure, and so on: all jumbled into the theater waiting for a thin beam of light, and a stream of vibrations from the paper cones of audio speakers, to reorganize the audience over the next two hours into a semicoherent entity. All of the emotional power of the experience comes from those fifteen thousand years of lived human lives; directed, sculpted, and channeled by a thin beam of light/sound whose objective power is small (only so many watts, after all), but whose coherence (if it is a good film) is very great (three hundred human-years of labor). The theater is the river delta where these two streams meet: Chaotic Power intersects Organized Coherence, and the former is given the coherence it longs for by the latter, as the latter is given flesh by the former.

The occasional pessimism about the future of cinema overlooks the perennial human urge—at least as old as language itself—to assemble in the fire-lit dark with like-minded strangers to listen to stories.

The cinematic experience is a re-creation of this ancient practice of theatrical renewal and bonding in modern terms, except that the flames of the Stone Age campfire have been replaced by the shifting images that are telling the story itself—flames that dance the same way every time the film is projected on the cave wall of the theater, but that kindle slightly different dreams in the mind of each beholder, fusing the permanency of literature with the spontaneity of theater. In the best sense, a *mass-intimacy* is created where the film speaks to the totality, but each member of the audience believes, sincerely, that the film is talking to him individually, with secret knowledge about things that only he knows.

So despite cinema's perennial uncertainty and the overall meager profit, we participate in cinema both as practitioners and audiences for reasons other than money. The cinema screen is a magic portal that gives us access, when things coalesce successfully, to a numinous *something*, deeper than our ordinary day-to-day existence, and which links us, despite the technologically advanced trappings, to our commonly shared human prehistoric past—and perhaps to our imagined future as well.

Pandian's phrase *teetering between jubilation and violence* hints at a darker question about the role of theater and music in society, something that has been discussed since Plato: Does the theatrical experience (and cinema is theater on steroids) provide a healing cathartic release of built-up tensions, or does it exacerbate the very tensions that it is depicting? Pandian goes into detail about this issue, examining what he calls the "nakedly commercial" and "belligerent masculinity" of many Tamil films (the audience at Tamil Nadu cinemas is mostly male) and posits it alongside the reported frequency of rape in Indian society, much of which has made international headlines. As, of course, has the gun culture of the United States and the frequent mass-killings at schools performed by disaffected or unbalanced young men who are frequently devoted to films that validate revenge by gunfire. This debate is long-standing and on-going: Does cinema influence behavior, or is it healthy cathartic release? On the *influence* side of the question, the $171 billion invested annually on television and Internet advertising in the United States would appear to be poorly spent unless the advertisers believed that their commercials actually influence the behavior of their intended audiences.

Reel World also catches its film tribes at a fascinating historical flex point: much of the audience for Tamil films is still firmly rooted in tra-dition—the book begins with a farmer irrigating his fields and singing a song from a recent film—but the impact of digital technology is rapidly transforming both the means of production as well as distribution and exhibition. The latter is particularly relevant, since Indian cinema, with its vibrant audience participation and heavy 35mm film prints, is vul-nerable to the atomization enabled by the proliferation of individually owned digital screens: tablets, phones, LCD displays. It will be fascinating to discover how all this resolves in the years to come, though the pattern elsewhere in the world is already becoming fairly clear.

On a more personal note, *Reel World* was particularly engaging to me because my mother was born in the Tamil region of Ceylon (present-day Sri Lanka) in 1907. She was the daughter of two Canadian doctors, Mary and Thomas Scott, who had emigrated in 1893 to manage the Green Memorial Hospital in Manipay, which lies just fifty miles from Tamil Nadu across the Palk Strait. My mother spoke Tamil when she was a little girl, and stories of her early childhood were full of the images and sounds, songs and smells of the vibrant Tamil life as persuasively presented in these evocative pages.

NOTE TO THE READER, ALSO A LISTENER AND SEER

This is a book about experience in a world that looks and feels so much like cinema—the sensory textures of this experience, and the circumstances of their crafting. Books on cinema typically focus on films already known for their critical value or popular appeal. They are usually written with the assumption that their readers would know something about these films.

This book, however, concerns a Tamil cinema still marginal in the contemporary world. More to the point, my choice of films is almost purely an accident of ethnographic circumstance: it so happened that I found myself in the midst of these projects as they unfolded.

What follows is therefore written with no assumption that you do know, or even should know, anything about these particular films. The chapters take up various cinematic moments as events in their own right, and my hope is that these stories will hold all that you may need as a reader. Still, though, I'm guessing that you might sometimes want a bit more—after all, the book seeks to think with the tangible sensations of cinema.

If and when such curiosity strikes, there is a website, www.reelworldbook.org, meant to accompany this book. There you'll find a number of photographs and film clips that may resonate with the words that follow here, each keyed to one section of a particular chapter.

These are images and sounds that confronted me ceaselessly in the writing of this book. But I'd like to think that you might also see and hear them, or something like them, even as you thumb through these pages. This is something that tends to happen in a world of pervasive cinema. I'm trusting that your faculties have gotten as restless and entangled as mine.

CHAPTER 1   Reel World

You could almost smell the onions, even before the bend in the road. Bulbs the size of castor pods, pressed into pairs along crimson ridges of dirt. The sun still hadn't cleared the summit of the mountains to the east. Rivulets of water crept slowly through the hollows of the field, leaving behind maroon trails of soft, wet earth. One corner of the orchard field was still dry, and these new bulbs would lend their shoots only in exchange for water.

Logandurai had been out here all night, running the small motor that powered his pumpset. Far upland from the common well, water seeped through the pipes at a lazy pace. Sometime before dawn, the electricity suddenly went out, when there were still four beds of onions left to irrigate. And so the farmer waited, anxiously, for the power to return.

He thought back to what he'd already done for this crop: all the plowing with his bulls; the travel to a distant city to buy these bulbs; a night of watering that would not end. Then the motor started to thrum once more. Picking up his spade, Logandurai started to cut channels in the dirt walls dividing one bed of plants from another. And as he worked, he began to sing— "With all this desire, I raised a bed of soil, and planted a single shoot."

People sing all the time, to their plants, to themselves, to each other. But here's what struck me when I ran into Logandurai that morning, in a tract of orchards deep in the south of Tamil Nadu. He'd found a tune to match the rhythm of his spade. The lyrics gave him a voice to describe what was happening just then, expressing all the hope and desire of that moment. And what made this possible was the popular Tamil film that had somehow surfaced in his recollections.[1]

Did Logandurai imagine himself as the young woman who sang these lines in the film, a bundle of green shoots in hand and her feet planted into the wet soil of a paddy field? Or did he imagine her, or someone like her, singing this song to someone like him? Grizzled, graying, with burnished skin and an easy smile, he was a handsome man. There was something about the build of his nose and jawline—when we first met, I thought immediately of Richard Gere.

But this middle-aged man in a fraying polyester shirt was not a Hollywood star. He was a farmer of modest means, eking out a living in an obscure village in south India. He worked with halters and plow blades, with paddy, bananas, and onions. He and his wife ate and slept on the floor of a room piled high with jute sacks of grain.

These were their conditions of life. And yet, despite its relentless difficulties, Logandurai could experience this life as a cinematic scene: not in a spirit of escape or denial but instead as the deepest expression of its hope.

What happened that morning in his orchard, over thirteen years ago, has been nagging at me ever since. How could something with such epic dimensions, cinema, slip into a space as intimate as this one, this narrow and fleeting gap between a body, a spade, some plants, and the earth and water among them? What could cinema express about the truth of such experience?

EXPERIENCE IN A WORLD OF CINEMA

Imagine this scene again. Imagine a camera mounted to the hood of a car as it rounds a bend, toward the same field. The crenellations of onion peel and dirt captured by a macro lens. The glints of light in the running water, thrown from an array of reflective panels pointed at the sky. The bulb of glass, encased in black metal, arcing down to meet the farmer's burnished face. The speakers planted into the loose soil, booming sounds for the man to mime. A heap of spades in case one breaks. Everyone bustling around the scene, careful of where their shadows fall. Someone beside a video monitor, already thinking of how to cut from one shot to another.

Did this happen? Could it happen? "Any person today can lay claim to being filmed," the German literary critic Walter Benjamin wrote in 1936.[2]

This is a book about experience in a world of cinema, a book about what happens to life when everything begins to look and feel like film. Cinema is experience of light and sound, but many other things as well: hope, wonder, desire, pleasure, the drift of dreams and imagination, the movement of rhythm and speed. Cinema has profoundly recast the scope of contemporary experience. Cinema can also help us understand its feel-

ing and texture. This book pursues such understanding by examining how
cinematic experience is crafted—the techniques that transform ordinary
spaces and moments like this one into elements of a cinematic world.

A cinematic world: I'm guessing that you might know what I mean by
this, even if it's been a long time since you've seen a film, even if you've
never been to a place as wild for cinema as modern India. I'm guessing
that something like this may have happened to you—

You're walking down the road on a damp and cloudy day. The music on
your headphones sounds as gloomy as the weather. As you listen, you can
see yourself walking. Those around you begin to look like extras on a set.[3]

You stay up watching French films on cable TV. You dream of leaving
your job, leaving an abusive husband, working in France for a while, and
coming back with enough money to buy a decent house for your kids.[4]

You see an explosion, a fireball, devastated buildings, and panicked
victims. Someone asks what happened. Dazed, you don't know what to
say. Then you find the words that everyone else is finding. "It was like a
movie."[5]

I first met Logandurai a few months before September 11, 2001, in
a village at the head of a remote agrarian valley in south India. Cinema
here was ubiquitous and inescapable. People kept saying things like this:
"My story is like cinema. . . . My life deserves a movie. . . . Hundred rupee
tickets, and I'd still pack the houses." Once I recorded the life of a middle-
aged man who worked in the valley's grape orchards. He asked me to trail
him through the countryside with a video camera, while he launched each
story at a different grove or meadow with the same salutation: "O my
dear fans . . ."

All of this was somewhat odd, but also strangely familiar. I grew up
in Los Angeles, a few miles from the "HOLLYWOOD" letters of the Santa
Monica Mountains. For years I expected the bathroom faucet to run red
with blood, like the gory Tamil thriller that my parents took me to one
weekend at the Montebello Public Library. Or, there was the summer of
1985, when a serial killer, the "Night Stalker," was on the loose in LA. I
remember watching from a window as my father stretched in the back-
yard after a run. I can still summon that dread, the sense of an impending catastrophe beyond the glass, the feeling of being stuck in molasses
as the inevitable would come, always in slow motion.

What should we make of such sensations, these feelings of being
caught up in some current of life as though it were a film? Some might
diagnose severe cases of such confusion between real life and cinema as
a very contemporary form of psychic disorder, a "Truman Show delusion."[6] One might seek to lead people suffering from this delusion back
to reality, in the way that Truman Burbank finally manages to pierce the

shell of the studio staging his life as reality television in the 1998 Holly-wood film *The Truman Show.*[7]

We often think of cinema in just this way: as a stream of images that obscure reality, screen us from the actual conditions of our lives, disable us from reflecting upon the truth of our experience. We tend to think of such an existence as a peculiarly modern fate, a consequence of being awash in a flood of media images. And we tend to assume that, as critics, our task is to lead people around the screen, to reveal whatever still remains invisible to them: *You may think you're just enjoying yourself, but you're also taking pleasure in the nation this film glorifies, the social class this film idealizes, the masculine violence this film celebrates.*

These problems are real. Critical perspective on them is essential. Too often, however, our critiques have relied upon naïve and flimsy distinctions between truth and fiction, reality and representation, the tangible matter of the world and mere images of it. Must we always seek to step beyond such representations in the name of understanding, and to implore others to do the same? This book seeks a different way of thinking with the worlds that cinema creates, a more intimate way of engaging the feelings of desire and fear that such media make possible.[8] "The act of seeing," as Vivian Sobchack reminds us in a meditation on film experience, "is an incarnate activity."[9]

Suppose that whatever we've done, felt, and thought has always happened in the thick of images. Suppose that reality itself is only this: a boundless multitude of impressions, endless slants of perspective. Suppose that the world is pervaded, even composed by such images: a spectator gazing at a screen and a farmer looking down at a field, to be sure, but also the water seeking a path along the crevices of that soil, the roots reaching down through the medium of that moisture, the pungent odors exploring that space of the air above. Suppose we took all such movements, whether human or not, as image-making activities, as jostling perspectives on a world and its potential for life. The French philosopher Gilles Deleuze proposed a name for this way of looking at things: "the universe as cinema in itself, a metacinema."[10]

Reel world, real world—the universe as a flux of images, and every film an experiment with its reality.[11] How does one grapple with the look and feel of such volatile environments? Our ordinary perception of things always ebbs and flows, coming in and out of focus. But there are those who live more intensely with these cinematic mechanisms, those who constantly work to modulate their force and texture. Say we plunged into the depths of some of their experiments—what would happen to us, and to our understanding of this life in a world of images?

The set is sweltering. Sweating faces, all around, wrapped in blue-green surgical masks—maybe for the swine flu panic in the morning papers, maybe for the paint fumes still heavy in the air. A black locomotive gleams wet under the lightboxes hanging from the rafters. They're rebuilding this colonial-era railway platform for *Madrasapattinam*, a historical romance between a young Englishwoman and an Indian washerman. Sketches and photographs litter the set: gathered over several years, pulled into plans over many weeks, molded into plastic, wood, and metal in a frantic burst of activity over the past few days.

They've already begun to shoot on one side of this unfinished arena, but then everything grinds to a halt. There's an angry rash spreading across the delicate ivory of the English heroine's face. The mood turns anxious, restless. Krishna scans his clipboard, plotting what to do while the problem is diagnosed. The words *Assistant Director* are lettered onto the back of his red Adidas T-shirt. He shakes his head, shares a wry laugh. "Anything can happen at any time."

Anything? Really? There are things I want to ask Krishna, but he's already somewhere else, and I'm just a visitor here, trying not to get in the way. I remember what Vishnu Vardhan, a young director and now a good friend, told me one evening at a café in the heart of old Madras (now called Chennai), on break from shooting a gory action thriller. The phone rings, and he imagines his son lying in a hospital bed. A horn sounds on the road behind him, and he can already feel the truck ripping into his car. A guy goes up on stunt wires, and Vishnu can already see the nails in the rafters driving into his head. An SMS buzzes in his pocket—"Hello sir, I have some 9mm pistols, if you are free, I will come show you"—and he can already sense the watchful eyes that mistake these stunt guns for a terrorist arsenal.

Anything can happen at any time. There is much to worry about in this sense of the radical potential that any moment may bear, but such openness can also be confronted as a field of unexpected promise. This is a book about creation in a world of enduring flux, what William E. Connolly calls "a world of becoming . . . marked by surprising turns in time, uncanny experiences, and the possibility of human participation to some degree in larger processes of creativity that both include and surpass the human estate."[12]

Think of that familiar sense of accumulating and even threatening novelty that marks so much of our contemporary experience. How does newness emerge in such a world? What does it take to make a life in the midst of such emergence? How does experience keep pace with the

boundless change visible wherever we turn? This book pursues such questions through the creation of Tamil cinema in south India.

Wherever I followed filmmakers like Krishna and Vishnu—the streets and studios of Chennai, the sandstone plateaus of central Karnataka, the soaring bridges of Kuala Lumpur, the mountains of Switzerland, or the deserts beyond Dubai—I found a milieu of tremendous uncertainty. Consider the enormous complexity of filmmaking as a technical and material process. Accidents come in endless varieties: the excitement that crests and wanes with every new story; the protean play of light, wind, and other natural forces shadowing every take; the unforeseeable needs that inevitably trail shot footage into editing and composing studios; the constant failure of actors and equipment to act and react as they should. Directors, cameramen, designers, and editors struggled with this caprice, but I also found them constantly anticipating and improvising with chance events. Everything that was interesting about their cinema seemed to grow from this openness to fluid circumstance.[13]

For many decades, across the wide span of global cinema, there was only one sustained anthropological study of film production: Hortense Powdermaker's *Hollywood: The Dream Factory*, published in 1950.[14] The book still deserves a close reading, rife as it is with startling and unexpected insights: "The Melanesian puts his faith in coercing the supernatural through using a magical formula, which consists of a spell and rite handed down by tradition. Hollywood people have their formulas too: stars, gimmicks, traditional plots."[15]

The parallel is bracing, this juxtaposition between the contemporary

Los Angeleno and an islander of the South Pacific. But this anthropologist had rested her hopes for the future of cinema on the eventual overcoming of such kinship: "The magical thinking and system of production which flows from it," Powdermaker writes, "are probably no more necessary to making movies than the corn dance of the Pueblo Indians is needed to making corn grow."[16]

Modernity has long been described as a triumph of reason over passion, as a mastery of nature's contingency. But I write at a time when this victory seems neither as assured nor as desirable. Filmmaking is compelling precisely because it splices together forms of thinking and feeling, encouraging an openness to the magical powers and dangers of a world resistant to human control. To be sure, filmmakers have strategies at their disposal, techniques designed to provoke particular feelings and sensations. All this depends, however, on how deeply they themselves are affected by their own productions. No one may be found here manipulating automatons from the safe distance of a remote-control panel. Cinema draws its force from the affective lives of its makers: from the immersion of filmmakers themselves in cinematic currents of feeling.[17]

Tamil filmmakers are often hailed in local media as *kalai brahmakkal*, "creator-gods of the arts." But like so many of the gods of Hindu India, these are individuals engaged in gambles with fate.[18] There are no systematic forms of audience research that the Tamil film industry relies upon: no market surveys, test screenings, quantitative exit polls. Instead, and at every stage, these films are composed by individuals who take their own felt sensations—however flighty and unpredictable—as proxies for the likely reactions of their eventual audiences. A faith in the promise of experience, however fickle: this is why filmmaking is such a compelling arena to examine what it means to inhabit a world of chance.[19]

Like cinema itself, this is a book that grows from the perils and rewards of serendipity: a handful of lucky breaks and countless missed opportunities, profound gifts of trust at the risk of betrayal, kinships that took root unexpectedly when slammed doors were pried back open.[20] Over the past eight years, I've had the chance to work closely with many central exponents of Tamil cinema—directors, cinematographers, actors, composers—but also more marginal yet essential technicians, like choreographers, stuntmen, poets, and digital compositors.[21] Although I've spoken with hundreds of Tamil filmmakers and many more of their fans, this book depends most heavily on short stints of anthropological fieldwork with seventeen Tamil film projects at different stages of production. Each chapter of this book takes one cinematic craft as an opening into a distinctive mode of experience.

"Our fields of experience have no more definite boundaries than have our fields of view," William James wrote in 1904. "Both are fringed forever by a *more* that continuously develops, and that continuously supersedes them as life proceeds."[22] Each chapter of this book takes up one such horizon of experience to traverse and explore: imagination, for example, or color, voice, and love. The first few chapters broach these modes through preliminary stages of filmmaking: the scripting of a story and the pitches made to a producer, the building of a set and the scouting of locations. The next few engage different dimensions of shooting: cinematography, direction, and acting. The scene then shifts to various kinds of studio work with completed footage—music, voice dubbing, editing, and visual effects—before closing with the release of a completed film and further reflections on this anthropological engagement with creative process.[23]

Although this is a book about the invention of things like cinema, the kind of creativity at stake here doesn't come from somewhere deep inside those unique people we like to call "artists."[24] The idea of the creative genius is still too strong, too magnetic, too misleading, giving too much credence to the intellect and its intentions. Unlike the "making of" features that come with every well-packaged DVD these days, the voices and views of filmmakers here are constantly swamped by the tides and horizons in which they work. From writers' dens to dubbing studios, from outdoor shoots to intricate sets, what we find, again and again, is another face of a creative world, expressing itself differently through every sound, every feeling, every image, every cut.[25] Creation is a field of channels, flows, and relays, an attunement, in the words of Friedrich Nietzsche, to "the world as a work of art that gives birth to itself."[26]

To engage creation in this manner is to resist the commonplace notion that human beings make things by imposing their forms and ideas upon the inchoate matter of the natural world.[27] I try to work instead with "a sense of the real itself as protean and perennially unfinished, at once malleable and imbued with its own forces and determinations," as Stuart McLean puts it, "a continuity between human creativity and the processes shaping the material universe."[28] Painting, poetry, music, dance, sculpture, and photography—whether these or any other of the myriad arts that together constitute what we call cinema, what we find are ways of participating in the creative process and potential of a larger universe beyond the human.

ON LOCATION IN KOLLYWOOD

A red-carpet night at the Nehru Indoor Stadium in Chennai. Almost every celebrity from the world of Tamil cinema seems to be gathered here this evening, smiling for the cameras that pivot from all angles and the

crowds of fans that cheer from the stands, gamely dismissing the flocks
of mosquitoes from the Cooum's nearby sludge. Sponsored by a detergent
manufacturer and staged for broadcast on the Vijay TV satellite channel,
the occasion celebrates fifty years in film for one of Tamil cinema's most
famous and beloved figures: the actor, writer, and director Kamal Haasan.

The title of the event flashes again and again from the video screens
ringing the stage: "World Hero Kamal: A Continuing History." Throughout the night, speakers on the stage look back and forth between southern India and southern California. Here's what the host proclaims: "Tamil
cinema introduced you to our people. You introduced Tamil cinema to
the world!" Then a senior director who worked with Kamal Haasan in
the 1980s adds this: "You never tried to make Kodambakkam into Hollywood. You wanted to make Hollywood into Kodambakkam!" Later there's
a speech by Venu Ravichandran, who had given the actor the title *Ulaga
Nayakan*, or "World Hero." Everyone knows him as "Oscar" Ravichandran,
after the name of his Chennai production company, Oscar Films, a word
that he began to spell "Aascar" when the Academy of Motion Pictures
Arts and Sciences protested in 2008.[29]

Not Hollywood, not even Bollywood, but Kollywood, based in the
studios and byways of the Kodambakkam area of western Chennai. Although Indian cinema seems synonymous these days with Mumbai's
Hindi-language Bollywood productions, most of India's films are produced each year by regional film industries working in vernacular languages such as Telugu, Tamil, Kannada, and Bengali. In 2011, for example,
India's Central Board of Film Certification cleared 1,255 feature films for
release: 206 in Hindi, followed by 192 in Telugu, 185 in Tamil, and the remainder in twenty-one other languages and dialects.[30] The Motion Picture Association of America, meanwhile, rated 758 films for release that
year.[31]

The history of cinema in India began with touring exhibitions of
drama, music, short films, and vaudeville performances at the outset of
the twentieth century, and silent feature films that drew diverse audiences into the new cinema halls of colonial India. Then, in the 1930s,
native Indian film productions exploded in number and scale.[32] The first
"Tamil talkies," so to speak, were produced in Calcutta and Bombay, relying on directors, actors, and musicians from different parts of India
and presenting songs and dialogues in several languages at once.[33] These
cosmopolitan legacies persist even now. This book engages films remade
from Telugu into Tamil and from Tamil into Hindi, an editor who works
between offices in Chennai and Hyderabad, a Gujarati cameraman who
processes his Tamil films in Mumbai, and a Tamil composer best known
for channeling the sounds of American hip-hop.

Still, the cultural and political distinctiveness of Tamil cinema is undeniable.[34] The consolidation of Tamil film production in the sound film studios of Madras by the 1940s coincided with the rise of Dravidian cultural nationalism.[35] Between the 1950s and the 1970s, the film studios of Madras emerged as powerful players in the Tamil political landscape. Popular films made by votaries of the ruling Dravidian political parties showcased heroes such as M. G. Ramachandran as saviors of the common people, garbing them in party colors and symbols.[36] Since 1967, the post of chief minister in the state of Tamil Nadu has been held almost continuously by men and women from Tamil cinema: two screenwriters, an actor, and two actresses. And the fan clubs that mobilize in the name of major stars operate almost like party organizations themselves.[37]

Most work on Tamil cinema has focused on these political features. But Tamil films also appeal to their audiences in a more diffuse and all the more powerful manner, by re-creating on-screen the circumstances and concerns of ordinary life in the region. One of the most distinctive qualities of recent Tamil cinema is its concern for *nativity*, a word that the industry uses as a shorthand for everyday habits, customs, and spaces. Pursuit of the everyday has taken Tamil filmmakers far beyond the studio confines of Kodambakkam, into the shoreline quarters and slum alleyways of Chennai and into countryside tracts far from that capital city. Most contemporary Tamil films are suffused with prosaic elements of cultural heritage: vulgar idioms of slang and humor, localized forms of bodily gesture and dress, practices as routine and banal as irrigating plants or pouring out glasses of tea from a wood-planked stall.

As with so much of India's globalization since the 1990s, Tamil cinema has also turned toward more distant horizons of hope and desire: the cities of Europe, the Middle East, and Southeast Asia, for example, where some of the films in this book were shot. But, at the same time, villages, small towns, and metropolitan margins of south India maintain a hold on contemporary Tamil film. Cinema here bends itself toward ordinary life, while ordinary life hankers after cinema, to the point where these domains become hard to distinguish. Recall my friend Logandurai, singing a film song set in a village not far from his. Logandurai's own village in southern Tamil Nadu, Kullappa Goundan Patti, was the site of one Tamil film shot and released in the mid-1980s. Logandurai even had a cameo in that production, *Rasathi Rosakili*. He played a farmer, someone like himself, teaching one of the actresses how to carry grain atop her head.[38]

"Everyone wants to be emperor of Rome," Kamal Haasan told me one morning at his house on Eldams Road. "Who becomes a centurion?" There is no doubt something profoundly anarchic about this enterprise of popular cinema in India, recognized officially as an industry as late as 2000. Young men—more rarely, young women—come as apprentices into trades as varied as cinematography, choreography, and editing with almost no formal training. Tamil production houses come and go each year. Fates are wagered on luck and timing.

But there are also many new and interesting things happening in the thick of this tumult. Pirated DVDs from around the world offer fresh perspectives on familiar places. Many speak now of a "New Wave" of gritty and experimental Tamil films, conversant with contemporary developments in global cinema yet faithful all the same to the vicissitudes of life in south India.[39] The work of this younger generation of emerging filmmakers lies at the heart of this book.

A few months after the night that lauded "World Hero Kamal," I attended a much smaller event in Chennai celebrating the launch of a new film by a young director. The program began with a familiar invocation to the goddess of the Tamil language. But then there was something I'd never heard before, a song in praise of cinema itself:

Restless into dream into seed into story
into bud into fruit into language into light
into body into space into gain, o endless
wealth of gifts! O god before our eyes!
O godscreen, whom we call Cinema!
We bow first to you! A bow for the
screen! Our bow for the screen![40]

These opening lines had a profoundly mythic quality about them—cinema as cosmogony, as the genesis of a universe.[41] The poem went on to celebrate famous names in the history of Tamil film and Indian cinema more generally, but also figures as widely dispersed as Thomas Alva Edison, the Lumière brothers, Charlie Chaplin, Akira Kurosawa, and Alfred Hitchcock.

There are many such things throughout this book that might be unique to this corner of the globe, and I try throughout to excavate the significance of this local culture and context. But I also try to think and dream as far and wide as I can with these Indian filmmakers, however crude their circumstances and productions may seem to distant eyes.[42] As the words of this poem attest, there are aspirations here of a global scope and questions concerning the very nature of things.

"Craftsmanship is a mode of thought," Ananda Coomaraswamy insisted a century ago, challenging those habits of mind that distinguished Western art from Eastern craft, lofty spiritual endeavors from merely material preoccupations.[43] This study of Tamil filmmaking may convey something about creative craft and industry in contemporary India.

But we might also find ourselves thinking about creative experience as such—not just theirs, but even ours.

ON WRITING: CINEMA, FICTION, ETHNOGRAPHY

Throughout my research for this project, I met the same question time and again: "When are you going to make your own film?" Everyone I spent time with could see that I was also picking up techniques—secrets, even—like all the assistants and apprentices working on the sets and in the studios of others, waiting for the chance to craft a film of their own. There was the sense that I must also have the same desire, that this madness for filmmaking had seized me too.

My answer to the question always went like this: "I don't want to make films! I like writing books. I'm writing a book about cinema. I don't want to make cinema myself."

Over time, though, this reply began to feel hollow. Why insist on this difference between books and cinema? What was at stake in using this medium to tell stories about that one? What should a book about cinema look and feel like, especially if its focus would be the look and feel of film?

These questions were gnawing at me one morning on the road to Tiru-vannamalai, a temple town nestled against a scrubby hill slope fifty kilometers southeast of Chennai. I was on my way to see a Tamil director, Mysskin, who had bunkered down at a spa there to work on a new script, a story of international espionage.

The road cut through urbanizing peripheries and fields of rice and sugarcane, a dry riverbed and the ruins of a medieval fortress. But these were geographic details I barely registered. My head was buried in the book that Mysskin had lent me, a novella about war in the Caucasus. Here's how Tolstoy begins *Hadji Murat*, the last of his works:

> I was returning home through the fields. It was the very height of sum-mer. The meadows had been mown, and the rye was just about to be cut.
>
> There is a delightful selection of flowers at that time of the year: red, white, and pink clover, fragrant and fluffy; impudent daisies; milky-white "she-loves-me, she-loves-me-nots" with their bright yel-low centres and their fusty, heady smell; yellow rape with its honeyed scent; lilac and white tulip-like campanula, tall and erect; creeping sweet peas; neat scabious, yellow, red, pink, and lilac; plantain with a hint of pink down and a faint, pleasant smell; cornflowers, a bright deep blue in the sun and when young, but pale blue and flushed with red in the evening and when ageing; and the delicate almond-scented bindweed flowers that wither straight away.

I had gathered a large bunch of different flowers and was walking home when in a ditch I noticed in full bloom a wonderful crimson thistle of the sort that is called in Russia a "Tatar" which people take pains to avoid when mowing, and which, when it is accidentally cut down, is thrown out of the hay by the mowers so that they do not prick their hands on it. I took it into my head to pick this thistle and put it in the middle of the bunch. I climbed down into the ditch and, driving off the fuzzy bumble-bee that had sunk itself into the heart of the flower where it had fallen into a sweet and languorous sleep, I set about picking the flower. But this was very difficult: not only did the stem prick me on all sides, even through the handkerchief in which I wrapped my hand, but it was so terribly strong that I struggled with it for some five minutes, tearing through the fibres one at a time. When I finally plucked the flower off, the stem was already quite ragged, and the flower no longer seemed so fresh and pretty either. Moreover, in its coarseness and clumsiness it did not go with the delicate flowers of the bunch. I felt regret at having needlessly ruined a flower which had been fine in its place, and I threw it away.[44]

By that morning on the way to Tiruvannamalai, I already knew this passage well. On more than one occasion, I'd heard Mysskin read aloud these opening pages of *Hadji Murad* to his assistant directors, lingering on the cadence and texture of Tolstoy's language. The director's passion for literature was well known; he had even borrowed a name for himself from the protagonist of Dostoevsky's *The Idiot*, Prince Mishkin. "What I like about Tolstoy," he once told a few of us, marveling once more at the description of this persistent thistle flower, "is that his images just pour and overflow."

Look again at how the Russian writer sets the scene for his novella. Someone in the distance, walking through fields of hay and rye. Then a quick series of vivid close-ups: clover, daisies, campanulas, cornflowers. Pull back, and you see them being gathered. Pull in again, and you see one more that went unnoticed, the Tatar thistle. Someone crouches to pick the thistle. Watch it prickle against a handkerchief. A struggle ensues. Then you see the flower once more, frayed, wilted, tossed away in sorrow.

Like cinema, the language brims with visual energy. This shouldn't be surprising, as Tolstoy was deeply intrigued by the transformative powers of vision and visual technology.[45] In his 1898 diary, for example, he sketched a narrative strategy for *Hadji Murat* that would proceed as a montage of successive perspectives: "There is an English toy—the peep show—beneath glass there first appears one thing, then another. *That* is how to show Kh[adzhi]-M[urat]: as a husband, a fanatic, and so forth."[46]

Many of Tolstoy's most prominent Western contemporaries and suc-
cessors—writers from James Joyce to Vladimir Nabokov, Gertrude Stein
to William Faulkner—were fascinated by cinema and brought diverse
techniques of cinematic expression to their novels. Devices like sceno-
graphic description, perspectival montage, and temporal discontinuity
have completely recast modern prose fiction.[47] Writing this book on
cinema, I have also tried to grapple with the value of such cinematic experiments in narrative form and voice.

I've done this as an anthropologist, as an heir to a peculiar twentieth-
century tradition of quasi-literary realist prose called ethnography. Here
too cinematic tones are unmistakable. Recall this famous passage from
Bronislaw Malinowski's 1922 *Argonauts of the Western Pacific*, likely the
most influential image of anthropological fieldwork to this day:

> Imagine yourself suddenly set down surrounded by all your gear, alone
> on a tropical beach close to a native village, while the launch or dinghy
> which has brought you sails away out of sight. Since you take up your
> abode in the compound of some neighbouring white man, trader or
> missionary, you have nothing to do, but to start at once on your ethno-
> graphic work. Imagine further that you are a beginner, without previ-
> ous experience, with nothing to guide you and no one to help you. For
> the white man is temporarily absent, or else unable or unwilling to
> waste any of his time on you. This exactly describes my first initiation
> into field work on the south coast of New Guinea.[48]

The dramatic scene of isolation that Malinowski sketches in this passage
was no doubt staged.[49] Consider, nevertheless, its cinematic quality, the
way that a foreign observer is pulled into a novel world, cutting back and
forth between perspective on that world—gear, beach, dinghy, neigh-
bors, New Guinea—and perspective on this character within it, as if initiation into anthropology was an invitation into a well-edited film.[50] As
it happens, Malinowski recalled his final days here having "rushed along
with Moving Pictures speed."[51]

Such rhetorical flourishes may lead you to suspect the scientific com-
mitments of their author. Anthropology, however, is an anomalous science, one that has long staked its claim to truth on the vicissitudes of
sensory and embodied experience.[52] Many in the discipline now acknowledge our ethnographic works as fictions—not in the sense that they are
false or unreal but instead because they fashion anew worlds of life and
thought, rather than simply reproducing some reality that already exists
(*fictio* in Latin: something made, shaped, molded).[53] This acknowledgment has nurtured diverse experiments with writing in contemporary

anthropology, works that spill into genres as diverse as memoir, poetry, novel, and natural history.[54] The chapters that follow likewise pursue various kinds of resonance between ethnographic writing and cinematic experience.[55]

Cinema may seem an especially intractable medium to think and write with, given the turbulence of its sensations and the jagged succession of its images.[56] Why tether an enterprise as serious as critical reflection to things as fickle as images, feelings, and sensory impressions? Indeed, as the filmmaker and anthropologist Lucien Castaing-Taylor has noted, "iconophobia" is typical of intellectual responses to the mercurial powers of such media.[57]

Suppose, however, that we began with a different picture of the relationship between thinking and feeling, thought and sensation. Think of what Deleuze writes in *Difference and Repetition*: "Something in the world forces us to think. This something is an object not of recognition but of a fundamental *encounter*. What is encountered may be Socrates, a temple or a demon. It may be grasped in a range of affective tones: wonder, love, hatred, suffering. In whichever tone, its primary characteristic is that it can only be sensed."[58]

If we take seriously this idea, that thinking can happen only in and among the things of the world, then we might find ourselves in a rather different relationship with whatever it is that we think and write about. Cinema might become more than another object of thought, awaiting its turn in the grist mill of rational decomposition. We might instead begin to confront cinema itself as a medium of thought, as a way of thinking with the visceral force of moving images.[59] This, in fact, is one of the essential principles of cinematic montage: a "dynamization of the inertia of perception," as Sergei Eisenstein put it, through the juxtaposition of contrary forms.[60] How best to articulate that mode of thought and expression with our own?

In what follows, I've tried to work with some of the formal properties of cinema—image and sensation, rhythm and tempo, structures of anticipation and displacement—as means of thinking through the experiential textures of the medium. Each chapter is composed as a montage of scenes, questions, and sensory impressions. Each cuts from angle to angle on a situation as it unfolds, as its characters confront the shifting tides of circumstance. The import of these successive perspectives often falls into the gaps that come between them, a risky move, to be sure, when it comes to scholarly writing. But I write like this as a way of underscoring the germinal quality of these situations, to try to show how encounters with the unexpected can generate novel forms of thought and experience: for filmmakers and the environments they engage, for an-thropologists and the milieus in which they work, for readers and the narrative worlds they enter.[61]

Recall how Michael Taussig described the montage form of shamanic ritual in the Putumayo Amazon: "alterations, cracks, displacements, and swerves all evening long. . . . In the cracks and swerves, a universe opens out."[62] Here, I think, lies the most crucial significance of the sensory and affective turn that so many disciplines have taken in recent years: a chance to confront and engage the open-ended unfinishedness of life, to follow the happening of things as they happen, to fold the uncertainty and vulnerability of living relations into the very substance of our intel-lectual work.[63]

With these developments in mind, this book explores the affective life of practices such as storytelling, shooting, cutting, and composing, but also seeks to convey in its written form—to evoke, embody, express, exude—something of their creative and disruptive force.[64] A chapter on desire comes as a torrent of impassioned words; parallel columns con-found the distinction between past and present in a chapter on time; a staccato series of eighty-six terse cuts composes a picture of cinematic speed. And, as you'll also see, the book keeps breaking throughout from retrospective narration into episodes unfolding in the present tense.

I fall back upon such devices as means of narrowing the gulf between the writing and what it concerns, as ways of trying to write from a stand-point of immanence, from *within* the world this book is about—to try to think like cinema thinks, to tap resources for thought in the very texture and momentum of its sensory material.[65] This too is a long-standing con-ceit of anthropological science—think of what Claude Lévi-Strauss wrote so hopefully of the orchestral form and feeling of his *Mythologiques*: "When the reader has crossed the bounds of irritation and boredom and is moving away from the book, he will find himself carried toward that music which is to be found in myth."[66]

That morning in Tiruvannamalai, Mysskin had actually forgotten that I was coming, and he'd gone off to look for a nearby crocodile farm. When-ever writing, he confessed later that day, "I have to forget myself." There is always the chance, in work like his and ours, of waylaying something along the way: an expectation, an argument, the indulgence of a viewer or a reader. But these are the risks we court in working with such trans-formative powers, in seeking to craft what Michel Foucault once called an "experience book," something that "has the function of wrenching the subject from itself."[67]

Experience is a matter of experiments with life, an arena of conjec-tures, trials, and difficult lessons.[68] What follows is a series of experiments in cinematic experience: trials undertaken by certain Indian filmmakers and also by an anthropologist wandering and writing in their midst. In fact, I should warn you now, before we get any deeper—some of these ventures are bound to fail.

AN ECOLOGY OF CINEMA

Trailing the making of popular Tamil films, this book has wound up following a series of stories told of contemporary life. Many of these cinematic tales are dystopic portraits of naïve hope and unexpected betrayal in the cities and countryside of modern India. Their spirit often resonates with "the big picture" of these times, to borrow an idiom for perspective born in an age of cinema.[69] Aspirations have a far more tenuous hold on the promise of a better future than they have had at more optimistic moments. Momentum seems to be stalling for all but a few. The "creative destruction" of modern advancement appears to have reached a fevered and unviable pitch.[70]

Many have begun to identify our time as the apotheosis of the Anthropocene, a geological age of human domination.[71] Some of the most unsettling anxieties of the present, Dipesh Chakrabarty observes, concern the prospective chaos of "futures we cannot visualize."[72] And yet we are flooded daily with attempts to do just this, with endless and overwhelming images of disaster and collapse at a planetary scale. Indeed, we might best identify this moment as the era of the *anthroposcene*, as a time whose spirit and mood are most indebted to such images of a pervasive and encompassing human agency, for better or for worse. "The age of the world picture," Martin Heidegger called it in 1938: "Everywhere and in the most varied forms and disguises the gigantic is making its appearance."[73]

Rising seas, burning forests, wide swaths of urban rubble: such images can be paralyzing, especially when they convey the sense of inevitable things happening at a distance impossible to span. Who is responsible for these things? How do we grapple with such problems, without denying the chance for a livable future to those who have had far less of a hand in their genesis? What place do other living beings, things, and forces have in our strategies for survival? Where to seek possibility, maybe even hope, in the face of looming catastrophe?[74]

So much seems to turn, both ethically and politically, on the cultivation of new forms of perspective—on learning to see beyond the conceits of human agency and its sometimes murderous consequences. "What is this world beyond us and the sociocultural worlds we construct?," Eduardo Kohn has encouraged anthropologists to ask.[75] Cinema can help us with this task, help to wrest our thinking away from stubborn habits

of focusing most closely on what people want from, and do to, the world. Cinema offers a way instead "to carry perception into things," as Deleuze put it, "to put perception into matter."[76]

This potential—lodged, in fact, with all such arts of perception and sensation—is a promise realized most fully when we approach cinema as something more than an archive of finished forms and tales. Say we hope to find new ways of reconciling human aims and intentions with the precarious vitality of this globe on which we find ourselves; there is no better way to do this than to examine how such accommodations with the world are put into practice—in the making of, say, a modern human artifact as powerful and complex as cinema.

"The creature that wins against its environment destroys itself," Gregory Bateson observed in his reflections on the "ecology" of mind.[77] With this ecology of cinema, I try to put the medium back into the world, back into the environment from which it arises, the web of relations through which it grows.[78] A world of agents of all kinds, human and animal, metallic and machinic, earthly and atmospheric. A world of actions that are constantly acted upon by forces and feelings from all quarters. A world of experiences that always seem to turn on the challenge of the unexpected. A world whose reality remains elusive and intangible, teeming with the shades of possible forms of life.[79]

Creation is speculation—with the germinal and unfinished nature of reality, with the substance of what you might call its ontology.[80] As with cinema, so with this book, a series of wagers made on the redemptive potential of the world at hand. What if these images haven't actually

slipped so far from the organic life of our bodies and minds as we might
otherwise think? What if a medium like cinema could actually lead us
back into the world and whatever prospects for survival it might still
bear? What if we could learn to think and abide with these images and
forces of a fractured earth—what if?

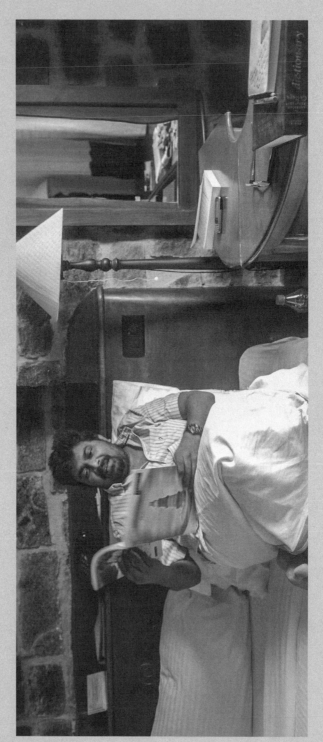

CHAPTER 2 Dreams

I see a wall papered over with handwritten notes. There's a somber man, J.K., lost in thought. He hears a knock at the door, steps out into the night. Someone on a motorbike lights a cigarette. Bushes rustle. A boy appears in a baboon mask. J.K. walks quickly, pursued by a line of stalkers, a row of knives. He steps onto a metal bridge, fingering the nail clipper in his pocket. They crouch, approach him one by one. Is he dreaming? Am I? "People always fight like this in Mysskin's movies," a voice nearby says softly. I can feel the lumps in my seat at the Loehmann's Indian movie theater in Falls Church, Virginia. On the screen, someone else has fallen to the stoic man and his diminutive blade.

································ ⊢ ································

From the very beginnings of cinema, films have felt like dreams. Bodies at rest in the darkness of some space, plunged into reverie by a fragmentary stream of images—"Every dream becomes real, uncanny ghosts appear from nothing and disappear into nothing, mermaids swim through the waves, and little elves climb out of the Easter lilies," the psychologist Hugo Munsterberg mused in 1916.[1]

Many of the earliest American and European films promised their audiences a magical means of gazing into the hidden worlds of sleepers and dreamers.[2] But for film critics, the trancelike quality of cinematic spectatorship has long been a cause for alarm. Take Hortense Powdermaker, who portrayed Hollywood as a "dream factory" in her 1950 study of American cinema, lamenting its "mass production of prefabricated daydreams."[3] Or Christian Metz, who argued that the "outer machine" of the film industry depended upon the workings of an "inner machine," a psychic harness taking viewers straight to the box office ticket counter to seek out their pleasures.[4]

Substantiate

are these alarmist?

We often think of dreams as delusions, as beguiling departures from reality. What happens here is fleeting, elusive, leaving nothing more than scattered impressions to piece together. Understanding itself is often taken to demand an awakening from such inchoate images, finding the right distance and perspective on them, ordering and investing them with meaning and clarity. As Amira Mittermaier puts it, "Civilized dreamers wake up and realize that *it was only a dream*."[5]

At the same time, as Mittermaier has shown of dream cultures in contemporary Egypt, there are also traditions of thinking and working with dreams that take such experience as means of revelation, as paths to an elusive truth, as ways of unveiling a reality that remains otherwise invisible. "Thanks to the camera," Walter Benjamin wrote, "the individual perceptions of the psychotic or the dreamer can be appropriated by collective perception."[6]

How do films gain these oneiric powers of vision? And can we say something about these powers without dispelling their revelatory force in the telling?

> Restless at a keyboard, I wonder how to compose this chapter. Thoughts drift between the screen and the window beside it. In the daydreaming that we also call writing, an idea comes. What if this chapter moved back and forth between dreaming and wakefulness, between reveries and more sober reflections? Could this be a way of staging that unsettling intimacy of dream and reality that cinema depends upon?

Remember this. Sometimes you know, when you're dreaming, that you're dreaming. Watch a film too, and you come in and out of wakefulness, slip in and out of consciousness of what is happening and where. "Every moviegoer will have observed that spells of trance-like absorption alternate with moments in which the drugging effect of the medium seems to wear off," Siegfried Kracauer writes. "Now he gets lost in the flow of images and intimate reveries, now he feels he is drifting ashore again."[7]

Kracauer's words speak to that moment in Virginia, when a nearby voice suddenly reminded me that I was in a movie theater, absorbed in someone else's dream as if my own. Say we followed this movement and its shifting tides, this passage in and out of dreamlike states—what more could we learn about these moving images, about the circumstances in which they arise and the stories they propel?

> *Yuddham Sei* is nearly over. Detective J. Krishnamurthy, J.K., crouches over the dying body of his friend Judas, a mortuary pathologist. Pairs of severed arms have been littering the city. Now Judas, drenched in blood, tells J.K. why. His story unfolds as a chain of macabre visions, the tremulous

dreamlife of a predatory society: a daughter huddled on the road beside her home . . . her suicide after a brutal gang rape . . . the madness of the family keeping vigil beside her body . . . the network of assailants they pursue by night . . . their implements of a torturous and implacable revenge . . . "There's a terrible beast nesting in every conscience," Judas says. "This is what happens when it comes out, J.K."

Dreams, like films, invite us to tell stories. And I too have a story to tell here. I want to say something about how stories such as this one come into being—how such films arise, what can happen when such dreams appear as well. Stories and films, films and dreams, dreams and stories: it is hard to know where to begin, how to proceed from one to the next. But perhaps this difficulty isn't mine alone.

Perhaps it has to do with the murky genesis of all such things, with the obscurity of that place that Sigmund Freud named "the dream's navel, the spot where it reaches down into the unknown," in "a tangle of dream thoughts which cannot be unravelled. . . . It is at some point where this meshwork is particularly close that the dream-wish grows up, like a mushroom out of its mycelium."[8]

Beastly lair or not, the dangers of exploration here are clear. To think on dreams, to think in and with them, is to risk entanglement.[9] Dreams create worlds that are all too real, like the hallucinatory universe that comes into being with the telling of any good story or the unspooling of any good film.

Take this one, for example, *Yuddham Sei*, story of dreams, story of a world composed by dreams. Here's a story about the emergence of that dreamworld, the story of that story.[10]

I knock on the door. The director is in khaki shorts, a rumpled T-shirt. He looks disheveled. "I've been in a mental torpor," Mysskin admits, sinking into a blue couch. We talk about the critics who savaged his last film and the producer who paid for another script, only to shelve it. The room is dark, the shades are drawn. A sketch of a wolf howls from the wall, lines of white on a layer of gleaming black. More ominous are the heaps of books everywhere, piled onto the couch and floor, swelling from the desk, spilling onto every flatness—novels, plays, and memoirs, books of poetry, painting, philosophy, physics, stacks threatening still to grow. "I'm feeling very tired," the director says. "I just feel like sleeping."

Mysskin and I first met in the summer of 2009, soon after he began to develop a story line for *Yuddham Sei* [Wage war].[11] Although this was only his fourth project, the director was already known for certain signature gestures: long and languid shots, scenes framed by partial and often puzzling perspectives, suggestive cuts that left you to imagine much of what was happening. Some of his predilections met at times with mockery: the sunglasses that he never removed in public, or the woman in a yellow sari who danced for a song in each of his films. But all the same, he had also developed a fiercely devoted following.

Black-and-white portraits of two Japanese directors looked down at us as we sat together that first afternoon: Akira Kurosawa and Takeshi Kitano. Mysskin was candid in his disdain for Indian films, having trained his own eyes elsewhere. There was also his unruly passion for books, distinguishing him from most others I met in the world of Tamil cinema. Mysskin insisted that when it came to composing shots, he had learned more from Gabriel García Márquez than from Alfred Hitchcock. He had fallen into filmmaking from a bookstore sales job, when a director browsing the aisles at Landmark Books was so startled by the sweeping suggestions of this eager young sales associate that he invited him to work as an assistant director.

A mood of magical realism pervades all of Mysskin's films. "I always wanted to make dreams. I never wanted to make movies, actually," the director once told me. In any case, he went on to argue, "people come to cinema to see dreams with open eyes." Mysskin saw this interest less as a denial or betrayal of reality than a way of attending to its unseen faces. I can't count the times that I've heard him say, flush with excitement, something like this when I stepped up to greet him: "Just now, one miracle happened."

> One morning, I'm already awake before the alarm sounds. "I just had a weird dream," Sanchita tells me. In the dream, she was in grad school again, taking a class with a Swedish model. He said he wanted her to do a project on the topic of "anthropology without anxiety." She told him this was impossible. "My husband is an anthropologist. He's always anxious in the field." Suddenly, the whole class was at the Grand Canyon. She wandered off, thinking to herself about the project, "There are all these power relations that get played out when you're in the field. There's no way to do anthropology without being anxious." As I listen to her dream, streaks of light filter through the blinds. "What are you thinking?" she asks. Although the images elude me, I have the strong sensation that I've already been thinking about Mysskin this morning.

When we first met, Mysskin was still working from the second floor of a rented house in West Mambalam. Two months back, he and his assistants had spent ten days in a lodge at the southern tip of India, floating a potential story for his next film. Now their days and nights were spent in discussion, working out flaws and loopholes in the structure they'd devised. The director hoped to have a screenplay written and approved by a producer by the end of that month. His previous film, *Nandalala*, remained unreleased, and cash was tight in their modest office.

I had just arrived in India—with Sanchita and our six-month-old son, Karun—for eight months of fieldwork on Tamil cinema. Our time in India that year was limited, but it suddenly seemed that I could focus on just this one upcoming film, *Yuddham Sei*, from start to finish over these eight months, from its gestation as a story to its theatrical release. As a narrative arc for the book I hoped to write, the idea was intolerably exciting.

I put the idea forward to Mysskin's associate Srikanth, who described himself as the director's "caretaker" rather than his manager. We began to exchange e-mails and SMS messages:

> Let me c how anand, we r asked 2 present d script by d producer, so discussion going full swing. I wil c if they hv breaks in between.

Srikanth told me that he was "literally hiding" the director and his team from the outside world so that they could work out the kinks in the story. "I want them to get enclosed," he said.

The space of the office seemed to be built around this imperative. The stairs led up to a narrow landing outside the front door, where would-be directors, actors, and other technicians appeared hopefully each day for a chance to pitch themselves. The wicker chairs inside made a place for newspapers, cigarettes, and the occasional interview. Beyond that hall was a closed wooden door with the words NO PERMISSION printed in big block letters. This was where Mysskin and his assistant directors secluded themselves for their discussions.

What was happening to the story inside that room? The question was tantalizing to ponder, but that closeted space, like Freud's unconscious, was barred from view.

"Nothing is actually happening now," Mysskin assured me.

"That's precisely the creative essence of this moment," I tried to persuade him.

Would his assistants speak freely or censor themselves in my presence, he worried.

"Take me on as one of them," I told him.

Finally he confessed his own curiosity about anthropology and brought out books by Marcel Mauss and Claude Lévi-Strauss.

All of a sudden, I too was "in."

> "An elephant is chasing me," Mysskin tells me one morning, describing a dream he had just had. "I'm running, running, running everywhere. Running through the forest and it's chasing. Running through a building and it's

chasing. Getting into a river and it's chasing, chasing, chasing. I'm so tired, I want to surrender. 'Okay, you want to kill me?' But it doesn't kill me. It just hugs me. I don't know what that is." He's been complaining all morning about being a misfit in this industry, I remind him, about being misunderstood. "Over a period of time, people lose the ability to wonder," the director muses. We spend some time interpreting his dream, then drift into silence. "I'll go and lie down for some time," he says.

The discussion room is cluttered with debris: clipboards and a torn denim cap; a hardcover edition of Hokusai's *One Hundred Poets* and a DVD of *Taxi Driver*; a telescope; a broken showerhead; an image of Salman Rushdie pinned to the wall. All the space in the middle is taken up by a small ring of mismatched chairs, one of which seems to have been nailed together with a few unfinished planks of wood. There's a case of film reels tucked under the television and a sheaf of expense vouchers piled on a table in the corner.

Mysskin is right: it's hard to say that anything in particular is happening here, at least visibly so. The director talks at length about whatever comes to mind. His words are often trailed by silence, sometimes by a quiet comment or question from one of the six or seven assistants gathered around him. Interruptions are frequent—phone calls, SMS messages, the echo of the doorbell outside. Talk slips in and out of gravity and focus, with many sudden shifts of register: jokes about someone's girlfriend, complaints about the air, calls for tea or water.

Everyone is familiar with the "one-line" that condenses the film into a single image: "A detective follows demons into hell, only to discover they are actually angels." One of Mysskin's assistants, Dhivya, explains that they're working out problems with the "spine" of the story—laying elements down, brick by brick, looking for cracks in the architecture. He has a laptop with a draft of the structure, while the others sit with notebooks and pens. Every now and then, Mysskin likes something that is said. "Write it down!" he exclaims, to no one in particular.

Film is "a production of a man awake presented to a man awake," Christian Metz has argued; it "cannot help being 'constructed,' logical, and felt as such."[12] To be sure, the director and his assistants are thinking carefully here. "We give ideas, ask questions, make him think in a different way," Dhivya explains. "We have to put him on the right track." But it is impossible to draw clear lines between sleep and wakefulness, conscious thought and unconscious impulse, when it comes to what happens in this room. It's more like the dreamspace of the unconscious as Stefania Pandolfo has described it: "a limbo of the unborn and unrealized, an intermediate frontier zone populated with larvae, or with sylphs."[13]

I too find myself nodding off through the long spells of silence. "Let the unconscious work," Mysskin advises us. "Don't just keep knocking on the door." Where is this unconscious that the director invokes so often? We may think of dreams as the idiosyncratic visions of private individuals, but people also come to share dreams through mediums such as conversation and cinema.[14] In fact, this is just what seems to be happening here, as one film's story slowly gains form and flesh: a circle of minds, dreaming for each other, and for others still to come.

> "Things we don't see in real life, we see in film," the director tells his assistants. Dhivya, interrupting, describes a dream he had that morning. There was water gushing down a street, as though a flood was coming. Mysskin, sitting in a chair in the middle of the road, sent him to buy a pair of shoes. The chief minister's daughter was getting married that day, and someone said he deserved this tsunami for all his sins. "Very interesting images," Mysskin says. "Dream interpretation is a must for every scriptwriter. That's why I tell you to read Freud."

At the time, Mysskin had seven ADs, or assistant directors: Dhivya had recently graduated from the L. V. Prasad Film and Television Academy, Vadivel had been working as an editor for the Tamil weekly *Ananda Vikatan*, Swami had worked at an advertising agency and at Landmark Books, like Mysskin. Their responsibilities were indefinite, impossible to specify, everything from running errands and massaging the director's head to working out plotlines, shoot logistics, and rough cuts for his films. Directing, like most trades in Tamil cinema, was organized on an apprenticeship basis. These assistants would stay with Mysskin for a few years, with the hope of eventually writing a story of their own and securing a producer to finance its making.

Ring the office doorbell, hoping for a chance to join the director, and you'd receive a list of ten books to read and a request to return only when you had: Hesse's *Siddhartha*, a play by Ibsen, *Chronicle of a Death Foretold* by García Márquez, and a handful of others.[15] Mysskin's ADs were devoted to his bookish imagination of filmmaking. I once stepped into the discussion room to find a silence broken only by the hum of the air conditioner and the rustle of turning pages: four assistants reading from four different novels, passing around a beaten-up English dictionary.

"You've taken a journey—forget your friends, forget your parents," Mysskin told them one afternoon, sipping from a glass of bubbly orange Fanta. He and his assistants cooked and ate together each day, drank together and caroused in the office at night. But the life of an AD could also be brutally exploitative, with punishing hours in exchange for minimal pay and recognition. Mysskin often spoke of being treated as a slave himself in the past, while acknowledging that he was a "despotic" direc- tor on his own sets.

I brought up these working conditions once with his assistant Swami, but the reply he made was startling: "It's not work, actually. It's more like playing."

Playing? "When you play piano, play guitar, you enjoy it, no?" he ex- plained. "Every day, I'm learning, I'm playing something. Some instru- ment—inside my heart, I'm playing."

> With the shuffle of feet down the black depths of the stairs, it's already like a nightmare. A cello calls with a guttural thrum, a sound that feels like stroking flesh. A bare yellow bulb reveals a pudgy man with a gentle face. His fingers play lightly over the gleaming instruments laid out on a table: pliers, knives, tongs, scissors. Toying for a moment with a power drill, he settles for the chainsaw. There is rhythm in the voice that shudders now in terror. You can see that other man, bound to a chair. You hear the serrated blade chop wetly through his arms. A plaything hangs just above his head: a child's doll with soft blond curls and round red feet, eyes as empty as a pair of black holes.

Yuddham Sei will follow a trail of severed arms, packed neatly into card- board boxes and placed on public grounds throughout the city of Chen- nai. The sundered limbs are the handiwork of a respectable, middle-class family: Purushottaman and Annapoorni, one a cardiac surgeon and the other a chemistry professor, along with a son studying for the Indian civil service. "It's less of a whodunit than a whydunit," Mysskin explains. What motivates these gruesome acts?

The question preoccupies the director and his assistants. Keeping vigil over the raped body of their daughter for three full days, the family has become "hyperviolent," Mysskin muses one afternoon. And so they de- cide to kill her assailants, one by one, and to show off their tormented bodies. "With that child, their humanity died. Their pity, their society consciousness, all that died, all of it began to stink." The rancid image appeals to him—"Write it!" he exclaims—but the problem persists: "Go deeper into the motive, why are they displaying?"

"They are showing how the villains have behaved," Dhivya suggests. But the director remains unconvinced. "Travel into their minds," he re- sponds, feigning skepticism. Such acts are rarely committed. He repeats the question: "Why this barbarous display?"

"Could this be a warning to other children," Swami asks, "that this could happen to you?" But Mysskin reminds him that these are "ideal citi- zens" who have carried out "something very inhuman." "There is a limit to what I can bear," they seem to be saying.

Vadivel brings up the case of Auto Shankar, a notorious Chennai serial killer of the 1980s. Sundar, meanwhile, the youngest and quietest among the assistants, has penned a suggestion in his notebook: "The script analyzes the animal inside us."

"Let's just travel and see," Mysskin says. "Is it that submerged animal, always wanting to come out?" And what kind of animal is it anyway? A cat, a rat? A lion, or a dinosaur?

"Generally, all people," Dhivya begins to say, but the director cuts him off. "Don't generalize. Go deep. Take a scalpel. Cut it, look at that." He brings up an incident from Henri Charrière's memoir of incarceration in French Guiana, *Papillon*. An inmate beats two others to death and smears their brains all over a wall, after learning that they've killed and eaten his cat.

"What made him do this display? 'It's these brains that made you do it' — is that what he was thinking?" The director yawns. "I will sleep today like anything," he pronounces, before checking his phone once again and calling for tea.

J.K. sinks into a wooden armchair, eyes closed, head keeled back, feet propped up onto a pile of books. Deep in sleep, or lost in thought, he doesn't notice the young man and woman who've stepped into his house. Now, stunned, he can see: they've brought the one key to finding his own missing sister. Was he dreaming, or is he now? Whose dream is this anyway? Books lie tossed in disheveled heaps, nearly engulfing the man in their midst. Do they belong to the dark yet hopeful world of this taciturn protagonist? Or, like the wizard in "The Circular Ruins" of Jorge Luis Borges, has the detective been dreaming his own maker into being?

In a lecture delivered in Vienna in 1907, Freud speculated on the affinity between dreaming and creative writing. Like the dreams we have at night, Freud argued, stories and daydreams are fantasies of unfulfilled wishes. This is why "His Majesty the Ego" propels every narrative of heroic exploits: with their stories, writers continue to indulge in their own childhood play, in adventures that remain otherwise repressed by the realities of adult life.[16]

Is *Yuddham Sei*'s J.K. this kind of hero, doing what would otherwise be impossible for the film's writer and director? In some ways, these two men are profoundly unlike each other: J.K. hardly speaks, while Mysskin is known for his dangerously unchained tongue. But there are also those peculiar moments that provoke a certain identification between the character and his creator — how J.K. calls up Kurosawa's *Rashomon* to make sense of his investigation, or the way that Judas jokes about his friend, this detective: "I think you read a lot of fiction." When they would later shoot this scene of a dozing J.K., in fact, the director will scatter six hundred of his own books onto the floor of the set.

In the month I spend with Mysskin and his ADs, these are elements yet to be scripted. Still, the farther they delve into the minds of the film's avenging family, the more evident it becomes that they are working from the vantage point of the detective himself. Early on they had decided to shift from "traveling with the family" to "traveling with J.K.," that is, substituting a linear narration of the family's travails and subsequent vengeance for a nonlinear presentation of the severed limbs first, followed by a gradual revealing of the backstory. Now their discussion, like J.K.'s investigation, pursues the tracks of an unfolding inquiry.

Late one morning, for example, Dhivya proposes a modification to the opening scenes: Why not introduce J.K. a little later, after three of the villains have already been killed? Mysskin objects. "Who is the protagonist of the movie?" he asks. "Naturally, you have to introduce the hero immediately. We are going along with him, from the birth of the story."

The director and his assistants have some sense of what will need to happen at the beginning and the end of the film. The creation of its story, however, has mostly to do with the range of possible movement between these two moments and the importance of preserving a place for surprise along the way. "Let the characters dictate what will happen," Mysskin says, whenever one of his assistants proposes a plot turn that seems to foreclose the unexpected too quickly. "We will travel a little wild."

There is always something childlike in his excitement whenever Mysskin says such things. And he has made intensely personal films in the past, such as *Nandalala*, in which Mysskin himself plays a mentally disturbed man-child modeled on one of his own brothers.[17] Still, it would be misleading to find in such figures a simple projection of their writer's deepest wishes. Dreaming with these characters is a creative and transformative movement—more the opening of a spiral than the closing of a circle.

"Dreaming may well be . . . a sort of thought run wild," Eduardo Kohn writes, musing on dreams in the Ecuadorian Amazon, "a form of thinking unfettered from its own intentions and therefore susceptible to the play of forms in which it has become immersed."[18]

Chronicle of a Death Foretold begins with a dream difficult to decipher. Santiago Nazar dreams of traveling through a grove of trees in a gentle drizzle. Then he wakes with the feeling of being spattered with bird shit. Later, to Clotilde Armenta, he seems to be dressed in aluminum. "He already looked like a ghost," she reports. She, like everyone else in that Caribbean town except for Nazar himself, has already heard that he will be killed this morning. They share a reality that he cannot reach, as though he is the protagonist of their collective dream. But where does this leave the teller of the tale? For many years after that leaden morning, the narrator recounts, "the cocks of dawn would catch us trying to give order to the chain of many chance events that had made absurdity possible."[19]

The producers that Mysskin and Srikanth are courting have asked for a brief synopsis of the film they propose to make. So, one afternoon, the director asks each of his ADs to tell the story in less than ten lines. What follows feels to me like Kurosawa's *Rashomon*—six different recountings of the same events they have witnessed together. I also notice, as does the director, that most of them tell the story as a logical sequence, beginning with the earliest happenings in time—the troubles of that family—rather than with the events that are proposed to begin the film itself.

"Now look, how does the story begin?" Mysskin asks, when the last of his assistants has completed his narration. "A series of murders take place. An officer is deputed to investigate them." The story is a mystery, he reminds his ADs. "When you tell a story, where you place the audience is essential. The audience will follow the protagonist's point of view. What is happening? What is happening? What is happening?"

The director calls up an image that often surfaces in his discussions of screenwriting. "Suppose we wanted to take the train from here to Madurai. What are the major cities? Chengalpattu, Villupuram, Trichy, Dindigul, that's all." In the same way, Mysskin suggests, they have to work now to identify a few "major transition points" that mark the route their story will take, "what pushes the story from one place to another."

It strikes me that they are working to establish the architecture of a dream, something like a practice of interpretation. Freud wrote of "trains of thought starting out from more than one centre," jammed together as a mass in dreams, "almost like pack-ice."[20] Interpretation was an endeavor to restore the proper conjunctions between these thought-trains, investing them with logical order and temporal clarity, almost like an effort of sequencing.

From the standpoint of this way of working on dreams, gaps and breaks are residual, fissures that remain wherever understanding remains incomplete or impossible, wherever interpretation has failed to lay down its tracks. This is an idea sustained by Mysskin's image of the journey by train. But it is also complicated by other things that the director says.

For the audience to follow along with the film, for example, its structure must remain open and unfinished: some space must be reserved for their interpretive imagination. Too much form is dangerous, even deadening. Mysskin speaks of Kurosawa, bursting out of his hut with a belated revelation at the age of eighty. "I've finally understood the essence of cinema!" he supposedly exclaimed. "The movie exists in the space *between* two shots."[21]

> Akira Kurosawa steps into a painting of a bridge in southern France, looking for Vincent van Gogh. He finds the painter absorbed in the yellow of a dry summer field. "All of nature has its own beauty," van Gogh tells him. "I just lose myself in it. And then, as if it's in a dream, the scene just paints itself for me." Kurosawa looks beseechingly, holding his own cap meekly in hand, until the painter strides out of view. The filmmaker trails him through landscapes of paint, thick daubs of stroke and color. He almost catches van Gogh cresting a path through a wheat field. But then a flock of crows suddenly take flight, and the scene resolves into a painting once more, an image fixed at a distance. Kurosawa, who is carrying two canvases and an easel himself, never once sets them down to paint.[22]

Mysskin is infamous for his public rants and tirades concerning the condition of contemporary Tamil cinema. His own films, however, have little room for lengthy discourses of this kind. The oratorical flourishes so dominant in Tamil films—sustaining, among other things, many decades of movement back and forth between scriptwriting and electoral politics—give way in Mysskin's work to a poetry of visual force. Images propel these stories rather than a character's speeches about what has happened or ought to happen still.

"When writing a story, images must come," the director says: writing is a process of working with images rather than one of lending images to words already formed. But when these images come is a matter of chance, a game that is wagered on terms of their own.

When he was writing scenes for *Nandalala*, Mysskin says, he looked down a tea estate road for three full days, wondering what would appear next in the film. Then, one afternoon, as he turned to face the other direction, a question came suddenly to mind: "What if four girls are coming along on bicycles?" It was this image that eventually opened the followed scene.

One afternoon, the director breaks a lengthy silence with a recollection of this incident. Their discussion of *Yuddham Sei* has now been stalling, often. For over a month, they have been trying to write the film in the absence of certain essential images. The "network," for example, that abducts and rapes Purushottaman's daughter—this word, *network*, is an abstraction they often use, but it remains unclear why this gang pursues young women. Are they pornographers? Why not hire prostitutes instead of kidnapping these girls? And what does J.K.'s missing sister have to do with all this? Over many days, the same questions keep resurfacing.

The director tries to put a buoyant spin on the impasse. "Not writer's block, but writer's rest," he says. "I'm traveling from Chennai to Madurai. I get down in Villupuram, then I have a tea. It's a very important thing in the journey. You have to get down."

Mysskin speaks of images as a kind of sustenance. Still, in their absence, and despite all the jovial play and banter, a certain sense of disquiet is palpable in the small office. Talks with the producers remain inconclusive. "There is a sluggishness," Srikanth admits.

> Mysskin can't remember the dream he had this morning, but certain images remain. An auto rickshaw. Someone crouching behind it, making a repair. A girl coming along that road. Who is she? J.K.'s sister, he wakes up thinking. As the director tells his ADs what he saw, one dream evolves into another. A girl gets into an auto rickshaw. It breaks down on a small road. The driver pulls out some kind of spray. Cut. Another girl steps onto a road, the same road. She walks past the auto, turns, sees a girl lying in the back. She has a suspicion. She quietly notes down the number plate. The driver sees her. The auto drives up to her. She looks. Cut. Dissolve. "My unconscious has spit some image," Mysskin says. "I've thrown it out there. Now we have to see—what kind of line to follow from here?"

With the dream comes a possible route beyond their impasse, through this image of a coincidence: J.K.'s sister is kidnapped, almost by accident, by the same people who abduct Purushottaman's daughter, on the very same night. Tracking one series of riddles, the detective, without realizing it, is pursuing the mystery of his own missing sister.

This may be contrived, even a cliché, Mysskin and his assistants know. Still, this is how they are "traveling" now, with the idea that this incident will open the film. "I'll just throw my dice and see," says the director. And as they talk, other images begin to surface: J.K. standing under a lamp-post, brooding on the spot where his sister disappeared. A hand hanging from a chain, bloodied and tortured. The peace of the city at night, sleeping through these cruelties.

The next day, a feeling of movement is palpable. When I arrive at the office, Mysskin is working out in his room upstairs. He sits for discussion with a bowl of oats and milk. They work through the beginning of the story, scene by scene and shot by shot. "Fine, super," the director says at each juncture between sequences. "It's going quickly quickly quickly, isn't it?"

To be sure, this pace often flags over the next two weeks. Neverthe-

less, on one of these afternoons, they finally approach the conclusion of the film. Another image pursues the director now: a boy, Purushottaman's son, walking away in an airport, stamped passport in hand. Flight will give this character a way to forget everything, the director argues, lending the film itself a feeling of satisfaction. "When you watch a film, it should relieve your unconscious."

Mysskin says something very similar about dreams as well: "The dream frees my unconscious. It cools me, relieves my tension." And he attributes these ideas to David Mamet, from whose book, *On Directing Film*, he often quotes. Intriguingly, however, Mamet actually says something rather different: "The purpose of technique is to free the unconscious."[23] For the American playwright, creative play is unleashed as a by-product of plodding pursuits, methodical procedure. For the Indian director, dreams themselves can accomplish this need.

It may be tempting to attribute this deviation to an error of reading or recollection. But there is much more at stake here than this. In fact, here lies an essential clue to the mode of creation at work in Mysskin's laboratory. The director is doing something different with dreams than the Viennese psychological tradition he invokes so often.

"Night is falling, dreamtime approaching: a process of closing inward, in destructive circles or spirals, is disrupted and blocked," David Shulman writes in a meditation on the dreamlike quality of the sixth-century Tamil Buddhist epic *Manimekalai*, a work that Mysskin too reads avidly. "This, in a word, is the promise of the dream . . . entering the story, releasing the self in dream."[24] Therapy here doesn't operate *on* dreams. These literary visions are themselves therapeutic—they make possible the creation of a world beyond some private wound.

Dreams can change things, yes, but they also make for fickle companions. *Yuddham Sei*, for a time, is mine as well as theirs. I report daily to West

Mambalam. And I dream, sometimes darkly, about a book that would follow the life of this sober tale. "We will churn up something beautiful and exciting," Srikanth promises. Then, one morning, everything has already changed without my knowing it. Mysskin pulls me aside, describes some other dream that has suddenly come to life, some greater fable he has the chance to tell. "Do you see how this cinema industry is?" he asks me, wonderingly, before leaping into that new project and dispelling my dream of shadowing this one. In time, he will return to complete this tale. But I am already somewhere else, trailing other stories.

CHAPTER 3   **Hope**

So I begin to wander from office to office, pitching this project, casting characters, populating the world of a book yet to be. Days pass in the company of the glossy headshots in the *Variety* south Indian cinema directory. "Can you come right now?" someone says unexpectedly. I throw stuff into a bag, rush out the door, but then, in the car, the phone rings again, me just a few minutes now from wherever they are, wherever they were—something's come up and they're already nearly someplace else, we'll surely meet soon, they avow. All of them, it seems, are moving continuously, chasing an elusive possibility: the chance to sit someone else down, to share a compelling story, the kind whose feeling might surpass the sheer evanescence of the moment. Now and then, I see how this happens—passage into the stream of something unfolding, something with an open future, something with the momentum of hope.

.... ⊢ ....

Tuesday, September 22, 2009. Moser Baer Entertainment's Chennai office occupies a narrow tower beside the Nungambakkam Police Station. It's cold inside, despite the English-language signs that hang over the cubicles: "Switch off all air conditioners when not in use. Save energy, save money, save the planet."

One of the walls has marker board traces from a video marketing strategy session: a diagram of a supply chain extending from the company to its distributors, wholesalers, and customers. Other walls carry photographs of erstwhile Tamil film stars in kingly garb and a poster identifying the ten commandments of success: "Smile. Call people by name. Speak and act as if everything you do were a genuine pleasure. . . ."

The chief operating officer, G. Dhananjayan, produces films for Moser Baer. He has a small room to himself at the back of the office. He gives me a quick smile when I step into that room this morning, gesturing toward a seat in the corner. "Today we have a lot of meetings," he says, "exploratory meetings with directors."

We wait, G.D. absorbed in both of his phones while I tap out notes to myself on the small screen of my iPod. Then they begin to come in, one by one—.

Sasi comes into the room with a young child, his daughter. G.D. leans over to greet her, asks why her father seems so tense. She hesitates for a few seconds, then says one word: "Story." Sasi has already directed *Poo* (Flower) for Moser Baer, one of the most sensitive evocations of a woman's desires that you can find in Tamil cinema. Now he's at work most days in a small room of his own downstairs, trying to write a film with a better chance of box office success.

There's a knock on the door. "Sir, Mr. Anbu Mani has come." He doesn't have a script, the man, an actor himself, admits, but he can tell the story in twenty minutes. "Okay, tell," says G.D. The tale opens with a poor boy who wants to be a cricket player. Dissolve, and he's a young man, still running, still trying to become a hero. Then he dies abruptly. G.D. promises to call Anbu Mani after thinking it over. Once he's gone, he asks me what I thought. "It bothered me that some of the most hopeful moments were complete fantasy," I tell him. "I found it too depressing," G.D. agrees. "Enough bad things happen in the world as it is."

Mahesh walks in next, carrying a glossy magazine profile of the Telugu-language film that he's been shooting. G.D. quickly explains my presence in the corner: "He is my associate." Would the producer like to buy the rights to remake his film in Tamil, Mahesh asks. "I'll give you half an hour," G.D. responds. "What's the story? Tell me." But what Mahesh has to say doesn't take more than ten minutes. As he is ushered out, G.D. promises vaguely to watch the Telugu version.

Kumaravelan has a comedy in mind, a story about a pious tobacconist in New York City whose son back home in India shares his secret foibles. There might be something funny about the story, but the man is mumbling his way too quickly through the lewdest bits. Kumaravelan apologizes when he suddenly reaches the end of his tale: "Comedy is hard to convey succinctly." G.D. gives him a warm and noncommittal smile. "Just give me some time. We will catch up."

Siva comes soon after lunch. Dressed in fraying jeans, he has a smell of souring coconut oil. His story has a metacinematic twist: a man wakes up from a coma, immediately begins to write a script to float with Moser Baer. But G.D., listening, dislikes the events of this film-within-a-film, especially its cruelty and voyeurism. He begins to lecture Siva. Audiences are bound to reject this: "You can't show things that typically happen in such a negative light."

Rajan is the last to appear. A stout guy with a shirt unbuttoned deep into his chest, he looks every bit the rowdy villain of his "action script." There is something captivating about his storytelling, though, the booming echo and singsong cadence of his speech, the rising of its pitch to a high and even breathless note with every crucial turn, the forceful gestures of his arms and hands. More than an hour has passed by the time he reaches the midpoint interval of his tale. G.D. arranges for Rajan to return the next day to narrate the second half.

Wedged into a corner, I watch the producer react to this continual stream of stories: the way he leans back in his chair at times with a focused look on his face, how he removes his eyeglasses to toy with them now and then, how his attention often strays to the various screens flashing from his desk.

"Hope depends on some other agency—a god, fate, chance, an other—for its fulfillment," Vincent Crapanzano observes.[1] These storytellers may speak as animatedly as they wish, but the fate of their tales depends upon the producer taking in their pitches. And he in turn is also one who hopes, one who works with the vagaries of yet another agency in mind, some hazy sense of what his market requires.

The producer remains equivocal. The process keeps them all waiting. It remains a mystery whether anything at all will happen with these tales.

There are places in the modern world that demand an almost impossible patience for the promise of the future. India is one of those places. Take Nehru's celebrated speech on the cusp of India's independence from Great Britain in 1947. "The future that beckons to us now," he said to the Indian Constituent Assembly, "is not one of ease or resting but of incessant striving so that we may fulfil the pledges we have so often taken."[2] Nehru's words depict a whorl in time, sketching a present pulled forward by the future already given shape in the expectations of the past.

Although this was an address broadcast by radio, cinema has been a far more potent vehicle for the transmission of such hopes in modern India, as elsewhere, and many have been alarmed by what the medium has done to our horizons of aspiration. A nation purged of its social enemies, the labor markets beckoning from distant countries, even the domestic tableaus set out for dramatic suicidal departures from the promise of such life—cinema casts a long shadow over so many such spaces of hope and despair.[3]

Think of what the German philosopher Ernst Bloch argued in the colossal study of human aspiration he published in the 1950s, *The Principle of Hope*. Bloch identified a degree of utopian potential in cinema, in its powerful movements of wish and dream. But he also made some harsh criticisms of the Hollywood cinema of his time and the swindling nature of its kitschy pleasures. "The happy end within a completely unchanged world," Bloch wrote, was only a tool for "ideological stupefaction."[4]

Consider what happens in one Tamil film that G. Dhananjayan produced for Moser Baer Entertainment in 2009, *Kanden Kadhalai* (I Found Love).[5] A remake of a 2007 Hindi hit, the film opens with a sad young man at the head of a corporate boardroom table, scarcely aware of the heated discussion around him. Shakthi Rajasekar is the heir to a lucrative conglomerate. But his lover has just left him for an arranged marriage, and his mother is carrying on an affair with the company accountant.

Shakthi suddenly picks up and leaves the building, renouncing the trappings of his commercial life—the smartphone, the keys to the gleaming Mercedes, the white tie and the silver cufflinks on his dark suit sleeves, all dropped without a glance as he walks listlessly away. This renunciation of material aspirations, however, is nothing more than an opening ruse. Soon enough Shakthi meets and falls in love with someone else, a zany and irreverent young woman who appreciates the bounty of something he conveniently forgot to throw away: his wallet.

The first song of their romance—a peppy number called "I Can Feel a New Breeze Blowing"—plays almost like a round of advertisements for the film's brand partners. Flush with cash from a gleaming ATM, Shakthi takes Anjali for a spin on a pink TVS Scooty and leads her into an Aircel retail showroom to pick up a brand new phone.

"You're an original piece," Shakthi raves to a bubbly Anjali, and indeed, both love and commerce find their footing here in hope. The young CEO partners with Aircel to launch a new line of phone cards named after his lover, and the product leads the value of his company to leap fivefold.

"Without the hope you gave me," Shakthi says to Anjali late in the film, "my company would have fallen apart. . . . The eight new products I launched, all successful, how? That magic of seeing everything in some other way."

The Tamil word that I've translated here as "hope," *nambikkai*, can also be expressed in English as faith, trust, confidence, and assurance—qualities essential to the operation of any marketplace.[6] But how could something so fraught with uncertainty be trusted to yield an assured return? What accounts for the buoyancy of that slogan—"It's time to move on"—plastered across the film's Aircel showroom? Is there any substance to such assurances beyond the market wares they're designed to hawk?

Hope is "prospective momentum," Hirokazu Miyazaki writes, a way of moving things along "in anticipation of what has not-yet become."[7] Such momentum runs fully through the life of cinema, as it does with any manufactured commodity.[8] There are the countless projections that make up the production of a commercial film and the plans and conjectures that guide its release. There is the diverse field of aspirations that each film must meet in the world of its release, and the ignominy that comes from failing to win a place among these wants. Structures of anticipation—of looking forward, looking ahead—shape the making, marketing, and reception of every film. Cinema depends upon the operation of a market in hope.

Moser Baer's G. Dhananjayan first came into cinema as a marketer of goods. With an MBA from Mumbai, he worked as a sales manager in the paint, telecom, and music industries for fifteen years before joining Moser Baer to oversee their retail line of home DVDs. As an outsider to the film industry but a lifelong cinephile—he often spoke of weekly childhood visits with his mother to their small-town movie theater north of Chennai—G.D. leaped at the chance to produce films himself when Moser Baer decided to enter the field of film production in 2007.

Very soon after we first met, G.D. began to draw a triangle onto a page of his daily planner. "Filmmaking is a process," he explained, dividing up the figure into a stack of five horizontal slabs, "a process of step-by-step activity." The script was the foundation. Then came the cast and technicians, then the shooting and the studio work, and finally, at the apex of the triangle, marketing and distribution. All of these layers, the producer declared authoritatively, "add value" to the project.

"What drives me?" G.D. asked himself out loud as we began to talk that first afternoon, offering up a pithy picture of his ambitions: "To make good cinema at lowest cost." On my way home from his office, I called Arya, the Tamil actor who had first put us in touch, to report on the conversation. "He's the one sensible guy in the industry," Arya responded with a knowing laugh.

At the very least, this was true of how G.D. dressed: metallic eyeglasses, shiny black shoes and belted slacks, a ballpoint pen tucked always into the pocket of his blue Oxford shirt. After just two years and a handful of productions, he was already reputed as a producer of distinctive—if not always successful—films. One of his first projects, *Poo*, was awarded a special prize from the government of Tamil Nadu in 2008 for "portraying women in an elevated manner."

Here too G.D. had a formula to share: "Don't compromise on art, but

don't make arty films. Don't compromise on commerce, but don't make commercial films."

It was sometimes difficult to place the man in the midst of these words, which came as a quick and abundant stream and often seemed glib, even automatic. G.D. prided himself on being able to keep up with everything, like answering every last e-mail immediately. More often than not, in his office, he was looking at the screen of his laptop as we spoke or attending to one of two phones kept always in hand. He typically spoke in haste, reacting impatiently to what I was saying, as though he was talking beyond the present moment that we shared.

These same mannerisms, though, also seemed like expressions of the hope that G.D. sought in Tamil cinema. Sheer momentum—this was how he seemed to shuttle from call to call, deal to deal, and meeting to meeting between Moser Baer's offices in Chennai, Mumbai, and Delhi. "You can have me for the next forty-five minutes," he told me one evening, ushering me into an airport taxi. I was able to pose a few quick questions, digital recorder in hand, before ducking out at a gas station along the way.

Why the hurry? Where did he want to go, really? As is so often the case with hope, there was a certain kind of utopian promise that the producer seemed to be chasing. Moser Baer Entertainment's chief operating officer had come of age in a time that embraced the free market as the cure to so many of India's ills. And he was working now at a moment when many corporations promised to do the same for Indian cinema—to rescue the industry from the pitfalls of its own production.

H

Tamil films are made for an audience centered in one populous state at the southern end of India. With the meager yield of ancillary revenue streams such as audio and television rights, film producers depend for the most part on the expectations that draw the Tamil moviegoing audience (50 percent of whom are young men, and 20 percent young women) toward box office ticket counters. In 2009, 81 percent of the industry's revenue came from ticket sales on 1,357 domestic screens.[9] Everything turns on the promise of a good opening, the first few days of a theatrical release, before pirated DVDs and upcoming productions dislodge these films from their theater slots.

Those who produce films for this market face many other challenges. Budgets for Tamil cinema have skyrocketed in recent years. Financing is difficult to secure, with banks understandably wary of cinema's risks. And distributors, who shouldered much of the burden of financing Tamil film production in past decades, now are largely unwilling to guarantee a minimum level of revenue for most films they release. Until the 1970s, Tamil films were produced by studios in Madras as well as other, smaller towns such as Coimbatore, Salem, and Madurai.[10] Only one of these early studios, AVM Productions, has survived into the twenty-first century as an active center of film production.

Dhananjayan reflected on these challenges in the articles he often wrote for *Galatta Cinema*, a glossy English-language monthly. One of these columns, called "A Year of Buoyancy," noted that 131 Tamil films were released in 2009, more than ever before, but that only 19 of them recovered the costs of their production and release, with hardly a few managing to earn a profit.[11] Most of these failed productions were made by "rank newcomers . . . who are entering for the fame and name the industry offers, without going through the learning curve," the producer wrote. "Let us hope," he added gamely, "that the challenges faced by the industry in 2009 are seriously addressed by the concerned authorities and associations to help the industry grow better than other industries in the country."

It was only in the year 2000 that commercial entertainment won official recognition in India as a legitimate industrial activity.[12] Subsequent years saw the entry of many of India's leading business conglomerates into the business of film and television production. Many observers lauded these developments as a chance to "professionalize" cinema through more organized and transparent operations, greater accountability to investors, and a tighter integration of production, distribution, and exhibition. "With newer markets and the growth of multiplexes, Tamil cinema has become a sunrise industry," argued one Pyramid Saimira executive in 2007. The company owned 250 theater screens in south India and was planning a major push into film production ventures.[13]

As Pyramid Saimira and other companies—many of which were head-quartered in Mumbai—began to make lucrative offers to prominent Tamil directors and actors, established Tamil producers argued that these spiraling expenditures had put Tamil cinema on an even more precarious footing. Deriding them as "outsiders" and "corporate raiders," the Tamil Film Producers' Council (TFPC) decreed in 2008 that Tamil films could be produced for release only by entities registered with the TFPC or partnered with one of its members.[14] This was how Moser Baer, a New Delhi–based company that had been manufacturing floppy diskettes and compact discs since the 1980s, entered the Tamil film industry, through a marriage of convenience with "Blue Ocean Entertainment," a novel Chennai entity newly registered with the TFPC.

Moser Baer's *Kanden Kadhalai* was one of 2009's few successful Tamil productions. The film opened with three dramatic production banners of literally global proportions: for Moser Baer Entertainment, a rainbow-colored comet rushing to join a blue planet, before resolving into the slogan "Hello happiness!"; then, for Blue Ocean Entertainment, the "O" an orb once again that encircled a surfer and a massive, curling wave; last, for Sun Pictures—a new offshoot of the Sun Network media and entertainment empire, which had bought and distributed the film—a globe composed of letters and girdled by reels of film, dissolving into an image of the Earth as a gleaming sphere of solid gold. Three vehicles of terrestrial ambition, all of which had suspended their film production and distribution operations by 2011—hardly the blink of an eye on the planetary scale they evoked so proudly.[15]

The corporate makeover of Tamil cinema never took place as hoped and feared. Most of these concerns—Pyramid Saimira, Adlabs, Ayngaran International—lost enormous sums of money before shutting down their operations within a few short years. A series of box-office disasters forced Moser Baer as well to suspend filmmaking operations in the spring of 2010, and when I returned to Chennai later that summer, G.D. was back to marketing their inventory of DVDs.

"Do you have any ideas about entertainment technology?" he asked almost as soon as we met again one night that summer. All of a sudden, it seemed, so many of his friends in the industry were captivated by the iPad.

⊣

Aspiration concerns the promise of space as well as time, Jocelyn Chua
argues in a recent study of suicide in the south Indian state of Kerala.
She writes of a young man named Abraham in the city of Thiruvanantha-
puram, who dreamed of leaving Kerala for work elsewhere—perhaps to
the Gulf, like so many of his peers. The closure of various routes drove
him to despair. But then, Chua reports, he perked up once again with a
new plan to leave the city for film school in Pune. "This would be his big
break, he assured me. This would be his ticket out."[16]

Countless numbers come to Chennai too with such hopes—to apprentice with an admired director, to study dance and make it as an actor, to
pitch a story to someone with a sympathetic ear and a production budget
to muster. G.D. was often sought out by such aspirants. And those who
managed to secure a meeting were sometimes surprised by what they
found. As a film agent had apparently warned him once, the producer
was too accessible, too willing to speak with anyone, "not like a producer
at all."

He may have been a peddler of candy floss hopes. And it might have
been a corporate ethos of audits and disclosures that was mostly responsible for his exceptional candor. Still, for an anthropologist loitering hopefully with so many others on the edges of Tamil cinema, G.D.'s
voluble nature was an invaluable gift.

"Come in, sit," he would say whenever I knocked on his office door,
throwing various charts, plans, articles, and images in my direction. He
was working on a book himself, a compendium of landmark films in the
history of Tamil cinema, and it turned out that both of us were pursuing
similar leads. "You're not connecting with me, I'm connecting with you,"
G.D. insisted one afternoon at the Moser Baer office. There were "inputs"
that he was also hoping to obtain from me.

G.D. left Moser Baer for UTV Motion Pictures in 2011, a Mumbai-based
corporation controlled by the Walt Disney Company, where, to this day,
he continues to produce films in Tamil and other south Indian languages.
The story that I have to tell here, however, has to do with that earlier
moment in his career as a producer, when his efforts seemed so closely
bound up with the prosperity of that now moribund brand that he was
known most widely as "Moser Baer Dhananjayan."

Inputs and outputs, projects and connections—how does one write
about a time since lost as though its hope still lives, as though it remains
indeed, in *Kanden Kadhalai*'s language, a new breeze blowing?

Hirokazu Miyazaki describes hope as a means of transforming knowledge, of reorienting what is known of the world by replicating past moments of unfulfilled hope on the novel terrain of the present. Hope, in
other words, is more than an object of knowledge or examination. Hope

is a matter of method, a way of enlivening the past once again by finding a form to recapitulate its momentum.[17]

There are many ways of practicing such hope, cinema being one among them. But we anthropologists also have a way of working with the momentum of emergence, in the very texture of our writing. We know it as the "ethnographic" present: a habit of writing about what has already happened as an ongoing flux of experience, one in which lives and thoughts may yet assume unexpected and perhaps even unknown forms.[18]

Let's go back to that now-shuttered office.

·· H ··

Wednesday, September 23, 2009. From where I'm sitting in a corner of G.D.'s room at the Moser Baer office in Nungambakkam, I can see his eyes flick distractedly across a computer screen. The *Kanden Kadhalai* release is still a few weeks away, and he needs to deliver the final version of the film soon to Sun Pictures, the company to which he has just sold the rights to distribute the film.

"Madam!" G.D. exclaims with great fondness and enthusiasm to someone on the phone. Curious, listening as best I can from the corner of his room, I figure that it must be Tamannah Bhatia, *Kanden Kadhalai*'s lead actress. "It's looking rocking!" he tells her cheerfully. "This film will prove you as an actress. . . . You've done the second half amazingly well. . . . We've got a huge hit in our hands. . . . Let's wait and hope, but the audience will love the film."

What begins on a note of praise takes another turn, when the producer asks the actress whether she's seen a film that released recently in the Telugu language. "It's a nice cute film with a lot of action, but also nice family scenes," he tells her, before asking whether she'd have any interest in doing the lead role for a Tamil remake of the film. I can't guess how she's reacted to his proposal. But the conversation ends with his promise to send over a DVD.

The producer as a dealmaker. Try to imagine the world of filmmaking, and it's hard to put aside this familiar figure of both veneration and suspicion. In Tamil cinema, there are producers who call themselves "proposal makers." AVM Productions' M. Saravanan, for example, told me how he puts together each prospective film project as a "basket" of marketable names: lead actor, director, composer, and so on. Or, as another, strikingly corpulent producer once put it to me, "A film is like a buffet—it has to have something for everyone to eat."

G.D., meanwhile, is neither basket maker nor buffet chef. "I'm a creative producer," he says, "all the time involved in production, production,

production." His task, as he sees it, is to guide each stage of a film through his "distant control and distant vision." What he describes sounds like a process of divination, one that begins with the future promised in the recesses of every script.

Stories and scripts have a rather ambiguous value in Tamil cinema. It is widely held that the leading male actor in a Tamil film—the hero, so to speak—determines the scope of its box-office opening. Many producers work with this idea in mind: trying first to commit these men to particular dates, and only then developing stories appropriate for them. Not too long ago, I am told, a well-known producer led his star and crew to Hong Kong for twenty full days without a complete script in hand. They had booked the star well in advance for those three weeks and were hoping just to shoot something worth keeping as the story itself was hammered out.

There are also questions concerning the value of a written script. Tamil directors are expected to have mastered the art of verbal storytelling. Tales told aloud lead each film through the totality of its production: from the sweeping pitches made to prospective producers, actors, and technicians, to the smaller narratives that guide the composition of particular shots, scenes, and sounds.[19] "If there's no confusion in the narration, they can deliver it," G.D. tells me. "If they say 'Sir, sir, sir, I forgot one scene,' then I know they've lost it."

As a corporate producer, G.D. won't commit to a pitch without receiving and reading a written script. There's a spiral-bound heap of them in his office, piled on a shelf behind his desk. "There's no compulsion to make a film," he says. "My company hasn't given me a target to make some number of films. 'If you get a good script, if you believe it is commercially viable, make the film,' that is what my company told me."

Then he reaches behind his desk for one of these sheaves. "I want to give you one assignment," he says.

⊢

Although, as a teacher, I give out assignments all the time, this is homework I know little about. I spend a day at a café in Anna Nagar, paging slowly through the handwritten bundle, reminding myself of what G.D. had said in his *Galatta Cinema* column the previous month: "Film production must begin only when there is a strong script in hand. Half the battle of the box office is won if that is achieved."

Then there are those questions he encouraged me to ask: "Is it entertaining? Is it engaging? Is it realistic? Is it identifiable? Is there something new about it?"

A few days later, we meet up once again. I'm still not sure whether this is just a pedagogic exercise that the producer has put me through, or an actual vetting.

There's a lot that appeals to me about the story, a tale of a renegade kid who becomes a crusading teacher, only to get stabbed to death by his best friend over a girl they've both secretly loved for years.[20] But I also don't want to seem too naïve about something with no real potential. Playing it safe, I hem and haw about the script: "The climax was a little predictable, as though his fall was destined. You're taken very, very high and suddenly dropped down."

As it turns out, though, G.D. himself likes the story. "This is the core of the film," he tells me: "It's possible to bring about change at a grassroots level if one desires to do it." He acknowledges that the script needs more work, but still, he insists, it engages continuously.

Our exchange is drawing to a close. The producer means to leave the office. But then, as it turns out, the writer of the script himself has just stepped into the lobby.

.... ⊢ ....

P. Ramesh is thin, with eyeglasses and a closely trimmed beard. There's something slightly dated about the decorative tags hanging from his T-shirt. He's brought a DVD of a few sample scenes that he and his friends have shot for the film, his first. "I feel like a kid who's just written an exam," he tells me with a slight and nervous laugh.

We step into the conference room, which has a large flat-panel TV mounted to the wall. The producer likes what he sees. "When can you narrate?" G.D. asks.

"I've always got it stored in my mind," assures Ramesh, who has worked as an assistant for two well-known Tamil directors.

"Good. Why don't you come back to the office at nine p.m. sharp?"

The producer has arranged to have the story told to him aloud after the Censor Board screening of *Kanden Kadhalai* that evening at a nearby preview theater. By the time we all reassemble at the Moser Baer office, everyone but an office boy and the night watchman have gone home for the evening.

"Ready? Shoot," the producer says. And the young storyteller begins to speak.

One night in the town of Thirumangalam, Madurai District. At a dosai stall, with the sound of oil sizzling, we show a tight close-up of a man's hand resting on the edge of a banana leaf. The hero, Manikandan.

"Someone asked me this, Alagu: 'Will you die with that pen in your hand?' 'I'll teach these kids to think for themselves, even if it kills me,' I said."

"'Good morning sir. Did you read the paper this morning, sir? Did you see that article about the pesticides, sir?' Do you know how it feels when those kids ask me these things, Alagu? It makes me feel like Arjun in *Mudhalvan*. We've got to help these kids, no matter what the others say."

"Ask all the flowers in my garden at home" . . . It's the SMS ringtone on his mobile phone. He turns it over, looks at the screen. Then, washing his hands, he taps a message with the keys: "I'm with Alagu. He wanted to see me. You eat. I'll be home soon."

Ramesh pauses as the office boy puts down small cups of lemon tea for the three of us. G.D. has already been smiling, leaning back in his chair to listen, head cocked slightly to the left. There's an indulgence in his smile, as though he is enjoying the unfolding of something that is already his. Ramesh begins to speak again.

Manikandan, he touches the phone to his cheek. "My sweet little thing. Forget about reading or writing, I didn't even brush my teeth until I met her. Kamala, the new teacher's daughter. I never thought what it meant to be a man, until she stepped into our classroom that day. Can you believe it, Alagu, all these years later, the three of us teaching together at the same school?"

Manikandan looks down at his phone. Some heavy music begins to play—*dampa dappa dampa dappa*. Film title. Fade out.

Daytime. *Chak chak chak chak*, two feet, pedaling a bicycle furiously down a dirt road, the spokes in his wheels spinning like the staves in a fighter's hands. The camera follows him, panning up from those feet and wheels. There's a boy in khaki shorts and a tattered shirt, his hair matted and sticky with sweat. He quickly turns back to look—it's Manikandan, as a boy.

Look behind him, and there's the headmaster of his school, chasing after Manikandan in a jeep. Manikandan is pedaling, pedaling along that road, bouncing over the rocks and stones, leaving behind a cloud of dust. The jeep is catching up to him.

Just outside the town, he sees a path that cuts through the thorny bushes. He takes the turn, still pedaling as quickly as he can. He turns to look, but the jeep is gone. Then, suddenly, up ahead, he sees the jeep pull up, stop in front of him, blocking the path.

He looks to the left, looks to the right. The bushes are thick, there's no way to cut between them. The path is narrow, he can't turn around. Is there some other way out?

Then, from his point of view, an intercut: Vijay racing his motorbike in

Thirumalai, coming to such a quick halt that his rear tire pops in the air. There's a shot of this. Manikandan tries to pop up his wheel like this, just before the jeep.

Dank! He hits the jeep, goes flying over top, into the bushes on the other side of the jeep.

Cut, and what we see is the headmaster's office, an exterior shot. Inside, the legs of a boy all scratched up and bleeding, Manikandan's legs.

As Ramesh continues, G.D. remains focused—laughing quietly to himself, hardly shifting in his seat, yawning only once as the story unfolds. Now and then he pens a few words onto the notebook on his desk.

Ramesh is a fluid and convincing storyteller. He modulates the tone and timbre of his voice for different characters and uses his hands to convey both their actions within the story and the space of the frame in which he imagines them. Phrase by phrase, what he says seems remarkably close to the written script that I remember reading.

At the midpoint interval in the tale, we take a break. When the producer steps into the bathroom, Ramesh looks to me with a gesture of hope, cupping both hands together before his face, as if in prayer, eyes turned upward toward the ceiling of the room.

⊢

Hope isn't always desirable, Adam Reed reminds us in a study of inmates awaiting sentencing at a Papua New Guinea prison: "In their accounts, the prospective momentum of waiting for court often seems relentless, overwhelming, and exhausting."[21] As I read these words, I think again of Ramesh, caught in the same yearning for well over a decade now, waiting, as he says, for someone to address him with a single judgment: "You're a director."

A few days after his session with the Moser Baer COO, Ramesh and I meet at a café on the third floor of a Mega Mart department store in Valasaravakkam. He tells me more about the small town in southern Tamil Nadu where he grew up, how he came across Chennai's Kodambakkam bridge into cinema over twelve years ago and doesn't ever want to go back. We talk about the other production offices where he's also pitched this story, about producers who had given him fifteen minutes to try to tell it.

Dhananjayan, who listened until midnight that night, seems different. "I went with a little hope and a little fear," Ramesh says. "Now, every day, when I tear a page off the daily calendar, it's not just paper tearing. It's also my heart that tears with each page."

⊢

For the project to move forward, the press of Ramesh's heart must somehow find an echo in the momentum of the company's ambitions. G.D. has numerous "corrections" that he's asked the aspiring director to make, various ways of trying to make the story more plausible, timely, and appealing. Once again, G.D. tries to keep in mind the wishes of his audience. Will they reject Manikandan's sudden turnaround from wayward youth to crusading teacher? Will they find this turn too "preachy"? And who will they accept in such a role?

These questions arise once more when Ramesh narrates his story to the entire Moser Baer production and marketing team a few weeks later. Although G.D. doesn't use the word *hope*, his management-speak relies upon its promise. "Is there a connectivity?" the producer asks his team, encouraging them to imagine how audiences would react to the film. One of these guys lauds the first half: "The flow is so beautiful. I was so hungry, but I didn't feel like getting up." But they all agree that the second half lags, needing something else, maybe a little comedy.

Their conversation remains open-ended. What scuttles the project, ultimately, is the disinterest shown by the most likely male lead they have in hand, *Kanden Kadhalai*'s young hero, whose own aspirations are turned elsewhere.

"The film has no depth in love," G.D. reports to Ramesh, describing the actor's reactions. "It is a one-track script revolving around public service. . . . He also felt that it will not elevate his career further and will be, at best, like one of his earlier films."

At Moser Baer, talk about the project slowly subsides. One day Ramesh calls me to ask whether I have any news to report. But what can I say about a future that deserves to remain an open road?

"May your struggle go well," I tell him, desperate, wanting to get off the phone.

.... ⊢ ....

There was a story on cassette I sometimes heard at night as a child, a musical version of the tale of Pandora's jar. Even now, when I see the word *hope*, I can hear the muted echo of some of those lines: "Hope is a gentle raindrop from the sky. . . . Hope is a handshake, when you need a friend. . . . Hope is a smile, it's a song to sing."

It may indeed be difficult to decide what hope is. But perhaps you can see by now what hope can do. Hope moves things along: commodities from hand to hand, projects from stage to stage, feelings from person to person. Without such hope, there is no cinema. This has nothing to do with whether a given story is optimistic in its narrative arc. The question is whether that story—leavened with whatever its proportions of aspiration and despair—can sustain the movement and momentum that spell commercial success.

Ramesh's script hasn't yet been made. But, in the midst of those discussions of its potential market promise, Moser Baer did put out that other film that the company took on, *Kanden Kadhalai*. The release began, as always, with a *puja* in the office: a stack of film canisters set before a gallery of Hindu gods and a banana leaf heaped with coconuts, bananas, and puffed rice. Circling these items with a camphor flame, the producer gave the film's director a sweet *laddu* to eat, and a blessing: "You'll be working on your next film within a month."

"There is nothing guaranteed in film production," G.D. later told me. "It's trial and error. So many mistakes can happen. The only force that can help you overcome those errors is God."

In the face of such profound uncertainty, a ritual performed with the gods in mind isn't all that surprising. But for the producer, *God* was a name for the feelings accumulated by all those who stood there together, praying for the success of the film. "Without that positive energy," he said, "even the Earth couldn't float."

Floating how, I'm not exactly sure—like the trio of lotus flowers perhaps, bearing the gods Ganesha, Lakshmi, and Saraswati through cosmic waters in the image at the heart of that makeshift corporate shrine. But then there's also that other vessel to consider, Pandora's jar.

At stake in the ancient Greek myth of Pandora, recorded for posterity in the epic poems of Hesiod, is the condition of human beings on this Earth. Pandora herself was a poisoned gift, given to men by gods irate at their theft of fire. With her jar came all the evils of mortal life: sickness, struggle, old age, and death. But, as we also know, something else remained within that container, a presence that Hesiod named Elpis, hope.

With the millennia that have since passed, this figure, Elpis, remains somewhat of an enigma. Jean-Pierre Vernant has argued that our word *hope* fails to capture the range of its qualities, for there are expectations here of both good and evil, an essential ambiguity of future horizons when the conditions of life are fundamentally uncertain. "It wavers between the dreams of the presumptuous and the terrors of the fearful," Vernant writes—both hope and dread, always cross-hatched, known only through the menace of waiting.[22]

Hope and also dread, ambition as well as affliction—these vessels too have something of Pandora's jar about them, these canisters of film, awaiting release.

CHAPTER 4 Space

I've been coming to this city—Chennai, Madras—for as long as I can remember. I didn't realize how little of it I'd actually seen until I began wandering with these filmmakers. That garden in Porur that sometimes doubles as a tenement block or village bazaar. The streets deserted of all but refuse, dogs, and blanketed souls on the outskirts of a night shoot. The luminary offices tucked into unassuming bungalows, their black SUVs barely hinting at the deals being closed inside. I spent weeks trying to get into one of those offices. Each time I came by, they told me the director was someplace else. Singapore. Bangalore. London. In a sense, they were lying, but there was also a grain of truth to what they said. Finishing his script behind that door, he was engrossed in the life of all these places, quietly searching for semblances of those cities in this one, for ciphers to read the trajectory of this space.

·· ⊢ ··

The director inside that office, M. Sasikumar, was working on his second film, *Easan*—a story about what can befall those who come to unknown cities, the kind of story that we've been hearing for a long time now in India and other places.[1]

There's a family in a village called Easanur, in the arid plains of southern Tamil Nadu: a girl and a boy, devoted like their father to the memory of a mother lost many years ago. Poorani is accepted into the Institute of Fashion Technology in Chennai. Her father moves there with both of them. "Their future is what's most important," he tells one of his skeptical relations in the village.

The city is indifferent to the tribulations of these migrants. Still, they somehow find their way. The father has a job. The boy, Easan, has his textbooks and video games. Poorani, mute from birth, at first sits quietly in

one corner of the college, hunched over her sketches. Then she falls in with a new crowd of friends. She loosens the tight braids in her hair, begins to wear jeans and sunglasses. The driving guitar chords of a song make for a soundtrack to these changes: "Here, a new world draws you in . . . here, a new image paves your way . . . here, new intoxications appear before your eyes."

Poorani's sketches gain new form and color. Then, one afternoon, she is whisked away to a birthday party for one of her new friends at a posh house in south Chennai. The son of a powerful minister is also there. He and another boy goad her to take a drink. They follow her upstairs and rape her behind a locked door. Violent scenes from an English film, maybe *Transporter*, play loudly on a screen in that dark room.

Poorani's father, devastated, blends a bottleful of pills into three glasses of coffee the next morning. Her story ends with this act—what we can only call an honor killing—as does his own. Only Easan survives to avenge them both.

"Is this a place fit to live?" Easan asks a policeman about the city. "Our father shouldered us here with all of his dreams and our desires. Do you know what our village is like? Do you know how we lived there?"

··· ┤ ···

"Space is social morphology," Henri Lefebvre writes. "It is to lived experience what form itself is to the living organism, and just as intimately bound up with function and structure."[2] We tend to think of space as something abstract, empty, and virtually formless: as a vacant stage or surface waiting to be filled by things and lives of one kind or another. Lefebvre asks us to take space instead as a matter of dynamic social forms and processes, as a way of conceiving and organizing things and relations, as a tissue of support for certain forms of life at the expense of others.

Think of Easan, in the film that bears his name, judging city and village by the lives they make possible and impossible, by what these different environments do in propelling prosperity or ruin. The village of Easanur, the film suggests, sustained a harmony between the inside and the outside, the psychic and the physical. The environment itself—ponds, trees, temples, and fields—is seen to exude care and compassion. "Without letting sadness touch me," the brother sings of his sister, "she protects me on this soil."

In Chennai, however, it seems as though that reliable tether between visible faces and invisible depths has somehow been severed. Disturbing events take place behind screens of various kinds, occluded time and again by something that passes over the scene: fixed obstacles, vague and blurry forms, crisscrossed lines of shade and doubt. The city is a space of danger and betrayal. Nothing is as it seems.

Recall the utopian ideal that animates so much of modern cinema and the modern city alike: open space as a visual scene to be mastered by the unencumbered eye of a spectator. The scene of a film may be imagined to belong to its viewers in the same way that an urban scene belongs to its inhabitants: through the projection of a spatial reach and depth potentially available for anyone's pleasure, experience, and control.[3]

Films like *Easan* confound this fantasy. Here, purchase on the city is always brokered through murky networks of dependency, influence, and exploitation.

H

Tamil popular literature has long warned the unsuspecting of the dangers and deceits of Chennai.[4] But this idea of the city as an amalgam of ominous images and appearances has much to do as well with its cinematic history: with the deep archive of filmic allegories for the betrayal of expectation in modern urban life, the long-standing status of the city as a destination for visiting filmgoers, and the dependence for decades of south Indian film production on its many studios.[5]

When the Tamil writer Sundara Ramaswamy first visited the city from his native Nagercoil in the late 1940s, he searched first for Gemini Studios and the iconic pair of cherubic heralds that opened their films. "After protracted wandering I reached the Gemini twins around one in the afternoon," Ramaswamy recalled. "Naked and with plump little bellies they were as beautiful as in the pictures. Only the gloss was missing and that was not a little disappointing."[6]

The world of such signs and images, Henri Lefebvre argues, is a "fraudulent world," entrapping the imagination in an illusory play and obscuring any real possibility of transforming its space.[7] Think of the many images that seal Poorani's fate in the Tamil film *Easan*: the image-world of fashion that took her family from their village to the city; the illusions of a certain style of life that drew her into a toxic circle of friendship; the spectacle of an invulnerable metropolitan masculinity that seems, for the film, to make sense of her brutal rape; the ideal of feminine honor and dignity that led her father to poison them both; the image of a heroic avenger that drives the remainder of the film's story; the idea of the city that led its makers to construct such a depraved picture of urban space. "After its fashion," Lefebvre writes, "the image kills."[8]

All the same, *Easan* also reminds us, it is such images that propel so much of contemporary life in a city like Chennai: images to reach, images to try to live with, images that court death and dying but also help to make a living. What does it mean to live and die in a space of such images, for the denizens of such a city, for the characters of such a film, for those who seek to make the one into the other? What does it take to make a home in the midst of such perilous and beguiling forms?[9]

Let's keep one thing in mind: space is always unfinished, a dimension of "loose ends and ongoing stories," as Doreen Massey writes, "full of holes, of disconnections, of tentative half-formed first encounters."[10] A space of images is a space in the making, a field of places for potential scenes, of gaps and margins where they come together and come apart. In these gaps lie its resources for life, its potential to sustain both existence and expression. Think, for example, of the space in which a film emerges.

································ H ································

Through the 1970s, most Tamil films were produced on studio floors in and around Kodambakkam in western Chennai. Toward the close of that decade, Tamil filmmakers began to shoot on location in and beyond the city. Those with independent financial backing found it cheaper to work beyond the networks of integrated studio production. They relied upon smaller and more mobile cameras, and new audio facilities to dub and sync sounds with visual footage shot elsewhere. They were also responding to the cultural force of Dravidian nationalist politics, which had cultivated fresh concerns for the authenticity of Tamil cultural heritage and expression.

This rise of location shooting was a crucial development in the character of modern Tamil cinema, an important foundation for its distinctive look and texture. The practice was described in vernacular Tamil weeklies in the 1980s as *velippura padappidippu*, a translation into Tamil of the phrase *outdoor shooting* that might be expressed most precisely in English as "the capturing of images in outside space."[11]

Beyond their manifest interest in the outdoor and the outside, these shoots also promised access to hitherto unexplored "insides" of ordinary Tamil life: forms of intimate experience that were best expressed by the environments to which they belonged.[12] Searching out folk habits and customs, regional forms of language and dialect, caste-inflected bodily gestures and dress, and the local sounds and rhythms of diverse rural milieus, these newer films sought to convey the "nativity"—the specificity and originality—of the Tamil countryside.[13]

This development is widely credited to the Tamil director Bharathiraja and his 1976 debut film *Pathinaru Vayathinile* [At the age of sixteen]. One afternoon at his Chennai production office, buried within an apartment complex on the former grounds of Gemini Studios, the director told me how he'd grown "fed up" with the artificial houses, roofs, and plows that had composed village sets in Chennai's studios.

"What happened in my village was entirely different," he said, describing his native environs west of the southern city of Madurai. "There was no reality in that. That's why I first took the camera outside. I didn't feel the soul—the soul, you know?" The director described a process of mixing or merging his own feelings with the living environment in which he was working. "Location itself is a character," he told me. "Then only can you merge with life. . . . It will speak, the location will speak to you."

Another one of the director's early films from 1980, *Kallukkul Eeram* [Moisture within the stone], strikingly conveys this kinship between an outward space of work and an inward space of feeling. Bharathiraja plays the part of a director in the film, shooting a romance in a riverside village. His character's heart has been hardened by the memory of an amorous betrayal, and the filmmakers enter the village as if a distant and alien space.[14] These inward and outward boundaries are slowly breached through the forces of curiosity, need, and love. The director finds his own imagination embodied in the smitten daughter of the village washerman, always circling around the fields, meadows, and shorelines where he shoots. The stony heart of the director softens. Inner and outer worlds collide and commingle through the expression of cinematic space.[15]

"Until the age of twenty-one, I lived on that soil," Bharathiraja told me. "There's nothing else that remains fresh for me." This idea of *man vasanai*—the "scent of the soil" particular to a region, the life of feelings and deeds most closely associated with that place—has deeply influenced the character of Tamil cinema over the past few decades. Films set in the villages and towns of southern Tamil Nadu, for example, typically oscillate between earnest sentimentalism and atavistic violence, as if to say that this is what people here are like.[16] Take the film that M. Sasikumar made just before *Easan*, his first production, *Subramaniyapuram*.[17]

The sound of a gentle voice drifts down the dusty lane of a Madurai neighborhood, musing on the music of a woman's eyes. The year is 1980. *Kallukkul Eeram* has just been released, and one of the composer Ilaiyaraja's most popular tracks from the film is playing on a roadside gramophone. A bearded young man in bellbottoms courts the shy young woman who lives in a towering house across the lane. He hears the song once more, a few days later, when she appears at a door within the house. "On the heart sown with seed, a citron has ripened," a woman's voice now sings, as the two exchange avid looks unseen by her uncle nearby. The space resounds with what is expressed in their eyes.

These are moments from Sasikumar's first film, *Subramaniyapuram*. The film is a tale of betrayal set in the 1980s: the young man and his friends will be goaded unwittingly into murder, and the young woman will expose her lover to death in order to save her own family. Made on a small budget and released in 2008, the film was a tremendous hit. Critics and audiences alike appreciated its meticulous attention to the details of life in Madurai at the time: black rotary telephones, cyclostyled invitations to temple festivals, even the bags of torn-up lottery tickets that cinema hall audiences would hurl into the air at the on-screen appearance of a star like Rajni Kanth.

I watched the film with a friend at the Cine Priya theater in Madurai one afternoon soon after its release. The excitement in that hall was palpable and unsettling. Our theater erupted in a cacophony of whistling when the film portrayed the release of Rajni Kanth's *Murattu Kalai* in 1980. We could see another Madurai cinema hall that looked and felt so much like the one we were in, packed with bodies that teetered between jubilation and violence. It was impossible to distinguish the whistling of the loudspeakers from the sound of those around us, an unnerving feeling of immediacy that returned once again when the film's villain was crudely beheaded on-screen. Joy was everywhere, impossible to place.

My friend, a writer and social activist, shook his head with the sense that nothing had changed in Madurai. "Subramaniyapuram is here," he said.

Sasikumar, who directed, produced, and acted in the film, knew this was happening all over the state. "Everywhere, the whole auditorium claps when I sever his head in that auto rickshaw," he said when we met for the first time at his production office in Chennai. "This is what our epics say: 'Destroy the evil one.'"

The director grew up in a village slowly encompassed by an expanding Madurai. His family owned a fabric business in the town and a movie theater along one of the main roads. In boarding school in the Kodaikanal hills, he watched films by Satyajit Ray and wrote and directed his own plays and skits. Back in Madurai for college, he joined the Yadhartha (Realistic) Film Society, then later worked as an assistant director for a film that his uncle produced.

A certain kind of realism was essential to *Subramaniyapuram* as Sasikumar conceived and produced it. What the film expressed, he told me, was the culture and concerns of the region. "The whole of Subramaniyapuram is the character," he said. By lingering on local festivals, conflicts, spectacles, and styles, "we're talking about who lives there, what kind of people live in that area."

I was struck by the affinity between what the director was saying and the Western anthropological tradition, which has long taken culture as an expression of national soil and place.[18] "We also go to these places, we live with those people, and then we write about them," I told him. "You're also talking about bringing a place to life with your movie."

Sasikumar and his crew were planning another project now, a "city subject," as he put it, the film that would eventually become *Easan*. The challenge they faced was this: how to express the character of a very different kind of space.

⊢

One morning in early November, a little over a year later, I'm wedged into a small red Skoda sedan with Sasikumar's coproducer, production manager, and cameraman, scouting locations in south Chennai.

They will be traveling with the director that night to Rome, where *Subramaniyapuram* has been selected for the Asiatica Film Mediale Festival. Production on this urban drama is scheduled to begin soon after their return. Shooting will start with a one-day "test shoot," and they are trying to identify a space suitable for this purpose.

Test shoots are often undertaken to explore the suitability of an actor, a film stock, or a visual look. What Sasi has in mind, however, is much larger in scope: a chance for the whole film crew—everyone from the director to the production crew—to practice working together in an organized manner. Rather than attempting any individual scenes, Sasi hopes to establish an overall "mood" for the film to follow.

The director is parsimonious with the screenplay. Only a handful of individuals know the story in detail, while most others—even the central actors in the film—know almost nothing about their roles. Because this film will cut between very different places—rave parties, business lounges, police stations, and so on—choosing the right backdrop for the test shoot is critical. What the cinematographer Kadhir describes sounds like the staging of an experimental space: "How will the characters and the location merge together?"

At first, the spatial field is wide open. Sasi has asked the production manager, Uday, to scout out abandoned factories, colonial-era bungalows, and older, two-story office buildings. Uday has been surveying the city with a digital camera, along with one of the director's assistants, a young man named Mahan.

"The director's mind is like a wild river," Mahan tells me. His task is to flow with its wishes, however obscure, rather than block their passage. They are looking for a place that might accommodate its contours of thinking and feeling.

The city, meanwhile, poses its own obstacles. Our morning in south Chennai begins at the National Institute of Fashion Technology. We walk through the campus with the film's art director, R. K. Nagaraj, who points out a few good "blocks" or backdrops where he has shot advertisements in the past. Then we drive to Chetpet to look at the grounds of two affluent schools. Film shoots are never permitted within these buildings, we are told, and exorbitant fees are required to use even their exteriors as backdrops. The coproducer tells the others how he'd once persuaded a diocesan bishop to allow them to shoot a Church of South India hospital for *Subramaniyapuram*.

"We should have never tried to go beyond Madurai," he says ruefully, with a markedly southern Tamil twang to his voice. Everyone laughs in appreciation.

·· H ··

A place for a mind like a wild river — Gregory Bateson contested the idea of the mind as something that lies "within" an individual person: "Suppose I am a blind man, and I use a stick. I go tap, tap, tap. Where do *I* start? Is my mental system bounded at the handle of the stick? Is it bounded by my skin? Does it start halfway up the stick?"

"These are nonsense questions," Bateson argued. "The way to delineate the system is to draw the limiting line in such a way that you do not cut any of these pathways in ways which leave things inexplicable."[19] To understand the mind of someone blindly feeling out a street, you have to acknowledge its tentative presence throughout that space, in the feet that step, the stick that taps, the pavement that meets the tapping stick.

Bateson's insights into this broader "ecology" of mind help me understand what Sasi's film crew is doing as they seek out a location for their unmade film. It isn't a matter of giving an outward form to an inward space, of finding a physical replica of an image or backdrop that the director has already composed in his head. Instead, they are looking for someplace more active, immersive — a geography of sympathetic elements, a space to sustain the thinking-out of the film, its open-ended movement of expression.

A week or so later, I meet up with Sasi and the others once again, at a disused gas cylinder factory along the East Coast Road south of Chennai. This place is owned by an acquaintance of Samudrakani, the director's close friend and one of the lead actors in the film they plan to make. Sasi walks quietly through the compound with Kadhir and Nagaraj. They examine both of the factory sheds, the defunct equipment lying about, and the view beyond one of the windows. "This is okay," Sasi murmurs to his cameraman after a few minutes. Then later, to me, with more confidence, "We have enough space to play on this ground."

The place is one that Mahan had scouted, one of thirty or forty places he had inspected around the city. He knew that the director wanted a broken-down factory, a place that looked old, somewhere with a lot of space. I marvel at how well he guessed what might appeal to Sasi.

"What's the mind like?" Mahan asks by way of reply. "It thinks, it calculates, it goes inside, into all those places that people can't go."

This, again, is the mind as river, as confluence, but it's something bigger than any one person now, a current embodied by the crew and by the landscape in which they will try to work out the film. "Take the man to the place that the mind is going," Mahan says.

⊢

The factory is mostly empty by the time Sasi and his crew begin their stint of work here. There's a pair of sprawling open sheds within the compound, each framed by wooden rafters, concrete supports, and sheets of corrugated tin. Between them is a gravel expanse strewn with weeds and massive cubes of rusted steel. Stray bits of equipment litter the sheds — machines and instruments of unknown usage, painted in flaking coats of blue and green.

The air is ripe and heavy with the smell of garbage, heaped up in the stagnant water ringing the site. Flies are swarming and settling everywhere.

The factory manager offers to straighten out some of the debris and equipment littering the sheds. "Don't rearrange anything," Sasi tells him. "However you've left those things, let all of it remain that way."

What they hope to do here is to find a way of improvising with the tangible qualities of a foreign space. "When we go," the director speculates to his cameraman in jest, thinking ahead to the day of the shoot, "all those things will have disappeared by then."

⊢

The test shoot begins on November 18, a day fixed with the director's astrological forecast in mind. The priest, Meenakshi Sundaram, hails from the Viswakarma caste of artisans. He sets several coconuts, banana leaves, incense sticks, and other ritual implements on a small desk within one of the sheds. A large image of Ganesha faces east. A clapboard, chalked with the word *Pooja*, stands beside a bound copy of the film's script.

A few minutes before 10 a.m., the priest sets alight a piece of camphor on a plate of ash. Everyone faces him quietly as he utters the incantations of a *jana vasika puja*, a ritual meant to attract and captivate people. "'This is good,' people should say when they watch the film," Meenakshi Sundaram explains.

The priest also pays respects to the gods of the eight directions. He has set up the desk on the cracked concrete floor of the shed as a *brahmasthanam*, the space of Brahma that composes the architectural center of a Brahmanical Hindu temple. The prototypical arrangement of such temples in India is meant to close and fix a space of worship.[20] Here, however, the physical space is too large to plot its center. Zones of ongoing activity keep opening around the makeshift shrine. There is also all the dirt and brush beyond the shed, where the priest must go to sanctify the first shot of the day.

"As if you've drawn a line, that's how you should be," Meenakshi Sundaram says, describing how he's insisted upon the importance of this date. But what happens here troubles any such distinction that might be drawn between order and disorder. Threats, in fact, are essential to the appeal of this space, as the director himself acknowledges: "Before going to war, we practice on our own ground."

.... ⊢ ....

There is no shot list or any other tangible indication of a plan for the day. While the priest prepares to consecrate the center of the space, the director and cameraman pick their way through the brush and rubble on one corner of the compound.

"First shot here," Sasi tells Kadhir. And the camera frames a pair of men, conversing among hulking scraps of metal. One stands stiffly, with the posture of an officer. The other looks like a politician, clad all in white. In the dark lenses of his gold-rimmed sunglasses, you can see the cigarette he's lighting for the cop.

The filmmakers move into one of the tin-roofed sheds. "Let's let them walk," Sasi says, and the cop and the politician begin to take slow and dramatic strides side by side down the long concrete floor, toward the camera at the other end of the shed.

Again and again, they walk with each other, but also, in many senses, they walk with the director: he literally steps with them and toward them; they gradually fall into step with the mood of the film; and his own feel for the film changes as they walk. "As they come walking," Sasi later explains, describing the appeal of this lengthy space of unfolding movement, "I will change myself, and I will change them."

Walking is a spatial practice that opens the space of the city to various kinds of appropriation, experimentation, and transgression, Michel de Certeau has written. "To walk," he muses, "is to lack a place."[21] This is how Sasi and his crew seem to occupy the factory, their shoot evolving as

a meandering stroll or amble through its space. Time and again through-out the day, two questions keep revealing new corners of the factory for potential shots: "Shall we try this? Or, shall we do something like this?"

The sky thunders and there are reports of heavy rain in Chennai. "We'll shoot in the rain," Sasi declares, and Kadhir, observing that the tin roof may leak, makes a gleeful retort: "As it drips, drop by drop, we'll have them walk in that as well!"

"Real, live, industrial, raw"—this is how the director describes the space. Most essentially, he finds it new, rife with potential powers that remain untapped.[22] Standing within a small office structure in one of the sheds, examining the detritus heaped inside, Sasi sees a den for the film's villains to scheme and conspire: "Someone must be sitting here. . . . Here, someone else will be standing."

The film crew opens the roof of this dilapidated structure to daylight, and its sides are wrapped with wire mesh and cobwebs. They make a plan to shoot the white-clad politician within this office, from the outside and through the mesh, before breaking quickly for lunch.

A. L. Alagappan, who plays this menacing figure, tells me that this is how he's seen Sasikumar work on location: "As soon as he goes there, whatever he thinks, that is developed into a shot." Alagappan is a veteran producer himself, with over forty years of experience in Tamil cinema. What he sees with Sasi reminds him most of Bharathiraja, whose first films Alagappan had helped to finance and distribute in the late 1970s. "Stop the car!" Bharathiraja would suddenly say. "There's something about this sunrise. Let's shoot this."

Space is both a field of action and a basis of action, Lefebvre has written: projects and intentions are undertaken and exercised in particular places, but the energies that propel these activities also come from—

course through—these places.²³ For newcomers to acting like Alagappan
and most other central characters in the production, the space is one of
fear and trepidation, the test shoot meant to draw them in. But the factory and its crumbling enclosures are much more than a passive backdrop for their acting—these spatial elements are protagonists essential
to the shoot.²⁴

Late that morning, the film's music director, James Vasanthan, suddenly
appears, with his wife and a bouquet of flowers in hand. The intention he
expresses is striking. "Naturally, it is the space that makes me evolve the
kind of genre that will suit the film," he tells me.

"The space creates the music," Vasanthan insists, but we are chatting
over the din of a soundscape already charged with the force of his music.
Throughout the shoot, wherever the camera goes, it is trailed by a pair of
speakers that blast the driving guitar chords that Vasanthan composed
specifically for the test shoot. It feels "tremendously exciting," Alagappan
says, "as if something is about to happen."

Sasi wants this mood that fills the factory sheds to ease the anxiety of
those acting here for the first time. But I can also sense its importance
for the director himself, who requests that certain moments in the audio
track be cued for each shot they take. The music plays even when they re-
wind the video feed to review these takes, with Sasi instructing the play-
back operator to sync each recorded shot with sound at the precise moment when he signals "Go!" with his hand.²⁵

Vasanthan's track is 1:40 minutes in duration. The film involves gangsters, youngsters, and city nightlife, he knows, and his music begins with
distorted guitars, forceful beats, and an ominous piano. But then, nearly
halfway through the sequence, these sounds fade into a melodic interlude, the slow crescendo of its violins conveying the hopes of a very different kind of place. The tempo breaks once more into a feverish rush,
but the violins remain, carrying some of that hope forward to the end of
the track.

"Two different emotions, a contrast," the composer explains. "It gives
a provision for the director to come out with the softer parts of the film."

As there is nothing suitably soft within the moribund factory, the art
director is tasked with creating another, smaller environment under the
high rafters of the shed, where a few shots will be taken to match the mel-
low interlude. Nagaraj, who describes himself as "half artist, half architect, half interior designer," works with a team of craftsmen to build an
L-shaped pair of compact walls, painted in a quiet white and blue.

One wall is fitted with a prayer cabinet at which a boy and girl will stand with clasped hands, the other a window into which he will leap when she isn't looking. Fully enveloped with thick black cloth as they shoot, these ten-by-twelve-feet walls compose a world within a world, a fragmentary glimpse of home resurfacing unexpectedly.

"An area like Madurai," Sasi says to Nagaraj, describing how he wants this displaced shard of home to look.

⊢

These images and sounds are eventually cut and composed into what the director and his crew call a "trailer," a two-minute sequence never intended for public release but meant instead to guide the filmmakers themselves as they work on producing *Easan*. Relying on Vasanthan's track, the test shoot visuals, and another day of experimental shooting on the Pondicherry coastline, the trailer tells a story in three moods or movements: intrigue, innocence, and vengeance.

Many unrelated images compose these moods: two men and a cigarette, a praying boy and girl, a violent scuffle in that derelict office, and so on. The integrity of the story depends upon the coherence of a certain space of experience, the feeling of a city.

"This is how I made the film," Sasi says one afternoon the following year as we watch the trailer together on his laptop, a few months after *Easan*'s box-office release. It's obvious, from the deftness with which he finds and opens the file, that he's watched and shown it often.

"It was inside me, in my mind," he says, describing how they had gone on to make *Easan* in the months that followed the test shoot. We watch the final image of the trailer together: blood trickling down the length of a knife plunged into the earth, as a shadowy figure walks away in silence. "This is the story," Sasi says. "This shot is the story."

⊢

Whose knife, whose blood, whose earth, whose shadow? There is much more to the world of the film than this one image or the brief trailer that it concludes so mysteriously. And yet it is clear that so much of *Easan* was anticipated in this microcosm of a full form yet to come. Take the way this dark film's flashback midway to a tranquil life in Easanur almost precisely matches the composer's placement of a buoyant musical interlude at the midpoint of the trailer's audio track. In both instances, you come back to a violent urban milieu suffused with the sensation of those shattered hopes.

Or consider the scene in which so much of the eventual film's action takes place: a factory compound in Porur that looks and feels like the defunct gas cylinder factory on the East Coast Road. Working here, the

filmmakers rebuilt an office structure matched exactly to the dilapidated, mesh-covered enclosure found in that first trial site. It's as if the film was fashioned in a space of imagination opened by the test shoot and trailer.

As a landscape of dream and imagination, the image of the city draws together elements displaced from somewhere else. It may not be surprising, then, to find shades of this one factory dispersed throughout that world. Early in the film, the site is seized by Alagappan's character, the villainous politician, and you see him first through the blurry wire mesh of its office enclosure. But then see how the same kind of nebulous form interposes itself wherever *Easan* looks into the city: as an assassin approaches an apartment building . . . as a business tycoon plots a land deal . . . as the politician plans to confound it . . . as a police officer visits a suspect at a hospital . . . as Easan murders the politician's son for raping his sister, Poorani.

Every space in the city begins to look and feel like that factory's wire enclosure, as murky and obscure as the space in which the director set his villains on the first day of the shoot. And as you trail these lived abstractions, this series of meshwork forms throughout the different scenes composing that world, what the filmmakers were doing on that first day also comes into sharper focus.

"Sometimes the house grows and spreads," Gaston Bachelard writes, "so that, in order to live in it, greater elasticity of daydreaming, a day-dream that is less clearly outlined, are needed."[26] I think that what these filmmakers sought in the space of these forms was something like a shel-ter for the film, a place to house its dynamic and expanding movement of expression.

"We have enough space to play on this ground," Sasi said so buoy-antly. At the time, he hadn't mentioned Poorani—a woman out of place in his Chennai, and a minor player in the disastrous showing that the film would ultimately make.

CHAPTER 5 Art

The warehouse is down the road from the Liberty Theatre in Kodambakkam, across the street from a new hotel called Cine City. "You name it, I have it," says the proprietor of Azim Cine Decors, "police stations, courts, houses, durbars, hospital parts, operation tables, skeletons, dental work. . . ." The palanquins from a famous movie of the 1950s still go out for historical films and merchant weddings. Yet much has changed with the disappearance of the studios and the turn to working on location with whatever is available there. We pick our way through dusty and neglected shelves of books, beakers, chandeliers, computer monitors, Buddhas, and Shivas; it feels like Siegfried Kracauer's tour of the "ruins of the universe" at the UFA Film City in Weimar Germany in the 1930s. "The old and the new, copies and originals, are piled up in a disorganized heap like bones in catacombs," Kracauer wrote.[1] Through what occult arts do such slumbering things come back to life?

······································ ⊢ ····································

A fleeting impression in the midst of life. We were rocketing down the East Coast Road, south of Chennai, for a weekend at the beach. Through the window of the taxi, I took in a flat expanse of white sand along a lakeshore. There were tiny men on the edge of that speckled plain, manipulating what looked like giant thimbles of various colors.

"Looks like they're carrying a huge butterfly," Sanchita said in passing. We kept talking. Then, a few seconds later, I suddenly realized what we'd just seen.

"That's Rajeevan's set!" I told her. "Can we turn around for just one picture?"

"No," she said, firmly. Karun was asleep and nestled against my arm, and this work on cinema had already dragged me from them in too many ways.

Three days later, when we came back up the same road, the set was

already gone. A lone tractor plied the sand, heaped with scraps of wood
and metal. Debris of many hues still littered the shore.

·· ⊢ ··

"Experience," wrote John Dewey, "is the fulfillment of an organism in
its struggles and achievements in a world of things. . . . It is art in its
germ." We tend to think of art as something that transcends the stuff of
the world, the needs and tumult of ordinary life. But the American philosopher put forward a different idea in his 1934 work, *Art as Experience*.
Art is already present in life, always and everywhere, as a potential for
its growth and fulfillment, like the rippling of a pond or the writhing of
a serpent. "Art," Dewey argued, "is prefigured in the very processes of
living."[2]

This is something that Rajeevan knows. There was the modernist
light fixture that he once put together from a pair of plywood discs and
a ripped-up undershirt. The animatronic bandicoot that he built with a
rubber mold and repurposed construction toys. The crimson Buddha that
had migrated from the sanctum of a temple in a historical epic to the edge
of a garden pond in a contemporary political satire.

Once he and I were standing beside an unpaved lane in the western
reaches of Chennai, chatting. Over his shoulder, I could see men and
women ambling down that road, past a book stand and provisions stores,
a pair of dosai stalls and a mansion in fading yellow paint. Behind me
was a roadside Hindu shrine, people relaxing on its steps. I asked when
he would take me to the set he'd just built. Rajeevan laughed. We were
already there: it was everything bustling around us.

·· ⊢ ··

Every art director has stories like this, tales of forms with a phantom fullness. Sabu Cyril, the senior art director Rajeevan had apprenticed with,
once tricked a famous actor into taking a wedding hall for a hospital.
Rembon, one of Rajeevan's former assistants, used to wrap palmyra seeds
and whittled bits of soap into candy wrappers as a child, watching gleefully as his friends gulped down his bitter creations. Rajeevan himself
told me how, as a boy, he would squeeze bananas from the bunches hanging in shops, arranging the flaccid peels to make them look full.

Rajeevan grew up painting in oils and watercolors. He hailed from a
matriarchal Nambiar family in Kerala, and two of his mother's brothers
were also painters. When the art director was eight, he told me, he
brought into class a pastel drawing of a bunch of grapes. The teacher al-

leged that someone else had drawn it for him, and Rajeevan, who stutters still, couldn't find the words to retort to her accusation. Then his uncle dragged the boy back into the classroom and asked him to draw the grapes again before her.

"There are certain episodes in life that you can't forget. This was one of them."

The story was colorful, like many of Rajeevan's tales. He had long been nursing quiet ambitions to make a film of his own. Admitted into a program in visual communication at Loyola College in Chennai on the strength of a sketch he'd made of the college president, he worked in computer animation and advertising for many years. Then, in 2001, a friend asked him to help with a film set. "Cinema pulls you," he told me. "That's how I got dragged into it."

Rajeevan was constantly getting calls now from producers and directors, always working on several films at once. The work was arduous. Sometimes I saw him hobbling around stiffly, a back brace tucked under his shirt. Then there were the Slims he always smoked. "I'm not getting any slimmer myself," the art director said with a rueful smile.

H

Cinema pulls, drags, traps, ensnares—it captivates. For the anthropologist Alfred Gell, this is one of the most significant things that artworks can do. "Gazing at the picture, my jaw drops, in admiration—and defeat," writes Gell, reflecting on Vermeer's 1670 painting *The Lacemaker*. He stands before the work, trying to retrace how it was made. Up to a point, Gell can imagine himself as the artist and the painting as the product of his own hand. But then the work defeats explanation, begins to appear as a "magical, supernatural, occurrence." The viewer is captivated: "I am left suspended between two worlds."[3]

Gell's examples of this effect range widely, from European gallery encounters such as this one to the demoralizing effect that prow-board canoe carvings could have on their spectators in the Trobriand Islands of the South Pacific. Although he makes no mention of it, you can easily imagine cinema in the same terms. Think of the consummate world unfolding upon that enveloping screen. How did they do this? Almost before you've had the chance to ask this question, the film has landed you somewhere else.

I remember the vaguely hallucinatory feeling that stayed with me for several hours after I watched *Inception*, the 2010 film directed by Christopher Nolan. When I think back on the film now, I have hazy and disconnected impressions of various kinds: wooden shutters, red velvet, concrete rubble. But I can't reassemble this world in my imagination. I crave the chance to submit to its sway once more. The film has an agency that surpasses my own.

When I first saw *Inception* late one night at the Inox Multiplex in Chennai, I happened to run into Rajeevan in the line for popcorn. The next morning, he told me that he and his friends had stayed up until 4 a.m., talking about the film. "It looks so real," he said. "You start believing it, actually. It's not the crap that you get here."

They were captivated. Still, though, Rajeevan admitted, there were certain questions that bothered him as he watched. He liked the unfinished warehouse space, for example, where the team of mercenary dreamers are training their architect recruit. "Oh, nice place. . . . Is it real?" Then he began to notice edges around certain things, pillars that must have been placed there as frames. The idea kept nagging at him. "It's a set."

··· H ···

We were chatting about *Inception* on the edge of a small studio floor at AVM Studios. Rajeevan was here to build a set for a nightclub song sequence. The film was a small-budget production, meant to introduce the younger brother of a leading Tamil actor. "They have no money!" Rajeevan complained. They'd given him just 2 lakhs (about $4,000) to work with.

The art department, as his trade is known in Tamil cinema, can easily be the most significant or the most neglected expense in the making of these films. Ask Rajeevan or any of his peers where their responsibilities lie, and almost without fail their answers will fall back upon the word *everything*: all that appears within a frame beyond the actors themselves.

Who are these actors, one may well wonder. Art directors work with a profound sense of the activity and vitality of things, the life of feeling and sensation that colors, textures, forms, and curves lend each cinematic image.[4] But they must also wrestle with a more restricted imagination of the most essential actors in a film: the human, generally male, protagonists and antagonists at the heart of each story.

"None of that will show," a director might say, brushing off an art director's attention to props and other smaller elements. "Will they be looking at the hero, or what's behind him? Enough, enough, as long as the actor shows, that's enough."

The bind is a typical one, but its challenges are accentuated here by the difficulties of wringing something good enough from so many scattered pieces of plastic, wood, and metal. "Either you compromise on the cost or you compromise on your creativity," Rajeevan said. "Holding these two things together is pretty difficult."

The construction of this particular set, like all of his sets, was ultimately in the hands of the *maistry*, or foreman, who oversaw all of his operations on a contract basis. "Multimillionaire," the art director joked, pointing out the man in a starched white shirt and checkered *lungi*, a thick gold band conspicuous on his hand. "He's buying a BMW."

The foreman, Rajalingam, had devised various ways of creating a nightclub ambience with the minuscule budget they were allotted: they were using the lights that they already had on hand, and they had repurposed four giant papier-mâché statues that Rajalingam had built two years back for a Telugu film. Headless now, with their feet sawed off, the statues were guarding each corner of a dance floor paved with glass and foam.

"There are people with no money, and people with lots of it," Rajeevan told me; some asked for sets that would come up and go down in just a few days, and others commissioned projects that would last for weeks. As we watched the carpenters put up psychedelic patterns on the walls, I asked what else he had coming up.

The art director said that he was going to Badami, in northern Karnataka, to build a bridge for the climax of an action film. My ears perked up immediately, but Rajeevan downplayed what he had to do there: "There's nothing creative in it, nothing aesthetic. It's just a bridge." Then he began to tell me, more excitedly, about the acid vat he was designing for a horror film south of Chennai.

.... ⊢ ....

"A literal origin, a beginning from ground zero, a birth"—in the discourse of avant-garde art, writes Rosalind Krauss, this is how the originality of an artwork is conceived.[5] We all know the idea of the artist as a creative genius, as the fount of something utterly new. It's an idea central to the image of the visionary production designer in Hollywood cinema, the role that corresponds most closely to that of the art director in Indian films.[6]

There are reasons why this ideal of art, as the creation of something without precedent in the world, is especially potent and vexing when it comes to places like India. Since the late nineteenth century, foreign observers have associated artistic production in India with craft traditions and the decorative arts rather than the making of art for its own sake. Those who style themselves as artists in the modern sense are still dismissed too easily as pretenders, belatedly seeking to "catch up" with developments already under way in more advanced places.[7]

I think of an exchange I once had with Rajeevan. "I want to work until I've made a mark," he told me.

"How will you know that you have?" I asked.

He brought up his former mentor, Sabu Cyril. "They say that he can do anything. Just that."

With art direction as with art, however, this idea of creative freedom is always skewed to the tastes of a marketplace—in commercial cinema, one abounding in failures yet intolerant of them. Pressures for repetition run through every collaboration: from the countless designs taken as references from books, websites, and other films, to the re-creation of entire scenes or films. Repetition is seen as a blueprint for success, a way of cutting out the costs of experimentation.

The bridge in Karnataka, for example, was meant for a Tamil remake of a Telugu-language blockbuster, S. S. Rajamouli's 2006 film, *Vikramarkudu*. A Tamil production house, Studio Green, had picked up the rights to the film as a vehicle for the actor Karthi Sivakumar, a budding hero and the producer's cousin. "I hate remakes," the art director griped. "You're doing something that's already been done. . . . You're copying someone else's work."

Rajeevan had done many outlandish and outsized things. He shot to fame for the wooden chalet he built on a Sri Lankan lakeshore. There was a song that he'd set in the midst of plywood frames, canvas sheets, and guy ropes—as though it took place on the *backside* of a studio set rather than within it. For another Studio Green project, he reconstructed an entire village devastated by the 2004 Indian Ocean tsunami.

"I like doing realistic work," Rajeevan said. "But not a metal bridge, man. What I'm doing is a makeshift metal bridge."

As he spoke, I was captivated by the idea of watching the art director concoct something extraordinary. And what I'd seen of *Vikramarkudu* frankly looked awful. I thought of waiting until a more promising project came along. But then I began to wonder: Could nothing new arise from this repetition of something old?

· ⊢ ·

"There is in New York," Claude Lévi-Strauss wrote in 1943, "a magic place where all the dreams of childhood hold a rendezvous, where century old tree trunks sing or speak, where indefinable objects lie in wait for the visitor with an anxious stare." The young anthropologist was reporting, rather breathlessly, on a visit to the gallery of native Northwest Coast art at the American Museum of Natural History. "Would it not be astonishing," he mused, "if these objects which speak, dance and eat should not conserve, even in the prison of the Museum, a little of their vibrating life?"[8]

What was this life that Lévi-Strauss had in mind, and where, in the body of these objects, did it lie? Although he likened these masks, statues, and ornamental beams and boxes to the work of Picasso, Lévi-Strauss emphasized that these creations corresponded to the rhythms of a vast and enduring indigenous culture. And this was not the only way these artifacts conveyed a force surpassing the creative agency of any one human artist. There was also a power of transmutation intrinsic to the material forms themselves: "Passing from vitrine to vitrine, from object to object, from one corner to another of the same object sometimes," he wrote, "one has the feeling of passing from Egypt to the 12th century, from the wooden horses of the merry-go-rounds to the Sassanides, from the Palace of Versailles . . . to the Congo forest."[9]

Decades later, in *The Way of the Masks*, Lévi-Strauss returned once more to the enigma of those Salish, Kwakiutl, and Tsimshian masks and headdresses from the Pacific Northwest. A mask, like any artwork, he argued, never represents anything on its own. Instead, what it does is to transform the field of masks as a whole, all those other masks, both real and potential, that also exist alongside it. Creation is always a dialogue with the past, with the form and force of what already exists.

"When [the artist] thinks he is expressing himself spontaneously, creating an original work," Lévi-Strauss suggested, "he is answering other past or present, actual or potential, creators. Whether one knows it or not, one never walks alone along the path of creativity."[10]

Back in Chennai, I called Kingfisher Airlines and booked a flight to Hubli in northern Karnataka.

.... ⊢ ....

At 4 a.m., a wakeup call from Rajeevan: "Good afternoon!"

Yesterday we'd both missed the 6 a.m. flight to Hubli. I'd woken in a panic to find daylight streaming through the window four minutes before the departure time. The art director had also overslept, but he was more sanguine; the truck taking up iron beams, wooden planks, and other materials for the bridge was itself a day late. "In this industry, chance is everything."

Meanwhile, plans for the structure have already shifted. What you see in the Telugu film *Vikramarkudu* are just a few planks laid across a ravine on a rickety metal frame. Now one of Rajeevan's assistants is hanging onto a sketch for something more elaborate: a bridge composed of rusted girders, held in place by a lattice truss and a taut network of cables.

On the way to Badami from the Hubli airport, we stop for breakfast at a roadside diner. The art director seems fidgety. He's made something out of a few luggage tags and a roll of plastic lying on the table, something that fans out, like a flower.

Does the project seem more appealing now? Rajeevan's face wrinkles into a small frown. He pulls together the tips of his fingers, then casts

them out as though it doesn't matter where they wind up. "It's the same
bridge," he says. "Only the shape is different."

·· H ··

Later that afternoon, I'm trailing the art director across a plateau of crumbling sandstone, high above the ruins of a medieval fortress. On a rocky outcrop lie more recent remains, a mortared foundation from the 2006 Telugu film set.

Look across, and the gorge has the semblance of a gash in the face of the earth. The span is narrow, daring you to jump across, to try to see if you can make it. But then you look down, and the land drops giddily away, maybe a couple hundred feet below.

Rajeevan, in shorts, flip-flops, and a wide-brimmed hat, paces along the edge, thinking about the bridge. "Shall we put it here?" he asks the stunt master and cameraman drifting along beside him. They have another spot in mind, which the art director agrees is better. "It looks more eerie there. The eerier it is, the better the impact."

"Art direction is just logic and common sense," Rajeevan tells me. But it's hard not to feel a sense of trepidation at what they're doing. Not one of them is an engineer, and gusts of wind sweep relentlessly along the outcrops. I keep my distance from the edge.

"Call everyone for a puja," the art director tells his master welder, Sathish, pointing out the spot where their construction will begin. But Sathish refuses to comply. Today is Tuesday, an inauspicious day to begin anything at all, let alone something so precarious.

The fate of the structure depends most upon his craftsmen, and their moral authority prevails. Work is postponed until the next morning.[11]

·· H ··

Sathish is thirty-seven. He's been welding since he was twelve. "Until the set goes up," he tells me, "there is nothing fixed in cinema." Locations keep changing. Even the ritual benedictions of the puja can happen again and again, as plans and strategies continue to shift. Through these tides, the master welder remains fixed on the safety of his crew and the approval of the art director. "For us, the art director is the most important, even more than the producer or director."

Rajeevan is sitting on an outcrop now, the next day, as Sathish's men raise a tarpaulin over their equipment. "Get me a pencil and a piece of paper," he calls out to the master welder. "See this," he tells Sathish, drawing him an image of the forty-foot truss they've begun to build and a scheme for laying it across the chasm of the ravine.

"There's no other way to do it," Rajeevan says, holding out his sketch to

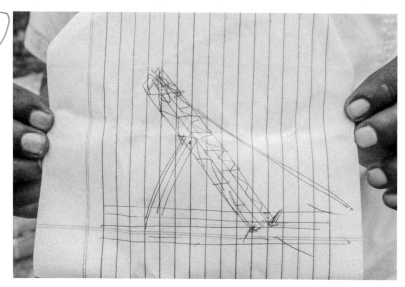

the film's director, Siva, who is lying on the rock behind him. "We make the truss. We let it down. Then we slowly loosen the rope support. I hope it works."

Day by day the art director leaves a continuous trail of such sketches, drawn on clipboards, in notebooks, even on the rocks around us. "I just make some scribbles," Rajeevan says dismissively when I ask about these drawings. But they're obviously essential to this process of construction. "Whenever we want to create something new," his assistant Prabha tells me, "it's with these sketches that we explain."

What strikes me most about these line drawings is how different each seems from those that have come before it. Some mark camera angles. Others, like this one, propose ways of tackling a construction challenge. Still others record architectural features that have since been abandoned. There is no place on the set—no clipboard, folder, or pocket—where they come to rest and accumulate. At each pivotal moment, another one appears, then disappears.

"To be original," writes Bruno Latour, "means necessarily to be the *origin* of a lineage."[12] This is precisely how creation appears to be unfolding here: as a chain of related images, each of which turns in a slightly different direction. These sketches are less models to copy than paths to follow—means of sustaining some momentum of movement, traversing the thickets of what is happening.[13]

"Here's the truss I've made," Rajeevan tells the film's producer one afternoon, holding out another sketch of the fragmentary structure. As with any other field of creation in Tamil cinema, his art is celebrated in the industry as a matter of individual vision and skill. But what happens here is much more dispersed, more like a scattering of busy workshops, a field of manual crafts folded into the manufacture of a contemporary digital artifact.

There are the seventeen welders, for example, who traveled here overnight by van from Chennai. Wearing plastic sheets and vinyl hats to ward off the rain, they work with slivers of iron cut down with a gas-powered blowtorch. One of them has just stamped on a scorpion lurking in a corner of their tarpaulin on the ridge. He shrugs. "Good luck for us, bad luck for it."

Down below, under the shelter of a sandstone overhang, the carpenters are examining some close-up photographs of axes and swords from *Vikramarkudu*. Working with small beams and plywood boards, they are expected to fashion wooden copies of these wooden copies.

Farther on, past a tangle of low brush, the molders are squatting around a pair of square plaster molds. Impressed upon the mottled surface of the ravine wall behind them, the molds are being replicated now with coconut fiber and more plaster. How can two small molds be enough to simulate such a large and irregular surface of rock? "We'll spread the mortar to make it work," one of them says, adding an explanation with a clever smile. "It's like editing."

Some of the painters have already begun to work on the finished copies of the molds, down at the base of the gorge. Red, yellow, and black watercolors to match the rock, with a spray of diesel and Japan black lacquer to hold the colors in place. "It's all a work of trickery, isn't it?" one of the painters, Krishna, jokes, his lungi soaked in the maroon liquid of his bucket.

·· ⊢ ·······································

What, though, are they doing out here anyway? All these makeshift workshops, nestled into various crevices of the sandstone cliffs, confound the distinction that is often drawn between studio sets and outdoor environments. Take the bridge that they're assembling, for example. Rajeevan calls it "a slightly bigger prop, just an element in an area." But then I overhear him on the phone. "I'm in Badami. We're putting up a set." What is it: a prop or a set?

Everything seems to turn on how you understand the "art" in such activities. Take this art to entail a transcendence of the natural world, an overcoming of what exists as it is, and what they're doing here may seem like very little indeed: filling out the landscape with scattered artifacts rather than remaking it fully to suit the demands of a creative vision.

But suppose you understood the relationship between art and nature in a different, less antagonistic manner. Think of Dewey, who had this to say about "naturalism" in art: "All which can be expressed is some aspect of the relation of man and his environment, and . . . this subject-matter attains its most perfect wedding with form when the basic rhythms that characterize the interaction of the two are depended upon and trusted with abandon."[14] What would it mean to "set" a film upon the basic rhythms of life?

Take walking, for example — the swinging to-and-fro of bipedal beings like ourselves. The rhythms of this movement have everything to do with the molded squares of plaster, coconut fiber, and watercolor paint that some of the craftsmen are fashioning. These ragged panels are meant, more than anything else, to disguise a stairway that the carpenters are building down into the base of the ravine, where much of the action will be staged.

The actors and crew will need these stairs simply to walk down to a spot where they will shoot. But the plywood steps and casuarina poles that compose this walkway must also disappear somehow; what the camera sees, as it moves, can be only those forms of movement appropriate to this terrain. "We can make something like a boulder here," Rajeevan tells his master carpenter; the face of the stairway will blend into the rubbled landscape.

As the art director sees it, a set is an "ambience created to shoot a film." But what he has in mind when he says this is something that serves as an active support more than a purely passive stage or backdrop: something, that is, that acts and reacts with the action that takes place upon it. The set is the space in which those of the film live and breathe, and the space from which the film will act upon the lives of those who watch it.

··· H ···

A quiet morning atop the cliffs. The skies are overcast but dry. There's a monkey rustling through the branches on the other side of the ravine. On this side, the welders are waiting for the power to come back on.

Rajeevan suddenly breaks the silence. "I've been thinking of creating clouds," he says, looking out at the rocks, "but I've never been able to do it." He's tried using cotton and dry ice, but nothing so far has worked well enough. He thinks he might make a trip out to California, pay a visit to George Lucas's Industrial Light & Magic.

"Being up here is making me a little philosophical," I say, looking down from the outcrop to the plunging depths of the gorge. The dizziness of

those depths reminds me of Kant and what he suggests about the sublime: that the terror we feel at towering mountains and deep ravines has mostly to do with our own minds, with the pull of imagination toward ideas of the infinite, the immeasurable, the abyssal.[15]

I remember what happened when a sudden gust of wind picked up one of Rajeevan's fake rock "puffs" and swept it over the edge. I made to grab it, without thinking, then found myself riveted by the horror of what I'd almost just accomplished. What if I had reached that gusting foam boulder? What if it had tumbled me along with it into the gorge?

If the art director has such feelings, he doesn't say. "Yeah, yeah, yeah, no big deal," he replies, distractedly, when I gesture toward these towering cliffs, asking whether he could build something so massive himself. For the film, his task is to give the semblance of a frightful infinity. For the shoot, his task is to give the semblance of measure and control.

.... ⊢ ....

Still, though, I know he's nervous. "We could have done all this indoors," he says on the rocks later, shaking his head. The depths below us? "We could have matte-painted it," he insists, waving the walkie-talkie in his hand. "We don't have the safety equipment here."

What they have to do is somehow lever across the ravine the hulking iron structure that the welders have built, to get it to sit on the lip of those rocks across the cleft without plummeting it or anyone else into the chasm below.

"None of us are engineers," Rajeevan concedes. But then he says this on the phone, with a gravity both alarming and absurd, when the moment finally arrives one cloudy morning: "Can I call you later? We're laying a bridge."

The voices of welders, carpenters, and local laborers rise and fall in rhythm over the gorge: *thallu thallu thallu.* Push, push, push. There are beams to grab onto and thick braids of nylon cord. The sunlight breaking through the clouds overhead has an epic quality. Gusts of wind send caps fluttering into the abyss. Rajeevan is also pushing, as am I, whenever I put down my camera. It feels like Werner Herzog's *Fitzcarraldo.*

A movement of slipping, creaking, stopping, and hanging. Then, with a booming clang, the truss comes to rest on an outcrop across the ravine. Cheers come bursting from both sides. "It's done," Rajeevan calls out. "Beers for everyone!"

Sathish is also proud. He wants my photographs on a CD. "I wasn't afraid, sir," he says. "I knew it, that we would lift it."

The art director and the stunt master are already walking around one

side of the structure, plotting how to use its space. Then a tape measure slips out of Rajeevan's hands and goes clattering over the edge. The faint thump of its landing beats back up to the lip of the gorge.

⊢

"Seem interesting to you now?" I ask Rajeevan, thinking back to his concerns about copying something that had been done before. His smile plays at a reluctant confession: "O—kay." He's planning on leaving the iron of the bridge unpainted, letting it develop a rusted tone akin to the sandstone rock. Coils of red rope will be wound along the railings.

We are talking now about the aesthetics of the construction. "It has to look nice," the art director concedes, but he also insists that beauty is less important here than the "practicality" of the set, "how it works." This is precisely what Alfred Gell had argued with regard to art: what matters most is "efficacy," the "capacity to accomplish tasks."[16] Artworks are active objects, things with powers, like persons in their ability to make other things happen. They have what Jane Bennett calls "Thing-Power: the curious ability of inanimate things to animate, to act, to produce effects dramatic and subtle."[17]

The bridge they've built is already doing this. Its presence has transformed the feel of these rugged cliffs, high above the small town of Badami. "It looks like a proper government bridge," some begin to worry, wondering whether, in the film, such a sturdy construction will seem implausible and out of place on this terrain.

Until now, experience of this landscape has been dominated by the force of gravity, pulling ever away to the depths of the earth below. Against this force is that of the bridge, a novel center of attraction. For those on the crew, crossing the chasm and its precipitous drop has suddenly become a routine and casual act, the landscape become an inhabited place, strewn with the detritus of human activity. Crumpled teacups take refuge in the thickets around the bridge.

.... **H** ....

In the film that they've been making here, *Siruthai*, the scene is terrifying. It may be the brutish guy with the axe, cutting apart the bridge so wantonly in his haste to kill the hero. It may be the child who dangles so precariously from one of its broken edges. Or the dizzying speed with which the camera keeps diving into the depths of the gorge.

"Appa, I'm scared," the little girl calls out, fingers clinging to a slender railing, as fragments of the fractured structure keep plunging into the chasm. There is a sensation of vertigo—hers, yours, whomevers. The bridge itself becomes this sensation, swaying and whipping wildly as it breaks into pieces over the abyss.[18]

I know there was a crane suspending these actors over the ravine with thick protective cables. I know they had also built a "dummy bridge," somewhere nearby, to stage these stunts over a much more modest drop. I know that these figures knocked and tumbling from the bridge are dolls that Rajeevan had designed to do just this. I know all this, and yet, as I watch, I keep forgetting. Things are moving too quickly. The threat remains, of falling.

Reviews of the film single out the art director's work on the fearsome bridge as "magnificent," "breathtaking." When I mention this to Rajeevan, he just laughs—a modest reaction with an ominous charge.

"In art, and in painting, as in music," Deleuze writes, "it is not a matter of reproducing or inventing forms, but of capturing forces."[19]

.... **H** ....

Sometime later, I have a dream. I'm walking into a space with a vaulted ceiling, something like a cavernous old-style movie hall. Inside there's a steep hillside, boulders tumbling down the slope. The scene is for a shepherd, leading his goats up the mountain. Then he's beside me, and we walk together, barefoot, up the hill.

Someone has thought very carefully about the shepherd's comfort. Cascading down the entire face of tumbling boulders is a long expanse of lime-green carpeting, wrapped precisely over the round contours of the rocks.

The carpeting looks absurd from here, as we walk through it, the shepherd and I, but I know this doesn't matter; on the screen, it will look like grass. I notice the small bunches of slender yellow flowers tucked artfully, here and there, into the plush green fabric.

"It must be Rajeevan," I think to myself, admiring the visual contrast.

Then I'm outside again, back in the light, in the midst of an anonymous crowd. Someone has dumped a cigarette, some plastic wrappers, other garbage into the shoes that I left outside. I try to knock it all out, but the refuse congeals into a thick gray slurry, pooling in the heel of my shoe.

I write to Rajeevan of what I saw. He writes back a few hours later —

Ha ha ha ha ha . . . . U must have watched "Raiders of the Lost Ark" and many other such films in the recent past i guess. . . . . . wake up dude. . . . its morning . . . LOL!!!

CHAPTER 6 Love

The first Tamil movies I remember watching were on Sunday afternoons at the Montebello Public Library in southern California. This was in the early 1980s, before you could buy them on VHS. I remember wondering why those men and women kept dancing together around trees and mountaintops. Then I began spending years in Tamil Nadu, watching these films myself, listening to rural women sing of their husbands as philandering parakeets nestled in the leaves of distant groves. The images stayed with me. Once I came back to California for a few delightful weeks. "This is the dream sequence, the song-and-dance routine," I said to a friend. "No, Anand," she insisted, gently but firmly, "this is actually your life." Still, it was strange, that summer, cruising around Oakland, hearing those Tamil film songs in everything I saw, finding some far-off landscape ever and again for the vexations and raptures of love.

.... ⊢ ....

His name is Anbu, *love*. Love is righteous. Love is fierce. Love is playful, sweet, and deadly. Love turns everything upside down, only to bring it all back to where it ought to be. So it goes in this 2007 Tamil film, *Malaikottai*.[1]

Love is all these things, yes. Love is also a tall guy pedaling a cycle through the dusty lanes of the town of Trichy, looking for someone, something. Love, in fact, is looking for love.

Love finds someone to love on a rooftop terrace in the clamorous heart of the city: a young woman clad in red and white, shaking out a sari to dry. A swish of the fabric sends droplets flying. Slowly, they glide across that smoggy terrace, gathering strength from the voices suddenly humming in the air.

Love closes his eyes. The droplets caress his face. Love, suddenly, is somewhere else: on a ridge overlook-

ing verdant slopes and snow-clad peaks, some vast space of possibility that engulfs the two of them. As the music picks up the rhythm of a song, they begin to dance. The voice belongs to Love, but its feelings are every-where, pervading the space around them.

> Life, my life, the moment that I saw you, I froze
> This bond, I felt it, the moment that you saw me,
> To live in your eyes . . . like camphor, love, I melted
> You're that song I always hear, do you know?
> You're my bloom, always budding, do you know?
> I'm that breeze you always feel, will you know?
> I'm the speech in all your silence, will you feel it?

Love and his beloved, a man and a woman, a heterosexual pair bobbing into union. But there's also something odd, even queer, about this love of Love's, this feeling that melts so readily into song, bloom, breeze, speech, and everything else in that unknown place, before returning, once again and so abruptly, to the grimy streets of Trichy.

⊢

Love, writes Lauren Berlant, is a queer feeling. Love is a matter of plots and norms, conventions repeated endlessly with every new avowal of its existence, chaotic and uncertain feelings that always seem to end up in the same old forms of marriage and reproduction. There is a rhythm and a shape to this movement between form and formlessness, Berlant suggests, a certain picture of what life and its fulfillment should feel like. But love can also drift into more enigmatic and untenable couplings. "Love is queered," she argues, "when we see that there is no world that admits how it actually works as a principle of living."[2]

Berlant pens her critical reflections with certain impasses in mind, limits that govern the experience of love in the modern West, which seems always to veer toward the love that individuals may nurture for themselves. But what of such feelings elsewhere, in places like Trichy, for example?[3] Think of what the anthropologist Margaret Trawick found in one Tamil family: a love that flowed as "a web maintained by unrelieved tensions, an architecture of conflicting desires, its symmetry a symmetry of imbalance, its cyclicity that of a hunter following his own tracks."[4] What would it mean to live out what seems to be so patently unlivable?

I think of the love that I encountered in the villages of Tamil Nadu's Cumbum Valley some years ago: an astonishing span of clandestine liaisons, sometimes craning toward the promise of marital life but also pursued with no such pretensions, consummated through furtive movements of running and hiding, through encounters that took place in shady orchards, narrow alleyways, and abandoned houses, indulging feelings that so often spilled beyond, confounded, and defied the taboos of age, caste, gender, homosexuality, even incest.[5]

Love there was a feeling that always seemed to carry a queering charge or potential. And so much of this had to do with the dangers presented by cinema, with the desires intensified by an age of cinema, with temptations borne especially along the currents of its songs—songs that tore themselves so far, so often, from the worlds to which their protagonists belonged.

⊢

There are the places, native or otherwise, in which films like *Malaikottai* are set. Then there are those moments that leap into startlingly different situations. The song-and-dance sequence has long been a prevalent feature of Indian cinema, creating a space for things that may otherwise remain unseen and unsaid. This is a "peculiarly *queer* form," Gayatri Gopinath argues, one that "falls outside the exigencies of narrative coherence and closure."[6]

Songs affirm that there is more to love in cinema than connubial union between hero and heroine or, for that matter, between a story and its audience, offering attractions that may have little to do with the plot and fate of a film's central characters.[7] These songs play at times on the charge of men or women cavorting, hand-in-hand, among themselves, which is why critics such as Gopinath find them rupturing the normative heterosexuality of Indian cinema. But there are also more diffuse and impersonal forms of pleasure and even love at work in such moments, often having to do with the very environments in which these songs take place.

Lakes and forests, tea estates and hill stations: until the 1990s, Indian filmmakers staged scenes of romantic attraction in the midst of such grounds of regional and national tourism. With India's economic liberalization at that time, however, also came a momentous globalization of filmic locales. Indian film crews began to seek out far-flung localities in Europe, Asia, Africa, the South Pacific, and the Americas—spaces of desire and fantasy, and often themselves emerging destinations for middle-class Indian tourists.[8]

One enterprise has had more to do with these developments than any other: Travelmasters India, a Chennai-based travel agency that has planned hundreds of overseas expeditions for Indian film crews over the past twenty years—over two hundred in Switzerland alone. "Can you find these colors in India?" the company's managing director, N. Ramji, asked me emphatically one afternoon, gesturing to the image of an ochre dune

in Namibia, where he'd just organized a Tamil film shoot. He recited a
litany of practical and aesthetic factors that drew Indian filmmakers to
such places overseas. "Logistically, it's closer to go to Switzerland than to
Kullu Manali" (in the Himalayas).

On Ramji's desk was a gleaming magenta globe and a scale model of a Cathay Pacific jetliner. He quickly understood that as an anthropologist, I would want, as he put it, "to get embedded in a shoot." He had another upcoming shoot that might have gone to Istanbul or Capetown, until a glitch in visa planning had pointed them once again in the direction of Switzerland, where they would soon be headed.

A few days later, with Ramji's considerate help, I was on a flight from Chennai to Zurich with sixteen members of the *Malaikottai* cast and crew.

⊢

At a certain moment early in *Malaikottai*, Anbu, played by the Tamil actor Vishal, is startled awake by the sound of an airplane passing low over the bus in which he's dozing. As his head cranes beyond the bus window, you can see him following the plane with his eyes for a long time, as though its unknown destination has captured his imagination.

The film takes its name from the rock fort that overlooks the town of Trichy, in central Tamil Nadu. Anbu, required to report here each morning to a local police station, finds an urban milieu of wanton cruelty and sadistic violence. All of this he will master almost single-handedly, walloping countless thugs with dramatic flair.

"It's nothing but a money-maker," one of *Malaikottai*'s producers admitted quietly to me, dismissing his own film and suggesting that my time might be better spent somewhere else. There is no question that so much of the film hews closely to a certain picture of what the young males for whom it was made might want, fantasies constantly turning on the appeal of aggressive and heroic men to vulnerable and defenseless women.

At the same time, however, there are many things about *Malaikottai* that confound this formula, often having to do with the unmanning of manly men. Take the police inspector, for example, Anbu's uncle, whose valorous bluster is nothing more than a cover for an unrequited romance. Or Anbu himself, who toys with a campy femininity—high voice, batted eyes, swaying hips—at many moments in the film. The most unambiguously masculine figures in the tale are its villains, all bound for inexorable defeat.

With all of his vigorous and decisive action, in fact, Anbu's headlong descent into love is marked most clearly by a condition of passivity and susceptibility. You see him shaken suddenly awake by that passing plane.

Then he's jolted by the collision of his bus with a car. Then he's startled by the glimpse of that young woman, Malar, on a nearby rooftop terrace. And then, soon enough, he is literally and magically moved by those fly-ing droplets of water, to somewhere else far away.

We are suddenly in the space of a song. "Life, my life, that moment I saw you. . . ."

⊢

Love, lingering on his beloved, finds he's drifted somewhere unexpected, somewhere other than Trichy. Still, why Switzerland? "Greens . . . love mood," the director of the film, Bhoopathy Pandian, mutters rather enig-matically when I ask him this question on a set one afternoon in Chen-nai. But we have no more than a few seconds to talk about this, as he has decided not to fly out to Zurich himself.

Concern for color persists as his crew meanders through the rural land-scape around Interlaken, where they have decided to shoot the song. "We want something that's endlessly green," the producer explains right away to their Swiss location manager. Cameraman Vaidhi has also pinned his hopes on spaces of "the purest green." And the location manager, Peter, caters to the desires embodied in their Indian English argot, pointing out such spots on a map: "We might be able to catch some greens here."

Each morning, they seek out green fields, flowering meadows, and tree-lined roads. Peter doubles as their bus driver, and decisions about where to shoot are made literally on the spot, as the sudden glimpse of an attractive view through the windows puts a halt to the ongoing flow of discussion. The movements they choreograph fill each of these scenes with energetic intensity, and techniques are devised to suggest that the landscape itself is admiring these moves—the blurred outlines of a single flower or a sinuous log in a corner of the frame, for example, as though the vision of love had erupted organically from within these fields.

Stopping the bus at one hilltop crossroads, shrouded now in rain and mist, Peter tries gamely to persuade his passengers that this is a place never seen before in Tamil cinema. The cameraman retorts with a sar-donic joke—"Hey, they shot *Karagatta Karan* right here!"—while the actor Vishal chimes in with some famous lyrics from this well-known Tamil feature, a classic village nativity film of the 1980s: "Hey oriole dear, hey cuckoo dear, here's some news for you—today's the day that some-one's coming to wed you with a garland."

⊢

They are, in fact, romancing the landscape itself.[9] But this is a love dif-ficult to nurture and sustain. The filmmakers have come into this affair with a particular ideal in mind, blithely presuming that the environment would bend itself to their needs. "Switzerland is like an outdoor studio," the young producer had confidently pronounced at the outset of the trip. The next few days, however, leave them rattled and frustrated by the very elements they are courting.

A premonition of the difficulties ahead came as early as the Zurich airport immigration counter, where an official responded ominously to a description of their plans with the two words "Bad weather." They had landed in central Europe in early August with an image of long summer days and sunny blue skies, only to find themselves interrupted by incessant bouts of rain. There are times it comes down so hard that they can't leave the bus at all to shoot.

Landslides strand the bus one evening, overrunning the roads around a lake where they are working. "I am sick of this place," the producer, Ajay, says darkly, having long since abandoned his fantasies of an outdoor studio. Meanwhile, the assistant choreographer, Kokila, admits that she hasn't even brought her camera with her on this trip, already her fourth Swiss shoot. "Who would want to see these pictures?"

Caught between rain and boredom, the crew's mood ebbs and flows with the weather.

·· **H** ··································

"This bond, I felt it, the moment that you saw me," Anbu sings. For most of the song, as Anbu and Malar lead each other through verdant fields and cobbled courtyards, the boy is looking at and singing to that girl. But at this moment, early in the song, when Anbu appears to give voice to precisely these words—*unarnthene*, "I felt it"—he is gazing not in her direction but upward, into the sky above, his face beaming and basking in the light of an unseen sun, as if fully immersed in the feeling of its warmth.

Take this too as a moment of love, a fantasy of intercourse, so to speak: With whom, with what? In an intriguing discussion of bodily orientation (ordinary, straight, sexual, and otherwise) Sara Ahmed challenges the way that orientation is reduced so easily to the question of sexual objects and practices. The "queer" object of desire may be understood more expansively, she suggests, as "the one out of line, on a slant, the odd and strange one . . . encountered as slipping away, as threatening to become out of reach."[10]

Slipping away, threatening to pass out of reach—like the sun, always, during those few fateful days of chase through Switzerland by the *Malaikottai* crew. Like most Tamil film crews shooting outdoors beyond India, they have cut their costs by working without the aid of mechanical lights,

relying entirely on what they can capture from the skies. For that one shot of a basking Anbu, for example, they use three reflectors made of vinyl and Styrofoam to bounce all available light onto Vishal's blissful face.

"It's opened! Quickly, quickly!" they say with each gap that surfaces through the passing clouds, a rush that lapses again and again into a familiar lament: "It closed, just like that." The sun itself is addressed as a person—he—in so many of their exchanges, with all the ambivalence of love and hate, tides of hope and bitter despair.

The rain finally breaks decisively on the final day of their weeklong shoot, as they work on a ridge overlooking the Grindelwald Alpenvogel Park. "Changing and changing, it keeps showing different locations," Vaidhi beams. They go on to can over seventy shots by sundown, including that image of Anbu soaked in sunlight.

"It shows, it shows, the Swissness shows!" the choreographer exclaims, as they frame one final silhouette of the dancers within a copse of trees and the gathering dusk.

Is this love, this embrace of place that they are seeking? The song ends with Anbu clasping not Malar but the Alps themselves, legs splayed open, arms cast wide, losing himself in the fullness of these snow-clad slopes, suspended in the air as though the moment will not pass, which of course it must. Back to Trichy.

⊢

Something strange and fortuitous happened as I was walking to work some time ago, as I was walking to my office, in fact, to try to begin writing this chapter on love. It was a humid day of cloudy skies, moisture clinging to the air as it often does in Baltimore in the summer. I was stepping down the forest path as I do each day, thinking about nothing in particular, least of all the stony ground beneath my feet.

But there it was that day, something black, maybe five, maybe six feet long, slithering slowly across the path, winding sinuously between the stones like a thick, glistening span of worm. Just a rat snake, nothing poisonous, nothing deadly, but enough to leave me riveted, palpitating, robbed of my forward momentum.

When I began walking once again, I found myself in a world become flesh. That slithering body, its echo was everywhere around me: winding roots, overhanging branches, vines and stems reaching out into the air, all of this was pervaded by that snaking movement, by its tingling promise to rupture the limits of my body.[11] There was, to be sure, a mild feeling of terror in all this, as I rushed through the woods to reach the asphalt road, but this was inextricable from the electric delight of such a rare encounter.

This too, love? Think of the countless poets tormented by a vision of the beloved at every turn. How easy is it to distinguish love from other ways of becoming overly entangled in some environment of overwhelming feeling? "Libidinal desire, the carnal caress . . . is an interchange with an other whose surface intersects its own," writes Elizabeth Grosz, an other whose universe need not even be human or animal. "It is in this sense that we make love to worlds."[12]

By the time I walked back home that day, a few hours later, the sensation had already passed. Vines were vines, branches branches, and I myself again, with little risk of coming undone. And yet the challenge, however odd, say, queer, remained. Love as a force that could engulf and envelop from nowhere and everywhere at once, only to recede once more without a trace: what does it mean to find yourself bound to something so fugitive as an atmosphere?

··· ⊢ ···································

Not far from Interlaken lies the Alpine saddle of Jungfraujoch, marketed to tourists from India and elsewhere as the "Top of Europe." Once the *Malaikottai* shoot has ended, I take the train up to Jungfraujoch to stop in at Hotel Bollywood, its wall-to-wall Indian film posters catering to a global clientele with passions for Indian and Swiss spectacles alike.

From the lobby, I place a call to Ramji at the Travelmasters office in Chennai, wondering whether I ought to return now to India or go somewhere else instead. He suggests that I fly to the United Arab Emirates, where he has just organized a song shoot for another Tamil film project.

It may be nothing more than an altitude-related headache, but I too am somehow tired of Switzerland. Two nights later, I land in Dubai, haunted by second thoughts—at 11:20 p.m., as we touch down, the pilots report a ground temperature of 104 degrees Fahrenheit.

Just after sunrise the next morning, I'm squeezed into one of several SUVs heading into the desert southeast of the city. This crew is here to shoot two songs for a film called *Nam Nadu* [Our country], centered on the political ascent of a nominally young party activist.[13] The character, Muthalagan, is played by the veteran Tamil actor Sarath Kumar; the actor's plans to float a political party of his own in Tamil Nadu give the project the unmistakable feeling of a promotional vehicle.[14]

Early in the film, a soft-spoken young schoolteacher named Gowri will implore Muthalagan to help fight the construction of a soda-bottling plant in her native village. Once he succeeds, the film will cut to a quiet office, where Gowri, alone, will call him on the phone. "I need to tell you something important," she would say with a shy laugh. "It wouldn't be good to say it on the phone. Can I see you in person?"

And as she asks this question, the film will have already gone somewhere else, to the image of Gowri striding through sand in a racy black outfit, while the gentle tones of a flute give way to a boisterous Arabic melody.

⊢

This song also gives body to a fantasy of union—in this case, hers. "It's whatever she likes inside her heart, which she won't tell anybody," an assistant choreographer, Arun, explains one evening in Dubai. The chorus, which comes first and most often in a woman's voice, makes this clear: "In the hearts of both, friction, friction, life's friction."

The movements the choreographers have devised leave little to the imagination when it comes to the kind of friction intended here. But oddly, the three environments where they choose to shoot the song seem rather unsuitable for physical pleasure. Heaping sand dunes, a rocky dam surrounded by craggy peaks, a white sand beach ringed by a stone barrier: all of these places seem hard, rough, and uncomfortable.

What the crew asks of their location manager only compounds the enigma. Immediately on reaching the dunes the first morning of the shoot, for example, the film's producer sharply declares, "This is not a real desert." The lead choreographer, Shanthi, dismisses the few green shrubs nestled in the sand as "rubbish," asking for a backdrop devoid of these "patches."

The following day, a series of shots are framed against the coarse rubble face of a nearby dam. The spot is precarious, difficult to walk upon, let alone mount a steady camera. And yet Shanthi applauds the cinematographer for managing to frame hero and heroine against the rubble as well as a jagged range of mountains in the distance. "It's nice, no? It's hard."

From the standpoint of the Swiss "greens" that I've just left behind, all of this is deeply puzzling. But then Arun explains that these places are meant to convey a different mood of love, a feeling more rough and rugged. "She's saying 'I will come and mix myself with you,' something sexy, like that. Green, trees, that'll make the scene too soft."

H

The sound booming across the space of these rocks and dunes has a hard and insistent edge of its own. "Call, and I will come," that woman's voice sings over a distorted guitar. "I will give you a thousand things. You're a sea of bliss, for she, this stream, to join."

These lyrics rely upon a Tamil poetics of devoted love, echoing the literary portrayal of gods and kings as objects of erotic longing for enchanted female devotees.[15] It's as though the song sanctifies terrestrial political struggle—in all of its manifest desire and evident friction—into a cosmic erotics of divine union.

Practically speaking, however, the deity in question is hardly reachable. The aging actor Sarath Kumar pulls the film's young heroine to him sharply on cue. But for the most part, the body he couples with most closely is his own cell phone, as he fields countless calls concerning his nascent political party back in Chennai.

There is also the caustic heat of the environment. Data about summer temperatures in Dubai have somehow been miscommunicated; even for an Indian film crew accustomed to working in challenging physical

circumstances, it is surprisingly, unbearably hot. Some of the crew soak caps and kerchiefs with water to cover their heads. Cartons and bottles of buttermilk are passed around in regular rounds, along with faintly chilled water. Umbrellas are snatched back and forth and sometimes disappear. In spite of all this, people are vomiting from the brutal heat. "This isn't life at all," one of the makeup men plaintively declares, gazing out at the desiccated terrain from the temporary comfort of one of the air-conditioned SUVs.

A fierce wind, one afternoon, blows coarse sand into everyone's face during a rehearsal, sweeping up caps and lyric sheets in the lacerating currents of air. "No need to move, this itself moves us," the taciturn director quietly intones.

The circumstances lead the hero to disappear into his trailer and hotel room for hours on end, leaving others to joke, nervously, that the song would be less a "duet" than a "diet."

·· ᚺ ···

Urasal urasal, friction, friction, the loudspeakers keep insisting, but the movements of the heroine and her hero remain weak and chaste. He is distracted, she awkward and hesitant, and both have wilted under the futile shade of their umbrellas.

There is an obvious deficiency of erotic charge between the leading pair. But, the filmmakers also have on hand a troupe of Russian belly dancers. These women in sequins and tassels are placed at times along the undulating ridges of the landscape, as though they draw their fluidity from the sand itself. For other shots, they are invited to almost engulf the hapless heroine with their twisting limbs, passing over, through their own bodies, the intensity of the desert.

The dancers are meant to magnify the erotic appeal of the song's reluctant and elusive hero. But looking back at the song that was shot here, these dancers seem, at times, to be doing something rather different from this. Look at Gowri as she imagines herself in their midst. For those few seconds, at the very least, she seems to be glorying in the company of those flying limbs and grains.

"Just your style, girls, just freestyle!" Shanthi calls out. She admits that these women are "the life of the song." The belly dancers provoke a hush of awe, one afternoon, when they boldly change into bikinis on the very edge of the shoot, relaxing into the shallow teal water of the Hatta Dam. "They're bathing. What a life," Shanthi says wistfully, as the men on the crew, still sweating, try not to stare too avidly.

·· ┤ ···

"As the sun with its hot rays and the moon with its cool ones might slip from their orbits and meet," the medieval Tamil literary critic Nakkiranar wrote, "these two will meet."[16] His was a commentary on a treatise of classical Tamil love poetry. A young man and woman spy each other in a mountain grove. The forces of love they encounter here are palpable, elemental, pulling together their bodies and many other things in their wake.

He sees her as a flowering vine, asks the bees for blossoms as fragrant as her hair. She wonders whether he's a wood sprite, marveling at the golden blooms of a kino tree. "At the very sight of it, she feels a swelling love. . . . She lets her heart flow wherever it flows, among all the things it wants," Nakkiranar writes.[17] Here love is a drifting movement of attraction, spilling easily beyond these dyadic pairs: man and woman, work and critic, spectator and object of vision.

"We should read popular Indian films," Lalitha Gopalan argues, "from the point of view of a cinephiliac, one that is based on an ambivalent relationship to cinema: love and hate."[18] Let me admit something: I've been struggling in this chapter with the limits of my own cinephilia, with two films that I find difficult to watch, let alone love. What drew me to them was less the hankering of a faithful devotee than the vicissitudes of ethnographic encounter. Wanting to learn something about film shoots overseas, these were the films I stumbled upon.

Both *Malaikottai* and *Nam Nadu* are steeped, like so many Tamil films, in a belligerent masculinity, a temperament portrayed as both bane and salvation of vulnerable women. These are nakedly commercial films, whose amorous entanglements between men and women are meant to secure another kind of marital contract, intended to consummate an-other kind of romance: the love that may brew between a screen and an audience before it.

Sometimes this works; *Malaikottai* was a box-office hit, *Nam Nadu* a resounding flop, like the political venture it was meant to fire up. Thankfully, though, in cinema as in life, there is much more to love than the promise of a happy ending.

Love is fugitive, as the poets of Tamil Nadu have long insisted, stealing ever away through the elemental drift of attachment.

CHAPTER 7 **Desire**

I never knew, with this fieldwork, whether what I left would remain as it was when I came back. Or rather, what these erratic encounters taught was the likelihood that things would stray from their expected course. One week, Sanchita and Karun had gone off to Kerala. I was alone and unmoored in our Anna Nagar flat—alone may not be the right word, as there were too many baleful presences just beyond my reach, working everywhere out of sight in the visible breadth of the city. I paced the balcony, drank well before lunch, passed the afternoons in fitful sleep, trying to do anything but to will the phone once more to ring. "Just go with the current," one of these filmmakers advised, when I expressed the impossibility of living with the sheer uncertainty of their world. They knew me as the guy who had a water bottle always swinging from his back, as though possessed by a fear of thirst. I tried to imagine what it might be like to lose myself in that current of desire, an endless exhalation of want, the rolling intensity of a scream.

.... ⊢ ....

Dusk is already falling when we pull into the parking lot and I point out the actress and the taxi driver says that she's the reason for his divorce, that Tamil director, sitting now on one of the plush lawns of the MGM Beach Resort, picking at a plate of French fries as his crew remakes a guest cottage into a nuptial boudoir, still waiting for the satiny sheets stuck on a lorry somewhere in Chennai, thinking about what was printed in the papers just this morning, more news of his impending divorce, about what his wife had said when she left him, that he wasn't stable, wasn't reliable, "how could I be stable?" he turns to ask me, "I can't be stable, I have to *live* somebody else, otherwise I can't make my films," telling me to imagine some filmmaker, any filmmaker, "two wed-

dings, four weddings, three weddings, countless affairs, because you're not yourself, you can't be yourself, you can't have a steady life," his words beginning to tumble now in a rush of recollections, "you've been a gangster, you've been a king, you've been a slum guy, you've been a decent guy, I've been that girl, this girl, in a given film I play some seventy, sixty, fifty, forty characters, and this is my ninth movie, so nine times fifty, you can calculate how many characters I've played," he says, "you can see why all filmmakers are mad, some people talk to trees, they have to let it out somewhere," and as I listen, I begin to wonder, what is it that they have to let out, all these men that he has in mind, expression, emission, is it the spunk of genius or something else for this director, Selvaraghavan, for whom, as he says, filmmaking is literally orgasm, multiple orgasms, more intense than a hundred orgasms, this man whose films are so flagrantly sexual, like *Thulluvadho Ilamai*, Youth, How It Leaps, his first, a coming-of-age story crammed with brothels, porn, and amorous predilections of all kinds, one man winking suggestively at a trio of boys, a girl alone running her hand down, down the length of her own dress, the forest tryst she has with her schoolboy friend, "so that's how much you're itching for it?" her confidante chides, a line that set the Thambi's Theatre crowd around me screaming and hollering a decade ago in rural Cumbum, the hall packed with young men and no women for what was said about the pornographic tones of the film, nominally directed by Selva's father, but a story really put, Selva says, into his own tender hands of twenty-one years, "hell," he says, "every night I used to come back and cry," too many people awaiting instructions, too little control over the technicians, until suddenly, "something happened on one of those days," suddenly there was "somebody else yelling inside me," someone else bursting out, "someone bold and arrogant, he just goes in, 'I want this shot, do it, push! no, I want it that way!' he screams," some presence you might describe as a person but is really more like a thing, something not to judge whether good or bad, something not to caution or censure for its injury or harm, "coming like a rush, you just do it, you just become it" he says, it, this it, let's call this "it" something, *desire*, "for it is a matter of flows, of stocks, of breaks in and fluctuations of flows,"[1] something to undo its subject, something to exceed its object, something that wants only to make things and break things, "after a point, nothing else exists for me, I don't care much about anything else" Selva says, knowing only too well what they say about him, that he's mad, that he's arrogant and eccentric, "an awful person nobody can call a good husband or a good son," and yet so many of them seem to adore his films, looking past—maybe riveted by—whatever they find distasteful or repellent in these stories of cou-

pling and decoupling, union and divorce, sex and death, films that seem
somehow to tap, even machine the rush of feeling that Selva describes,
like what happened a few years back at the Sangam Theatre in Chennai,
the opening day of his sixth film, *Ayirathil Oruvan* [One in a thousand],
all 887 seats sold out for the 11:15 a.m. show, a thunderous crowd of
young men mostly, roaring and whistling for that song that came an hour
into the film, *un mela asai than*, "yeah, it's desire for you," whose desire,
my desire, your desire, their desire, those guys in the hall or that guy on
the screen or that rowdy pair of girls flanking and mounting him that
voice never said, singing into being a desire that belonged to no one in
particular but was everywhere at once, a desire that settled delighted on
the spectacle of that threesome but seeped as well into everything else,
the desert, the thirst, the booze gold and meat, an encompassing landscape of delirious want, "delirium is cosmic," says Deleuze, "this is the
great secret of delirium, we become delirious with the whole world,"[2] as
with the aftermath of that drunken revel onscreen, as that desire passed
more fully into madness, as the film descended into caverns spattered
with blood and human flesh, haunted by the depraved heirs and followers
of a Chola prince exiled to that island eight centuries back, as the ruckus
in the theater subsided, as it grew into a palpable feeling of unease, as all
of us fell into a silent longing for daybreak, for sunlight, for punctuation—for something other than another fucking comma please!—for a
release that wouldn't come, the film dawdling still in that night of pillage,
rape, and gunfire, then dipping into an abrupt and startling blackness, "is
it over?" puzzled voices calling out in the theater, sober and uncertain,
still awash in that fate, in that "cultivation of desire,"[3] that production of
desire, that erotics of affliction and delectation, desire like a machine
winding up and sputtering out, the cinema as a "desiring-machine,"[4] a
collective production, all those elements of conjuncture and disjuncture,
unleashing pulses and fluxes of various kinds, passing through an audience and the world, undoing their integrity and the solidity of that world,
desire bordering on delirium, as with so many of Selvaraghavan's films,
like this one too, now under way at the MGM Beach Resort, a film without
a name, or at least a name that has stayed with it for very long, "Shri
Films Production No. 1" is what the clapboard reads for a shooting schedule that began in a basement studio just a few days back, a film, it seems,
that had started up all at once, Selva still writing the script in the corners
of that house, casting additional roles between each take, for "everywhere else," as his art director says, "the sun rises in the morning and sets
at night, but not here, things here, they suddenly happen, all at once,"
something wry and sardonic about what he says and how he laughs but a
commotion all the same that the director had wanted, "we're throwing

out everything we've learned," he told me, speaking of French New Wave cinema, "trying to do something new," his heroine reading between takes from François Truffaut's *The Films in My Life*, his cameraman Ramji improvising long and uninterrupted shots with a handheld camera trembling with the tension of what was happening, a shoot, in fact, unlike anything else I'd seen before, more private, more intense, Selva and Ramji always huddled close to the video screen in a swirl of smoke, offering no more than a murmur of assent to an okay take, mostly calling instead for more of this, less of that, one, two, five, nine, fourteen, the take count building relentlessly for this director who acts out each scene himself, who projects with his own face and body what he wants from his players, like the argument they staged around the dining room of that house in T. Nagar, "he doesn't even deserve to look in my fucking face, are you fucking mad?" that young woman screaming, "I'll arrange the marriage only if you like him, what am I gonna do, grab you by the neck and shove you at him?" her father belting back, Selva telling the father that he should feel the fury in his bones, telling the daughter that she had to lose herself completely, the director gesticulating wildly with his own clenched fists, letting out a raw growl of rage—zhzhzhzhrrr!—that left him parched and needing water and muttering something to himself about losing energy, the father admitting that he was exhausted himself, "she's banging the table saying 'Fuck!' and automatically, you get pumped up, it flows, you have to feed off that energy," and the more he spoke, the more the shoot began to feel like an economy of energetics, some system of flows, blocks, transfers and relays, "plus-minus and you have current flowing through the shot," Selva, once a mechanical engineer, told me, "nobody wants to see plus-plus or minus-minus," like Sergei Eisenstein, I said to him, "conflict as the fundamental principle for the existence of every art-work,"[5] but Selva said he hasn't heard of Eisenstein, only Einstein, and so we got to talking about other things, like what they would do here, at this resort, for another scene in the film, the art director now inside the guest cottage, painting a wall with swirls of blue for an episode of misfired seduction, a scene, Selva says, that will "propel the entire first half of the film," plus-minus, minus-plus, "people are never gonna believe that these two will live together," their desires pulling to opposing poles, the actor stripped down already into his boxer shorts and clambering eagerly into bed with a glass of champagne as the actress steps wearily out of the bathroom and fixes him with a look that passes from horror to disgust to despair to rage, "so you think two people having sex is some kind of game, I know nothing about you, to have sex with someone I know nothing about, what, do you think of me as a prostitute or something?" she screams, "I can hardly stand, my whole body hurts, there's so much else you could have asked me, 'dear, you haven't eaten since this morning, can I get you something to eat . . . you look tired, why don't you sleep . . . you said you had a headache, how is it now . . . can I cut you some fruit,' not one damn bit of this, instead, 'come, lie down with me,' you say, tearing off your clothes just like that, and you call yourself a man?" and as the director leads them through the scene, living out each of these characters himself, I can see what he means about an impossible stability, for there he goes, first with earnest glee on that rumpled bed, then with bug-eyed rage in a corner of the room, leaping, in a matter of seconds or even less, from one place into the other, one mood and then the other, one character into another, a subject undone by these predicates, these "successions of catatonic states and periods of extreme haste, of suspensions and shootings, coexistences of variable speeds, blocs of becoming, leaps across voids,"[6] desire much more than a personal feeling to fulfill, the director much less than the operator of this machine, the director, in fact, as someone operated himself, someone directed, bisected, and dissected by all those relays, blockages, and flows, by the canister of film that needs to be changed, by the pocket phone that suddenly rings, by the glycerin nagging at the heroine's eyes, interruptions warping and confounding whatever lies unspoken between the director and the actress, his wanting that she wants what he wants, his wanting that he wants what she wants, "see, any woman, standing and standing from the morning, standing for four hours, you're dead tired, you can't go on, you come in and he's sitting there, at least he could have spoken to you for five minutes, 'how are you, okay, sit down,' but nothing, just 'come, come, come,' you're totally frustrated," Selva tells her, exasperation beaming from his face, but she is somehow missing from the mirror of his gaze, and so they try another take, and then another and another, and this is how it goes, night after night, as this small scene of desire sputters into life, the director wanting more from her than from anyone else in that crowded cottage, most especially the actor, his brother, a beloved star and a fixture in Selva's films who just shrugs off what is expected of him here ("he tells me what he wants and I can easily Xerox it"), preparing for each bare-chested shot with a few quick pushups while the tension mounts between the director and the actress, "hit him nicely," he's insisting, "don't fake it, I need an emotional outbreak, it should come like a storm," but it's not until the next morning that the brewing storm lands, the director just past shouting when I walk in the door, the actor buried under the bedclothes while the director and actress argue beside the bed, she, sighing "I wouldn't do that myself, but if this is what you want, I'll do it for you," he, muttering, "I can't shoot like this," someone handing her a tissue for her reddening eyes, the actor imploring the director not to cancel the shoot, each of them locked for most of the day within their dressing room strongholds, finally coming out to work into that night, but only that one night, not the next night, or the one that follows, or even the night after that, for there is rain more rain and even more rain in Chennai, drowning out their plans for another scene, and by the time the rain lets up the actor is gone, the director's back to editing another project, and the actress who knows as they've hardly let me speak to her for more than a minute at a time, more than a year going by before I read, in the papers, that she's walked out of the project at last, and that Selva is directing another film now, *Mayakkam Enna*, Why the Tumult, a new film that will bear, less like a scar than a sluice, all the force of this movie that barely happened, all the rage, the disdain, the nearly imperceptible twitching of want, all this feeling borne onward into yet another world, yet another trial, "desire," writes Deleuze, "never needs interpreting, it is it which experiments,"[7] or, as Selva says, "it's like jumping into the sea, you have to keep swimming, it's too late now to swim back."[8]

CHAPTER 8 Light

Like the primeval convulsions of the cosmos, all of this has got to begin somewhere, with the coming of a universe into light. It happened one night on a grimy street corner in north Chennai, before a makeshift shrine and a pair of store-front shutters advertising Coca-Cola. It was the first night of a film shoot, and everyone was waiting for the cameraman, who finally showed up at ten. In a crucial sense, nothing here could begin without him. And like all such auspicious beings in India, he was greeted with a garland when he arrived. Still, we should be careful about likening him to those gods who can make things appear all at once from nothing.[1] After all, the camera was already there, waiting, adorned by the crew with another garland and anointed with sandalwood and vermil-ion. Then there was the light itself, flickering from the camphor flame passed slowly along the roundness of its lens. Camera and cameraman, a pair of seers—what would they do with the light they faced? "No longer is it a matter of speaking about space and light," writes Maurice Merleau-Ponty, "but of making space and light, which are there, speak to us."[2]

Night has fallen on the colonial world of *Madrasapatti-nam* [The city of Madras].[3] The day of India's indepen-dence from Britain—August 15, 1947—is just a few hours away. Activists of the Indian National Congress Party are massing outside Central Station, awaiting the victorious return of their leaders from Delhi. Their white tunics glow softly in blue under the moonlight. The arches of the station flood the courtyard with a yel-low radiance, a portent of the coming dawn.

A young man and woman duck and weave through the milling crowd, looking for each other. Amy Wilkin-son, daughter of the governor of Madras, is desperate to remain here with her Indian lover, Parithi, a Tamil washerman with a penchant for wrestling. The station at night is a medley of deep shadows and bright pools of light. As the police try to chase her down, Amy finds refuge behind one shadowy pillar, then another, before breaking into the moonlit streets of Madras.

The colonial city is a space meant to be grasped and enjoyed with the eyes, brimming with bright advertisements, sculpted façades and prospects, ornate architectural motifs. Countless gas and electric lamps draw attention to these details.[4] Amy knows the city well. She has toured it with Parithi, capturing its many spectacles with a handheld Agfa camera.

Now everything seems to lie with the light yet to come. There's a song in the air as they run hand in hand through the patchwork darkness of the city at night, pursued by gleaming bayonets: "Life will go on when that moment dawns, when this endless meld of light and dark gives way."

Look again at those white-clad activists massing in the station courtyard. The light is playing on them, acting through them, bringing this moment and all of its promise into reach.

⌐

Light invites an epic scale of imagination. There's the sun, that vast sphere at an inconceivable distance, responsible for almost everything we see. There is also the modern image of humankind as *naturalis lux*, being of light, radiating the truth of the world.[5] Think of the clock tower beaming into the night atop this train station in colonial India: one among the many manifestations of the European Enlightenment's promise to shed light on the true nature of things.

This promise in modern times has relied upon visual devices of various kinds: scientific technologies of vision, instruments of ambient lighting, media such as cinema that bring together these devices in an encompassing play of light and shadow. Light has been pursued to the infinitesimal scale of the photon, and yet its ultimate nature continues to elude our knowledge and control. Our eyes are both active and passive, aggressive and receptive, bending light to their purposes but also struggling with the force of what they see. The light of the world envelops and encompasses the light of the mind.[6]

Here are two men, for example, a director and a cameraman, looking over a sketch. The image outlines a space yet to be built, the set that will eventually become *Madrasapattinam*'s train station. The director, A. L. Vijay, speaks in a lively fashion, sketching vivid images of what will unfold here: Parithi and his gang running to the platform/cut/the station master holding up his hand/cut/the train for Delhi already gone/cut/Parithi looking sad/cut/then seeing Amy hiding in a train car/cut/his running to catch her/cut.

"It'll be deadly, that emotion," the director says with an almost glee-ful smile, describing how the dejected washerman will feel at the sudden sight of his young English lover. "It'll be grand," the cameraman, Nirav Shah, agrees in a measured and confident tone.

What does Nirav see, as he listens closely to the director's story? In the station's patchwork of light and shadow, the tension lies along one edge: the shifting line between what is visible and what is palpable though in-visible still. The cameraman can see Parithi's despondent eyes flickering across the span of the station, then suddenly alighting upon Amy's pres-ence in one of the compartments. He sees Parithi's face gleaming with re-lief, the light playing on Parithi's face. Everything else begins to fade into the darkness around the frame.

"We'll play it on Parithi," Nirav tells Vijay.

We tend to think of human consciousness as a beam of light on the opacity native to the natural world.[7] But the cameraman does not intend to shed light on what remains invisible without his help. His task is some-thing more modest in its orientation: to bring into focus and reach the light that is already there.

⊢

Cinematography is known in Tamil cinema as *olippathivu*, literally an im-pression or recording of light. The term itself is highly suggestive: camera-men work to capture something already in motion, light that comes from somewhere else. "Light is more than just a medium," as Mikkel Bille and Tim Sorensen observe. "Light evokes agency."[8]

In mythological and devotional films, rays of light are sometimes de-picted as streaming from the eyes of gods and goddesses.[9] Whether or not they attribute its power to such divine origins, cameramen work with light as a potent substance: flowing, leaking, seeping, spilling, always edg-ing beyond their control.

In this cinematic milieu, studio floors are scarce, sets costly to build, electrical lights expensive to rent and staff. Most shots begin with the light available in a given environment, to be filled, bounced, filtered, or reflected as possible and necessary. Control is a persistent concern. More than anywhere else in a film production, the fortunes of the camera crew depend upon the vagaries of natural elements. Day by day, countless mo-ments pass as camera assistants gaze into the sky with polarized eye-pieces, waiting for clouds to open into some degree or quality of light.

Given these circumstances, I was all the more surprised to see a glossy black invitation lying on a desk in Mysskin's office one afternoon, embla-zoned with the confident slogan "Lightning will strike!" The event adver-tised was the Indian launch of a lighting system developed in Hollywood nearly twenty years before, a high-wattage electronic special effects device called Lightning Strikes. *Madrasapattinam*'s cameraman was spearheading the launch, along with an entrepreneurial team calling themselves The Lighthouse.

The launch was held at Prasad Studios, the walls of the studio floor painted with thick, dark clouds. Many Tamil directors, cameramen, and other technicians were on hand, seated before a bank of press videographers in the back. Standing onstage beside a broken pillar and a lone tree, Nirav orchestrated a demonstration of the system. Until now, he observed, they'd all been flashing an arc light to simulate lightning; the light would build and fade slowly and was difficult to cue with a shot. Lightning Strikes, however, promised "lightning at the right time. Exactly at the right emotional moment you want it, you can have it."

Nirav called out "Strike!" with dramatic emphasis, and almost immediately, we were all cast in the flickering intensity of a white burst of light. The American inventor of the device, David Pringle, came onstage to echo what Nirav had said: "The light is very bright, very controllable, and makes dramatic scenes more dramatic, scary scenes more scary, explosive scenes more explosive." They dimmed the lights to bring the studio floor into darkness and played promotional clips from many of the Hollywood films that had used the system.

I slipped out of the studio just as Tim Robbins was escaping from jail on a stormy night, hands raised triumphantly against a lightning-ridden sky. I found myself wondering whose triumph was being celebrated on the screen, and on the stage. Is this what cinema ultimately promised, ever more mastery of the world through a fuller mastery of its light?

Nirav was someone I already knew quite well, as he'd shot several of the films that I'd been shadowing over the past few years. We first met in 2007, when he was shooting Vishnu Vardhan's *Billa* in Malaysia. On my first day with them, a fierce rainstorm suddenly engulfed the Buddhist temple complex where they were working. They waited at first for the storm to pass, then decided to improvise a few shots of the heroine practicing T'ai Chi against the driving rain and mist.

"In Hollywood," Nirav speculated, "they get their own sun if they want. They've got the time, the expertise, the money." Circumstances here demanded accommodation to light and environment, "a little bit of control, and a lot of acceptance."

I learned more about this attitude one sunny day a couple of years later. We were standing on the marshy fringes of Pozhal Lake, north of Chennai, where he was shooting for a spoof film called *Tamil Padam*

[Tamil movie]. They'd just staged an altercation on the edge of the water, a crane-mounted camera gliding in low over its glistening surface. Equipment and crew were all perched in ankle-deep water because their cables could extend no farther.

Nirav rehearsed the swooping movement of the crane's rig with his own extended arm and hand. He called for a polarizing filter to deepen the clear sky's blue and to cut its reflection on the lake. He noticed a fallen tree trunk and had it planted vertically to break up the wide openness of the space. And then, on one of their longest takes, a crow came sailing through the frame. "Super," the cameraman said to the director. "It's come together beautifully. Even that crow came in."

None of this was planned in advance, Nirav confessed when they broke for lunch. He hadn't even seen the place until that morning and had to guess what equipment he might need for the day. "It's an Indian way of accepting what is there in front of you," he reflected, as we picked our way along the low grass on the edge of the lake. "We are reacting to the moment, reacting to the location, reacting to the light. . . . Everything is working out on its own."

For the cameraman, this approach was "a spiritual thing," brought on by the exigencies of filmmaking. "The film industry does that to you," he said. "Day by day, you live in the moment. You develop a Zen-like attitude." I wasn't sure what he meant by Zen, and nor, perhaps, was he.[10] Still, I knew that diverse strands of Indian religion and philosophy had long taken knowledge of the world to demand a certain kind of vision. In Indian Buddhist literature, for example, the mind is described as essentially luminous by nature, its ordinary obstructions and afflictions susceptible to the piercing light of wisdom.[11] Nirav himself spoke of seeing past obstacles, working with a more expansive awareness of what was present.

"This doesn't happen every day," he admitted. Nor was he always as pleased with what happened as he had been that morning. These were lessons that had come with time. "You reach a point where you can't crib anymore. Then you say 'Fuck it! I just want to be happy about what I'm doing.'"

That afternoon at Pozhal Lake, he and the others worked as long as they could, until a sudden downpour forced an abrupt end to the shoot.

H

In all honesty, Nirav was hardly the poised and pious sage. He often seemed restless and distracted on sets, reaching immediately for one of two phones at each break between shots. He was also an incorrigible flirt, with a boyish and irreverent sense of humor. I remember one stunt that consumed him for an entire day on a tea estate in southern Kerala, involving a recorded fart, a maxed-out loudspeaker, and a shy young assistant director who was apparently having gas trouble. "See how we're spoiling the peace of the hills," the cameraman said to me with a devilish smile.

How could I reconcile such gags with his penchant for philosophical musings? "Both are true, both can exist in the same space," Nirav would assure with an earnest look of innocence.

The question may well arise: Was this guy just bullshitting me? Still, in the many months over many years that I hung around him as he worked, not once did I try to look through his viewfinder at the world visible through it. Unlike almost anywhere else on a working film set, here was a viewpoint that seemed fundamentally sacred, private, inviolable.[12]

Nirav had studied commerce in a Chennai college for just a few months before dropping out to try to make films. To direct, he would have had to apprentice for at least seven or eight years before getting a break, while he'd likely have to assist with a cameraman for no more than five. "I'm the type of person who gets bored very easily," he told me, and so he approached P. C. Sreeram for a chance to assist him.

Sreeram was one of the most creative and influential living cinematographers in India, a man who had trained most of Tamil cinema's leading contemporary cameramen. "I don't know anything about film," the young man admitted to the veteran when they first met. Sreeram told him to come back in a few months. Nirav waited. He watched films and bought old issues of *American Cinematographer* on the pavements of Mount Road,

Anrevey
tot

where they were dumped and sold in bulk by weight. "I had a lot of catching up to do," he recalled.

I'd met Sreeram myself a few times. "I was a very disturbed boy," the
senior cameraman once told me, describing how, as a child, he found
solace and company only in the photographic "camera diaries" he recorded for himself. Later too, he said, "whatever happened was within
the four frames. Cinema was the only way I felt at home." There was
something spiritual in this for Sreeram, "another energy" that pulled him
ever deeper into the world, but this was something he didn't want to talk
very much about.

Nirav, meanwhile, was born and raised as a Svetambara Jain. Over-
hearing dialogues between his grandmother and others, he had contem-
plated "giving up this material world" in his early teens to become a Jain
renunciant himself. But then, "somewhere down the line I realized that
if I leave everything and go now, I wouldn't have left anything. It would
have been renouncing nothing."[13]

The younger Nirav concluded that he'd have to live out more of this
life before trying to give it up. And now he was fully caught up in its
momentum.

.... ⊢ ....

Colonial Central Station is rebuilt for *Madrasapattinam* on two different
sets. The exterior façade and hallways are built on an open lot at Mohan
Studios, station walls raised with wooden scaffolds and framed with thick
canvas cloth. With design elements gleaned from historical works and
photographs of the existing station, the art direction team builds the bot-
tom half of the massive building at 100 percent scale. The top half will be
superimposed later onto shot footage by a visual effects company based
in Mumbai.

"You wouldn't have expected something so humongous," Nirav says
as we walk through the half-finished structure, jostled by the clanging
of wood and metal. He spends many minutes looking up at its soaring
armature. "You have to be true to the lighting of that period, you have
to imagine what it would have been like," he explains. As we step across
the plywood flooring of the set, under the waning sunlight of a cloudless
evening, Nirav imagines harsh spots of individual light cast upon this
surface, surrounded by expanses of deep shadow. "The sources back then
were just bare bulbs," he reminds me.

As an Indian director of photography, Nirav's responsibilities are technical as well as conceptual, encompassing the selection and position of
individual lighting elements. Back on the set a few nights later, he and his

camera crew undertake a test run to examine the workings of their patch-work light design. A light-meter reading suggests that their first design will not suffice, and Nirav decides to use a number of arclights to bounce brighter patches of light throughout the station.

"We should do it simply," Nirav tells one of his assistants, Bakyaraj, a young man who's been working with the cinematographer for the past two years. A shy and taciturn sort, he walks around the set with his head craned upward, eyes squinting into the light, passing on instructions to the foreman of the lighting crew. These men tie lights to the scaffold-ing with thick lengths of braided cord, making their own judgments con-cerning the proper height, angle, direction, and placement of individual lights. Bakyaraj shows the foreman what is wanted, cupping his fingers slightly and moving his hand forward at an angle, as if it stands for both the source of each light and the direction of its movement.

As night falls once more, the station's arches glow in the yellow light of the workmen's lamps. "Unbeatable!" the director, Vijay, exclaims, en-thralled by this glimpse of what the space might come to look like. Nirav, meanwhile, continues to pace through its corridors and hallways, look-ing up and around at its visual textures and shadows. "The first time you walk in, it looks huge," he says. "Then it becomes smaller, and smaller, and smaller."

Follow the cameraman through the shifting contours of a space like this one, and you might come to appreciate what James J. Gibson pro-posed as an "ecological" approach to visual perception. "The optic array flows in time," Gibson wrote. "One sees the environment not just with the eyes but with the eyes in the head on the shoulders of a body that gets about."[14] The visible is always much more than what appears before a geo-metric point in space, for seeing bodies are moving bodies.

Here, on the film set, everything is orchestrated to lend integrity to the perception of two such seeing and moving beings: the cameraman and the camera. As the lighting crew arranges the light that falls onto the various surfaces of the station, these sweating and anonymous men seemingly become little more than the luminous devices they manipu-late. I can hear Nirav call out instructions like these: "PAR can, come to the center. . . . Softie, come. . . . Come a little more. . . . Yes, okay. . . . Cam-era, come."

H

So Parithi and his friends rush into the train station, fearing that Amy has already left for Delhi. They push their way through the chanting crowds of activists. "What platform to Delhi?" one of the young men runs to ask a railway officer.

There is a massive wooden board looming over the tracks and platforms, listing the various trains. At first, this is all we can see. Then the film slowly takes us over the board.

We see three long rows of lamps, suspended from cords above the platforms. There's a thick, gray plume of smoke, curling into the dim rafters. There's a round white clock, which reads 11:20. We see the black locomotive pulling into the platform to the right, round face lit with a blinding sphere of light. Waiting to greet the train are porters in red; they look like small and humble figures from up here. Parithi and his friends suddenly appear to the left, casting long shadows as they race along the tracks.

The train comes down one side of what we can see, while they run up the other side. As our perspective on the scene continues to rise, one more lamp descends smoothly from above, reminding us again that we are looking down from the high vault of the station. Rows of lights form lines of perspective, converging on the tracks lost to darkness at the distant heart of the image. For a moment—and no more, as vantage on the scene will shift very soon—the film feels like the inside of some intricate and beautiful piece of machinery, gears and counterweights turning and pulling against each other with a smooth and balanced consistency.

The image is composed on a small studio floor at Prasad Studios, the second of the two sets that double as Central Station. Work on the space continues even as shooting begins here, the set crew hoisting up black lightboxes, painting lines of PVC piping to double as the railway tracks, and positioning blue screens against the studio walls for the visual effects work that will lend the station its interior scale and depth.

Nirav shouts out instructions through a surgical mask, meant to ward off fumes still evaporating from the freshly painted locomotive. At first, he's frustrated. "You can't really enjoy it," he says, complaining about the painters and carpenters bustling throughout the compound. "I need to be able to see the frame. I need everybody out of it and to be able to see it for a while."

The shot list for Scene No. 69B, fixed to the clipboards of the assistant directors, marks the need for an image that will stage the drama within the station: "5. Empty frame. Camera on left platform. Back shot of Parithi and gang running on the platform. A train is seen arriving camera right." But the use of the wooden board to slowly reveal the station's interior from above is improvised on the fly. The cinematographer selects a 14mm wide-angle lens to convey the breadth of the space. "Fantastic, sir!" the director exclaims, throwing his arm around Nirav's shoulder.

"You're trying to frame it like you're shooting a landscape," Nirav later explains. "That's the thought behind it, you want that scale, like you're shooting a mountain."

Cinematography has often been described as a kind of "painting with light" — such, for example, was the title of the handbook written by the renowned cameraman John Alton in 1949. Was Nirav "painting" with light when he composed scenes such as this one? "I haven't done it yet," he says with a laugh.[15]

There are Tamil cameramen who describe themselves as sculptors or painters of light.[16] Many others have come into cinematography from photography, and remain in the habit of seeing photographic frames wherever they turn. Nirav, meanwhile, has a different sense of what he is meant to see and do. "I am a storyteller," he says. "I will react to the story, I will react to what the story needs."

Here, for the cameraman, what is needed is a visceral reminder of their story's epic scale, something conveyed most powerfully through a slow unveiling of its span. "These fuckers have done the whole Central Station," Nirav imagines his audience saying. "You have to do this sometimes. The *Titanic*, it's such a big ship, it's sinking, people are dying."

⊢

Amy has slipped out of the train compartment where she was hiding. She doesn't know yet that Parithi is also here, looking for her. But then she spots the troop of policemen who've also been searching for her. The station is crowded with others who've spilled out of the train, and she can duck and hide among them. Although it's nearly midnight, bright lights beam from the station walls and the rafters overhead. What will she do? She darts from pillar to pillar, in and out of the crowd, until she breaks into the moonlit plaza outside.

This is the movement that Nirav must convey. The scene is brimming with excited political activists, charged by the promise of independence. But the light is also acting in powerful and unexpected ways. "See those shadows acting on the floor, where that guy is walking?" Nirav points out, as we pass together through the set. What will the cameraman do with this play of light and shadow? "These things are never written in stone," he says. "You go along and keep changing the strategy. But your basic idea remains the same."

Beginning with the framework of lights already fixed throughout the outdoor set, the cameraman plots what more are needed for the backdrop of these particular shots. "I think they would have had lights in the corridor," Nirav speculates. "Now, I can decide how much the light should come out. Or how much of the outside light should hit it."

He squints through a cupped hand to see what passes beyond the square black fabric of one skimmer. "I'm just seeing what the light is doing," he explains. "When you see it with the naked eye, there's too much other stuff."

He calls for the camera, and here's what becomes visible through its rectangular frame: Amy ducking out of view behind the first pillar, then suddenly creeping up along its shadowy face. There's a small, 300-watt arclight trained on this spot, its illumination broken up by lines of darkness through the use of a "shadow cutter." There are policemen and others passing in and out of small pools of light on the other side of the pillar.

"She's hiding from them. Just trying to create a little bit of drama with the shadows," Nirav says.

As Amy runs to the second pillar, the shadow of a wrought-iron fence reaches across the station floor, cast by a platform-mounted light on one corner of the set. A smaller light makes a bright spot through which the policemen run, followed quickly by Amy. She remains fully within this beam once she reaches the pillar, where concern plays over the whole of her face.

"Shadow, shadow, shadow . . . And then you will see her properly," the cameraman explains. "This is mainstream cinema. You want the audience to fall in love with the heroine."

Amy catches her breath for a few seconds at the third pillar. Her face is now bathed in a soft light of a texture different from anything else in the station. This is moonlight, cast at first from a helium balloon suspended high above the station courtyard, then supplemented—when the balloon malfunctions, inundated by the seasonal rains—with another daylight hoisted high above the scene by crane.

"She enters this blue light for a bit," Nirav suggests, "and then she disappears."

"Light itself is always invisible," the physicist Arthur Zajonc has written.[17] Although we never see light itself, we confront the things upon which light falls with a tactile gaze, taking in its powers in the tangible terms of feeling and texture.[18]

Just beyond Amy, Parithi, and the policemen who pursue them, the cameraman is also chasing something. It comes in and out of range, in and out of focus, in and out of darkness as he works. The feeling of the film: it's there but remains elusive.

"The tension was there," Nirav says, stepping away from a viewfinder trained onto one of these pillars. "I could feel it."

⊢

Then comes that song, as Amy and Parithi flee through the dark streets of the city. "Light will come in the east once more, as morning puts an end to the black darkness," a chorus of voices promises in a stirring and defiant mood. Layers of smoke and shadow create a moody atmosphere. Most everything happens with a haunting slowness, dim and blurry figures moving against nebulous spheres of white light. The lovers leap over a high wall back into the deserted station, running along the tracks, alongside a train, and then over its compartments.

"I love shooting in the dark," Nirav says while they set up these shots one evening on the Prasad Studios floor. "I could do this for days." Amy and Parithi run along a smoky platform lit from behind with one, unseen light: a 4,000-watt Arri flicker-free hydrargyrum medium-arc iodide (HMI) daylight. Nothing more than their silhouettes and shadows are visible against that harsh and searching light, which casts a white glow on the walls of the train compartment.

When arclights were first introduced on the gas-lit streets of Europe in the late nineteenth century, they were often likened to artificial suns.[19] Nirav has such powers at his disposal—"I could have lit the shit out of that place"—but he wants to make the lighting as pure as possible in pursuit of the scene's dramatic charge. "Whatever you can achieve with ten lights, there's a possibility you can achieve it with just one light, in the right spot," he tells me.

The dark images they compose here gesture toward the work of the cinematographer Gordon Willis, widely known as a "Prince of Darkness," as well as that of V. K. Murthy, a pioneering Indian cameraman whose moody and impressionistic visuals owed much to the aesthetics of German Expressionist cinema.[20] Nirav admires them both. "Whatever I'm doing is a sum total of everything that I have seen till now, stuff that is subconsciously there," he admits, "every film, every photograph that I've ever seen."

Visual impressions have been made upon his mind, the cameraman suggests, without his having known or realized it; this is also how he understands his own images to work. "Why should I tell you that you should feel a certain way?" Nirav asks. "I should make you feel that way, without your knowing it. . . . It's a psychological game. As a cameraman, what you're playing with the audience is a game."

What Nirav says echoes certain arguments made about the psychology of cinema. In an influential essay published in 1970, Jean-Louis Baudry described cinema as a world fashioned for the eye of a subject. The camera creates a unified point of view: something much more than physical, consolidating the very identity, activity, and understanding of its onlookers. This, for Baudry, was the foundation of cinema's ideological efficacy. Though they do not know it, cinematic spectators are "chained, captured, or captivated" by the light they find reflected within its dark chambers, by its "moving beams from an already veiled light source."[21]

This is no doubt part of what is happening in this song from *Madrasapattinam*, which celebrates the poignancy of a nation's tumultuous birth. But there are countless other things happening here as well. Think again about that light. "You have black and white happening at the same time," the cameraman observes. "You're not really sure what is happening."

Here, as he does so often, Nirav speaks in the second person: you. It's not entirely clear whose perspective and experience he's speaking about now: that of the camera, the cameraman, the audience, the story, or the characters or the tracks along which they run. All of this is possible, likely, implicated in what he says. There is no seer here—not even the cameraman himself—independent of what is seen, operating at a controlling distance from the object.

The space of the game collapses into the visible texture of the image. Everyone is lost within its depths of light and shadow.

⊢

"Victory to Mahatma Gandhi!" the director calls out on his mike, leading his freedom fighters through the station once more. Then he suddenly remembers today's date, August 15. "Freedom Day," he says with a laugh of surprise. "We're shooting on the same day." The time is 11:40 p.m. Within the confines of the studio floor, days and nights keep bleeding into each other.

Nirav's eyes are red with exhaustion. On breaks, which come unpredictably, he's been following a discussion thread on the CML-PRO cinematography listserv with his iPhone. "The set is running late, the actor's thrown a wobbly and the director has opened his second bottle of whiskey, yet you need to light the next scene," a Dutch cinematographer writes. "Do you have any tricks, cultural, drugs, alcohol . . . ? What do you do?"

There's a long response by Oliver Stapleton, a British cinematographer known for his work on films such as *My Beautiful Laundrette* and

The Grifters. Writing from Melbourne, where he's shooting for Guillermo del Toro, Stapleton observes, "Great Cinematography pretty much always comes from people with Artistic Vision." At the same time, he advises, "don't behave like a painter in a loft." The tumult and commotion of the set must be approached with disciplined and unflappable mental distance, and here, like many others on this discussion thread, Stapleton affirms the value of Zen and other lessons of "the Eastern Masters."[22]

"I haven't read much philosophy, I've never read anything," Nirav admits, as we walk together from Prasad Studios to the outdoor set across the street, talking about these remarks. And there is no "school of photography" to which he cleaves. "Trying to keep your life simple, trying to keep your lighting simple," this is as much as the cameraman is willing to put forward in the form of principles. "I think if it's going to be taught to you, it won't stay with you for too long. If you arrive at it on your own, I think it'll last much longer."

Two years later, we meet again one evening beside the Gandhi statue at Marina Beach. As always, Nirav has been busy. We talk about the enthusiastic reception of his work for director Vijay's most recent release, *Deiva Thirumagal*. "You're a magician," a friend of his had apparently said, deeply moved by the film. Nirav disagreed, and what he goes on to say has the beauty of philosophical vision. He speaks slowly and quietly as we sit together under Gandhi's looming bronze frame:

> I am not a magician. I am the medium. The magic is all there. I'm not creating anything. With my limited knowledge and my limited sense, I'm trying to capture whatever is there. I didn't create the blue sky, I didn't create the green of the grass. I didn't create the clouds and all that. It's just how you look at it. If you look at it wide-eyed, it seems magical. If you're in a fuck-all mood, it looks trashy. You can crib about it, you can say "Ah, the light is crappy," or you can say "The light is beautiful." On a sixteen-hour day, I can't say "Let's wait for the right light." I don't know if it's going to happen. The idea is to be open and receptive and alert about what's around me. Happy accidents are happening all the time. So if you're open to it, you will capture it. And if you're not, then you won't.

There's a lucidity to what he says. I have much to ponder, little to add. We chat for a few minutes before I get into a taxi, and he wanders farther down the beach. As the car pulls away from the pavement, I can see him scrolling through his phone, still restless, looking for something reflected in the light of that small screen.

Color

Happy accidents are happening all the time, Nirav said. What
did it mean to be open to them? The challenge lay in thinking
with the vicissitudes of the sensible, in and among the things
of the world, the flux of qualities and textures that carried its
light. Like color, for example. On another night in Chennai, I
was crammed into the back of a production van with Nirav
and a team of directors, scouting locations for a different film.
Beyond the tinted windows flashed the electric hues of the
bazaars. "What about, you know, that color, like magenta,"
one of the directors began to say. "No, not magenta, actually . . . deep like purple, but not bluish, more red, what's that
color?" What was that color that he was thinking of, as they
mused on the nocturnal visage of these streets? None of us
could say. To think and work with light's colors is to toy with
a stubborn medium, one that often defies the lineaments of
expectation. Colors linger and stray beyond the things they
mark, like the inchoate tugs of sensation itself.

·· ⊢ ··

I've just arrived at Greenspring Station, though there
aren't any springs, green or otherwise, as far as I can
see. It's a sunny summer day. The retinas of my eyes
need examination. Within one of the hospital's faintly
lit consultation rooms, a technician has me remove the
pair of soft plastic contact lenses. She pours a few drops
of fluid into each eye. As I wait for the doctor to come
and as my pupils begin to dilate, the world resolves into
vague fields of muted color and indistinct spheres of
light.

I've been looking through thick, transparent lenses
from the age of six—eyeglasses for a long time and,
more recently, contact lenses. The sense of a world without focus has always been terrifying. Haircuts, for example—without those eyeglasses wrapped around my

face, the bright mirrors of the salon revealed nothing of what was happening to my head.

Today, though, I find myself in a buoyant and experimental mood. It must be the book in my bag, Goethe's 1810 *Theory of Colours*, packed with hundreds of observations of the poet's own reactions to color and light. I take out my laptop, a pair of earphones, a Tamil DVD. My eyes are still naked, stripped of their plastic armor, their foveae washed in brightness. The controls are hard to manage, even when I squint and frown. Then the film begins to play.

There are dabs and streams of light and color, pulsing through a shifting depth of darkness. At first, long-standing habits get the best of me, dwelling on the puzzles posed by these images: Whose face, what scene, what next? Then I can feel something begin to slacken, loosen. The questions subside, and I succumb to the openness of movement.

Fireflies of many hues dart, stream, and dance through the blackness. Contours give way to abstract series and echoes. Tinted blocks loom and recede beyond these blurry edges: lime-green, blood-red, the orange of a persimmon, the cool green water of some tropical lagoon. But there are only so many such words and things that I can summon.[1] These shades are like petals that have inundated the landscapes surrounding them, spilling fields of riotous tone.

Then everything ends in a sparkling crash of light. Here's the ophthalmologist's office once more, with its quiet shades of mauve, gray, tan, and mustard. A melancholy sigh rises from my chest, taking me by surprise.

Our eyes, Goethe suggests, need experience of diverse colors: "The eye especially demands completeness, and seeks to eke out the colorific circle in itself."[2]

· H ·

The film is called *Va, Quarter Cutting*.[3] There's hardly a story to speak of: one night in Chennai, a guy named Sura on his way to Saudi Arabia, wandering the city with his sister's fiancé, Marthandan, searching for a bottle of booze before he goes. Critics dismissed the film as a faltering knockoff of *Harold and Kumar Go to White Castle*. But it feels to me more like a film by Jean-Pierre Jeunet, a surreal world of unearthly hues, eclectic characters, and whimsical happenings.

The film's young directors, Pushkar and Gayathri, are such a genial and easygoing pair that you might just want to kick back with them over beers. "We're also Westerners," they told me some years ago, lounging against crimson bolsters in their smoky flat in Nungambakkam. Born and raised in Chennai, both had studied film in the United States. When they returned, they found themselves surprised and fascinated by the ambience of familiar places and habits. "The little things we took for granted were super cool, super charming," Gayathri said. "Kitsch, pop culture," Pushkar added, stubbing out a cigarette. "When you come back, you see it with a different eye."

Like their first film, *Oram Po*, a breezy tale of a clandestine circuit of auto rickshaw racers in Chennai, *Quarter Cutting* was shot almost fully within the city. I trailed the duo one night on a route that crisscrossed Chennai for several hours. They were on a "tech recce" for *Quarter Cutting* with their cameraman, Nirav Shah, scouting and planning locations for the film's first shooting schedule. Touring these unseen corners of Chennai was intriguing, especially given the odd, almost obsessive concern with color that kept resurfacing at every turn.

Under an ornate tower on a congested side street in Parry's Corner, for example: "There won't be any blue, will there?" Gayathri asked, uneasily, to which Nirav assured, "We'll do something else, green."

Or beside the cracked and faded pink of a high wall in a narrow residential alley: "We'll paint it maroon," Pushkar mused, gazing at the sea green wall it faced.

Or planning a frame on a road overlooking the shipping containers and cargo cranes at the Royapuram port: "I don't want to break the yellow," Nirav said, gesturing toward the painted arrows curving along the road below our feet.

Or riding in that production van toward Koyambedu bus station, when Nirav warned that these warm colors might get boring in isolation: "What about, you know, that color, like magenta?" Pushkar asked. "We'll use blacks to fill in the frame, Gayathri suggested. "We'll go with a dark red tone."

Maroon, green, and yellow, magenta, black, and red. We were in Madrasapattinam, the port city that had launched a thousand ships of dyed chintzes and calicoes to a Europe that hadn't yet learned to properly fix colors to cloth.[4] I didn't know the story, hadn't seen the script. Why all these colors? And why not blue?

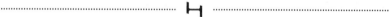

"Savage nations, uneducated people, and children have a great predilection for vivid colors," Goethe observes in his treatise on color, concluding a discussion of "pathological" forms of perception such as color blindness and hallucinatory impressions of color. There's something startling about this juxtaposition, this implication that a fondness for bright colors is a kind of sickness, contrary to the healthy eyes of "people of refinement."[5]

The artist and critic David Batchelor calls this "chromophobia": raw
color purged from Western culture as an alien phenomenon, dangerously
recalcitrant and resistant to control. Long imagined as feminine, vulgar,
and primitive by nature, color was to be "learned, ordered, subordinated
and tamed" through modern science and industry.[6]

At the same time, however, there is a modern history of chromo*philia*:
the lust for exotic colors that propelled Western colonialism in Asia,
underwrote the trade in African slaves, and made colored compounds
available for scientific extraction and refinement. "This distaste for vivid
color is actually an unstable mix of attraction *and* repulsion," Michael
Taussig writes; color has been denounced for the very reasons that it has
provoked ceaseless invention and experimentation.[7]

In Western cinema for many years, color remained suspect for its anarchic qualities and tendencies.[8] Shifts from black-and-white to color were
often made in the classical Hollywood cinema of the 1930s and 1940s to
signal the irruption of a world apart: states of dream, delusion, and in-
sanity.[9] In the face of such impressions, Technicolor, the American company that pioneered color cinema in the early decades of the twentieth
century, took great pains to argue that proper use of color was an essential foundation of cinematic realism.

Natalie Kalmus, the obligatory color consultant deputed to oversee
films employing the Technicolor process, outlined their endeavor "to portray life and nature as it really is." In an influential article titled "Color
Consciousness" published in a leading cinema trade journal in 1935, Kalmus described a union of scientific method and aesthetic judgment in the
development of color cinema. "We must study color harmony, the appro-
priateness of color to certain situations, the appeal of color to the emotions," she wrote. "We must constantly practice color restraint."[10]

Despite such ambitions, Technicolor productions remained intensely
saturated and imprecise in their coloration for many years, and the process was used most often in Hollywood for genres with little need for
realism, such as fantasies, westerns, and musicals.[11] In Tamil cinema too,
color film was first used in a song-and-dance scene for T. R. Raghunath's
otherwise black-and-white 1955 film, *Kanavane Kankanda Deivam*.[12] Then
there was a Tamil adaptation of the fantasy tale of Ali Baba and the forty
thieves, shot fully on color film and released the next year.

Fantasy's colors are portals into another world, composing an alternate universe with a nature of its own. Take *Quarter Cutting*'s land of
lurid reds and eerie greens, where everything gleams with scarlet rich-
ness and the vaporous glow of citrine, where there is hardly any blue to
be seen. Here, it would seem, even the sky breaks into streams of saffron

each morning before cooling into a soupy green—as if light's own wavelengths had been realigned, as if one family of shades had fallen out of the rainbow altogether.

"Color," Jeffrey Jerome Cohen writes, "is not some intangible quality that arrives belatedly to the composition but a material impress, an agency and partner, a thing made of other things through which worlds arrive."[13]

Here's a film crew, setting up *Quarter Cutting*'s first shots late one night beside a deserted restaurant in north Chennai. The scene is pivotal: this is where Sura and Marthandan will learn why every wine shop here is closed this night, where they will indeed discover—as Sura mutters to himself before these shuttered storefronts—"something wrong" in the life of the city.

The dirty gray of the metal shutters has been painted over in rusty red; above, the blue signboards for the Winner Café have been replaced by the bright green boards of a government wine shop. Nirav is working with various colored lights and filters. A sheet of green plastic covers a bank of four tube lights on the right of the street corner, while a piece of orange plastic flaps from a tungsten lamp looking down on the road.

There is light, and tinted screens through which to pass it, but more is needed still to ensure an expression of color. Angles of refraction are essential. At first, the light bounces too directly onto the ribbed surface of the red shutters, glinting at the camera in white. "That color has to come out more," Nirav tells one of his assistants. "Put it that way, and it won't come."

He holds both of his arms out from his body, then widens them as he brings them down, opening a space for the redness he wants. The gesture serves as a small but lucid reminder: color is a movement of expression, an intensification of what already exists.

"The painter recaptures . . . the vibration of appearances which is the cradle of things," Merleau-Ponty writes in a meditation on color and brushstroke in the work of Cézanne.[14] It may seem strange to turn from this unnatural glimpse of Chennai to the landscapes of Aix-en-Provence that Cézanne had painted, but there is a certain kindred sensibility that Merleau-Ponty's words evoke.

For the French philosopher, what was most significant about the painter was his exploration of perception as a kind of embodied movement with the world. Successive distortions of perspective, colors spilling over one another, reveal "the structure of the landscape as an emerging organism." Color conveys the active and radiant life of things, which is why, as Merleau-Ponty writes, "expressing what *exists* is an endless task."[15]

Deep within the crowd gathered on that street corner, Pushkar is dressed in a maroon corduroy shirt, a few shades darker than Sura's rusty garb. Gayathri, nearby, has a teal kurta with flowers of many hues. Everyone can see the contrasting colors that play so forcefully against each other within the frame that Nirav has established. On the fifth take, Gayathri smiles at the colors she glimpses on the monitor.

"It's warm," she tells the cinematographer.

"I'm going to use that tone throughout the film," Nirav assures her.

On the way to the next set of closed wine shop shutters they'll be shooting, Gayathri describes the warm color palette they've chosen for the film. "All around, you'll see it," she says, talking about these colors. "Look around in India—you'll be looking at the road, suddenly you'll see a woman walking by in a loud yellow sari."

She points to another shuttered storefront across the street: "There, that shutter, opposite us—it was already painted completely red."

They are drawing together, focusing, and deepening the colors scattered throughout this urban landscape, she tells me: "We'll look at what is there, and concentrate all that together." I can already see, as we speak above the midnight din of their generators, how this process is remaking the city as an otherworldly space, as a landscape alien to itself.

⊢

The film eventually looks like a peculiar reversal of figure and ground: as though it's happening *within* one of the vivid chromolithographic prints of goddesses, kings, and commodities plastered onto so many of its walls—as though these colors of the film have been printed onto posters that spill beyond their own framed borders.[16]

Given the total pervasion of these colors, it's hardly surprising that there's only one moment in *Quarter Cutting* when anyone says anything about them.

An ice-cream vendor in a cardinal shirt is parked on a deserted road. Bright red signs convey what else he's had to offer—plenty of black-market booze—until just a few minutes earlier, when a crowd of rich kids wiped out his stock.

Sura is dismayed, Marthandan suddenly peckish.

"Give me a popsicle," he says, ducking under the cart's lurid canopy.

The vendor reaches into his icebox and hands him one.

"No," says Marthandan, refusing the yellow popsicle. "Pink." His face melts with childlike glee as he reaches for the wooden stick, coated this time with rosy ice.

Colors are always fixed to something. The pink syrup of Marthandan's popsicle is frozen into a wedge of ice. There's a thick red coat of paint on the bars that frame the cart, and its various plastic surfaces glow with chemical dyes. These colors compose the scene of a movie, their chromatic tones recorded onto thin layers of color-sensitive film through the action of a silver halide emulsion and chemical dye-coupling agents.

Quarter Cutting is shot on a new brand of color film stock, Fujifilm Eterna Vivid 500, introduced globally just a few months before the film's shooting schedule begins. Promotional materials for the stock describe material characteristics that will minimize reflection, improve sharpness, and enhance the definition of colors reproduced by the film. Fujifilm promises a "highly saturated palette" that will extend "sharp, intense color into the realm of night scenes."[17]

Here is color in the language of marketing, a ubiquitous form of contemporary soothsaying. But, as Taussig writes, color is a "polymorphous magical substance," always veering into unanticipated qualities and textures along with the things in which it is expected to inhere. Take the massive vats of indigo dye in colonial India, harnessing color for industrial Britain and much of the rest of the world. Observers were mesmerized by the slippery hues of these dye works, Taussig notes, as beaten sheaves of indigo took river water from clear to orange to green to lemon to blue. "Color here will not stand still," he writes. "Indeed, it is not so much color that is changing here in the indigo vat, but change itself that is on view."[18]

Something like this also happens as the shoot for *Quarter Cutting* unfolds, as the intensified colors of the nocturnal environment are fixed to reels of Fujifilm stock. The filmmakers must work by conjecture, for the video monitor is an unreliable guide to what is happening within the lightproof body of their Arriflex 435 camera. While they ride from one shuttered wine shop backdrop to another, Pushkar asks Nirav whether he thinks these tones are coming across. "The red could have been more red, the green could have been more green," the cameraman admits in a speculative tone.

There are things whose presence or absence must be fixed in place before the camera itself. Color, however, will endure in its vagaries well beyond this stage, deep into the laboratory processing of the film. What still remains is the color grading, where, as Nirav projects with a confidence I find surprising, "you can do whatever you want."

ㅂ

A shipping yard somewhere in Chennai. Marthandan has had it with Sura and their quixotic expedition. Plump, bespectacled, now furious, he

drags Sura into an alley between the cargo containers, swinging wildly at
him. Light glints from these corrugated boxes and their prismatic lines of
metallic hue. Despite all the tumult onscreen, there is no sound, except
for the voices murmuring quietly in the dark studio where we're watching
the scene, and the steady clicks that turn one shade into another.

We are now somewhere within the Chennai division of Reliance Media-
Works, a few months after *Quarter Cutting* has been fully shot, a few days
after the film has been trimmed and edited. The room feels chilly, almost
pressurized with a steady influx of cold air. Pushkar and Gayathri are on
thick leather couches, facing the screen. Nirav is sitting at the Baselight
color-grading console beside Nilesh Sawant, the film's colorist. Nilesh has
just come from the Reliance office in Mumbai, where he's already begun
working on the film. As they scroll through the scenes, reactions to color
surface in a ragged mixture of English, Hindi, and Tamil.

Until recent years, the grading of cinematic color was a photochemi-
cal process: cinematographers would work together with technicians in
postproduction laboratories to filter and vary by primary color—red,
green, and blue, individually—the light that passed through an original
film negative onto the intermediate stock from which prints were made.
Now in India as in much of the world, filmmakers work primarily with
digital intermediate, or DI, images: high-resolution digital scans of shot
footage. The technology allows for the manipulation of film—and most
especially its color—at a much smaller and closely tailored scale of intervention.[19] As Pushkar puts it, "It's a more polished version of the apples
you've already seen."

The directors are mostly silent here, deferring to the cinematographer. On this first of many nights of color grading, the task is to establish
how much further they can extend what they've already done with the
tones of the film—"How much to push it, how much to hold it back," as
Nirav says. He asks the colorist to enrich the saturation of reds and yel-
lows, to deepen the green of the shadows, and to extend the contrast between these different hues: "Everywhere, we'll enhance the color slightly,
though you won't know."

Faced with an accumulating rain of minute instructions and suggestions from the cameraman, Nilesh gradually develops a sense of how this
peculiar film ought to look. "I understand now, what you want," he assures the cinematographer. Still, there's only so much he can do with his
many knobs and dials.

At the shipping yard, for example, the problem they confront is the insistent presence of the blue they intend to eradicate from the film: here,
in the illumination cast by one light in the distance and on some of the
shipping containers that Sura and Marthandan tussle between. "Select

the blue," Nirav says, pointing to the ultramarine shade of one of these containers. He murmurs his appreciation as this metal surface reappears in a lighter teal shade. But then, when the bumbling combatants spill back onto the road, Nirav once again sees a bluish darkness surrounding a white orb of light.

"Even if it goes whitish, it's okay," Pushkar calls out, expecting that the cameraman will try to lighten this color. But Nirav has another, more radical manipulation in mind. "Do a total hue shift," he tells the colorist, and the nocturnal sky suddenly assumes a greenish cast more typical of the film.

This move solves one problem, but it also creates another: the image begins to appear noisy and pixilated. "Desaturation would be better," Nilesh advises, and Nirav concedes: "It's too much of an opposite, we've started to get noise." The sky will retain its bluish tinge.

Nilesh has graded over fifty films, and this is his fifth project with Nirav. "Any color can be changed into any other color," he tells me, but only so long as that other color is already present somewhere in the image. One of his chief responsibilities is to ensure that no one tone dominates and overshadows the others. The colorist knows that these shades tend to bleed and spill into each other, especially when charged with high levels of saturation.

"Color is single," Walter Benjamin once observed in a fragment called "A Child's View of Color"—"not as a lifeless thing and a rigid individuality but as a winged creature that flits from one form to the next."[20]

.... **H** ....

Some time ago, Sanchita, Karun, and I were at the Hirschhorn Museum in Washington, DC. Slipping protective white socks over our shoes, we walked through an installation by Carlos Cruz-Diez called *Chromosaturation*. The artist had constructed three small rooms, each washed from above by a glowing bank of colored fluorescent tube lights: first green, then red, then blue.

Each of these colored spaces felt remarkably different. I remember the slight twinge of nausea that I felt in the green room, the sense of being pressed upon by heat from above in the red, and the involuntary sigh of relief that escaped me as I stepped into the soft blue of the final room. Basking in that cool light, my thoughts strayed to the unrelenting intensity of color that I'd soon be writing about. Was this why *Quarter Cutting* had done so poorly at the box office, because its audiences were denied such cerulean release?

I knew that these familiar euphemisms for color temperature— warmth and coolness for red and blue—had nothing to do with the physical properties of these respective wavelengths.[21] Still, the sensations somehow felt incontestable. So I caught up with Karun and took him through the rooms once more, asking how they made him feel. The child's answers skipped away in some other direction altogether.

"Sad," he said under the green. Then he said, "happy," looking up at the red. And then he pronounced the blue "grumpy," before running off to find his mother.

.... **⊢** ....

Arguments for the feelings provoked by colors rely upon both philosophical and physiological foundations. Goethe, for example, had harmonies of both kinds in mind when he wrote that "every decided colour does a certain violence to the eye, and forces the organ to opposition."[22] The color science that edged out monochromatic cinema drew upon such notions, as in the principles of moderation expounded by Technicolor's consultants. And these ideas circulate widely even now; Nirav works with the idea, for example, that "warm colors make you feel a certain way, cold colors make you feel a certain way, on a very subconscious level."

The color-grading studio can be thought of as a kind of sensory laboratory, a space of controlled experimentation with such sensations of color. The second night of *Quarter Cutting*'s grading, for example, begins with Sura and Marthandan in an open market, searching for a trader who deals in both dried fish and liquor. The image is already fixed onto the screen when we walk into the dark chamber together: Marthandan dangling his legs over the edge of a vegetable stall, singing to himself and smoking a cigarette as vendors pass by with woven baskets.

"I'm missing the green," Nirav reacts, almost immediately. "See if you can increase it a little more?" Nilesh creates a mask for the image, isolating the triangular zone of vegetable stalls at its center in order to manipulate their color independently. "Add the green," the cinematographer tells him, and then he asks the colorist to flash the modified hue off and on.

"It's good, isn't it?" Nirav says, almost to himself. Then he consults the others: "Which one do you like, Gayathri? Pushkar?"

Pushkar responds first—"The green one, definitely"—and Gayathri agrees: "The green is nice." They don't say why they like this, nor do they ask me, which is just as well, as I can't see any difference between the original and amplified green.

The filmmakers are working with aesthetic judgments, founded on the effects that colors can have on viewers like themselves, and on how these colors may affect each other. Later that night, they turn to a scene staged in an alleyway behind the marketplace, Marthandan consoling the fishmonger beside a pea-green wall as Sura looks on. "You can get a little

more warmth in this," Nirav tells the colorist, asking him to amplify the red in the shirts that both Sura and the fishmonger are wearing.

Nilesh resists, thinking of the wall behind them: "It will affect the green."

"Just a little," Nirav gently urges. "We'll see it again later."

These are strange tones, to be sure. There is an interplay of light and shadow in images such as this one, but the use of color confounds the sense of depth that such an interplay would otherwise evoke, as everything bursts forward equally with the charge of saturated intensity. This isn't something that bothers the cinematographer. "It doesn't have to look real or natural," he reminds the others. "Whatever works for the frame is fine."

How is color working in frames as peculiar as this one? The red and the green, antagonistic colors, exert pressure on each other. The filmmakers modulate these forces, pushing them as far as possible without precipitating a collapse in their tension. There is a kind of visual contortion being attempted in the color-grading studio, one that summons the tactile push of aggressive tones against each other. Expressed here is what Deleuze calls "a properly visual sense of touch, or a haptic sense of sight."[23]

Deleuze was thinking of the tortured canvases of the painter Francis Bacon, which, once again, like Cezanne's vistas, may seem to have little to do with this lighthearted jaunt through Chennai's midnight. But think of what he says about these paintings of wracked figures with nothing to narrate, no story to tell, through which something profound nonetheless keeps happening. We find the body escaping from itself in Bacon's paintings, Deleuze suggests, a dissipation of its flesh into fields of color. The sensation of color is a nervous wave, a vibratory movement, an event of transformative passage: "At one and the same time I *become* in the sensation and something *happens* through the sensation, one through the other, one in the other."[24]

Is this what they wanted to make happen, these makers of *Quarter Cutting*, as they cut blue so meticulously from the landscape of night?

————————————————————— H —————————————————————

There are films in which colors obviously mean something, in which they embody or stand in for a certain idea or possibility. Remember *The Wizard of Oz*, in which color belongs only to a magical land over the rainbow, somewhere, or *Pleasantville*, the first film to rely extensively upon digital intermediate technology, in which color appears as a full flowering of life.[25] In Tamil cinema, there are the political overtones of Dravidian red and black in any number of films, and the racial and sexual grammars of aspiration that pair dark and heroic men with light-skinned women.[26]

In the case of *Quarter Cutting*, though, it's difficult to decipher such meanings of color, if they are there to be decoded at all. I think of the mysterious man in a lime-green shirt that Marthandan stumbles into that night. "Why do you all just wander around, looking for a message in everything?" he chides Marthandan, before slapping him across the face and sending him off with a few words about getting what you want before you get beaten.

Here too, I think, the habit of seeking meanings can get us only so far. "You can use red for anger, rage," Gayathri pointed out to me, "but if everything is dark, and one red pops out, it's not anger anymore, it's joy." Even in the case of blue, she wanted to say only this: "This is not a serious script. You can experiment a little. At night, usually, your most obvious choice will be blue. We wanted it to look completely different, not something you're familiar with. I'm not able to articulate it properly. . . ."

Why not blue? She couldn't explain it, and frankly, nor can I. But I think that the vexing colors of her film demand a different mode of engagement, some other way of thinking with them than asking why. "Everything factual is already theory," Goethe insisted. "To understand this would be the greatest possible achievement. The blueness of the sky reveals the basic law of chromatics. Don't go looking for anything beyond phenomena: they are themselves what they teach, the doctrine."[27]

Take a look at the film if you get a chance. In the meantime, here is a fable, on what it's like to fall into a world of such lurid hues—

Amsterdam, I know, but I was there for a conference. The Dutch were in the running for the World Cup, their streets swarming with orange jerseys, lapping up in waves each night before the women boxed in pulsing red.

It might have been what they handed me at that café, but the scarlet light kept beating against my eyelids, sloshing and throbbing from the canals. What I wanted was a slice of pizza. What I wound up with was a falafel and a red can of Coke. The sidewalk stretched with every step. I tell you, it felt like *Quarter Cutting*.

Oh, by the way, I almost forgot—Sura did get that bottle of booze.

Time

As you might have noticed by now, I've also been pursuing certain contortions of form. We face the challenge of making these things sensible somehow—the light and the color of cinematic experience, its desire and its love, these dreams and the artifice that makes them real. But, despite whatever I try to do with the narrative form and force of these words, a rift endures. Vishnu Vardhan, a young Tamil director, often pushed me to think about the tension between life and language. "If you really want to understand us," he told me once, over dinner with Nirav at a hill resort in Munnar, "you have to make a film yourself." I think what Vishnu said that night had to do with more than matters of technique or familiarity. There was the fundamental question of time itself, lodged at the heart of what he said and most everything he did: the time in which things appeared unexpectedly, and the time that took these happenings to others as a flowing stream of images and sounds. Vishnu was telling me to gamble, as they did, on the promise of time. And I began to wonder—what if this writing, this medium of mine, could follow some of the twists and whorls through which things like cinema surface in their newness?

.... ㅏ ....

YOU HEAR the clatter of their shiny black shoes on the marble floor, as a team of police officers steps through the glass doors onto a busy road in Kuala Lumpur. "Mr. Jai, we've got Billa," one officer tells another with a confident smile. They don't actually have their fugitive yet, but every movement of sound and image conspires to give the sense of an inevitable capture. The battalion of police sedans that surround a towering apartment block. The SWAT team, clad fully in black with the word POLIS lettered onto their backs, filing one by one down the dark passageways of an abandoned building. Their rooftop silhouettes against a trail of skyscrapers. The sharp beams of light that swing from the snouts of their assault rifles. The steady beat of their heavy boots along the concrete floors. The driving pace of an electronic soundtrack, drums and organs syncopated with the press of shuffling feet and the rhythm of a passing helicopter. The geometric layers of stairways and hallways leading down to the fugitive's lair. The wail of a police siren somewhere in the distance. The train rolling past the waiting detectives, their impassive faces wrapped in dark glasses. You see the capture of a man with nowhere good to hide. But you can also see the capture of a moment by a sense of the inevitable, an imprisoning of time in a future that is already known and expected. Everything to come seems as implacable as the movement of these troops, any trace of their vulnerability obscured by the black that envelops

"KRRRR, that's how you feel it," the director says, scattering shards of broken tube lights onto the concrete floor for the SWAT team to crunch with their boots. They are shooting at Pekelling Flats, a complex of abandoned apartments in the heart of Kuala Lumpur. The film is *Billa*, a remake of a 1980 Tamil hit.[1] The contemporary version of this gangster film will be set in Malaysia, to give it, as the cameraman Nirav Shah says, "a slightly futuristic feel." The director Vishnu Vardhan seems to have that feeling himself this morning at Pekelling Flats. "Taka taka taka taka," he says to himself as he races along these stairs and hallways. Then he recalls this momentum for the members of his SWAT team, mostly composed of Malaysian extras. "Stand like this! Point here! Lasers like this! Positions, please! Be quick! Be quick! Action! Move in now!" Shots are directed at a rapid pace, which seems to have something to do with how the filmmakers imagine the city itself. "In terms of time zones, they are two and a half hours ahead of India," muses Ajith Kumar, the film's star, and the one who plays the fugitive gangster hiding in this building—"but in terms of development, they are fifty years ahead of us." As we chat, I can see the twin spires of the Petronas Towers looming behind his head. Day after day, we see different faces of these towers in the distance. The filmmakers keep choosing places to shoot in proximity to them. Look through their lenses, and it seems as though this icon of modernity must anchor every event here, as though every-

them fully. Take them as emissaries of a certain image of time, the idea of time as a movement through space, as relentless as these beats, as regular as the tick of a clock from point to point to point.

thing that happens must unfold in its shadow. There is something almost anxious in this compulsion, this insistent return to the base of the towers, some deep uncertainty about the very possibility of keeping, catching, up.

Things seem to be moving very quickly indeed these days, so much so that we can hardly keep up with their momentum. But what do we mean when we say such things? What are we saying when we talk of time—this time now, the time that we share, but also "time" itself—as a relentless, mechanical, even cruel force of change?

Imagine the hands juddering around the face of a clock, marking out each second with the same stiff thrust. Think of the countless other devices, schedules, tables, and routines that circulate and standardize this picture of an unrelenting advance. Imagine this time collapsing into space, beginning to look like nothing more than an empty container in which things are bound to happen with lawlike certainty. Now imagine yourself within that container. Is there any choice but to keep up or get left behind?

Something essential is obscured by this widespread manner of conceiving time, argued Henri Bergson in the early twentieth century: the very way in which time introduces newness into the world. "Time is here deprived of efficacy," Bergson observes with such ideas in mind, "and if it *does* nothing, it *is* nothing."[2]

Take time as a straight line that passes from one moment to the next, and the present loses all of its potential for novelty, fixed as it is between a past that has long since been superseded and a future that is already plotted and ordained. With such a picture of time, it is as though everything is given or laid out all at once: what is behind, what is ahead, what remains caught somewhere in between. Change would seem to be nothing more than a displacement in space, a change of coordinates, like going from Chennai to Kuala Lumpur.

Suppose, though, that these are misconceptions of time and its creative potential. Suppose that time is something else altogether: not a space of points to traverse but instead a continuous succession of overlapping states, ceaseless movements of flux and transformation, impossible to bound off from one another.[3] Follow some of these movements, allow them to seep into what you think and feel, Bergson suggests, and you might find yourself with a very different way of understanding what time can do. Time lets things develop into unforeseen forms. "Time is invention, or it is nothing at all."[4]

To perceive this creative quality of time, we may have to forget about those lines and arrows that appear to lead inexorably from one direction into another, and to think of time instead as a matter of spirals, loops, and circling whorls.[5] Bergson challenges the idea that the past inevitably gives way to the present, proposing instead that we consider time as a pair of arcing "jets . . . one of which falls back towards the past whilst the other springs forward towards the future."[6] There is always, in other words, a coincidence of what is present with what has already passed: every perception of an actual object draws an endless series of memories, enlivening this presence with the ripple of contrary qualities and textures.[7] These virtual depths of time give each moment its openness, its potential to sustain creative transformation.[8]

These are very abstract claims to make, diaphanous things to try to grasp—such are the perils of thinking with something as elusive as time. Here's an example, then: take cinema, or any other work of art. We are accustomed to thinking of such works in sequential terms: a film is first made, then later watched. Suppose, however, that we refused to grant this process the clarity of such direction. Suppose we took both these dimensions to unfold together in time: the events of a film and the events of their making.

Put them side by side. Watch them spiral into each other, these happenings in a cinematic present and the past in which they came to pass. What might we come to see about the creation of cinema, about the creative potential of time itself?[9]

.... ⊢ ....

SASHA AND BILLA face each other in a stark black space, leather jackets catching spare glints of light. "I like your courage," he says, extending a hand. She shakes it. She whips out a gun and fires. There are wisps of smoke. The tinkling of a bullet casing. Billa, dead, slowly falling backward. Then, there they are again, facing each other, Sasha still scowling. "Don't think," he tells her. "You've come to the right place." What? Cut. You see two bouquets of yellow roses, laid on a granite tombstone. You see Sasha standing there in a sober black dress, facing a

IT'S A HUMID summer day in Kuala Lumpur. The graveyard on the outskirts of the city is ridden with swarms of mosquitoes. *Billa* needs just a few seconds of footage here: the actress Nayantara, dressed in black, lost in thought before a pair of tombstones. To stage, compose, and expose these shots, however, takes nearly six hours. Cranes, tracks, and cameras keep shifting from point to point. Black cables snake back and forth among the graves. The stones are touched up for color and texture. Vishnu looks often into Nirav's viewfinder, thinking about the lay-

pair of graves. You see whose graves these are: her brother's and his fiancée's, both slain by Billa. There are the Petronas Towers again, looming in the distance. The pair of tombstones and the rose bouquets are reflected in the depths of Sasha's dark sunglasses. You hear the tinkles of shared laughter that Sasha remembers, sounds that gradually gain a tinny echo, as though they've been cast deep into a well. You understand something new about the depths reflected in her mirrored frames: these are abysses of time, not space, recollections of a shattered happiness that lap throughout her present like melancholy sighs of reverberation. You understand that there is something different about her experience of time. Sasha lives with two deaths already certain and another death yet to come. In the lingering depths of this temporal span, she is becoming something altogether new: Billa's killer, a would-be assassin, bent on revenge.

out of his frames. There are no storyboards or diagrams to consult and ponder. Each shot is blocked on the spot, each take following another in a jagged rhythm of anticipation and discontent. It's only my fourth day in Malaysia, and I find the flocking mosquitoes and heavy afternoon heat almost impossible to ignore. I see Vishnu sitting on one of the trolley tracks, waiting for the camera crew to set up the next shot. "How do you deal with all this?" I ask him—the enormous time and struggle involved in creating what will amount to no more than a few seconds of film. "It's simple," he replies, almost immediately, without a thought. "I'm traveling in reel time." Reel time? "Those four seconds of shots, it's that moment that you're living in. That moment. By the time it's lunch break, fuck! Lunch break and by the time you go, fuck! It's evening already. You travel in that thing actually. You won't actually know that the time is just flying."

⊢

Vishnu Vardhan was just over thirty at the time, less than a decade past his Loyola College BA in Visual Communication. Small in stature, with a tousled mop of hair on his head and a goatee trailing south in scraggly lines, he reminded me more than anything else of a grungy and unkempt Smurf. *Billa* was his fourth feature film.

The young director always seemed fidgety, restless, speaking in bursts of words and laughter that would abruptly take some unexpected turn. He was also one of the warmest and most generous people that I met in the world of Tamil cinema. Talking with Vishnu was always delightful, even a relief; he didn't seem to know himself where his words were going, as though they were bobbing along in a tide of pure and candid feeling.

What Vishnu said that day was startling. Though we were standing side by side, sharing in a conversation, his experience of this time suddenly seemed profoundly different from my own. This "moment" that

Vishnu described was not an instant to capture and fix all at once, like a photographic snapshot. Instead he was speaking of a span of time in which things were changing, and he and his film along with them. "I'm always in reel time," Vishnu confessed. "Suddenly I'll go somewhere else. I won't know where I am."

This drift in time was sometimes perplexing to others around him, Vishnu admitted. He often had to remind himself to keep looking at his watch, otherwise he would lose track of the clock schedules and hourly shifts that regulated labor and equipment contracts each day on set. All the same, this experience of reel time that Vishnu described seemed essential to his work as a director. He told me about how he would often stumble—"Fuck!"—into an unexpected situation, one whose novel qualities would somehow get absorbed into the body of his films. Like the cinematic character whose graveyard experience he was conjuring that day in Malaysia, *Billa*'s director lived in a time of emergent and transformative potential.

To be sure, Vishnu's words epitomized a certain ideal of creative or artistic flight that circulates widely in milieus such as filmmaking. You might even find them symptomatic of modern cinema's affair with contingency, its appeal to the compelling immediacy of a moment in the midst of the fleeting and ephemeral rush of feeling that we often associate with modern life.[10] There were certainly those in Tamil cinema who found this outlook vexing—like the producer, for example, who once waved a bound script before my face as he excoriated Vishnu and some of his peers with the dismissive judgment "I cannot work with indisciplined directors!"

From another standpoint, however, Vishnu's reel time might have less to do with the difference between disciplined and undisciplined individuals than with the fundamental nature of an improvisational activity like filmmaking. "Improvisation," Tim Ingold and Elizabeth Hallam write, "is inherently temporal. This is a time, however, that is not marked out by the oscillations of a perfectly repeating system such as a clock or metronome, or by the revolutions of the planets, but one that is lived and felt in the pulsating rhythms of life itself."[11]

The very word *improvisation* comes from the Latin *improvisus*, the unforeseen or unexpected. Although we tend to associate this open-ended relationship to time with certain arts such as jazz music or poetic jousting, or, in cinema, with certain styles of filmmaking such as cinéma vérité, it is arguably at work in any domain of creative life. A classical pianist finding her way through a score on stage is improvising just as much as a jazz musician, albeit in a rather different way.[12] And in the universe of film directors in which Vishnu was eking out a place, this was true even of someone as notoriously rigid and controlling as Alfred Hitchcock. "Unless we include improvisation and free play as components of Hitchcock's working method and routine," Sidney Gottlieb observes, "we will end up with a distorted notion of his way of making films."[13]

Cinema's images can help us grasp the transformative force of time, Deleuze argued, "how we inhabit time, how we move in it, in this form which carries us away, picks us up and enlarges us."[14] Think of *Billa*'s Sasha, for example, lost in an abyss of memory as she stands before those graves, a young woman resolving into a determined assassin as these waves of recollection and anticipation wash over her experience of a present moment. But it's one thing to say that certain moments in cinema—Deleuze called them "time-images"—can reveal these workings of time; it's another thing altogether to try to understand how these moments themselves come together as film.

Let's look more closely, then, at what happens when a director like Vishnu loses track of time: how the virtual horizons of reel time surface in what he does, sees, and feels as a director, and how these three domains of experience—action, perception, and affection—might help to convey the time in which cinema comes to be.[15]

·· ┤ ··

AN AUTO BODY workshop, somewhere in Kuala Lumpur, scene of an arms deal gone awry. Billa has a gleaming black trailer full of weapons: handguns, assault rifles, rocket launchers. But something unexpected happens: the police swoop in, threatening an arrest. The gangster remains unruffled. "You need me alive, but I need nothing from you," he tells them with a slight, almost pitying smile, slamming shut the trailer doors. Bullets clang and ricochet off the metal surface. Officer Anil Menon comes forward to pull them open, handgun drawn. Inside Billa is nowhere to be seen. Suddenly, Menon hears the rev of an engine somewhere, maybe behind a plate of smoked glass at the back. He panics, leaping out of the compartment, bracing himself against one of the

SRI MUDA Auto Works, southwest of Kuala Lumpur, scene of a shoot gone awry. Vishnu had wanted a factory floor for the scene, but the Malaysian location managers misunderstood, and the producer insisted he shoot here. The director is agitated, vexed, but resolves to make do: "That's my job, to make it look fucking good." When Billa's blue rally car bursts through a smoked glass plate, the crowd massed around the edges of the workshop breaks out into spontaneous applause. But the actor Anil Menon has mistaken his cue, leaping out of the trailer in surprise and alarm a full second before the car erupts through the shattering glass. Presented as a single shot, as the director had planned, the moment on replay looks comical rather than dramatic. A retake is impossible, as

heavy steel doors. A blue rally car bursts out of the trailer, shattering the glass plate behind which it was hidden. A gunfight ensues. Menon recovers composure, fires off a few rounds, but the gangster at the wheel escapes.

the producer's budget has sanctioned just a single glass plate. Vishnu is dismayed but quickly adapts, breaking up the action into a few successive shots that conceal this gap in time. "Just go with the flow," he tells himself, thinking ahead to the next shot.

H

Billa is a quintessential action film: a character is thrown into an overwhelming situation whose forces he is ultimately able to grasp and master.[16] This is what makes the film such a potent vehicle for its star, Ajith — at every turn, the gangster that he plays finds a way of conquering the unexpected circumstances in which he lands. His heroism is only magnified by the feckless quality of so many others around him, characters like the police officer Anil Menon, who has to scramble just to keep up with these shifting scenes of action.

This idea of mastery is not far from the way that we often picture the director of a film: as a creative "author," or *auteur,* someone who orchestrates action *on* a world, someone whose very command—"Action!" — can bring the environment around him into harmony with his aims and intentions, bending each circumstance to suit a vision that had already been shaped and readied before ever setting foot in that milieu.[17]

To be sure, Vishnu and his team of assistant directors brought such ideas about possible and desirable action into each of the situations in which they worked. But this wasn't all that happened on their shoots. On the grounds of Sri Muda Auto Works in Malaysia, as was the case almost everywhere else he shot, Vishnu seemed profoundly susceptible to the activity—the virtual action, the "vision" even—of the world around him. For better or for worse, on Vishnu's sets, new possibilities for action often seemed to erupt from the places themselves. This is what he meant by that phrase that he repeated so often, almost like an incantation: "Go with the flow."

This is a familiar cliché, steeped perhaps in the syrupy wisdom of the California coastline more than anything else. But regardless of its pedigree, the phrase had an enormous amount to do with the character of Vishnu's work as a director. "No matter whatever happens, no matter if everything goes wrong, you make sure that nothing stops," he told me once, elaborating on this philosophy of action: "My whole flow is like, you know, it's like a stream, you just go, you just go with it, you know. You just go with the flow. Either you flow with the location, or you flow with the nature, or you let everything blend together and you just . . . It's like a gushing thing, it's not like a planned thing, no, you just gush along, you just go." Like the onrushing stream of his own words, the act of directing plunged Vishnu into a continuous current of worldly activity. "You don't cut that flow," he said.

The flow of action that the director described did not imply simply capitulating to whatever happened as it did. Instead this orientation involved a kind of attunement to the possibilities invested in things as they occurred, an ability to seize upon the potential borne by accidents as they erupted, as they would almost inevitably. There was, in other words, a peculiar and almost paradoxical combination of both discipline and latitude at work here, akin to the rigorous techniques of improvising with disruption that are taught in contemporary American jazz schools, where, as Eitan Wilf describes it, "one's fingers take charge because they have been trained in the vocabulary of jazz."[18]

For Vishnu, therefore, acting and directing action was far from a matter of simply enacting the ideas and intentions that a director might bring to places like that Malaysian workshop. "What is the best I can do now?" he asked. "That will be running always in the mind." This one word *now* seemed essential to how the director engaged with the inescapable flux of such situations. The time of action mattered—how one would respond to those forces, elements, and arrangements that time could introduce at any moment.

⊢

SOMETIME LATER, back in Chennai. A guy and a girl stand by the sea, quarrelling over wedding plans. Karthik proposes a race: "If you win, I'll listen to you." They borrow a pair of children's bicycles, take off down a wide road flanking the beach. "Loser!" Sandhya teases, gliding right by him. You can see their avid faces. You can see them laughing as they wobble along on diminutive wheels. Then you see what they haven't noticed: a red kite, caught up in a lamppost farther along the road, trailing a string studded with jagged shards of glass. She pedals quickly, on the verge of winning their race. She turns back to him, smiling triumphantly. But there is

"EVERYTHING IS very happy, and *dabbak!* The girl dies," Vishnu explains. He's shooting now for *Sarvam*, his next film after *Billa*.[19] The bicycle race is staged at Eliot's Beach in southern Chennai. Permission to shoot has been a problem, and the filmmakers scan the roads for police between each quick guerrilla-style shot. I notice Vishnu looking at Karthik's Maruti Swift, parked beside the two small bicycles. Someone on the light crew is nearby, removing a black cutter used on the last shot. The man slowly walks the unwieldy screen between the director and that car, cutting for a moment through Vishnu's field of vision, provoking a sudden and angry outburst. "Come, man, to

still that strand of glass fluttering in the air, visible to you, invisible to her. Suddenly, she yells out in shock, falling. He runs to her, tripping over his cycle. There's blood all over her neck and hands, soaking through his thin white shirt. The scene is a lesson in the difference between ordinary and cinematic perception. Through the film, you see the emergence in time of an event neither seen nor foreseen by its subjects.

the outside, just standing in the frame like that!" the director exclaims. The light man is puzzled, as am I. There is no frame, there is no shot. The camera itself is idle, pointing somewhere else altogether. But what the director sees does not exactly belong to the present moment the rest of us share. The ordinary span of his perception has been extended by cinema; he looks at a virtual frame yet to be established by the film.

What we see in the world reflects what we want to do with it, Bergson argued in the early twentieth century. Our perception of what is present is always selective, subtractive, isolating objects upon which we hope to act and the qualities of those objects that would best support these actions.[20] Think of Sandhya, for example, trying to win that bicycle race, seeing only the empty road ahead and her lover trailing somewhere behind. Although she misses that stranded kite, its sudden and deadly appearance reminds us that there is always more to see and do at any given moment.

Writing at the dawn of cinema, Bergson used the example of the movie camera to convey the difficulty of perceiving time in its transformative flux. "We take snapshots of the passing reality," perceiving the world as a discontinuous series of static impressions in the same way that a rapidly unspooling series of photograms conveys the illusory impression of a moving image. "The mechanism of our ordinary knowledge," the philosopher wrote, "is of a cinematographic kind."[21] Much of Bergson's philosophical work wrestled with the deceptively simple challenge that such habits posed: that of grasping the essential mutability of reality.

What would it take to discern things that have such a virtual and intangible quality? Bergson himself, although critical of the cinematic camera, vested great significance in arts such as painting and sculpture. "Now and then," he wrote, "men arise whose senses or whose consciousness are less adherent to life. Nature has forgotten to attach their faculty of perceiving to their faculty of acting."[22] Those we call "artists" were less bent on submitting what they saw to the immediate demands of embodied existence. They could see what otherwise remained no more than an ephemeral presence, the real depths of time in its continuous flux.

Jean Rouch, the great ethnographic filmmaker, recalled that something like this would happen as he worked in West Africa, that the filmmaking would plunge him into some unfolding dimension of perceptual reality: "With a ciné-eye and a ciné-ear, I am a ciné-Rouch in a state of ciné-trance in the process of ciné-filming." Rouch described how, in his many collaborations with the migrants and workers of the region, they would together set off some riddle, charade, or enigma and then wait to see what would become of this disorder. "Cinema, the art of the instant and the instantaneous," Rouch suggested, "is, in my opinion, the art of patience, and the art of time."[23]

Contemporary Tamil directors like Vishnu worked in circumstances very different from these. Still, on location here, everything seemed to conspire to effect a radical break from the active demands of ordinary life. Directors were shielded from the sun by broad umbrellas, cooled by standing fans, and plied with continuous rounds of fruit juice, exotic teas, and favored snacks, as if to annul the distractions of the body. Assistant directors—bearing cell phones, laptops, notepads, cigarettes, and other accessories—were expected to respond at an instant to the improvisational urges of their bosses. These were taxing and often oppressive forms of hierarchy for many who worked on film sets. But they also sustained those practices of virtual perception that enabled filmmakers here to look beyond what we usually look for.

"I'm only looking at what is in the frame," Vishnu explained to me one afternoon, describing how he filtered out the bustle and commotion of the many people and things around him on a shoot. These frames of which he spoke surpassed a particular moment or instant, spilling far beyond the bodies and tools working to make them present. "In one frame you actually see another frame," he explained, "another frame of the same thing, another perspective of the same thing." To live with a film in its piecemeal fashioning was to perceive the virtual horizons of a world in motion.

Vishnu's shots always evolved with the life of each shoot. New perspectives on each scene were constantly surfacing, like the angle that he saw beside the parked Swift that morning at Eliot's Beach. The director's perception seemed to be moving in a continuous flow, reflecting the temporal depths of the cinematic frame itself. "The film is running through me," Vishnu said. Where it went next remained a surprise—even for him, its putative creator.

.... ┗┥ ....

THERE IS Sandhya's accident, and then her bloodied body, rushed by stretcher along a narrow hospital corridor. "You will be fine," Karthik

THE HOSPITAL is set on the ninth floor of an unfinished office tower, on the grounds of the old Gemini Studio complex in Chennai. Just be-

tries to assure her, as she passes beyond a pair of glass doors. But then you see her mother and father in the distance, crumpling in grief. You see everyone around Karthik begin to wail, when a doctor steps out to report on her demise. Karthik alone remains strangely composed, almost meditative. Seemingly unfeeling, he is caught in a spiral of time. "Just now," he tells his friend Krishna, "she was laughing happily and riding a cycle. That laughing face is still there, just like that before my eyes." Each time Karthik turns away from his friend, he gives voice to a different recollection: that such a tiny string had caught around her neck . . . that it was coated, though, with glass . . . that she had sped ahead on the larger cycle . . . that he could have pulled ahead of her, and . . . Karthik is still talking, mostly to himself, when Krishna pulls him away. It is only when he leans his head against a long white wall that we finally see him break down into sobbing tears. This feeling of grief erupts almost as a surprise. To feel it, Karthik has to remember what is happening at that very moment—as though it could be felt only by a return of time to itself.

fore the shoot begins, Vishnu walks me through the corridors, painted with a blinding white to convey the anxiety of the moment. More than anything, what the director wants from his actors today is feeling. "Let me feel it now!" he yells into a microphone, as they prepare the first take with the stretcher. Accidents erupt throughout the day, underscoring the chanciness of what they do: a glass door cracked by an errant nurse . . . an open doorway exposing set equipment to the frame . . . pieces of the camera falling away as the stretcher races along the hallways . . . emotional misfires on the part of the actors themselves . . . "We don't even know what is going to happen, we don't even know how it will look," Vishnu tells me, just before they try out the first shot down the narrow corridor. But then he also says this: if he will "feel it" in the shots they take here today, that feeling will come to him as a kind of déjà vu. "When you see it, there is a feeling of watching something which you've seen inside," the director says. A successful scene will echo or revive something that has already been felt before, as if time had come to spiral in on itself.

⊢

Affection is essential to the happening of cinema: the feelings that pass between the characters of a film, the feelings that they nurture in turn among their audiences. But this poignant moment in *Sarvam* reminds us that affection is much more than a feeling for others; the affective play of feelings also crucially involves a relationship with oneself. Here again comes the significance of time, for so much depends on the complex ways in which filmmakers are affected themselves by the time of their work.

Take, for example, the shooting of this tragic hospital scene. Director and cameraman, Vishnu and Nirav, speculated that this would be the most intense scene in the film. "They should cry," I caught Nirav saying confidently to Vishnu, as they flicked through digital stills of the completed scene two days after they had shot it. At the outset of that shoot, however, what the scene might make anyone feel remained entirely unclear.

Like the spiraling course of Karthik's own grief within the film, the affective power of the scene would develop only slowly, through something like an encounter with itself in time. "It's like it had already happened, but not exactly in the same way," Vishnu reflected, thinking of what he had scripted and what was now unfolding around us as we spoke. "Feeling it" for the director involved a strange kind of circuit: the sense that familiar feelings of his own were erupting into presence again in some other time and space.

Bergson again has illuminating things to say about this condition. Strange states of consciousness such as déjà vu, he argued, show us how past and present coexist simultaneously. "It is a recollection of the present moment in that actual moment itself," he wrote: "it is of the past in its form and of the present in its matter. It is *a memory of the present*."[24] What is palpably "felt" in such sensations, in other words, is the intensity of a spiraling relation between the actual and the virtual, a commingling of the present with the lingering remnants that make it otherwise. These sensations remind us that whatever we cherish most may be no more than a slip in the stream of time.[25]

There is an essential openness to the play of such affections, as Vishnu himself observed while we walked together through those hospital corridors: "If it is the same dialogue, with the same emotion, with the same way that he is doing, then everything is the same, it should work. But sometimes, it won't work. You won't know. Something is wrong but you won't, you can't understand what is wrong. That always happens. 'It's okay, but something is . . . ,' you say. 'Let's do one more.'"

Every take was a gamble with time, wagering the potential response of an eventual audience. Directing the course of a film, therefore, also involved being directed by the flow of time, having to rely upon its duration for the emergence of a novel feeling. One could never say exactly how and when this would happen.

Throughout the shoot that day, Vishnu's eyes were glued to a small video monitor where he watched the action unfolding around him. "Wild, huh?" he said as we watched one shot framed without a hitch late that afternoon. "I felt it in the first take itself," he told me, but even he couldn't have expected this feeling to come when it did.

┡

WITHIN A week of its release, *Sarvam*'s doom is evident. The afternoon show at Sathyam Cinemas in Royapettah is nearly deserted. In the next row, some college students mock a love song. A chase scene draws sighs of impatience. They snicker as Karthik weeps over Sandhya's death, just before the film's interval break. "What, have they finished the picture so quickly?" one of them asks sharply as they stand up together. They are laughing as they kill the film.

SOME YEARS past that afternoon at Sathyam Cinemas, some years beyond the day that screening found a place on this page, you are also here, reading. I can't imagine who you are, but I keep wondering what you'll make of all this. I take heart in a line from Calvino, repeat it to myself almost like a mantra, trying to lay hold of a being and a time and an encounter impossible to reach. "You are always a possible you," Calvino wrote—you are always a possible you.[26]

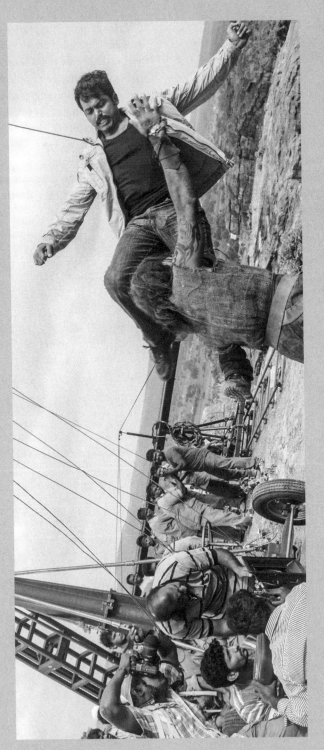

CHAPTER 11   **Imagination**

Something stubborn and unyielding rises up at times in the space between a film and its spectators, or a book and its reader: the presence of an intractable limit between one world and another. Yet this invisible barrier is constantly being ruptured too. Like that night that I tagged along with Push-kar, Gayathri, and Nirav on their tech recce for *Quarter Cutting*. As we walked through the narrow alleyways of an old residential quarter, speculating on the colors of those walls but not really talking to anyone else, the boys in the neigh-borhood quickly figured out we were there for a film. "Hey, run, come!" we heard their voices call out excitedly as they dashed along beside us. "They're shooting a movie! I'm the hero! I'm the villain!" Nothing was happening yet, but every-thing was already happening. Characters were congealing from the air around us, pulled into shape by longing and an-ticipation, by the work of imagination. "You're the god on the hill, the one who's taken hold of me," the fifteenth-century Te-lugu poet Annamayya declared. "For me, you are real, as real as I imagine."[1]

⊢

Swetha first sees "Rocket" Raja when he bursts into a shopping mall crowd. There's a man passed out on the floor among them. "Rocket landing!" Raja exclaims, and does something deftly with his fists to revive the man. They meet next at a lavish wedding at her uncle's house, where he leaps to nab a running thief.

She's entranced. "That day in the mall when you saved him," she says, "I saw Mother Teresa in your good deed. Today, when you caught this thief, I saw Netaji in your speed."[2]

He beams proudly, speaks magnanimously. And then, as she looks admiringly at the hero, you can see for a few seconds how she imagines him: a towering figure with clasped arms and a modest smile, rising alone into the distant heights of a deep blue sky, his body bathed in a halo of green and white light.

The vision leaves a glint in her eye, and she remains distracted by it. She comes back suddenly with a start, realizing that he's been trying to get her attention. This is the least of what she misses in the film *Siruthai* [Leopard].[3] He's already declared in song that he is "really, really not a good boy." He will steal her heart, among many other things.

H

Imagination is an alarmingly creative faculty. Imagination makes things appear—shadows of what was once before, impressions of things impossible or yet to be. These powers give reason to both veneration and suspicion. Are these images no more than illusory appearances, distractions from the reality of what is happening?[4]

The question poses itself especially forcefully when it comes to experiences like cinema, so clearly a departure from the space of the here and now. And the stakes grow even higher when we linger on industries like Tamil cinema, deeply invested in larger-than-life heroes whose outsized exploits fall utterly beyond the means of their adoring fans. Take what happened when this Tamil film, *Siruthai*, was released in January 2011.

Rocket Raja was one of two roles played in the film by Karthi Sivakumar, son of a venerable Tamil film actor and younger brother to one of the most popular stars in the industry. Though *Siruthai* was only Karthi's fourth release, he already had a huge base of avid fans. In Chennai alone on its opening weekend, the film screened 339 times. "House Full" boards were lit up almost everywhere.[5]

Loud drums, strings of firecrackers, and dancers in polyester tiger costumes greeted Karthi at some of these opening shows, his white Honda City with darkened windows slowly making its way through boisterous crowds of ebullient young men. He posed for a few photographs at each of the cinema halls, smiling graciously.

It was the weekend of the Pongal festival, an avidly sought window for Tamil film releases. The annual festival celebrates fields and lives flowing over with health and vitality—*pongal* is literally that which overflows, as with the rice and cane sugar that bubble over the lips of cooking pots throughout the region. Around the theaters, other liquids were overflowing, as young men in red T-shirts—members of Karthi's fan clubs— climbed the scaffolding behind lofty vinyl posters of the actor, spraying them with plastic packets of milk and fizzing bottles of beer.

The ritual was borrowed, bent, from the world of the Hindu temple, an *abhisheka* or bathing of the cinematic deity in consecrating fluids.[6] As

M. K. B. Santhosh, the young leader of a fan association later described to me, "Fifty or a hundred packets of milk, fifty beers . . . That whole road will run with milk and beer."

Santhosh took his initials from his father, a Chennai politician who vanished mysteriously a decade ago. His father helped pioneer the use of massive wooden cut-outs to venerate Tamil political leaders, and there was an unmistakable kinship between that public practice and the vinyl posters that his son now produced, some of which depicted Karthi in the manner of an erstwhile royal lord: bejeweled crown, proud sword, lavish garlands.[7]

Santhosh wasn't entirely sure why these images looked as they did. "We feel like doing it, we do it," he said. But the flow of his devotion spilled even further. "Do you know what else I want to do? When his next film comes, I want to make sir come on a horse-drawn carriage and make a round of the theaters. I have that desire."[8]

·· ⊢ ··

Imagination is a movement of overflow, a crossing of boundaries, a spilling beyond oneself. To say that imagination works in this manner is to acknowledge its peculiar reality, its intangible depth beyond the sheen of appearances, its shadowy existence between presence and absence, there and here, oneself and another. "At every crossing," as Vincent Crapanzano writes, "there is always a moment in which one is neither on one side nor on the other, neither what one was nor what one will be."[9]

What does it mean to dwell in this in-betweenness of imagination?

What happens when a writer pens someone else into being? Or when an actor brings a character to life?

Of all the roles to fill out a book on Tamil cinema, this one—the being of an actor—was the most difficult to "cast." Agents were difficult to reach. Directors quailed at the idea of introducing actors they'd worked with closely. Producers laughed knowingly, yet uselessly, about these troubles. Access was a practical problem and a terrifying prospect. How do you approach someone so readily imagined as god and king?

I made countless and regrettable attempts. Over time, in this cascade of failures, the idea of working with Karthi Sivakumar grew more alluring. The ruffians he played in *Paruthi Veeran* and *Ayirathil Oruvan* were charming. I could see how thousands of bodies erupted in enthusiasm at his appearance on a stage or screen. People in the industry praised his acting skills and easy demeanor. And he was a trained engineer, with a degree from upstate New York, not far from a college where I once taught.

I imagined telling him all this. I imagined him listening appreciatively.

I finally had a chance to meet Karthi's father, Sivakumar.[10] Clad in a crisp white pantsuit, the elder man was unexpectedly warm. He presented me with a few of his own books and DVDs, signing fond words into a copy of his autobiography.

In the face of such sincerity, I was embarrassed to ask for a chance to meet his son. Still, of course, I did. Karthi was shooting daily for *Siruthai*, the senior actor told me, but he promised to try to arrange a meeting when they took a break.

Sivakumar himself had acted in nearly two hundred Tamil films over the span of forty years, stories, he said, that pursued him still. "Literally, I stopped acting six years back. But every night, in my sleep, the shoots go on."

··· ┣┥ ···

The moment finally approached, two weeks later. I was loitering in a deserted bookstore near Gemini Flyover in Chennai, checking to see whether they'd sold any copies at all of my last book. In the lobby, I managed to catch Sivakumar on the phone. "I'm waiting for his call," he said. "As soon as it comes, I will call you."

I wandered around by taxi, waiting anxiously. Karthi would leave Chennai soon for Badami, to shoot the climactic action sequence for the film—over that bridge that you already know, the one that the art director Rajeevan was building. By that late summer of 2010, my own fieldwork for this book was nearing completion. To spend a few days with the actor in Karnataka—could that be enough for this most desperately incomplete chapter?

I thought of trying to pass the time at a nearby café. Then, idly fishing the phone out of my pocket once again, I saw the SMS:

7 o'clock is ok for u?

I rushed the driver along a narrow road, stopping only to buy some breath freshener for my parched mouth. I suddenly noticed the wrinkles on my shirt.

———————————————————— ⊢ ————————————————————

Karthi was more than I could have imagined: affable, sensible, talkative. "I always wanted to know what anthropologists do," he said with a friendly laugh.

I could hardly believe it.

We talked about New York. He'd written a master's thesis in industrial engineering: "Scheduling of Electronic Assemblies in a High-Mix Low-Volume Environment." Thinking back on that thesis, he said, had helped with the caprice of his work as an actor, the utterly unpredictable fit between oneself and a role to play.

"There won't be a breakthrough for six months," Karthi recalled. "The breakthrough will come in one day, and you would've finished the project in one week. It happened to me."

Although I didn't say it at the time, I knew exactly what he meant.

———————————————————— ⊢ ————————————————————

One cloudy morning ten days later, I'm on a plateau of crumbling sandstone in northern Karnataka, surrounded by undulating ridges of thorny bush, low grass, and outcrops of jagged rock. Among these clumps of grass and rock, men are shuffling cables, boxes, poles, and other gear, preparing for the shoot that will begin later today.

I suddenly notice Karthi sitting on a wide slab of red stone, clad in dark blue jeans and a simple gray jacket. I sit down beside him on the slab of rock, jutting from a steep face of the high plateau.

"Lovely place," he says.

"Are you ready?" I ask.

"It's coming slowly," he says. "You can't become Jackie Chan in a day."

He warns me that these scenes will lack emotional drama. "As an actor your contribution is small for the stunt sequences," he explains.

Still, there's something essential he must give, something he will think and talk about every day of the shoot: "You give intensity."

———————————————————— ⊢ ————————————————————

In Indian literary tradition, David Shulman suggests, the faculty of imagination—*bhavana*—is a locus of causality, a generative and productive force, a means of bringing things more fully into being by intensifying their reality. Such was the case with the fifteenth-century Telugu devotional poems of Annamayya, in which the god he praised comes into completeness through the imaginative activity of the devotee's mind.

"It is not the original image that the imagination finds," Shulman writes, "but, through the finding, something much fuller, something the imagination itself has driven to the surface and then shaped and deepened by seeing or reimagining it. That is why one needs the whole panoply of mirrors, memories, paintings, poems."[11]

Consider, for example, that implausible but ubiquitous form of mirroring found in Indian cinema, the "double role." Every successful actor here, it seems, seizes the chance to intensify the heroism of his persona by playing two (sometimes even more) roles at once. In the world of *Siruthai*, Karthi Sivakumar plays both cop and thief.

Rathnavel Pandian is a righteous police officer dispatched to tackle a gang of mountain bandits. He pursues this campaign with a fearsome snarl, hence the *siruthai*, or leopard, of the film's title. Rocket Raja is an irreverent pickpocket, absorbed in various exploits until one day the bandits mistake him—and why wouldn't they?—for the cop. The plot reveals Rathnavel's death and Raja's quest to avenge his doppelganger. The climax happens at the lair of the villains, where their leader, Bhadra, has kidnapped Raja's girlfriend and Rathnavel's orphaned daughter.

Siruthai is a faithful remake of a Telugu hit, produced by Karthi's cousins and chosen deliberately for its mass appeal. "This kind of mass commercial film," Karthi says, "when an actor can pull it off, it gives you another jump in the market."

Karthi has a vivid image of what his audience wants: "a hero in the film, not an actor." Many had been disappointed with the ending of *Ayirathil Oruvan* earlier that year, his character looking blankly as his world erupted in an orgy of indeterminate violence. "Why wasn't I doing anything about it? Why was I witnessing everything happening around me?"

This film will end very differently, the actor tells me. "It's very Hollywood. Hero comes in and saves the day." Rocket Raja begins the film as a selfish and comical character, but by the end, he will avenge the fallen cop with newfound valor.

I follow Karthi down a narrow rock path as he talks of these things. When the camera rolls, Raja struggles with mock emphasis to hold back the unseemly axe of the brutish villain. "This is just like the Jetix channel," he jokes to the frightened little girl that Bhadra holds tightly.[12] "See this dirty uncle? This is the villain. I'm the hero. What will the hero do to the villain?"

"He'll hit him!" she exclaims. And when he does, cheers erupt from a crowd of local men, women, and children watching the shoot from a nearby ridge. It's as though the world has already become that universe of masculine heroism.

.... H ....

I'm struck by the friendly conversation Karthi shares with Supreet Reddy, the actor playing Bhadra. Supreet presents a curious and mysterious figure. Clad in a brown jute vest and dirty black cloak, with a necklace of curved animal teeth draped around his neck, he retreats to a lone chair and umbrella on the edge of the shoot whenever he can, knotted strings of hair falling over his face as he taps the keys of a small mobile phone.

He speaks with a gruff voice that somehow feels soft at the same time. While he's played villains in over fifty south Indian films already, his brother works as an engineer in Seattle. "I like doing negative characters," Supreet says with a sardonic laugh. "The more cruel, the better for me."

His wooden axe looks frighteningly big beside the small girl playing Rathnavel's daughter. Curious, but no doubt with a trace of censure in my voice as well, I ask how he manages to threaten this child with death.

"If you got the chance," he asks, "would you want to do a positive or a negative role?"

"A positive role," I tell him. It's difficult to imagine myself otherwise.

He watches me closely, then asks when I'll return to India. "You can do a sadistic role," he advises. "Half the acting is in the eyes. Looking at you, I can see you doing a sadistic character."

I'm shaken by what he sees. My eyes keep drifting to the patches of plastic scar tissue peeling from his cheek. Then I recover some ethnographic composure. "What about Karthi?" I ask, lamely, already knowing where this will lead.

"He can only play a hero," Supreet declares. "Soft, no, his eyes?"

.... H ....

On a flat expanse of bare brown ground, Rocket Raja and Bhadra finally confront each other directly. They grapple with axe, stone, bare hands, and booted feet. This is the "solo fight" to which the film builds, and for close to a minute, there's hardly anyone else to see.

You can't always tell who or what is acting now in the film. Perspective on the scene jumps, darts, shakes, and spins wildly, cutting too quickly to distinguish blow from blow. The sounds of swift limbs and clanking metal lead or lag behind their visible movement. Spurting dirt, tattered cloth-ing, and whipping hair express the violence.

The scene is composed in bits and pieces over several days. Early each morning, thirty fighters gather to face the sun and silently pray. Three men make up the first row of this motley group: Karthi, Supreet, and Ganesh Kumar, the film's stunt master. Someone slices open a lime and squeezes its juice on the ground, and each approaches Ganesh to touch his suede boots or the earth before his feet. Karthi is the first to make this gesture of humility and respect. Everyone addresses Ganesh only as "Master."

The stunt master is a third-generation fighter in south Indian cinema, and he has fought in over two hundred films. "There's so much history," he tells me just after dawn one morning. He's not talking about the ar-chaeological site where they've been shooting this week—what he means instead is the history of blows recorded on his body: the knee crushed by an accident eight years back; his back trouble between discs L3 and L4; the sternum he's broken twice.

"You'll have certificates in your room to show what you've studied," he tells me. "We have x-rays and medical certificates."

Like a dance choreographer, Ganesh is constantly improvising moves. With a sporty bandanna around his neck, he works out darting blows suitable for a thief. "It's like a monkey's work," he says, describing the style he's developing for this accidental hero. Ganesh also has to keep in mind the physical condition of Karthi's body, the back problems, for example, that keep troubling the shoot. "We'll have to make it seem as though he's got it," he vows.

The plateau is strewn with equipment that will help with this sem-blance: thick mats of padding, rocks and branches built of foam, blood-red paint and pliable shoes, and the metal hooks and lines of black cable leading up to a forty-foot crane, towering over the horizon. On breaks between shots, stories are shared about such things from other shoots: moments of accident when they assumed a dangerous life of their own, snapping, swinging, falling, breaking away unexpectedly.

Attention will be focused here, however, on the action of the hero alone. "Are you doing spycam?" a voice calls out with friendly concern as I record some rehearsals on my iPhone. It's the director, Shiva, worried that my video might leak onto YouTube. There's just one thing he forbids me to record on video: this crane, as it lifts the hero for high leaps and kicks.

"Let them believe that Spiderman can fly," he says.

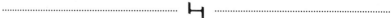

There are many extraordinary things Rocket Raja does in his battle with Bhadra. He aims a kick at the villain's chest, but Bhadra catches hold of his left knee. Raja leaps off the ground with his other foot, pivots upside-down high in the air, pins Bhadra's head between his own knees, turns down to grab Bhadra's legs with his arms, rolls the villain onto his back, comes up to grab one of his legs, and snaps it sideways with a painful jerk, all in a single movement. Physical laws of gravity, mass, and momentum are defied by the hero's body.

On one break, Karthi tells Ganesh how Akira Kurosawa gave fight scenes a new intensity by intercutting wide shots of such action with close-ups of the face. A palpable rage twitches on his own face as many of the shots here are composed and taken. Where does this intensity come from? "I just got hit in the face," Karthi says. "Yesterday, the last shot."

He speaks causally, as though this is quite straightforward, but I am puzzled. In what sense did he "just" get hit in the face? Just now, the makeup man had applied blood to his brow. When I ask about this, Karthi only smiles. "It's all make-believe, right? That's my job. I have to deliver. You're writing a book. You have to go page by page."

If this is indeed a matter of belief, where and how is this feeling conjured? Imagination is taken too easily as a matter of inward vision. Like cinema itself, imagination's images are composed through myriad techniques and technologies, active and dynamic relationships that minds and bodies assume with a wider environment for life.[13] In Egypt, the anthropologist Amira Mittermaier met people who brought up photographs, microscopes, telescopes, and x-rays to make sense of what they saw in dreams.[14] They invoked movies too, and indeed cinema has recast the very horizons of imagination in the contemporary world.

On the set for *Siruthai*, everything depends on the relationship between the hero and the world of activity around him. Take the high crane, for example, dangling the ropes and hooks with which Raja will execute his leaping overhead turn. There is talk of *The Karate Kid* as Karthi practices these moves on a thick foam mat covered by canvas and dirt. "As if you're doing it yourself," the stunt master advises. Karthi, learning how to lift one leg as if pushing off solely with the other, understands. "It should be done as if I'm doing it myself, without support."

All of these artifacts matter: the black vest around his chest, the steel rope clipped to it, the team of stuntmen pulling the rope back, and the crane through which it is laced. Still, the imaginative reach of this moment also depends on the building of a more private alliance with oneself: "Basically, you have to do exactly what you're going to do in every second of the entire action," Karthi says. "You have to do it yourself. The rope is there for help. You have to do it the way you will do it, thinking that you can jump, and you can. . . . At every point you should be conscious about yourself. . . . Your body, your hands, your legs, where exactly, what it is doing."

I marvel at this idea, that the hero must somehow focus his attention, second by second, entirely upon his own body. "It's not so great, anybody can do it," Karthi replies, quietly and with modesty, suggesting that it takes practice more than anything else.

But then he adds, "It's a lot easier compared to Jackie Chan, who does it himself." Even he, it seems, has his heroes. Does he believe that Jackie Chan can fly? Must he?

.... H ....

A chapter in Constantin Stanislavski's *Building a Character* describes exercises in moving with a fictive drop of mercury. "We all did the same," a student actor reports, "letting the imaginary mercury roll up and down our limbs, shoulders, chins, noses, then let it run out again." At one point, the student wonders, "Did we really feel its passage through our muscular system, or did we imagine that we felt the imaginary mercury coursing through us!" But there's little time here for such reflections; they must work ceaselessly on the movements, again and again.[15]

"I'm reading Stanislavski's book now," Karthi says one morning, naming this one, *Building a Character*.

"Is it useful?" I ask.

"Yeah," he says. "Every single thing in your body can help you to look like a different person. You should know how to use it."

Karthi echoes the Russian dramatist on the importance of habit, practice, and discipline. There's also the relationship between inward fiction and outward expression that Stanislavski nurtured as a matter of technique. "Imagination," he wrote, "while devoid of flesh and blood, has the ability to summon genuine actions from flesh and blood—from our bodies."[16]

For Karthi too, such experience is essential: "How deep you believe what's happening." There is something very peculiar in this, he admits, as the events are themselves unreal. "Your body is not paining. You did not [feel] a blow. But you stand there. You feel it." There's also the scrambled time in which these happenings are staged, for when the take begins, "you're in the middle of the action." How to react compellingly now to a punch landed two days ago?

"Playing a part means becoming a true character, not pretending to be someone else," Kirsten Hastrup observes in a study of Shakespearean actors.[17] Karthi speaks of imagining the life of the person he is playing and seeking a way of dwelling in that life. "Creating the situation again

and again, in my mind—that is what it is," he tells me. He closes his eyes
to practice this, "seeing myself from my point of view" as he thinks of
Rocket Raja's routines: coffee in the morning without brushing his teeth,
wandering the slum with his friends, sitting beside the sea and feeling
the heat of the sun.

"It is his nature which creates through him," Stanislavski wrote about
the actor's creation of a character: "he is only the instrument."[18] Karthi
too talks about the organic expression of an actor's selfhood, a personal
nature gaining depth and diversity—both inside and out—through such
practices of imagination. "You get more and more intricate towards it,"
he reflects. "I think you grow in layers."

I find what he says fascinating. All of this feels intensely familiar from
my own experience as an ethnographer, yet remains so inscrutable.

.... **ㅡ** ....

Closing on Bhadra beside a deep ravine and a narrow old bridge—the
one that Rajeevan and his crew put up—Raja lands a few swift kicks and
punches. His arm is bleeding, but his curled tongue juts out visibly from
an open mouth, casting a look of mischievous disdain. The gesture is a
familiar Tamil expression of heedless aggression, often identified with
lower-class men. "As you go into that mood and do it," Karthi explains,
"it will come naturally."

Working actively now with a gesture that expresses itself, the actor
modulates its force and meaning. "Was that funny?" he asks after one
take, ensuring that the gesture matches the narrative progression of the
sequence. "He's confident now, isn't he?" Karthi asks Ganesh. "He's not
yet afraid?" He hasn't yet seen, that is, the little girl dangling over the
edge of the precipice?

Gathering around the video monitor to review each take, actor, director, cameraman, and stunt master refine such expressions of feeling with
a language of mechanical adjustment: higher or lower, lesser or greater,
faster or slower, lighter or heavier. "The more you believe in the situation that is actually happening, [the more] your meter keeps increasing,"
Karthi says. "It's like the fan regulator, you know."

But although such talk suggests that imagination may be harnessed
and channeled, its workings also constantly surpass these moments of
control. Whatever happens in the film doesn't begin when the director
calls "Action," nor does it stop immediately after the director calls "Cut."
Instead, for Karthi, these situations keep trespassing the boundary between film and life.

Shot after shot, his face holds strangely in a frown or grimace lingering oddly out of place, as others bustle all around him with mirrors,

No title

notepads, lenses, and cables. The film slackens its hold on his imagination with visible and peculiar delay. "Because you are always straining
your mind," Karthi admits, "it does some things which you don't even
ask it to do."

Everything that happens here depends upon this play of imagination,
in which I am also caught as an observer. Karthi smiles at me one morning in the midst of a rehearsal. I smile back reflexively, beaming inwardly
at this shared moment of mutual recognition—after all, I'm a stranger
and he's the hero. But then I feel a slight blush of shame, as he turns away
with the look still playing on his face.

"Did you have a very active imagination as a child?" I later ask.

He laughs in acknowledgment. "Overimagination. I used to tell stories
to everybody. My own stories. Very James Bond–inspired."

A few minutes later, he lies down in the dirt beside a clear Plexiglas
panel, grasping a painted rock made of foam, preparing to gaze fiercely
at the reflective glass bulb of a camera lens swaddled in thick black cloth.

⊢

I don't know him very well. But from what I can see, he seems to live
in the midst of a ceaseless stream of stories. He's voluble and funny on
breaks. He sings to himself. We take a run together along the main road
one evening, and tales pass between us continuously. The impression he
conveys is one of overflow. Prabhu, his cousin, and one of the film's producers, agrees. "If you get him started, he'll talk to you for hours."

Karthi's father, Sivakumar, is also like this. Conversations with him are long and drifting. Once I pressed the father for some insight into the imagination of the child. His children didn't see very much of him at home, Sivakumar admitted: he left each morning at six, and returned at ten-thirty each night. But in those same twenty years, he added, Karthi watched almost a hundred films and characters that his father played. "All of this would be passing continuously into the subconscious mind."

He told the story of one film released when Karthi was two or three years old. Sivakumar played a Catholic priest. Someone came to confess a murder. To protect this secret, the priest declared himself responsible for the death. The entire village rushed to attack and lock him up. Only then did the murderer admit to the crime.

"Imagine seeing this film close up," Sivakumar said. "The boy is sitting before this screen. On the screen, they are beating the father with their slippers. There is a close-up of him bleeding. The way he cried and shouted then, sullying that theater! 'They're beating my *appa*, they're beating my *appa*!'"

Hurrying out of the theater in the midst of his own film's climax, the actor carried his son down the road to the beach and bought him some ice cream to try to calm him down. But the child continued to cry out. "Appa, appa, they're beating my appa!"

He tried to bring him back—"Hey, it's your appa here that's feeding you this!"—but the boy was inconsolable. "No, they beat my appa, they beat my appa!"

"When they magnify that and show it," Sivakumar said, "the father being beaten, the slippers coming down on him, when all that happens . . . The ice cream is sweet and good, but in his mind, the father is being beaten. All of that will reach within those children, no?"

—— H ——

"To live a hundred years in the hearts of a people," a tearful constable tells Rocket Raja at the midpoint of *Siruthai*, "it's enough to live for a single day." He speaks of Rathnavel Pandian, lying gravely wounded in a hospital ward. As the constable recounts the fallen cop's heroism, we catch glimpses of how Rathnavel has lived such a life, vanquishing the depraved authority of these demonic bandits. With rain, wind, time, and other cosmic forces on his side, and a spinning metallic disc in hand, the policeman slaughters countless foes and restores order under his rule. It is difficult not to imagine him as Vishnu, the avenging deity of Brahmanical Hinduism.[19]

In peninsular India, righteous gods and kings share a kinship dating back to the early centuries of the Common Era. In this age of cinema, many of the temples and monuments of that time have been revived as centers of veneration. Others survive as decaying objects of appeal, such as the local sites of touristic attraction marked so hopefully on the paper placemats laid out each morning at the Badami Court Hotel, where all of us are staying.

It is on a sandstone rise overlooking the archaeological ruins of Badami, erstwhile capital of the Chalukya Empire between the sixth and eighth centuries, that the tense finale of *Siruthai* is shot over several days. The museum commemorating this history is scarcely mentioned by the filmmakers, although everyone and everything must pass daily through its gates to reach the stone stairs leading up to the height of the plateau. Then there are the plentiful gangs of pigs, dripping black sewage onto the narrow, muddy lanes of what is Badami today, an acrid reminder of the impermanence of human exertion.

Karthi too is prone to such reflections. "As *appa* says," he muses one morning, "don't assume that things will remain as they are."

I remember an image like this in his father's autobiography. "Fame that cinema gives is like the transient clouds of Kodaikanal," Sivakumar writes. "It arrives unannounced and vanishes quite as suddenly."[20]

························· ⊢ ·························

Across the lime-green waters of the Badami lake are the remnants of Chalukya-era cave temples: Vaishnava, Saiva, and Jain. One afternoon, the pull of these distant black spheres strung along the cliffs proves irresistible, and I cross over for a look.

On one side of the lake, artisans are preparing the serrated discus that Rocket Raja will hurl to annihilate Bhadra. On the other side, in one of the caves, a stone Vishnu quells the lofty ambitions of the demon Bali with three steps through the immensity of the cosmos, a lesson in humility imparted through a cunning shift of perspective.[21] In one of his many arms, he bears his own steadfast discus.

The space has an air of epic grandeur and desolation. The vastness between the cliffs is like a resonance chamber, amplifying the sounds that carry across the water. Wet clothes slap sharply against the sandstone steps below. Then there's the fluctuating thrum of diesel generators and the words "Ready . . . take . . . action!" resounding even at this distance. The silhouette of a protective umbrella—an abiding visual sign of Indian kingship—bobs along the edge of the shoot, suggesting the presence of someone important.

From the wide-angle perspective of this viewpoint, though, everything about the film seems small, except for its sound. Although the stunt master's commands boom across the water, there are few signs of any of the activity they intend to provoke. People appear to be milling about slowly, the forty-foot crane among them dwarfed by the ruins of the Shivalaya temple on the northern edge of the rise. The word *action* does nothing to change the pace, direction, or momentum of what seems to be happening from here.

Meanwhile, a gang of Kannada boys has occupied a terrace below the caves, interrupting this reverie. They pose for their own cameras against the lake with jaunty hips and artful smiles, all of them heroes too.

This is relevant, but also irritating. There's nothing for me to do but wait and hope for one more glimpse of life in the vista beyond them. In this reverie, and from this distance, the entire span of it looks uncannily like a screen.

CHAPTER 12 **Pleasure**

They speak of them here as hero and heroine—that starring pair, a film's lead actor and actress. You hardly ever find, however, the symmetry that these titles imply. Take Tamannah Bhatia, who played Rocket Raja's lover Swetha in *Siruthai*—she too had adventurous stories to tell, of stunts and accidents encountered in distant locations, but little more was wanted of her on that set than to scream and run from the villains, to throw her arms around Karthi in joy and relief whenever he appeared on the scene. "Very limited characterization for female artistes in Tamil cinema," she soberly observed on a break from the shooting one afternoon. She, like so many of the young starlets who came in and out of the industry's limelight each year, was wanted mostly for the appeal of her beauty. These films, largely made by men for other men, indulged what Laura Mulvey described as "scopophilia"— the pleasure of looking at erotic objects, most especially women's bodies.[1] Consider what happens when an actress dances, as they are asked to do so often for these cameras.

.... ⊢ ....

There's a young woman named Priya, walking down a crowded road in Chennai with a classmate. Her final project in fashion design is on the thumb drive she's carrying. She loses it when a young man barrels into her, chasing after a kite, eyes turned upward. Ramesh has grown up in a slum, flunked grade after grade. They have little in common. Yet, as these things tend to go in Tamil cinema, they wind up in love.

Later a misunderstanding erupts between them, which takes some time to work out. One afternoon, their quarrels unresolved, Priya approaches Ramesh. She tells him to come to a bus station the next morning if he truly loves her. But the gangsters in his slum also have him marked now—you don't know if he'll survive the night.

The film, *Bana Kathadi* [Kite], is nearly over when this happens.[2] As Ramesh stands in the rubble beside a decaying tenement building, thinking over what Priya has just said, horns and drums begin to sound. It's suddenly nighttime, and a ragged yellow banner advertises dancers from the Bombay Stars Dance Company.

Their stage is small and bare, surrounded by cheap strings of light. There is a pale, pretty girl in a small mustard skirt and a smaller blue blouse, ringed by four bare-chested guys in black lungis. She dances with loose hips and a provocative smile. They follow her with forceful steps, reacting with comic surprise to each of her erotic overtures.

"Come inside and look," this unknown young woman beckons boldly, so unlike the chaste and demure Priya. "This vision of a shapely woman, dancing these unknown moves, how did she come to life?"

The sound of the song is hard and rough, slipping now and then into a tide of Arabian horns. You may well think of belly dancing with these tones, and indeed, there she is now, alone on that stage, torso rolling with those ripples of sound.

All around her, men are clapping as she dances.

⊢

Indian cinema is replete with troubling pleasures, difficult to acknowledge or affirm. "Even among regular (middle-class) film-goers," Rosie Thomas observes, "there appears to be huge resistance to admitting to finding pleasure in the form."[3] Commercial filmmaking turns on the promise of enjoyment. And yet this satisfaction can take quite alarming turns—think of how often social critics in India have charged its cinema with inciting religious, communal, nationalist, or misogynist violence.

Something like this happened in the late summer of 2013, when a photojournalist on assignment at an abandoned factory in south Mumbai was sexually assaulted by five men. Seeking to make sense of the horrific spate of high-profile gang rapes that this incident trailed, numerous voices blamed highly sexualized song-and-dance features for putting potential perpetrators in "a state of heightened provocation." As Dr. Manju Mehta of the Indian Association of Clinical Psychologists observed, "The emphasis on the (woman's) body, the suggestive lyrics, the dance movements—they are things that have the potential to stimulate and provoke ideas in certain sets of people."[4]

Mehta and other critics were most incensed by the so-called item numbers now a staple in Indian commercial cinema, in which an attractive and scantily dressed woman will suddenly appear to dance provocatively before a crowd of adoring men. Alluring and seductive women have long been opposed in Indian mythology, literature, and cinema to the vir-

tuous character of mothers, wives, and daughters. But this pull between 169
an ordinary world of family life and another world of danger, vice, and
temptation is played out most forcefully in these cinematic scenes of in-
toxicating pleasure.[5]

Set in bars, brothels, streetscapes, and courtyards, these song sequences have much in common with each other, whether they appear
in Tamil, Telugu, Hindi, or other Indian cinemas. Their music, lyrics, and
choreography attest to the transmission of courtesan salon performance
traditions—widely criminalized in the nineteenth and twentieth centuries—into modern cinema, along with the moral uncertainty of their
erotic charge. As Davesh Soneji writes of the depiction of a courtesan
dance performance in a 1956 Telugu film, such scenes leave "the viewer
confounded by a spectacle that animates the simultaneous desirability
and vilification of the courtesan and her art."[6] Sexuality is steeped here
with transgressive potential, threatening to spiral out of control.

The story of *Bana Kathadi* turns, in fact, on Priya's horrified discovery
one evening of Ramesh's apparently "low-class nature" when it comes to
matters of love and sex. Reaching into his shirt pocket for a rather sappy
gift, Ramesh pulls out a Moods condom package instead. It turns out that
the boy has nothing to do with the condom in question, but the seeds of
suspicion have already been sown.[7] Priya looks numbly away as a police
patrol seizes Ramesh, accusing him of attempted rape; their courtship, it
seems, is predicated on a disavowal of any interest in physical pleasure.

All the same, when the moment finally comes, late in the film, to clear
this misunderstanding and reconcile the young couple once again, it's
that bawdy song of sexual promise that suddenly intercedes. "Capture
and seduction, confrontation and mutual reinforcement," writes Michel
Foucault—"These attractions, these evasions, these circular incitements
have traced around bodies and sexes, not boundaries not to be crossed,
but *perpetual spirals of power and pleasure*."[8]

·· ╚╗ ··

"Our films have a particular pattern," the director Badri Venkatesh told
me one morning at the *Bana Kathadi* production office in 2009. Though he
had taught for many years at the Tamil Nadu Film Institute, this would
be his first feature film. They were about to begin choreographing and
shooting that song, "Ullara Poondhu Paru" [Come inside and look] and
had generously agreed to let me look on.

Venkatesh rehearsed the story of the film and described how the song
would come just before the climax, less as an interruption than as a way
of exerting control over the audience, focusing their attention at this crucial point. "I need the audience to regroup and come to me totally," he

said. "This song, this beat, when it hits the theater, you can't think of anything else, except for the movie. . . . You must make them dance."

The director knew that most of them would be young men. He was convinced that they would connect with the music of the film's popular composer, Yuvan Shankar Raja. Then there was the "item girl" herself, a model and trained dancer from Mumbai.

Venkatesh was wary of dressing what she would do in too much explanation: "We didn't want to have a very complex thing there. Just a simple, nice, catchy, item number, that's it." They thought of her as an enchantress, he added, casting a spell on those who watch her dance.

In one of the most influential essays in the history of film studies, Laura Mulvey dissects this kind of enjoyment. Visual pleasure in cinema, she argues, belongs to an active male subject, consolidating his authority and agency in the world against the alluring, threatening, yet ultimately passive spectacle of female presence. Narrative films domesticate and contain the anxieties provoked by the female image. At the same time, they can also lock the spectator into a certain posture of desire and fascination.[9]

"It is said that analysing pleasure, or beauty, destroys it," Mulvey writes, seeking to make impossible this form of masculine pleasure or satisfaction.[10] But, as Elizabeth Grosz has argued, pleasure need not always be taken to bring closure and completion to subjects of desire. Pleasure and pain are ways that the body registers the ongoing tussle of forces at work in the world, visceral sensations of flux and intensity. "Pleasure has the role of both force and counterforce, a mobile energy," Grosz writes, "capable of being bound into habituated, disciplined practices . . . but also, under the right circumstances, capable of unleashing the unpredictable forces of rebellion and transformation."[11]

Take the elements that come together in the crafting of a song like this one: that young woman's plunging bodice and suggestive hemline, to be sure, but also the pulsing thrust of the camera, the infectious attraction of the beat, the continuous movement of image and sound that yield so little time and place for a gaze to rest and enjoy what it beholds. There are certainly those alluring optical images that Mulvey had in mind in her critique of visual pleasure, but these images are caught up in a machinery that is more powerfully sonic, haptic, and carnal in its texture, qualities that make for more intimate and unpredictable forms of involvement.[12]

How are such pleasures developed, and what can they do? Take those who allow these forces and images to work most fully upon their own bodies and sensations: the dancers on that threadbare stage.

Her name is Debi Dutta. She's sitting beside a wall of mirrors in a small
dance studio in Saligramam, looking closely at a few stapled pages. It's
October 20, 2009, her first day of rehearsals, with the shoot itself still a
few days away.

Debi is a jazz and ballet dancer, originally from Calcutta. She knows
very little about the film, her first south Indian project, but no matter, as
the song is a world in itself. "I'm a beautiful girl, look at me"—this was
the terse brief they'd given her.

Lying nearby is a CD labeled "Bana item song." When I point this out,
she laughs. "That's what they call it here."

What Debi laughs off is that she's the "item" in this song, without even
a name to match her role in the film. "It's a little bit of a sexy tune," she
concedes. But she also says that she trusts the director, and the shots and
angles he'll take. "Though, technically, you call this an item song, I don't
find anything sleazy about it," she tells me.

Dressed in black pants and a simple white T-shirt, she mouths the
Tamil words to herself in one corner of the studio hall, trying to memo-
rize these unknown syllables. *Podatha vesham pottu, puthusaga vantha-
tharu? Yellarum solluvanga, yennoda nalla peru.* "Who's this that's come
now, with a look that no one's seen? Yes, they'll all proclaim it, my good
name is what they'll say."

Bobby, the choreographer, doesn't know how many times he's listened
to the song in the past two weeks, maybe a hundred, maybe five hundred. Yuvan Shankar Raja's music is "mind-blowing," he says. He speaks
as a fan, eager for this first chance to choreograph a dance for one of the
famous musician's songs.

Bobby wants the song to look glamorous and sexy without being vulgar. This is how he sketches the scene: A girl comes to a slum area to
dance. There are fifty or a hundred people watching. "They should enjoy
that," he says, "but without lust."

The young choreographer speaks of pleasure as *rasanai*, invoking ideas
of taste and refinement that have circulated for centuries in Indian aesthetic and dramaturgical tradition. "You might like to look at something,"
he says, "but you shouldn't want to possess it yourself."

Consider the influential remarks on the subject by the eleventh-
century Kashmiri mystic and philosopher Abhinavagupta. A spectator's
personal and individual sensations of pleasure and pain, he suggests, are
obstacles to the realization of *rasa*, to the enjoyment of poetry or dramatic performance. *Rasa*, the savor of such aesthetic experience, depends
instead upon the cultivation of heightened states of feeling.[13]

There are dramatic devices, gestures, expressions, and conditions that appeal to the hearts of sensitive spectators, observes Abhinavagupta, lifting ordinary and familiar states of feeling into purer and more universal forms.[14] These may be peculiar aspirations for a cinematic spectacle of seduction. Still, as he plans steps and gestures for something so conventionally and viscerally appealing, Bobby says he wants to extend the pleasure of its experience beyond the physical passions of individual men.

"Everyone should dance these movements," the choreographer says hopefully, seeking a route to shared enjoyment through the motion of his own body. "Children, elders . . . listening to this song, they should all dance."

H

For two full days, Bobby and his dancers rehearse with Debi, mostly at the DKS Waave Dance School. The word *rehearsal*, which they use themselves, is misleading, as their moves suddenly appear, gradually change, and gather in number by the hour.

"Sound," Bobby calls, and fragments of the song loop again and again. Standing in a corner of the single large hall that comprises the school, the dance master thinks quietly to himself, eyes closed and both index fingers fixed to the bridge of his nose in a pose of concentration.

"Boys, come," he says to his dancers, sipping from a can of Red Bull before facing the mirrored wall. Body tense and engaged, absorbed in his enjoyment, he begins to act out a series of steps for the others to follow.

As Bobby and his assistants call out numbers from 1 to 2 or 1 to 4, strokes and surges of movement pass through the music, the choreographer, his dancers, and the young woman the scene is arranged for.[15] A step, a turn of the hips, a flick of the wrist, a thrust of the chest—with each repetition, these gestures emerge as successive layers of an orchestral tide.

Vinod is one of these dancers. He came from Burma to India at the age of three, trained a few years ago at a nearby dance school, and has been dancing with Bobby for the past year. "I love Yuvan Shankar Raja," he says earnestly, invoking again the song's composer. "Only he gives a Westernized sound for an itemized song."

Whatever Vinod feels in the music carries him beyond each move they're developing, melting into other steps and slides whenever the music cuts abruptly and its force slowly subsides. Bobby's thoughts also keep drifting with the sound, taking in the character of the audience, the dignity of the production house, the judgments of the Censor Board, and the body of the woman in training.

As the music repeats, moves keep surfacing in new forms. "The song

comes to life when you hear it again and again," Bobby says. "You come
to see what it feels like."

⊢

After a few days of work in the dance studio, the crew shifts to T. R. Garden—a private estate west of Chennai where films and television serials are often filmed—for three nights of shooting. It's close to 5 p.m. when Bobby appears at T. R. Garden for the first of these three nights, wearing a blue T-shirt that reads "Minimum wage, maximum effort." Preparing to shoot in the gathering dusk, they will work until nearly six the next morning.

The art team has been trying to do as much as possible with the sets and props left behind by an earlier film crew some months ago. Bobby wanders through the space, lost in thought. Painted wooden planks, sheets of plastic, and strings of light create a stage for a series of evolving dramas about beauty, desire, and pleasure.

"He's changed all the steps," Debi complains cheerfully as she sits down on one break. "Magic, spells, and schemes, where do they begin?" she is now going to have to ask in front of a leftover rack of liquor bottles, pulling the heads of her male companions into the wine shop one by one. The action is deceptive, a feint—that's not the place she's meant to convey. She poses before a rectangular rack of flashing lights to reveal the answer. "The moon, even the sun, it's here they come to rest," the dancer says, gesturing up into the sky and then down toward her waist, hips thrusting up quickly to meet her pointing fingers.

Debi's lips also move with these Tamil words, but she's the only one here who can't understand what she's supposedly saying. The voice, recorded by the singer Roshini in a nearby studio, is sharp and brazen. As it bawls loudly and repeatedly through the space, distorted pulses of electronic sound echo the swing of its tones.

Deep bass beats edge heavily into noise. The sound is also dirty, raw, and carnal.

⊢

"She's a local girl, but she can also talk about life," the director Venkatesh tells me, explaining how they conceived the character that Debi is playing. There's a mythological depth to the seductive scene they're crafting here. As with so many other dancing girls in the world of Indian storytelling, there is a philosophy of pleasure and desire expressed in the words, movements, and gestures of this nameless temptress.

In ancient Greece, Foucault has argued, the ethics of pleasure concerned the forces and dynamics of *aphrodisia*, or sexual practice. It was never a question of whether a particular act was good or bad, whether it was right or wrong for men to take up with other men, with boys, or with anyone else other than their wives. Instead, Foucault writes, the Greeks wrestled with the problem of pleasure's intensity and the possibility of its moderation: "For classical Greek thought, this force [of sexual activity] was potentially excessive by nature, and the moral question was how to confront this force, how to control it and regulate its economy in a suitable way."[16]

The classical Indian science of pleasure, *kamasastra*, also grappled with related problems of force and control. The *Kamasutra*, like so many of the works that followed in its wake, understood enjoyment as an outgrowth of disciplined activity. "It is perhaps peculiar to conceive of the enjoyment of pleasures as entailing a conquest of one's senses," Daud Ali acknowledges. And yet, as he notes, this is precisely what was argued in these texts, that "the mind ruled the senses in the enjoyment of pleasure and it was in the mind that the experience of *kama* was thought to arise."[17]

It may come as no surprise that the courtesan has long been an iconic figure in this Indian tradition of pleasure's thought and practice, as she remains even now—an expert in the art of dissemblance, of luring the guileless with the promise of satisfaction, of winning dependents in the name of release, of promising pleasure to all but reserving its experience for those who truly understand the game being played.[18] In her cameo in this film, Debi's character dispenses advice of tenuous value, her singing and dancing appealing to mind and body in contradictory registers. "Gain or loss, there's nothing like that," she assures her audience. "In the dark of night, there's nothing to suffer."

In these words penned by the veteran Tamil songwriter Gangai Amaran, the dancer speaks with treacherous authority. "Costumes and ornaments, for whom are these things beautiful? Cover over and conceal it all, but this is only made of wax," she declares, dismissing the evident physical appeal of her own body. And yet, even as she says this, the dancer will slide sinuously among the men below the stage, in a movement that hints at the pleasure of melting.

At times, the charged relationship between lyrics and choreography takes on theatrical dimensions. "As the flower opens up, let all the bees swarm in," the dancer sings at one point in the song, surrounded by four shirtless young men. While these words trickle out slowly from her mouth, the men bend back, away from her, spreading out like a corolla of petals around a torus of attraction.

They too are puckishly handsome, these guys who move in most all of the ways that she does. And yet the contrast between her complexion and theirs—her visibility and theirs—is unequivocal. On the dim fringes of

the stage, they blend into each other too easily. Let your eyes wander ov
their bare, dark bodies and their mischievous smiles, but still, everythi:
conspires to draw you back to her.

·· ⊢ ··

On the sheaf of notes that the director's assistants carry around the set,
the song has been cut into 163 small bits to cover, shot by shot, hour by
hour. Late into the third night, Debi looks tired. The choreographer suggests she have a Power Horse instead of Red Bull.

Someone pulls him aside, gestures drily toward her. "What, master,
the tomato has wilted?"

He smiles. "We've been squeezing it for two days now," he says.

There's something alarmingly casual about the way the men here trade
in such fleshly puns. But *rasa* in India is literally taste, a gustatory pleasure, a matter of savoring subtle variations of flavor and sensation.

There are Debi's coquettish looks, her arched eyebrows and sidelong
glances. There are those glimpses of her deeply scooped bodice, which the
director wants to keep within the frame even as she moves so vigorously.
"Debi, bright!" the choreographer keeps shouting, as the camera closes
in on her face and body.

She is a woman surrounded by men: the four guys moving with her,
the clumps of technicians manning the equipment, and the crowd of
mostly men clapping to the beat on all sides below the stage—extras,
dressed in polyester shirts and cheap cotton lungis.

With each take, a voice booms over the mike with their cues. "Dance as
soon as the sound comes on! Just enjoy yourselves and do it! Clap your
hands! Everyone whistle! Enjoy yourselves! Jump up and down, and clap
your hands!"

I talk to some of them on a long break between shots. Their instructions are so odd. Are they actually enjoying themselves? One describes
the sound as "limbo varieties." A friend nearby is a lyricist, another a per-
cussionist. "Everyone has the capacity to enjoy music," one of them says.
He's worked as a film extra in Madras for nearly forty years now.

It somehow feels wrong to ask whether they find the woman herself
appealing. They never discuss her themselves, but I overhear someone
else nearby quietly murmuring a line from Selvaraghavan's *Ayirathil Oruvan*: "Yeah, it's desire for you."

·· ⊢ ··

"Let the girl just smile, and so many eyes will adore her," the dancer sings.
Everything about the song amplifies her sensual availability: aural, visual,
and physical. She lays her hand casually on the shoulder of one of the guys

on the scene as she and her dancers pass along a lane in the slum. He's fat and ungainly, dressed in a lurid yellow vest, but there he is, later, dancing on the stage with them.

This is while the cameras roll. Otherwise everyone keeps a respectful distance from Debi. She's on the set alone, unlike so many south Indian starlets in such spaces, trailed always on location by their mothers.[19] How does she feel, dancing in the midst of all these unknown men? "I don't notice," Debi tells me. "For me, they don't even exist."

But there's at least one moment that seems to break through her veneer of confidence. The film crew wants her to glide along the edge of a tank of water, the man in the yellow vest and the other dancers pressing close beside her as she moves. The fat man with the cameo is no extra, in fact, but a production manager for the film.

The dancer is discomfited, but acquiesces. "Just take it, take it," she tells me that she told herself. "They were too close, skin touching skin." She speaks to me in confidence, although I too am a voyeur here, another man looking on. Her candor is both wrenching and magnetic.

.... ⊢ ....

The mood changes once again, later that night, when Debi grabs the pole at the center of the stage. As the Arabian horns break into a solo melody of undulating tones, she winds around it again and again, curling herself against the narrow column wrapped in a slender blue cord of lights.

What she does with her hips and midriff looks somewhat like belly dancing, but the way she swings around it has the titillating feel of a strip club pole dance. Although no one else is visible within the frame, there are all those men watching from the sides as she dances. "A body trained hard at the gym," someone mumbles appreciatively.

Moving along with Debi on that stage is a camera, mounted to the long black boom of a "Jimmy Jib" crane. The camera dips, twists, turns, and darts with her, controlled remotely with a joystick by an operator seated behind a screen.

On a break, this middle-aged man, Niranjan, introduces himself as one of the first camera jib operators in India. He moves, ever so slightly, along with the heavy beat of the song as he works the slender joystick with his fingers.

"Give me the freedom, and I'll go anywhere inside," the operator de-clares with risqué gusto, but there is a certain amount of bluster in this ᴇll. It turns out that he is afraid to take the camera too low beside ᴇgs. "Short skirt," he insists, whenever someone asks if he could push ᴀngle further.[20]

LOTUS FIVESTAR DVD

H

Wherever the camera goes on its boom, Debi follows with her eyes. The intensity of her gaze is palpable and unnerving. She doesn't see Niranjan or any of the men as she dances around the pole, she tells me. Instead, in the flat, square mirror of the camera lens, she sees someone more susceptible, something that can be seduced more easily.

"The camera doesn't judge you. It doesn't have a brain," she says. "What is it thinking at the moment?" is not a question that she has to ask herself. She thinks of herself as alone in her room, enticing this inhuman eye.

The first two takes with the pole are awkward and stilted. "See, it's not vulgar," Bobby tries to assure her. "If it's vulgar, I'll tell you." Then, the next take brings loud whoops of joy from the choreographer.

"Let me see, I have no idea what I've done," Debi says. I see her smile coyly to herself as she looks down at the monitor, before heading straight to her dressing room without saying another word. The dancer seems both pleased and embarrassed, proud of something that took on a momentum of its own. "I have a little part in the song where I have my vision, and my sets, and my everything, instead of just following somebody else," she later tells me.

I begin to see how the dancer herself enjoys the song, what there is to enjoyment here beyond the grammar of woman and man, object and subject of pleasure. There is, no doubt, the fulfillment of a certain image of herself: the song makes her feel beautiful, sexy, and desirable in the eyes of these men. But there is another aspect to her pleasure in the tune, something aural and kinetic as well as visual, waves of movement lapping beyond these ocular images of herself.

"Even before I'm doing my moves, I feel like moving my shoulders, moving my legs," she says. "I'm already in the feel of the music."

"Were you born to look seven lifetimes away?" that dancer asked so impudently. I spent three nights with her at T. R. Garden. I wandered the periphery of that stage for hours on end, falling wearily into bed after dawn each morning. Those were days I hardly saw my wife of several years, my son of eleven months. Those were nights that I spent in the company of a beautiful young woman, absorbed in "her tresses swarmed by bees, the unique beauty of her bowed forehead, the beauty of her eyes shooting forth lances, the beauty of her legs, the beauty of her speech, the beauty of her garlanded shoulders, of her teeth . . ."[21]

Cut! This isn't right—whose dreams are these, anyway? These words of praise for a nineteenth-century courtesan in the erstwhile Ramnad Court of Tamil Nadu do fit the situation, and rightly so. Still, although the dancer and I did share quite a lot, now and then over the span of those nights, I was equally absorbed in the experience of those men around her, those who were conspiring to turn all eyes in her direction. Isn't this how these public scenes of seductive womanliness unfold so often, as a chance for men to share some world made possible by a woman in their midst?[22]

Those four guys dancing beside her, they all knew this, I think—always smiling, smirking, eyes widening in mock hope and disbelief at every bawdy turn in her voice. In the aesthetics of *rasa*, the erotic always shades into the comic. There was more than beauty to enjoy on that stage.

The dancers were fans of Yuvan's music, physically immersed in its shifting tides of beat and melody. And over those nights, that song also seeped into me. I'd heard it only once from beginning to end, that first morning, when the director played it on his car stereo. It sounded harsh and grating at first, though I dutifully nodded along with him. Then, over those days and nights, I began to hear it constantly, continuously in my head, even as I fell to fitful sleep each morning. I began to look forward to each familiar movement of sound and voice as it came. And as each small fragment was cued once more, I heard, and enjoyed, new details and minor tones that I hadn't noticed before.

This continued to happen long past the shoot itself. In fact, it's happening even now, as the song loops continuously through the writing of this chapter.

"There is something about vibration, even in the most primitive of creatures, that generates pleasurable or intensifying passions, excites organs, and invests movements with greater force or energy," Elizabeth Grosz reflects in a meditation on the natural history of pleasure. "Vibrations, waves, oscillations, resonances affect living bodies, not for any higher purpose but for pleasure alone."[23]

··· H ···

Bana Kathadi was released a few months after they shot that song. I caught a late show on the opening weekend at a shopping complex in south Chennai. The hall in which it screened was unusually small, but all the seats were occupied.

"If they get up and leave during this song, I've failed," the director had said to me. No one did this when the song began. Nor, however, were there any cheers or whistles as these drums and limbs began to beat.

The film was panned by critics and shunned by audiences. But the song by Yuvan Shankar Raja picked up its own legion of fans. Someone uploaded it to YouTube, and tens of thousands watched it online before the producers managed to have it removed.

"Awesome figure with a beautiful Ice ;) and a strawberry lips!" one YouTube comment declared with clumsy enthusiasm, leading whoever uploaded the clip to respond with an incredulous reply: "Are u a fruit seller?"

I can't help but think of something else that Abhinavagupta said: long after the spectacle itself, its pleasures remain on the lips, yet to be tasted fully.[24]

CHAPTER 13   **Sound**

The space was massive, quiet, empty. Yuvan is a small guy, but he looked even smaller here: a lone figure in a black leather jacket and fedora, wandering across a gray field of removable flooring pads, lit with stark and epic shadows by the halogen lights above. Now and then, digital shards of color suddenly appeared on the towering screen behind the stage. Each of them glowing with a portrait of the composer's legendary father, Ilaiyaraja, they hurtled toward the center of the screen to compose a mosaic of Yuvan's impassive face and dark mirrored sunglasses. The image was beautiful, but also unsettling: every digital glitch left the face open, vulnerable, unfinished. It was the night before Yuvan Shankar Raja's 2009 show at the Dubai International Cricket Stadium. Called "Southern Dreamz," it would be the first time anywhere in the world that the film composer showcased his own music in a live concert. They'd been planning the event for months. Yuvan wanted it to feel like Michael Jackson. Would he first appear in a circle of light? Could they lever a piano onto a rising pillar? Should he burst onto stage on a motorbike? I tried to imagine this immense space running over with pulsing lights, pounding beats, waving and leaping bodies. It was staggering, the idea that anchored this bustling arena of activity—the idea of an ocean of sound, spilling somehow from that small figure wandering through the vastness.

-------------------------------- ⊢ --------------------------------

"What does a sound typically lead us to ask about space?" Michel Chion writes. "Not 'Where is it?'—for sound 'is' in the air we breathe, or, if you will, as a perception it's in our head—but rather, 'Where does it come from?'"[1]

The question is a pervasive one in modern times, as sonic reproduction devices seem to make sounds erupt from nowhere and everywhere at once.[2] We tend to look and listen no further than the ubiquitous speakers and other machines that make this possible. Still, the question remains persistent and unsettling, as sounds drift ever farther from their apparent sources, both physical and natural. Where are they coming from, these unseen vibrations that have so much to do with the feeling of the worlds we inhabit?

This is why they line up in this Chennai sound studio lobby like nowhere else in Tamil cinema: directors, famous, aloof, and elusive, sitting side by side, sometimes even for hours on end, waiting for the young composer to surface from behind his heavy recording studio door. Restless, anxious, they field urgent calls from their production managers and pass the time with fitful gossip.

Inside, for all they know, he could be joking around with his engineers, browsing online for a stylish new phone, or pulling together one of their tracks. It doesn't matter, they have to accept that he can't be rushed. They take his work as a matter of divination—he can hear things, in their images and stories, which they can't place themselves, sounds they've heard but cannot identify, others they hope still to hear.

"Sound, music give life," one of these directors says to me with a reverent look in his eyes. "We take the camera through the darkness. There, *dang, dadang!* That sound gives fear. A piano, early in the morning, when the birds sing—it gives happiness, the flowering of that morning. Music can give happiness and fear. Music can bring surprise and summon tears."

⊢

He beams, thinking of her, weaving down the road on a motorbike as someone unseen begins to sing, "like a feather, I drift off, at the sound of your voice." He's batting on a playground, "like a child, I totter, when I feel your glance," as she paints her nails, "I got lost without losing my way at the touch of your hands, I dissolved without melting when I felt your breath." Smiling, teasing, talking, laughing, both of them pressed to their own phones, "this cruel love that's come, the wild desire it brought, like lightning inside before it went." Then she's on his bike, wind whipping through her hair. "When love comes to the edge of the eyes, even the tears turn sweet. Don't need a thing just you."

⊢

This song, "Iragai Pole" [Like a feather], spans a few minutes in the Tamil film *Nan Mahan Alla* [I'm no saint], released in August 2010.[3] Read these words to yourself out loud, follow them up and down as if they trailed the notes of a melody through a sheet of staff paper (as these lines do, sort of), but still, that voice is just a single track, only one instrument among so many others to trail.[4]

Imagine the page as a device like a diaphragm, a vibrating membrane meant to register on its physical surface something of the wavelike movements that compose a sonic world—whatever I try to do with the rhythm of these words, their tempo and flow, even the lilt and tilt of these lines across the page, so much of the song remains stranded somewhere else.[5] The chords. The syncopation of beats to hear and cuts to see. The soundscape made by the intertwining of these sounds and images.

The Canadian composer R. Murray Schafer proposed this term, *soundscape*, as a name for acoustic environments.[6] Listen closely to a film like *Nan Mahan Alla*, and you can hear what he calls the "keynote" tones of the space in which it's set: the constant buzz of car horns and motorbike engines, the sizzle of cooking dosas, the cacophony of televisions, the calling of crows and cell phone ringtones, and the crowds of people shouting over all the din. This is the "sonic jabberware" that Schafer laments, the relentless and ubiquitous noise of Chennai's urban modernity.[7]

These aural elements, however, come to prominence only during moments of relative silence in the film. This soundscape is a space of acoustic design, pulled together with louder and more forceful vibrations, sonic movements of anticipation, anxiety, and relief. In Tamil cinema, composers—known here as "music directors"—are most responsible for these auditory currents of feeling, borne along by the ebb and flow of the background score as well as the occasional song.

Every action in the film seems to come with a signature sound: the whining mischief of a guitar each time this guy flirts with that girl, or the *shehnai* that calls out mournfully whenever his father is pursued by that gang of hoodlums. Each return of a similar deed is signaled by a repetition of the same tones, thrown into various sequences, tempos, and instrumental arrangements, building up an architecture of sound.

Sometimes these sounds anticipate and foreshadow what is about to happen, like the ominous tinkle of piano notes that surface every time those hoodlums plot another act of violence. Then there are tones that muddy the surface of what appears to be taking place, such as the whistling melody that betrays so many of the hero's jests as acts of comical deceit.

Furious slashes of sound can topple, all at once, into murmuring pools of silence. But there is also music that laps along with the tides of what is happening, redoubling and intensifying its momentum—like that song, for example, "Like a Feather," composed and arranged in a quiet corner of the city that the film portrays so darkly.

.... ⊢ ....

The music for *Nan Mahan Alla* was composed by Yuvan Shankar Raja, one of the most popular and prolific of contemporary Tamil music directors. Yuvan is the younger son of the legendary film music composer Ilaiyaraja, a man said to have scored more than a thousand films and known for his pathbreaking fusions of Tamil folk melodies with Indian and Western classical traditions. As versatile as his father, Yuvan himself is known for his work with hip-hop sounds and electronic dance music, and for his appeal to the biggest market for Tamil film music: contemporary urban youth.

From the 1930s onward, the development of Tamil cinema has been closely bound up with the development of popular Tamil music. Gramophone recording companies were involved in the production and distribution of many early Tamil films. It was not uncommon for three-hour films to feature fifty or sixty songs in the first decade of Tamil "talkies."[8] To this day, most commercial Tamil music stems from cinema, and songs are essential vehicles of film promotion, through album sales, radio and television programming, and mobile ringtones.

The music director, therefore, is a crucial figure in the production of contemporary Tamil cinema, often besting the cinematographer with the distinction of immediately preceding the director and producer in the opening credits of a film.[9] A. R. Rahman, the most famous of Tamil music directors, is widely known as "the Mozart of Madras." He has had much to do with the aura that envelops these contemporary composers, an intensely soulful adulation not unlike the reverence for his eighteenth-century European namesake.[10]

The mystery of music's origins pervades talk about these composers. "It's not a factory, it's not a product," Yuvan's manager, Karthik, once told me, gesturing with a hand that met and fell gracefully away from his own head. "It has to come from his mind." His sound engineer, Guru, proposed Yuvan's speedy compositions as the gift of the goddess Saraswati, Hindu patron deity of music: "Where else does it come from?"

The association of popular Tamil music with Saraswati's divine blessings dates back to the marketing of gramophone recordings in the 1930s, Stephen Hughes has shown.[11] Whether from the composer's mind, the favor of the gods, or the commercial infrastructure that has drawn these wellsprings together so closely, everything turns on the riddle of what happens behind the soundproof doors of studios such as Yuvan's.

Karthik would stand guard in the hall outside, fielding countless phone calls and warding off restless visitors. Now and then, he told me, during moments of respite, his thoughts would drift to the idea of a trip to Salzburg, to the place of Mozart's birth.

I first met Yuvan while he was working on the music for an earlier Tamil film, *Yogi*, another dark vision of a Chennai underworld, released in 2009.[12] I wanted to get a sense of how he developed the background score for that film. It took months simply to work out when this might happen. As Karthik sometimes put it, with bemused and exaggerated emphasis, "It *all* depends on Mr. Yuvan's *mood*."

Then, one morning, the manager called to invite me to Kalasa Studio in the western Chennai neighborhood of Saligramam, where Yuvan and his sound crew were working at the time. "He will start the re-recording today."[13]

Around noon, the music director himself showed up, and I trailed him into the recording booth. Tucked into each corner of that large, pentagonal room was a separate workstation, Apple logos lit from the back of every screen. At the center was a digital recording console and mixing board, with cables snaking between the keyboards, hard drives and outlet boxes positioned everywhere else. It was the most intensively wired space I'd ever encountered in India.

Yuvan took a seat beside a Roland synthesizer, two aluminum cans — Coke Light and Red Bull — perched atop its black casing. One of the opening sequences of the film was playing again and again, in silence, on the screen before him: a fat, drunken man in a loose white shirt, beating on a serving boy at a roadside restaurant.

The music director called over his drummer, Kumar, who had come into the booth a few minutes earlier, fingers tapping some rhythm to himself as he chewed on a mouthful of betel nut. Yuvan sent him over to the *taiko* and *naqqara* drums they'd set up inside the soundproof recording space, where he wanted Kumar to try out a beat with a 4/4 time signature.

"Play," he called out to Kumar, as the TAKE sign lit up in red, asking for a series of variations in tempo and tone. They went from the taiko to the naqqara, then to a frame drum and some cymbals that Yuvan had him graze with a pair of wire brushes.

Now and then the composer gave voice to what he was hoping to hear, what he found missing from the drummer's beat: *ta tankun tinkun tinkun tankun tinkin tinkin ta tankun tank tinkun ta.*

"It's got a world feel, doesn't it?" Kumar mused at the console, as he listened to Yuvan layering together these overlapping beats. To me, these sounds didn't seem to have any obvious relationship to the visuals still playing from the studio monitors.

"There's a sound that the mind hears," Yuvan later said, describing what happens as he watches such scenes. "I hear some sort of sound, I keep in search of that. I try to create whatever I hear in my head."

⊢

What exactly did he hear, and where did these sounds come from? About this, he couldn't say very much. Yuvan was quiet, soft-spoken, often keeping his utterances to no more than a single word. Super. Cool. As he said once in the midst of a rare more voluble exchange, "I feel my music should speak, not me."

The studio itself seemed to conspire for silence. The recording booth was always cool, air-conditioned mildly and carpeted in a deep and muffling blue. Yuvan would dim the track lights, such that the illumination came mostly from the glow of their screens. It felt like the Zulu recording studio in South Africa that Louise Meintjes has written about, "an enclosed space, a dark-bounded interior, a private space with a secret life."[14]

"These complex interiors," Meintjes suggests, "play a part in generating an atmosphere of mystery and hidden potency, for they can be revealed—always only in part—to those who know how to access them, while they are hidden from ordinary view."[15] At Kalasa, the sound of running water played continually in the hall where visitors waited for their audience with Yuvan, spilling from an upturned mud pot, a *kalacam*, in the courtyard fountain. Kalasa, *kalacam*—a burbling flow of quiet, like the consecrated water poured from other *kalacams* onto the bodies of Hindu temple deities.

Within a few days, the basic principle at work here became clear: everyone else—sound engineers, musicians, managers, caterers, visiting directors and producers—was meant to be held to a certain degree of tension, such that the composer alone could relax. I found the situation remarkable, as I'd never met anyone else in the industry who could work in such a state of complete repose. It was in the way he shuffled slowly through the space of the studio. It was even in his jokes, which he told with an almost unnerving tone of calm.

Scoring film music used to be a "jolly" occasion, the sound engineer Guru once told me, describing the many sessions musicians who would cluster and chat for days on end in all the corners of the studio, their sounds and instruments always on call. Yuvan still often worked with smaller groups of musicians. The first few days of the *Yogi* score, however, like so much of their work now, found Yuvan at his own keyboard and

computer for the most part, manipulating libraries of electronic samples, stocks with names like "Goliath," "Symphia," and something called "Dystopian City."[16]

H

A dystopian city. Like the space occupied by that drunken man in *Yogi*, clad in white, wildly aggressive, beating up the serving boy before staggering out onto the deserted streets at night, his satchel overflowing with bundles of cash.

This is what you could see on the monitor. Then there was what Yuvan was doing, adding, sounding something like this: as the rage of that man rose up from the clank of utensils and the sobbing of that boy, you could hear the faint metallic tingle of a Thai gong, tailed by an electronic pulse then a brooding organ as he stumbled onto the road, the low strokes of the taiko coming in and out of sync with those images of the Chennai Marina at night, punctuating that sound that rose and fell like the siren of a passing police car, giving way once again to a deep machinic thrum that faded as he fell into the seat of a bus, the seat in which his throat, soon, would be gashed with red.

"Super," the drummer Kumar said, nodding his head in appreciation. "Each of the sounds overtakes another sound as it goes."

In his classic study of sound and sentiment among the forest-dwelling Kaluli of Papua New Guinea, Steven Feld grappled with the local concept of *dulugu ganalan*, or "lift-up-over-sounding." Human sonic activity here came constantly in and out of resonance with the continually shifting tide of that natural environment, Feld observed. "Unison or discretely bounded sounds do not appear in nature," he wrote. "All sounds are dense, multilayered, overlapping, alternating, and interlocking."[17]

Parts out of phase with each other: this is how sound becomes soundscape, how sounds convey the sense of an active place—perhaps a tropical forest, as in Feld's work, or, in *Yogi*, an urban wild-land habitat for predatory forms of life.[18]

⊢

A few days later, Ameer stepped into the studio booth. A well-known Tamil director, he had produced as well as starred in *Yogi*, which would be his debut as an actor. This was the fourth film that he and Yuvan would do together. Still, I could sense how the composer tensed up while the producer evaluated the nascent score with his audience in mind, making a number of suggestions of his own.

"It's his script. I'm here to give what he wants, and that's it," Yuvan said as he took a break outside. But later that evening, when I sat down beside him and his keyboards once again, I could see that something had changed. He kept scanning through various scenes. He fidgeted with his seat, playing around with the recline. Then he put the film aside and took up a pair of headphones, plunging himself into something else.

It seemed like a scene of creative impasse that I had just witnessed. But its gravity became clear only the next morning, when Karthik pulled me aside to ask gently whether I could stay away from the studio for just a few days.

I suddenly felt terrible, almost dizzy with the sense of being an interloper. I kept thinking back to the previous evening, to the way I'd sat beside the composer, scribbling busily into my own notepad as he struggled with his music. I continued to work while he had clearly been stuck. How much of this was my fault? It suddenly seemed appalling, the idea of the constant presence of someone like me.

Karthik laughed and patted me lightly on the back, assuring me that I'd done nothing wrong. "His mood will suddenly change," he tried to explain. But I had nothing more than an uneasy smile to share in return. I couldn't guess whether I'd be admitted again into that space, which felt all the more now like a temple to sound.

⊢

A year later, Kalasa is being renovated, and Yuvan is working from another nearby recording studio, his father's. I drop by one afternoon in June 2010, a day after landing again for more fieldwork in Chennai. Still repentant, I apologize for having been a distraction the previous year.

"It's nothing," Yuvan says.

We chat for a few minutes. I remain eager for more of a sense of how his sound and music develop in the studio environment. Yuvan talks about the tremendous expectations that have settled around his music with the immense popularity of his previous soundtrack, for the film *Paiyya*, one of the biggest Tamil albums of 2010. He tells me about the project he's working on now. Then, unexpectedly, he invites me to follow him into the recording booth. "Let's see how it goes."

Let's see how *what* goes: the studio work or my eavesdropping on it? This recording booth, much smaller than the one at Kalasa, is crammed with equipment of all kinds. Wearing a hoodie over his dark T-shirt and whistling a tune to himself, Yuvan steps over to the microphone tucked into one corner.

It looks to me as though he's preparing to sing, as he has done for some of his most popular tracks. I can see from the sheet resting on the music stand that the film is a Studio Green project, an upcoming film called *Nan Mahan Alla*.

"When love comes to the corner of the eyes," Yuvan warbles in a gruff falsetto, rehearsing what will come. Warming up as he goes along, he's humming at first, then singing softly to himself, then more emphatically, bouncing on his feet and tapping his thighs as the recording console begins to pick up his voice, earnest, boyish.

Guru, listening, corrects his rendition of the lyrics, which Yuvan is still learning. *Iragai pole*, not *siragu pole*—like a feather, not a wing.

⊢

After a few more takes, the house engineer hands Yuvan a thumb drive. The composer listens to a voice bathed now in the tones of an earlier version of the song, which the film's producers had disliked and asked him to redo. This music sounds tinny, flat, the voice drowned out by the urgent tempo of a dense and repetitive electronic melody. Yuvan strips almost all of it away and begins to work with other sounds.

Playing that first line—"Like a feather, I drift off"—again and again, the composer tries out various percussive tones on his keyboard. He layers a heavy beat over a spacey and atmospheric sound, bringing in deep reverberations of his own voice.

Then he adds what I can only describe as something blippening, working with its pitch as he plays around with knocks, taps, zaps, and scratches, thick beats with distorted edges. A metronome begins to tick with every new sound, striking at around a hundred beats per minute.

Wedged as inconspicuously as possible into one corner of the booth, I can't help but shake my own head and legs. It's the music running through my own limbs, but also a sense of wonder at unexpectedly finding myself in the midst of its creation.

Yuvan is now playing electric guitar chords on the Juno-G keyboard, backing a piano melody. He and I are alone in the booth.

"You like it?" he suddenly asks, looking out at me over the high edge of the recording console. "This is awesome, dude!" I blurt out, laughing.

How does it sound inside the studio? Something like this:

"Like lightning inside before it went" beat, beat, b-b-beat, b-b-b-beat, b-b-beat, blippening up, beat, b-b-beat, blippening back, beat, b-b-beat, hanh hanh hahanh, hanh hanh hahanh, b-b-beat . . .

Silence, keys tapping . . .

Drumkit, beat, guitar chords, beat, bass notes, beat . . .

Silence, keys tapping . . .

"Girl, we gown do this, we gown do this" . . .

"Ow woaw, ow woaw" . . .

"Ow" . . .

"Whoaw . . . Whoaw" . . .

Beat, beat, whoaw, b-b-beat, b-b-b-beat, whoaw, b-b-beat . . .

"Do you hear holes? Do you hear a hole, and know that it needs it?" I ask Yuvan when he takes a break from all this, thinking about this pause in a current of sound that seemed to me to be moving already, his looking for something to move it along otherwise, his finding it in a sample that sounds like a black American voice—*whoaw*—and his fitting it back into that succession of beats.

"Some . . . thing is there," Yuvan says. "So I go to the sampler. Okay, let's try this here, this effect."

"So you know something is missing? You feel something is missing?"

"Yeah, something is there," he says, cueing immediately what sounds like a church organ, playing first with one hand, then two. And then those lines once again. "Like a feather, I drift off, at the sound of your voice."

.... ⊢ ....

Whoaw. Did Yuvan hear a hole, or a whole? The song isn't made by filling in holes, by nullifying absences, it seems. The song already has a virtual fullness—these things, these sounds, are already there, here, spectral presences to listen for and body forth.

I realize that Yuvan hears far more than what seems to be resounding within the walls of this small room: not on the edges of the frequency spectrum, where we are accustomed to looking for what is inaudible to our ears, but deep at its heart, in the company of those sounds that we can already hear. It's like the silence into which the recording booth keeps lapsing: not empty or forlorn but suffused with the timbre of sounds yet to be.

Think of the intrinsic vulnerability of the ears, about which so much has been said—their inability to block what we wish them not to hear.[19] What must it be like to live and work in the midst of so many potential sounds, to draw harmonies from all this din?

"How do you spell *feather*?" the composer suddenly stops to ask me.

"F-e-a-t-h-e-r," I say, startled by the question.

Yuvan laughs softly to himself. "Yeah, sometimes you get the . . . what do you call that? Suddenly, before I can spell *which*, it'll be lost, w-h-i-c-h, you know? The spelling, the smallest thing, I'll forget."

"You work with sound, no?" I rush to tell him, moved by his candor and struck by the difference between his work of composition and my own. "I think some people think very visually, or they think in terms of sound. For me, it's just words."

I think of my own keyboard back home, clicking in tones that I scarcely know. What would it mean to write musically, to write with rhythm, to be sure, but also with pitch, melody?[20]

.... H ....

The next morning, Tanvi Shah gets a call from Yuvan Shankar Raja. "There's this song happening, why don't you come?" he says. At the studio, he plays her a few bars that precede the second verse. "This is where you have to sing."

"What do you want me to do?"

"Anything."

Tanvi is an avid cyclist, a Grammy-winning songwriter, and an heir to the granite company that supplied the stone for the Vietnam War Memorial in Washington, DC.[21] She used to sing in a choir that Yuvan would sometimes hire, which was how they began to work together some years ago.

"He's a really chilled-out dude," she says. "He's very encouraging."

Yuvan asks her to follow the melody with her voice and to throw in whatever words she can think of. Tanvi responds with choral tones, sounds that she insists are gibberish. "It's music, it's not language. There is no language." They record for six or seven takes, and her work is done within half an hour.

"There's something about that song," Tanvi later tells me. "I don't know what it is. I don't even understand half the lyrics, the Tamil. But you can't sit still."

.... H ....

Movement of sound, movement of a body that can't sit still—a good song is a transducer, turning energy of one kind into another. This is what happens in the recording studio, in ever so many ways, its boxes, wires, and devices leading waves of sound back and forth between physical vibration, electrical signal, digital code.[22]

"To think transductively," Stefan Helmreich writes, "is to pay attention to impedance and resistance in cyborg circuits, to the work that needs to be done so that signals can link machines and people together, at a range of scales, from the private to the public."[23] There is momentum, but also the constant threat of breakdown.

This is what happened in Dubai in December 2009, on the night of "Southern Dreamz." That concert took place just a few days after the Dubai World crisis, when it looked like the emirate might default on its real estate and construction debts. The venue remained empty long past the scheduled start of the show, most ticket-holders packed into a few of the cheapest galleries far from the stadium stage.

"Can I hear you, Dubai?" Yuvan, clad in a glossy hooded jumpsuit, kept calling out to the Indian migrants of modest means clustered in those galleries. Satisfying these masses had always been essential to the idea of the show; one of the songs was even planned as a salute to them, a line of men in hard hats and construction uniforms dancing in unison onstage as the singer exhorted everyone to stand tall in their struggles.

Sadly, though, they couldn't hear him very well at all. The sound was muffled and distorted at that distance, people there complained at the end of the show. And most of the songs were new and unknown to them, not the familiar hits they'd hoped to hear when they made the long journey by bus that night. The pleasure of the music was somehow lost in the cold wind whipping through the stadium that night.

⊢

When I return to Yuvan's studio just a little while after Tanvi's session, I have no idea what to expect. Would I spend the next three hours on this worn-out waiting room couch, staring at a portrait of Yuvan's father emblazoned with the slogan "Nothing but Music?" while the song itself is completed inside?

But suddenly, again, I'm in.

Yuvan, inside, is playing around with a tone that sounds like the Indian oboe played at Tamil weddings, confounding the soulful feeling of his own voice with zany and irreverent twists of sound. Kumar is cackling, loudly, over the music.

"The song is ripping," the drummer howls, and Yuvan points to me: "He was there from the start."

Soon enough, though, something is wrong. *Pip pip pi-ip* goes the o melody, but the bass notes are a tattered mess. The problem lies with of the massive black speakers in the booth, in the way that it's vibra no longer music but noise.

The house engineer chides them lightly for maxing out the sound levels—"Ripping song, ripping song, you keep saying, but you've gone and ripped through these!"—before calling in the studio technicians.

The drummer wants them to fix the speakers as quickly as possible, as his composer is in a creative mood. Yuvan, meanwhile, has his headphones on, the volume cranked so high that I can still hear almost everything he's doing. Kumar shares a story from his days with A. R. Rahman: "Even with his headphones, you could hear it going *basssu basssu*. You could feel it jarring you, that's how high the levels were for everyone."

I look over at Yuvan, still relaxing the tension of the whole of his body, turning himself into a tympanum, an eardrum, vibrating in sympathy with the body of that sound.

Then the composer lifts the headset off his ears, leans back in a slow stretch. The song is done, more or less anyway, subject to what the speakers in the BMW parked outside will say. I follow him back out into the lounge, where he's still tapping and thumping his hands onto the wall, the table, his jeans. "The hangover of that beat," Yuvan explains.

The song has come together in a little over twenty-four hours. I'm struck by how quickly it's taken shape. "You just have to be really loose in your head, willing to try anything," Yuvan tells me. The script, the characters, the film—he was thinking about none of these things. For a long time, he'd been wanting to mix together hip-hop and trance. "I was doing this song, and I got the hip-hop beat. Okay, let's do a trance backing for it."

"You never say 'I made it,'" I point out. "You always say 'I got it.' When you say you got it, where are you getting it from?"

"It just came to me, that's what the whole theory is about," Yuvan says. "I'm sort of a messenger. It just flows through me. Nobody can create something like this. It just comes, it's flowing through me. I'm just a mediator, in between."

What he says reminds me of what was just happening within that small recording booth: the activity of the studio itself, the speakers, the wires, the keyboards and samples, all those panels and instruments, modulating the frequency of vibrations throughout that room, relaxing and intensifying those streams of energy, all of which were passing through the composer in their midst, the man working to keep up somehow with the thumps of sound that he'd had a hand in making himself. A circuit of relays and modulations: Does the genesis of sound need nothing more than this?

"Do you ever wonder where these songs come from?" I ask again. Yuvan laughs, shaking his head. "No, that's something else entirely."

.... ⊢ ....

I was there from the start, the composer said, but I know this isn't true. The lyrics to "Like a Feather," for example, were already there when I stepped into the recording booth that first afternoon, printed on the sheet from which Yuvan was singing. And behind the lyrics themselves, I know, was a melody, a tune, something bereft of nearly all these sounds and words.

The lyricist, Yugabharathi, lives in a modest flat on the top floor of a Tamil Nadu Housing Board colony in Kodambakkam. His living room is dominated by a pair of looming bookcases, faced with glass and overstuffed with books and magazines of all kinds. "A writer's room!" I exclaim immediately when we meet, a few weeks after those days with Yuvan. We quickly slip into an intense dialogue about writing.

Poetry, Yugabharathi insists, is different from the writing of a lyric: "A poem appears on its own, but this is made for a tune." From the director, the lyricist learns of the characters and the mood of the situation they find themselves in. From the music director, the lyricist receives an outline of a melody. His task is to find words to suit both that melody and that situation.

He sings for me, quite beautifully, the tune of this song. *Thana naa naa nee-e-e, thana naa naa nee-e, thana naa naa nee-e-e, thaa nannannee.* Yuvan's manager had sent it over one day, recorded onto a CD in the composer's voice. Yugabharathi listened to the recording a few times that evening, singing it to himself before he went to sleep. Then, the next day, he composed the lyrics in a single sitting, just ten minutes of work.

I marvel at the suggestion that this could have happened so quickly. But the lyricist insists that all he does is follow a grammar of possible words and sounds. He talks about *yappu*, prosody, the many variations that present themselves with the same rhythm of expression, the same arrangement of accents, breaks, and copulas.

Thana naa naa nee-e-e, thana naa naa nee-e. The first line of the song could have gone in so many ways:

Iragai pole-e-e alaigire nee-e	Like a feather, I drift off
malai illaa mal-l -l	Even without rain, I'm getting
ninaigirenee-e	soaked
kanavil naanum-m-m	Even in my dreams, I'm all
kalaikirenee-e	messed up

kavithai pole-e-e alaigirenee-e	Like a poem, I drift off
manathai neeyum-m-m	My heart, too, so troubled by
kudaikirayee-e	you

"Like a shadow, like the heart, like a bond . . . You can keep saying all such things," the lyricist says. But the opening image is the most crucial, having to convey the essence of the song. To Yugabharathi, rain and dreams felt too conventional. He remembered a poem by Dharmu Sivaramu, something about a feather that wrote poems on the endless pages of the wind. He also knew that the character in the film was someone used to drifting aimlessly himself. And so he took up this image and pursued the route that opened up thereafter.

Yugabharathi shows me the small bedroom desk where he works: clock, phone, box of pencils, desktop computer. There's a stack of CDs, other tunes and songs, beside the desk. "We can't say," he muses, "how that word will appear, at that moment. There's no scientific explanation for this."

"It's like the happiness that comes when a stranger smiles at us, makes us smile, makes us smile at others," he adds. "Creation is like that."

Transmission, a contagious movement of sounds and smiles: *thana naa naa nee-e-e, thaa nannannee.* I want to hear the tune itself now, to track back, almost desperately, to this point of origin, the headwaters of this flow. But everywhere I turn, a recording of the original melody proves elusive.

Yugabharathi says he's misplaced the CD. Prabhu, the Studio Green producer, thinks it's on his laptop somewhere but will have to look. The director's office says they gave their copy back to Yuvan's people. The composer's guys say they can't share anything without his permission. And Yuvan himself is suddenly impossible to reach.

When I finally manage to catch the composer on the phone, after many weeks of trying, he says there's nothing to it. "It's just my voice and the chords, just the backing, that's all." I try wheedling and cajoling a copy or a listen in ever so many ways, until finally he admits something else and leaves it at that: "Actually, I can't give it to you."

I can't say what he means by this: whether it's a personal preference, a lack of physical access, or a matter of being disallowed somehow from sharing it himself. Nor will anyone involved in the composition of the tune — the director, the composer, one of his sound engineers — say much more than that it happened and that it went well.

The mystery abides. It begins to feel like something sacred, ineffable, this lost moment of genesis. The mystique of commerce is no doubt

Yuvanshankar Raja
@Raja_Yuvan

IRAGAI POLAY from NAAN MAHAN ALLA
is a KILLER song tripping on it for days!
Don rem when was da last tym I tripped on
my own song like this!

← Reply   ↻ Retweet   ★ Favorite   ••• More

12
RETWEETS

1
FAVORITE

9:45 PM - 28 Jun 10

work here, so essential to enlisting such music as a means of marketing film. But there is also the enigma of the creative process that is marked by the elusive tune, the sense of creation as a cascading flow of channels and displacements, echoes and reverberations.

"Music as we know it," writes David Shulman in a meditation on the experience of sound in Indian classical music, "is really a sort of sustained echo of something we cannot truly hear, something hushed and subtle, almost at the edge of silence."[24]

Perhaps the studio, in the end, is less a temple to sound than a monument to these powers that remain active and alive beyond the evidence of our senses.

.... ┣ ....

The song, meanwhile, is a hit. The *Nan Mahan Alla* soundtrack is released on the ThinkMusic label in July 2010, a few weeks before the film's debut. Reviews of the music single out "Iragai Pole" as the pick of the album. The song climbs quickly to the top of the Tamil FM radio charts, as the film itself draws avid crowds to the cinema halls of Tamil Nadu.

Yuvan joins Twitter around this time, quickly amassing hundreds of thousands of followers. One of his first tweets is about the song.

The tweet itself goes viral, suddenly reappearing everywhere, in press coverage about the film, about the music and the composer, even in Studio Green's own print ads for the film.[25]

"Iragai Pole is everyone's ringtone these days, ever since Yuvan tweeted about it," the actor Karthi says in one interview.[26] And indeed, for some time, this is how I keep hearing small fragments of the song, in Chennai,

Madurai, Badami, even back in Baltimore, when certain phone calls connect through the sound of that familiar melody, those first few words. The tune slips into the stream of countless other soundscapes.

Three old friends, trundling along a potholed road through the mountains when that song comes once again – "when I see you from afar, the rain spills lightly within my heart." Bose, videographer, points out where he'd shot some newlyweds on an outdoor jaunt, cueing his montage to the fall of beats like these, as if it was the song of their life yet to come, "saying just half of everything, feeling everything else inside." Malai, drifting off in the back, thinks of a girl he once knew, how he would ride, lovestruck, along a bumpy path through the paddy fields, imagining her with him, sharing his headphones, listening to the same song, "lost without losing my way, at the touch of your hands." And me, I'm drunk on it all, gaping at hills I haven't seen for years, places where I drifted and tottered, like a feather, like a child, wondering at the calling that drew me here, drew me away, drew me back again on the heels of this song, all of it knitted into the fabric of these sounds, gathered into the folds of these reverberations. "Come with me, and I'll have everything. Don't need a thing, just you, just you..."

Voice

I was born in the Bronx in the early 1970s. My father's parents waited eagerly for the home movies that would sometimes come to India from America, flickering images of my sister and me playing with stuffed animals and riding on wooden horses. My mother's parents had come to New York City for my birth. Mamamma spent days lying beside me, I've been told, in that small apartment on 233rd Street. "Will you be an American president or an Indian president? What will you be?" my grandmother asked again and again. "Unh," I said. Really, though, what could I say? What does it take to realize the life given voice by those who come before us?[1]

························· ⊢ ·························

The head of operations for the *Tamil Padam* film production team spies me sitting over a notebook at a café on Khader Nawaz Khan Road one afternoon in 2009. "You're Nirav's friend, aren't you?" Sushant asks, recalling my work with the film's cinematographer. They've wrapped up their shooting and are now in postproduction. "Can you do us a favor?"

I laugh at the idea of what he wants me to do, and insist that there must be others in Chennai far better suited for this task. "The director is looking for a black man," Sushant admits gravely. But he calls again, two days later, with the same request.

On Saturday morning, I arrive at Bharani Studios in Vadapalani, where the film's director, C. S. Amudhan, is already at work in one of the sound-dubbing studios. "You're going to dub for Obama today," Amudhan declares when I step into the dark and frosty space.

I sound nothing like the president, I profess, secretly tickled by the outlandishness of the idea. But the director assures this won't be a problem. "The audience won't have a frame of reference, they won't have heard Obama speak."

"Can you tweak it a bit?" I ask, skeptically, yet not without hope. "We can give it a bit of a baritone. Let's see how it sounds," he says.

·· ⊢ ··

The power of voice is a power of animation, bringing things and persons into unexpected life. We tend to think of this power as something deeply personal, bearing the essence of an individual. But voice always has about it an uncanny feeling of ventriloquism, the sense of being thrown from somewhere else. "The source of the voice can never be seen," Mladen Dolar writes. "The voice comes from inside the body, the belly, the stomach."[2]

Cinema only deepens this gulf between the sound of a voice and its source. As Michel Chion has shown, films are full of "acousmatic" elements issuing from somewhere outside the visual frame, things heard without being seen, "wandering along the surface, at once outside and inside, seeking a place to settle."[3] Unseen bodies, sudden eruptions, distant murmurs—so much of cinema's power depends on the movement of such sounds on and beyond the screen.[4]

Think of what happens in the opening minutes of C. S. Amudhan's 2010 film, *Tamil Padam* [Tamil movie].[5] Under a thatched roof and pouring rain, a young woman wails into the dark of night. A boy is born, but in a land infamous for its partisan love of sons, this one is strangely unwanted. "Here's fifty rupees," the father tells the midwife. "Finish off that little life."

A mournful flute implies that something awful will happen in these opening minutes of *Tamil Padam*. But the film is a spoof, the scene a parody of a wrenching Tamil movie about female infanticide from the 1990s.[6] There, a midwife reached for a bowl of milk-white sap from the deadly *kalli* cactus to poison a newborn girl with her first meal. Here, the midwife reaches instead for a shiny green Tetra Pak of P.R.S. Cactus Milk. "Pure! Hygienic!" the carton reads, slickly.

"Grandma, Grandma, wait a minute!" a young voice says as the old woman bends over the child with the carton's offerings. She looks up and around, unable to place its source. "Look here, Grandma, it's me, Mini-Superstar speaking!" the voice says again. She looks down with wide eyes, finally connecting the sound to the newborn infant on her lap.

"I'll go to Madras and truly become a great hero," chirps the voice, trying to convince her to spare his life.[7] The midwife is impressed with his verbal flair. "You're already speaking in punch lines!" she exclaims, vowing to save the child and take him to Madras herself.[8]

Years go by, and the child, Shiva, has indeed become a valiant, if somewhat diffident hero. One afternoon, his phone begins to buzz with pleas to undertake an undercover operation against some notorious Chennai gangsters. First the police commissioner. Then the chief minister of Tamil Nadu. Then the prime minister of India. Shiva rebuffs them all. Then the cell phone screen scrolls one more name: "Obama calling."

With a casual flicker of recognition, Shiva takes the call. The film lingers for a few seconds on the image of a dark silhouette standing before a flagpole, curtain, and American presidential seal.

"Okay, dude, I'll do it for you," Shiva tells Obama. "My regards to the family."

H

So there I am, sitting on a black leather couch in the Bharani Studios control room. At the console with the sound engineer, the director Amudhan asks to see Obama's lines. "We can enhance it," the director says, unimpressed with what they have so far.

"Shiva, please take up this assignment," he suggests, pencil in hand.

I have to object. "He wouldn't say assignment."

"Okay. Job, project, assignment, operation, something. Only you can kill Pan Parag Ravi and Swarnakka. Please do this for world peace."

"He won't say that," I blurt out again.

"Why?"

"*World peace* is very flat. No one actually says *world peace*. Beauty pageants talk about *world peace*. It's not a smart thing, to say that way."

"Or," the director proposes, "we'll say 'The people of America are counting on you.' There's no connection. It'll be funny."

I give in.

"When you say *Pan Parag Ravi*, you'll have to exaggerate your accent, you'll have to make it really Yankee Doodle," Amudhan tells me.

"Ravi."

"Roll your Rs more. R-r-avi."

I'm perplexed. "He wouldn't roll. We don't roll."

"That's okay. We'll exaggerate it. That's the funny bit. R-r-ravi . . . That's how people would think Americans talk."

After a few minutes, we agree on what to say. "Let's go for it," the director says.

"Just like that?" I ask nervously. "You don't want me to practice or anything?"

"I'm sure you'll get it the first time," he assures. "The second"—he snaps his fingers—"you see Obama on the screen, start talking. We'll give it a shot, let's see how it sounds."

I head through the heavy steel doors into the recording booth. "He speaks more pompously than Obama even," someone murmurs as I leave the room.

"See this," the director says to him, pointing out my audio recorder still lying on top of the recording console. "You shouldn't have said that just now."

——————————————————— H ———————————————————

How do you prepare to assume the voice of anyone else, let alone an American president? Say you're small, awkward, and clumsy, like me. Say you've always been teased about your supposedly foreign accents— Moroccan, French Canadian, Cambodian, South African, always winding up as though you were pretending to be an Indian.

I'd downloaded Obama's 2008 victory speech onto my iPod that morning. I'd listened again and again on the ride over to Bharani Studios, hoping that the driver couldn't hear me quietly try out a tenor, depth, and cadence of voice so unlike my own.

Through the double steel doors now into the recording booth, I stand behind a corner podium and mike, facing a large image of the faux-presidential silhouette. It doesn't help that the image looks nothing like Obama. It doesn't help that the actor playing Shiva also walks into the control room to lounge on the couch, just before the first take.

But when the recording begins, there is little time to fret, so little, in fact, that I miss my first cue. From then on, there's no chance to think of anything else but getting the lines right, modulating their speed to match the length of the shot.

"Perfect," the director said after just a couple takes, when the sound engineer plays the recording. I'm alarmed. "It sounds like me, not like Obama!" I can't help but blurt out. But all that matters for the film is that I sound American.

There are a few more adjustments. Obama throws in a Tamil-language plea to Mr. Shiva: *Americave ungala than nambirku*, All of America is counting on you. There are laughs and claps as I rehearse this line with an American twang. Someone suggests another line about Rambo and Schwarzenegger, but luckily, this last idea falls flat.

On my take once more, there is little left to do now but adjust the recording levels. When I step back into the control room, the director is already thinking ahead to dubbing voices for the next scene. Smiling, he offers to help me get a dubbing artiste union card. "You've got a career waiting for you here."

——————————————————— H ———————————————————

Sound in Indian cinema is rarely recorded on location at the same time that visual images are shot. Human voices are matched instead to speaking faces in the environment of the dubbing studio. There are nearly two thousand men and women registered with the dubbing artistes union in Chennai. Some are screen actors who join the union to assert the right to project their own voice onscreen. But most are specialists in oral performance, recruited by a "dubbing agent" to speak on behalf of bodies other than their own.

A few months later, on the grounds of another film studio complex close to Bharani Studios, I meet K. Vinayagamoorthy, dubbing agent for *Tamil Padam*. He reminds me that films are still known in Tamil as *pesum padam*, "talking pictures." Echoing modern Tamil theories of speech, Vinayagamoorthy insists that voice alone gives *uyir*—life—to film.[9]

We step into a modest canteen on the studio grounds to talk more about these ideas. For the dubbing agent, cinema demands two kinds of action: "acting in the light" and "acting in the dark," which his dubbing artistes perform. "This work is creative, sir," he insists. There is, for example, the challenge of "lip," that is, the visual movement of lips already recorded by the camera, for which the dubbing artiste must improvise a closely matching stream of words.

Back outside the canteen, we meet a couple of senior dubbing artistes who've dropped by the studio, looking for work. With them, my play for solidarity fails. One repeats my Tamil Obama line—*Americave ungala than nambirku*—back to me in a faux-American accent, making it known that I could dub this voice only because it accompanied a static presidential silhouette: there was no visible "lip."

The dubbing agent nevertheless enters my contact details onto his Nokia phone. He takes a photograph of my face, as if to fix a single person to the name and number the screen would call up. Nowhere else in India have I encountered this gesture, one that seems yet again to acknowledge the power of voice to conjure unexpected lives.

.... H ....

There was a young bespectacled woman at the mike when I walked into Bharani Studios that first morning. She was asked to scream as if she were the woman giving birth under a thatched roof in the opening scene of *Tamil Padam*.

The director found her too consistently pained on the first take. "A little buildup is needed," he'd said, "as though the sound is rising." I listened as the pitch of her voice kept peaking and quavering in visceral tension until the director was satisfied. "It's over, dear, thank you," he told her, and she was free to leave.

The dubbing artiste's name is Shaji. We meet one evening at her own small recording studio on a narrow lane west of Bharani Studios, the name of the enterprise painted in English block letters on the blue steel door: "Sound in Silence."

Shaji tells me that she was the niece of a screen actress, and that she'd grown up quietly acting out her aunt's roles as she watched her from a distance. We talk about the work she's been doing herself, dubbing continuously for films, television serials, cartoons, and other media in Chennai for the past several years.

"Our own lives will be forgotten," Shaji says. "When we see the screen, we become that. Until now, I am Shaji. Then I am Kavita. Then I am Sunitha."

Listening to her speak, I begin to see how voice can claim its own existence, its own life, independent of body and identity. "Even my own mother can't identify my voice," Shaji adds. "My voice will be telecast, and she won't know."

Her mother, it seems, would marvel at times, "Where did your voice go? It was nothing like your voice, girl. Don't lie. Was it you that spoke?"

H

The film, *Tamil Padam*, is a massive hit. I hear nine hundred bodies erupt in a roar of enthusiasm when a trailer for the film plays on a 70mm screen at Chennai's Sangam Theatre one afternoon in 2010.

Sixty-two seconds into the two-minute trailer, my lines resound through that cavernous hall: "Mr. Shiva, you gotta do this job. Only you can kill Pan Parag Ravi and Swarnakka. *Americave ungalai than nambirku*."

There I am, beaming in that dark space, but there is something unsettling in this pleasure, for I can't claim this voice as my own. It sounds like me. But so unlike the shouts and whistles erupting loudly here and there in that packed cinema hall, this voice echoes from everywhere at once. It does things I clearly couldn't do. And then suddenly it is gone.[10]

Something else happens in Los Angeles, when the film screens there a few months later. For my mother, everything always seems to come back to her children. Hearing my voice, she sees me in that presidential silhouette onscreen.

"That's my son!" she shouts into the space of the theater, as those around her shift uneasily in their seats.

Rhythm

The driver seems worried about the crowd in this industrial district north of Chennai. Boisterous ripples of sound
course through the young men massed in the lobby, piercing
whistles and cries of exultation. When the doors swing open,
it's impossible to do anything but surge with the tide into the
hall. A deafening clamor erupts when the star is seen on this
opening day of his latest film, streamers in the air and silhouettes of dancing fans thrown from the rows onto the screen.
The cheers and whistles crest and subside in waves throughout the film, lulled into regular spans of relative quiet, swelling
with the drums and horns whenever they come. The energy
endures even as the credits roll and these bodies spill again
into the lobby, mingling with those awaiting their turn, with
the surge yet to come. "To grasp a rhythm it is necessary to
have been grasped by it," Henri Lefebvre writes; "one must
let oneself go, give oneself over, abandon oneself to its duration."[1] Here and there throughout the city, there are film editors buried in the darkness of these cinema halls. Anonymous,
unremarkable, they study the movement of these crowds—
how long their cheers hold, when they lapse into sudden
silence—plotting a rhythm for the films yet to come.

⊢

"There's a problem here," Sreekar Prasad says as soon
as the director walks into the room. Gangly and bespectacled, the hair around his temples graying, Sreekar is
widely known as India's preeminent editor of film.

His studio is modest, taking up the top floor of a
small house in Saligramam. The front door is propped
wide open, allowing the humid air of the city to settle
over the old videocassettes strewn across the shelves,
warping their plastic covers. In the studio's one air-
conditioned room is an Avid Media Composer Adrena-
line system, before which Sreekar is sitting now with his
assistant Bavan.

In this room without a window, the editor looks into another world. On his screen a young man lies across a pair of railway tracks, wrists and ankles bound to the trestles with white cord. Although it's dark, you can see him panic in the light of a looming train, limbs jerking and shuddering violently against the cords. He continues to struggle as the train takes a sudden turn along a switch in the tracks, his face convulsing with a scream as it clatters past.

"His movement looks very feeble," Sreekar says to Sudha, the film's young director. And the train comes too suddenly, without any sense of an impending threat. This is just the opening sequence, but the editor feels that the film is already dragging.

There is nothing in the world without rhythm, Henri Lefebvre argues: nothing fixed or stable, only the pulse of movements lapping over each other like waves, exhalations of body and mind commingling with the drone of machines and the movements of society, the rustling of trees and the tremors of the cosmos.[2] To track these movements takes the work of a "rhythmanalyst," one who "calls on all his senses," who "draws on his breathing, the circulation of his blood, the beating of his heart," thinking with the cadences of his own body, catching hold of such rhythms in order to grasp the motion of an entire world.[3]

The French critic presents this sketch as a portrait of "someone who does not yet exist," as a description of a figure yet to come.[4] But perhaps he is wrong on just this point. Our rhythmanalyst is already here, on this narrow lane in Chennai, quietly editing a film.

The mood in the studio is calm and deliberate, nothing like what you see on the screen. The film cuts from railway tracks to cars and buses packed onto a crowded shoreline. Blades hack into iced slabs of fish. Bundles of cash pass hands. Cards get flicked onto the sand, blows rain down on a wailing boy, bananas are pounded into a beggar's mouth.

As he watches the footage, Sreekar rolls a spiked wooden acupressure ball in one hand, trying to keep his own mind relaxed. Then, as he slouches back into his chair to share what he's been thinking, you can see the tautness in his contemplation give way. There is a break, and the editor gets up to make green tea.

In the life of cinema, a rhythm of tense release.

⊢

Called *Drohi* [Traitor], the 2010 film begins with Samy tied onto railway tracks somewhere in Chennai, left there by his closest childhood friend, Karuna.[5]

"God hasn't just told me that I will die, he's even sent a timetable,"

Samy says as he's lying there. "By three this morning, twenty-one trains will go this way, one of them right over me. Can't trust anything in life, not a man, not even a train. A lesson life has taught me, a lesson that my area has taught me."

This soured friendship is the heart of the film. Samy and Karuna are from Royapuram, an area of north Chennai that the film presents as a violent and gritty slum. Every attempt to maintain some rhythm of daily life here is confounded by an act of betrayal. Karuna, pouring out *dosais* at a roadside stall, rushes madly through the streets one afternoon, suddenly panicking that Samy may have just attacked his girlfriend. Relationships in the film have a fleeting life, constantly upended by such gestures of masculine aggression and retaliation.

Drohi is directed by Sudha K. Prasad, one among a small handful of women directors in contemporary Tamil cinema. After assisting the legendary director Mani Ratnam for many years, Sudha had made a daring and improbable choice for her debut: a gory and brutal action film.

With the many films that Sreekar Prasad had edited for Mani Ratnam, turning to him was as natural as going from tenth to eleventh grade in the same school, Sudha told me. "I can trust this man," she said, joking about her editor as a "security blanket" for her first venture.

Sreekar, meanwhile, had invited me many months back to watch him edit a film. The idea was generous and exciting but difficult to work out in practice. He was working most days on Mani Ratnam's *Ravanan* somewhere within the inaccessible depths of Ratnam's Madras Talkies production house. *Drohi* would be edited at Sreekar's own studio, but it was difficult to say when the project would begin.

After weeks of delays, Sreekar sent me a long SMS one morning:

> I suddenly feel this film may not be good for the purpose ur looking, as it is going to happen in a very haphazard way due to me and the production dates which keep changing. The edit is going to happen in bits and pieces and in few hours at a time. Unfortunately I do not have a project which is continuously happening. I think should you try some other editor.

Flustered by the sight of this message, I managed to reach the editor on the phone and assured him that I would wait for whatever happened when it did.

In the life of cinema, a rhythm of fraught belief. Collaborative processes such as editing seemed to unfold here through a constant stream of confounded expectations. "You won't even know what will be happening," Sreekar once lamented. Friends would decide to make films together, then suddenly find themselves at loggerheads. Their films would stall, gaps and fissures open up, calling for the slow and patient suture of an editor's work.

························· H ·························

Two young boys catch their breaths on a corrugated tin roof, marveling at the wedding prank they've just pulled off. Karuna beams triumphantly at Samy. "That's why I've got you, Iyer!" he exclaims, grabbing his face and planting a kiss on his forehead. The drums are already beating as the two of them laugh, a child's voice chanting gleefully in time with its pulse.

Think of rhythm in cinema, and you might think of such sounds, a tide of beats and reverberations sweeping you along from mood to mood, moment to moment. It's difficult to talk about rhythm without calling up music and sound. "A movie is expected to peak as it goes," Sreekar says. "We'll make sure that the rhythm is such that it reaches a crescendo. I can't start a scene on a very high note and end it on a lower note."

There are ever so many ways that such cadences are worked into films. Take this small snippet, in *Drohi*, of a child's joyful chant: a tinny voice says the same thing, again and again—*nan nan nan nan nan nan nan naa na na naa naa naa*—but as the syllable returns, over and over again, the voice picks up in both tone and speed, spiraling upward with a hopeful lilt. The chant returns at later moments in the film, a refrain that reminds you each time of the promise that was lost with the destruction of Samy and Karuna's childhood friendship.

In the life of cinema, a rhythm of highs and lows. As a spectator, you have these rhythms to lead you from one scene into another. The film's editor, though, works without their guidance and counsel. In his hands, the film is mostly silent, a jagged pastiche of images in a rough and preliminary order. Nor is he one to edit to the beat of music, as many others do.[6] What, then, does he hear or feel within this silence?

"I have to build it up in a certain way," Sreekar says, "so that when you actually come to the point when you want to say something, it's felt."

On the corrugated rooftop, he pares down the laughter, slows the pace of Karuna's approach to Samy's forehead for a kiss. This moment, he explains to Sudha, is the "high point" of the scene. The editor is sculpting a peak, one in a chain of peaks and valleys, successive moments of anticipation and fulfillment.

························· H ·························

Over the past twenty-five years, Sreekar Prasad has edited many more than three hundred films in most Indian languages, although he has long since lost count of exactly how many. "Pace and rhythm," he notes on his website, digesting some of this experience: "Any work of editing devoid of these two qualities will inevitably damage the comfortable flow of a film."[7]

Sreekar seems to think of his editing almost like a kind of therapy, grappling with the accelerated rhythms of modern life, with the "neurasthenia" or nervous disorders long attributed by social critics to the nature of metropolitan existence.[8] The editor often laments the frenetic pace of contemporary MTV-style cutting, especially when such relentless images are projected onto a canvas as large as a cinema screen.

"Your brain is trying to get so much information, it becomes tired," he says. "You need a breather. . . . It can never be like this, this, this, this, this."

Is this what he means by rhythm too, a movement of alternation between this and that, this and that, one thing and then another? "Rhythm is something about the flow, you know. . . . So it also depends on the story line, but there is a certain, what do you call . . . You have to balance, between the performances, and the visual. . . . So you are always trying to create an atmosphere, of . . . I should take an example, then only will you understand."

It isn't easy to grasp at once what rhythm means for Sreekar. As an editor, he is rarely involved in the slick public narration and representation of his films. What he does within his small studio often remains unspoken. He struggles for words to make sense of his practice, offering sentences that trail off, break up midway, circle back once more to where they began. Every attempt to define rhythm seems to go somewhere else. And yet, through this broken language, suffused with cuts, something definitive begins to take shape.

"Rhythm is not meter or cadence," write Deleuze and Guattari. "There is nothing less rhythmic than a military march."[9] To be sure, rhythm depends upon the repetition of some element. What makes it rhythm, however, is not the reiteration itself, but the difference that is constantly produced with each of these iterations: the time of the unexpected, that is to say, within which such repetition unfolds.[10]

"No rhythm without repetition in time and space, without reprises, without returns, in short without measure," Lefebvre writes. "But," he too affirms, "there is no identical absolute repetition. . . . There is always something new and unforeseen that introduces itself into the repetitive: difference."[11]

Let me also restate—well, not quite the same, but close enough that you might begin to feel what I mean to say: *In the life of cinema, a rhythm to loop, repeat.*

Tatt tatatt tatattatt, tatatt tatatt tatatt.

"I should take an example, then only will you understand." The example upon which the editor's words alight is that of a conversation, the idea of a conversation like ours, back and forth between us, on film: "If I and you are speaking, there's a timing at which I am speaking, and you are answering. That timing is also paramount in the way that it's cut."

Actually, this is what he says, but it isn't all that is said:

He: There's a timing at which, if *x* person and *y* person, if I and you are speaking—
Me: Yeah.
He: —there's a timing at which I am speaking and you are answering.
Me: Yeah.
He: That timing is also paramount—
Me: Yeah.
He: —in the way that it's cut.
Me: Okay.
He: Although they're two different shots joined together—
Me: Yeah.
He: —it will feel very real. You will always feel that two characters are speaking. You won't feel that two cuts are being joined together to make two characters—
Me: Hah.
He: That timing. But if that timing isn't right, even if it's a second more or a second less—
Me: Yeah.
He: —suddenly, you will feel the disjoint. That's what the editor is supposed to control.

He, me, he, me, he, me, he, me. Can you see what the editor is doing, leading me to do unconsciously with him, without either of us realizing it? As we speak, his hands darting back and forth across the space between us, Sreekar steps me through a rhythm of ordinary life, reminds me of a rhythm that is already there, often disregarded, passed over too easily.[12]

"If the rhythm is wrong, if you have an unnatural pause, or if you have a late reaction, you'll immediately feel a disjoint with what is happening," he says. "If the rhythm is close to the actual rhythm of people, there's no way you're going to see it as a cut."

In the life of cinema, a rhythm of leap and cut. Experience is discontinuous, although these gaps are rarely perceived. Cuts, breaks, and joints compose the rhythm of ordinary life, like the edges of celluloid film that Sreekar used to bind together with cellophane tape in the years that he apprenticed with his father, Akkineni Sanjivi, a renowned editor himself.[13] These interruptions, ubiquitous yet invisible, are the foundation of Sreekar's practice.

"You shouldn't see the seams. The audience shouldn't be able to see the cut."

When Sreekar speaks of invisible cuts, he speaks with certain conventions of film editing in mind, conventions that have persisted, in modified forms, for over a century. Conceiving our own conversation as a fragment of film, the editor invokes a shot–reverse shot system of filmmaking — back and forth, seamlessly and continuously, between the image of one partner in a dialogue then the another — already prevalent in Hollywood cinema by 1915.[14] These techniques have seeped deeply into the grammar of Indian cinema, so much so that every film already anticipates such cuts and shifts by the time it first appears in an editor's studio.

"Cut, cut, cut — this is how we're going," Sudha had reminded one of her assistant directors, for example, at the CSI Middle School in Triplicane one Saturday morning when I had the chance to watch her shoot. With a small budget to work with and the mistakes of timing and judgment that often come with a first film, the director had been shooting under intense pressure. Rather than risk more errors with long and complex shots, she established each scene with one wide shot and a series of close-ups of individual characters.

"Okay for me," she called out again and again after just one take, asking the unit to move on to the next shot. *Takku takku takku*, I heard Sudha say, evoking the clipped rhythm of a Tamil euphemism for speed. "This is how we've got to finish."

They were shooting an essential scene that day, a pivotal event in the childhood flashback that propels *Drohi*'s tortuous course. Samy and Karuna's classroom is the scene of a savage murder that will drive these friends apart: their teacher is killed by a hoodlum before their eyes, leading the two boys to plot and carry out his murder in return. Later, a terrified Samy will betray his friend to the police, confessing Karuna's role in their act of vengeance.

At 4:30 that afternoon, Sudha passed her microphone to the stunt master, Dilip. "Next is the killing," the executive producer Jaya Kalyana warned me with a grimace on her face. The shots that followed were indeed brutal. "I hope I don't get hurt," the actress Pooja confessed with a slight laugh, describing the bruises she'd suffered on her previous film.

The crew, though, hardly seemed to linger on such worries. Time was the most pressing problem. Could they complete as many shots as needed before the clock ticked forward into a second, and more expensive, evening shift?

"Just five more minutes," Sudha tried to insist, as Dilip prepared yet another shot with a bloodied spade.

"How will you cut, then?" he retorted, walking off in frustration for a few minutes.

In the life of cinema, a rhythm of broken beats. Pooja's battered face, the blur of the spade in her dazed eyes, the shock of the children at the attack—the shots continued from still more angles.

.... ⊢ ....

Sreekar Prasad is watching now what happened that day in Triplicane, through the rough cut that Bavan has made of the footage. The editor doesn't look like he's doing very much—mostly scrolling back and forth through the scene, again and again.

After some time, he objects to the timing of Pooja's reaction to the decisive blow of the spade, the one that will kill her. It seems to come too late, but there's only a single take of the reaction available. Sreekar decides to reverse two shots: first you see her spinning head, then the spade that caused it.

"It's quite intense in your mind," he later says about such moments, "the mathematical calculation of so many things that are happening." Shot by shot, take after take, watching with angles, orders, performances, plotlines in mind, the available possibilities are nearly endless: "I can go from A to C, C to D, E to F, whichever angle I want." Borrowing a phrase from mathematics, the editor calls them "permutations and combinations."

These possibilities have always been there, but they are more accessible now with digital editing platforms such as the Avid on which Sreekar works. He first learned to cut physical reels of film on a Moviola machine in the early 1980s. Producers at the time often gave their editors no more than one print of each reel to work with. Cellophane tape and smudges of dirt would accumulate on the film as they worked.

"The cuts would stare at you," Sreekar says.

Now, however, on a digital editing platform, he finds that he can work more easily through a series of variations, sustained by a certain rhythm of thought: "Try *x*, try *y* also, try *z* also." Everything seems intensely, even impossibly open, as he quietly contemplates all that can be done and to what effect.

Then, suddenly, there is a halt to this current of thought, as he is caught by the sense of just one way to proceed: "When I crack it, when the formula is cracked, it's quite impossible to find another way to do it. I think the mind is like that."

In the life of cinema, a rhythm to feel and think. Editing is an intensely cerebral process, an effort to think along with the shifting course of an incipient film. "Every shot is a thought or a series of thoughts, expressed visually," Walter Murch has suggested. "When a thought begins to run out of steam, that's the point at which you cut."[15]

Spend some time with Murch, Prasad, or some other editor, and you might learn something about such movements of thought, as well as their limits. Halts come for various reasons. There are moments of realization. There are confounding encounters with the illogical. There is the inevitability of exhaustion, at which point it's time to break for tea.

.... ⊢ ....

Tube lights off, later that week, we're watching the first half together. The director, bursting into laughter every now and then, seems to be enjoying her film. The editor is quiet, steeped in thought, sitting back at a distance from the small screen. The enigmatic gestures that he makes with his hands seem like vestigial traces of long-gone machines: one hand wipes from left to right, another cups fingers and turns in an arc, as if rolling onward a knob or a reel.

Here are the images flickering on the screen. The flashback of Samy and Karuna's childhood continues until they murder the hoodlum who killed their teacher. Then you see Samy as a full-grown young man, on the railway tracks once again, thinking about something else: the many ways he has tortured Karuna ever since.

His erstwhile friend is in Delhi, interviewing for the Indian Police Service (IPS). Samy taunts him on the telephone, pretending that Karuna's sister is undressing before his eyes. Perhaps you wonder why Samy is being such a jerk. A second flashback to their childhood offers an explanation: Samy was chased down and raped by Karuna's friends after his betrayal at the police station, and the boy has been bent on revenge ever since.

An hour passes, and the lights in the studio come back on.

"It's working?" Sudha asks hopefully.

"This sort of thing will work," Sreekar says, gesturing toward the episode of the police interview. "Whenever they clash, it'll work."

But then the editor tries to find words for something else he experienced during this portion of the film: "Somewhere I felt, it felt, you want to get on with the story, one feeling was coming . . ."

They talk, working to make sense of this feeling of unease. The problem is the structure of the flashbacks, which leave Samy's rage unexplained and confusing for far too long. "You're making the audience wait, and you're making the audience think," Sreekar says. "I don't know whether this is a good idea for this sort of film, to sit and think why. . . . It's an entertainer, and an action flick. If I know this guy has *become* bad, I'll enjoy it better. I'll stick with him."

In the life of cinema, a rhythm to tempt and jolt. Sreekar suggests they move the rape of the boy to the initial flashback. Sudha argues, then relents. Her audience begins with her editor. She takes note of his smiles and grimaces.

H

The director knows that certain people will find this film crass and distasteful. "At the end of the day, they're going to ask, 'Did a woman director make this?' They're all going to hate me, women directors."

Still, as she and her editor agree, the film is not intended for people like themselves. "That world of down-market, underprivileged, that sort of world": this is what the film concerns, Sreekar says, and it is there that the film is meant to appeal.

The editor calls them "frontbenchers," those who are most likely to watch and enjoy *Drohi*: the young men of "low class" who crowd the cheapest seats at the front of cinema halls, making a spectacle of their own pleasure and displeasure for everyone seated behind them.

The director has another way of picturing them, calling up the familiar Indian classification of film theaters and audiences into three social grades of sensibility and refinement: metropolitan "A" theaters for well-to-do people, "C" theaters for poor and rural audiences, and "B" theaters for those in between. Regarding *Drohi*, Sudha simply says this: "It's a C center movie."[16]

Karuna, who flips dosais on a street corner stall while he waits for the results of his police interview, clearly belongs to that other world. The officer who interviews him in Delhi reminds him of just this: "Karuna, IPS . . . It's a disgrace just to hear this said, isn't it? Your father, just like you, began killing people at the age of ten."

How does the officer know this? Will the audience recognize the coincidence in his face, that the very man interviewing Karuna now in Delhi was the one who first arrested him as a child for murdering that Royapuram thug?

Editor and director debate the question. "I don't remember that I've

seen him before," Sreekar says, speaking with his frontbenchers in mind. Ultimately they decide to flash three images as reminders of the connection. "At least no confusions then for the B and C audience, which is my audience," Sudha declares.

This singsong phrase—B and C, B and C—often resurfaces as Sudha and Sreekar work together on *Drohi*: whenever they wonder whether something needs more explanation, whenever they speculate that something else can be left unexplained.

"No one will believe it," one of them says.

"B and C people will believe it," the other retorts.

In the life of cinema, a rhythm of fact and guess. The phrase, B and C, keeps resurfacing as a supposition and reminder, lending flesh to their conception of the film. Even so, a nagging question remains, returning now and then with redoubled force: Is this an accurate conception of that down-market world?

··· ⊢ ···

Here's another quarrel, one pioneer of montage arguing with another. In an essay first published in 1944, Sergei Eisenstein objects to the early American cinema of D. W. Griffith. "The structure that is reflected in the concept of Griffith montage is the structure of bourgeois society," Eisenstein argues: Griffith's films are populated by both rich and poor, but there is no tension between them, for they are taken for granted as parallel and eternally dissimilar lines."[17]

Such cinema has tempo, speed, Eisenstein concedes, but no rhythm: "True rhythm presupposes above all organic *unity*. Neither a successive mechanical alternation of cross-cuts, nor an interweaving of antagonistic themes, but above all a unity, which in the play of inner contradictions, through a shift of the play in the direction of tracing its organic pulse— that is what lies at the base of rhythm."[18]

As this language of organic pulse implies, Eisenstein has in mind a unity of life, a "dynamic concept of things" as constantly changing and evolving through a ceaseless play of conflict and contradiction. For the Soviet filmmaker, the mission of cinema is to aid in the perception of such tensions, and to stir them up further, by confronting spectators with "the collision of independent shots."[19]

Sreekar is also thinking with cinema, always thinking, as he edits, about what some film does or fails to do. But he doesn't style himself as a social critic; there is no pretense that a film like *Drohi* may propel its subjects to some critical or revolutionary understanding of themselves. Instead the film is pulled together with the organic movement of a certain world in mind, the "pulse" of a particular audience.

"It's for the masses, specifically for them," Sreekar says. He edits like a social psychologist, relying on his sense of their expectations, their habits of perception, and how much tension this "section" can tolerate without a break.

Here he is, watching Karuna approach Samy on a motorbike, over an hour into *Drohi*. Karuna, wearing a brand-new police uniform, is unfazed by Samy's usual gibes. He brandishes his IPS appointment letter, nearly pinning it to Samy's nose. "You've been thinking that you've won for seventeen years now, but I was the one winning all this time," gloats Karuna. As he slowly wheels around his bike to leave, Sreekar says one word to Sudha: "Interval."

"So many days, he's getting beaten, beaten, beaten, and then, one day, he hits back," the editor explains. He is working with a rhythm of expectation that traverses the line between the film and the social world it seeks to express. "I'm trying to see how I can control the characters to create the effect," Sreekar says. "Sort of like a remote control."

With points shaped like sickles, letters spelling "interval" materialize on the screen, as a smile slowly spreads across Karuna's face. *In the life of cinema, a rhythm to seize and grasp.*

Sort of like a remote control. Rhythm can be terrifying, especially with the powers built into the machines controlled by such devices, their capacity for manipulation from some unknown location, at a distance from the experience they yield.

Think of Freud's famous reflections on the trauma of the First World War: the widespread compulsions to repeat in dreams, again and again, the terror of new forms of mechanical injury and concussion, the bombs and shells raining down as instruments of remote and unseen assailants.[20] "Railway disasters" also did something like this, Freud observed.

Remember what Samy undergoes in *Drohi*, blindfolded, alone, bound to the tracks of a railway line as he waits for the one train that will careen across his body. Train after train veers just past his head as he recalls the rush of events that compose the film; the story itself unfolds in this state of captivity, a trail of recollections bound to the timetable of these locomotives.

Then, all at once, almost at the end of the film, the trains pass once more in a pulsing, minute-long montage: trains as streams of light and sound, crisscrossing the screen on diagonal routes, lapping over each other, overwhelming the screams of the body in their midst, flashing up with brief and shadowy images of the tortured past that landed Samy here.

What does our editor, our rhythmanalyst, want with this experience? Certainly not to free you from the throbbing tension of its movement. The sequence, this montage, was actually his idea—he put Samy there, and now he wants to put you there as well, to hold your attention on those trains, on the terror of their repetition, on the life that lingers between them.

In the life of cinema, a rhythm no death will break.

CHAPTER 16 Speed

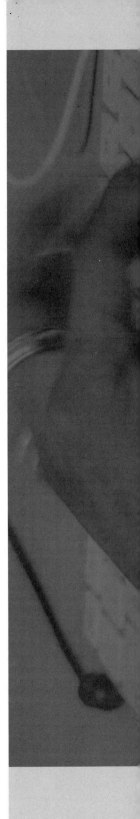

You know by now how these chapters have opened, each recounting some germinal episode of fieldwork, something that happened in the form of a problem or question. I don't mean to imply that such events cease once you leave "the field," wherever that is. It so happens, for example, that what follows was written in Los Angeles, a city that, to Jean Baudrillard, looked as though "it was invented with the screen in mind," a lived space that "seems to have stepped right out of the movies."[1] I wrote mostly in a café overlooking Ventura Boulevard, the steely glint of automobiles flashing from plate glass windows. "Speed is not a vegetal thing," Baudrillard said. "It is nearer to the mineral, to refraction through a crystal, and it is already the site of a catastrophe, of a squandering of time."[2] Each of those cars was a hurtling cocoon, a cosmos careening past those big sheets of glass. I must have been wired on their arrhythmia, for all of a sudden, there it was, a chapter in acceleration.

CUT

The director is a young guy in a checkered shirt. It's his first film, a comedy. I tell him why I'm tagging along with the editor. He smiles. "Will you have a chapter on notoriety?"

CUT

A white BMW 320d pulls into the driveway. Anthony warns me that he's unpredictable. "I may be working on one film, suddenly I may get bored and start working on something else, suddenly I might go hang out with my friends. You shouldn't feel that I've suddenly disappeared for three hours."

CUT

The Anthony cut. People talk about it. "This looks like an Anthony cut. Can you try an Anthony cut? Make that Anthony cut here." Anthony says he hates all this. "There's the hero, walking upside down. Then he's walking straight. Then he's walking upside down again. Why the fuck do you call this an Anthony cut?"

CUT

Here's the cut that Anthony's always talking about, in Guy Ritchie's *Snatch*. Two dons on the phone, one in America, one in London. One guy says, "Fuck you, asshole, I'm coming to London." Then, just four tiny shots. Chak! There's a shot of a taxi door opening. Tung! There's a flight shot. Vroom! There's another taxi. Tung! He's standing across from that guy. Zap, zap, zap, over.

CUT

Where to go now?

CUT

As a film passes through an editor's hands, possibilities for movement are nearly infinite. Take this one small juncture here. Should I tell you about Anthony's fondness for fast cuts? The explosive quality of his expressions? The trajectory of his practice? No matter what, we're bound to go somewhere else. "It's a way of storytelling," Anthony says. "You slightly confuse the audience, then bring them back on track."

CUT

There's the sleek Anthony of dark glasses and curling smoke, then there's the somewhat slovenly character shuffling around the office in baggy shorts and a rumpled T-shirt. He worked in advertising for a decade, learning how to use the Avid digital editing system without bothering to read the manual. "If I press this button, what happens to the visuals?" Now many of the biggest Tamil films pass through his studio.

CUT

(handwritten: read aloud)

More than anything else, Anthony is known here for speeding up films. Frequent cuts, ramped-up frame rates, scenes pared down to the barest necessity. "Nowadays, people are so hectic with their busy lives and their running about," the editor says. He steps into a cinema hall with two boxes of popcorn and this is what he sees: "These guys are changing. They don't want elaborate scenes. They want it just fast, and finished."

CUT

I don't quite believe him, but I know what he means. In the 1980s, in Los Angeles, we came of age with MTV. Who didn't know that line from *Top Gun*? "I feel the need . . . the need for speed." Arcade games like Pole Position gave a visceral sense of momentum. Roller coasters got faster each year. The stack of *Motor Trend* magazines climbed higher and higher from one of my closet shelves. "Speed," Enda Duffy writes, "has been the most empowering and excruciating new experience for people everywhere in twentieth-century modernity."[3]

CUT

Speed is a sensation, not sheer velocity as such but the impression of shifting from one velocity into another. Take this globe, deceptively immobile, whipping us through the cosmos at sixty-five thousand miles an hour. Who can tell that this is happening?

CUT

"A speed may be very slow, or even immobile, yet it is still speed," write Deleuze and Guattari.[4] Think of the last film you saw. Think of how quickly or slowly it might have taken you somewhere, without your going anywhere. How does this happen?

CUT

Three months pass before I see Anthony again. The BMW is gone. He was worried about getting it scratched, so he never drove it, he tells me. A rat bit through the diesel line. Another lay dead inside. He kept taking out the motorbike instead.

CUT

Anthony used to have a company called Cutting and Pasting. Now, with the director A. L. Vijay, he runs an editing studio in south Chennai called Frame Works. They've boarded up all the windows with sheets of plywood. They work at all hours. At least one of the assistants always seems to be asleep in the room downstairs.

CUT

Anthony is working on *Vinnaithandi Varuvaya* [Crossing the sky, will you come back?] with Vamsi, an assistant director. On the monitor, an earnest suitor. "I'd like to marry you," he says to someone. Anthony nixes the line. "It's understood. Just one look, then another look, then music playing, that's all. I'll be great." He cues the scene again with his fingers—snap!—to signal how the cut moves things along. Vamsi isn't sure. He calls his director on the phone. Anthony steps out for a smoke.

CUT

Someone else is in love with the same girl. He's traveling by jeep to see her. The editor ramps up the speed, wants to know what's next. "Come on," he growls. "I'm finally in the mood, now. Come on!" But there's nowhere else to go. They haven't even shot the next scene. Another cigarette. "You keep asking me to edit, then you keep telling me you haven't finished the shoot."

CUT

Because I'm THE REAL DEAL, able to edit this much after CROSSING THE SKY from RENIGUNTA and coming as far as MADRASAPATTINAM, I must be a ROBOT, or maybe just an ordinary GUY. . . . . Laugh out loud. (Those are film titles in capital letters.)

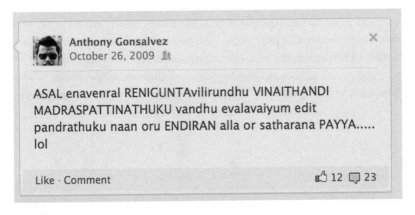

Anthony Gonsalvez
October 26, 2009

ASAL enavenral RENIGUNTAvilirundhu VINAITHANDI MADRASPATTINATHUKU vandhu evalavaiyum edit pandrathuku naan oru ENDIRAN alla or satharana PAYYA.....
lol

Like · Comment   👍 12 💬 23

CUT

Anthony and his crew are working on eight films at once. "Takatakataka-taka," the editor sputters to Vamsi. "I'll cut yours as I keep going between the other films."

CUT

Everything about Anthony seems to be as nonlinear as these digital systems. There are Steenbeck machines still gathering dust in the corners of many Indian editing studios, teeming with rollers for physical reels of film. Here the digital consoles let you pick out frames, shots, scenes, and sounds at will. The convenience of this technology is obvious, but there were advantages to the earlier machines. Steenbecks, Walter Murch says, gave editors a much better feel for their material by forcing them to scroll sequentially through each roll of shot film: "The real issue with speed is not just *how fast you can go*, but *where are you going so fast*?"[5]

CUT

Where did Anthony go?

CUT

Veera's across the hall, working on *Madrasapattinam*. When she started with Anthony four years back, she had no experience with editing. "Knowing the machine is not such a big deal," she says. Software, keyboard, the buttons to mark "in" and "out" points on the material, all of this is quickly learned, but judgments of pace take time to develop. "You should know how long to hold a shot, that's what's important."

CUT

Anthony's finally back at four; he's been working on an ad. There's another the next night, a ninety-second fable for Bhima Jewellers. The protagonist is a tomboy with a motorbike. "Faster is better," Anthony says. "More boyish." Then again, she also needs time to remember what it was like to be a young girl. "Every girl needs gold," a mellifluous voice croons in Malayalam. The editor cackles: "She's got so much fucking jewelry on her!"

CUT

Too fast, too slow, speed verges easily into a problem. "In extreme cases, if the stream of thought is too fast, it may lose itself, break into a torrent of superficial distractions and tangents, dissolve into a brilliant incoherence, a phantasmagoric, almost dreamlike delirium," writes Oliver Sacks on the breakneck momentum of Tourette's syndrome.[6]

CUT

What the editor does is modulate. "Just at the moment when this guy is like, 'Oh fuck, what is this now,' when he's just slightly getting restless, not consciously, subconsciously, when he is just about to get restless, that's when you have to cut it and go ahead," Anthony says. "Just ten frames extra can make it the wrong reaction."

CUT

The director Lingusamy and Anthony are watching rushes for *Paiyya*. There's an iPod wired into the speakers. The knob is turned so far up that the leather couch is thrumming with bass. All my exes live in Texas. There's a bad moon on the rise. If you like it then you shoulda put a ring on it. The editor taps, snaps, bounces in his chair, sings to the screen in a falsetto. "Put the AC on, it's too hot in here!" he yells out to someone. The tempo of his cutting can't possibly keep up with these beats.

CUT

Lingusamy keeps reaching for the AC's remote control, shutting it off. "What, boss, isn't it too cold in here?" he asks with an uneasy smile.

CUT

The studio walls are flimsy, white sheets of painted plywood. At every lull in the music, shouts spill over from the next room. "Are they editing a fight, or are they fighting?" Anthony wonders crossly. The stunt masters for *Asal* are in there, big guys with long, oily curls on their heads and thick gold chains draped against their chests. They look like the gangsters flailing on the screen in here, necks cracking in a Bombay marketplace.

CUT

Fight scenes in Tamil cinema alternate between exaggerated speed and slow-motion torpor. The editors call it "buildup," that sense of anticipation: "Come on, come on, just go and hit him, go and hit him." How much buildup does this market brawl need? "Dap dap dap dap dap, four guys standing there, zup zup zup zup zup, the fight, takatakatakataka takatakatakataka tktktktktktktktk zoom!" Anthony says. "Fight over."

CUT

"Mmm, let's see," the director murmurs. He goes back to the reviews of *Avatar* in today's papers.

CUT

Anthony is smoking, also fuming, on the couch outside. "If they allow me to edit, which they won't . . . You hit my guy, no? Touch me, you fucker. Touch me, let's see. And he pushes him thrice. And finally this guy gets irritated, fuck. Bang! He gives it to him. As soon as he does that, I can just jump-cut to five, six banging shots. Tap! Pup! Tup! Kutap! Tupak! Kutap! Kirup! And the last shot, one guy falls down. That's it, the flashback is over in twenty seconds."

CUT

I can't help but laugh. "Look at it that way, and your film will last just five minutes."

CUT

His whimsy, though, is infectious. After lunch I set off for *Renigunta*, another film of his, now in the theaters. "You won't like it. With two or three scenes, you'll just want to jump out," Anthony warns. It does lag sometimes. Guys get up from their seats, almost like clockwork, as the music wells up for a song about young love. I feel for the editor. A review in *The Hindu* lauded its "racy" drive without mentioning him once by name.

CUT

Morning again. The *Paiyya* fight has settled down to just three minutes. Lingusamy is pleased. "It's flown," the director pronounces, simply.

CUT

Shhhhhup! Vroom! A flock of pigeons scatter from the pavement of Victoria Terminus. This is how Anthony wants *Paiyya* now to establish Bombay. Puuaahhh! Flapping wings, ta ta ta ta ta.

CUT, CUT, CUT!

Anthony feels all this, yes, but he's also thinking. Here's what's on his mind, as he watches these rushes with Lingusamy: "Just look at how these pigeons go. I should've been born as a pigeon. No taxes to pay, doing as many girls as you want. . . . Look at me, watching these pigeons, thinking about taxes."

CUT

Shouting about a tax bill, quietly wondering whether he should call the auditor. Laughing his guts out, imagining catcalls that skewer his sense of humor. The editor is always split between many voices, many reactions. "I feel it that way. And at the same time, I ask myself, 'You're feeling it that way, do you think the audience will also feel it?'"

CUT

Now I'm the effusive one, tripping over a rush of words: "It's amazing, you're balancing reason and passion, feeling and understanding. You're both subjective and objective, inside and outside, you have to judge, you have to discriminate, you have to think about the logic, at the same time, you have to be able to go with it, with the feeling, you have to let yourself go."

CUT

"Correct. It just happens. Consciously or unconsciously, I don't know, but it just happens."

UNDERSTOOD

"It's understood." Whenever Anthony says this, which he does so often, whenever Anthony, saying this, ramps up the course of a film, what he has in mind, what he has a sense for, what he's working with is the speed of a course of thought, a thought inextricable from feeling, the flow of a sensation through the mind and body of an audience nowhere and everywhere at once.[7] Where is it understood, and by whom? We don't know, he never says.

CUT

"People won't understand," they kept telling him with *Renigunta*, overruling his cuts. He was livid. "Unless you fucking show them, how will you know whether they understand or not?" Sometimes he watches films in small-town theaters far from Madras. Even there, he says, guys in front of him say exactly what he's thinking himself: "This scene isn't even needed, brother, why are these motherfuckers torturing us like this?"

CUT

It's understood. Let me admit. This prickly article of faith makes my heart race. There was the temple priest that I once met in a village close to Madurai. With his long ponytail, gold earrings, and Gold Flake cigarettes, with his smoldering eyes and contemptuous drawl, Anga Thevar reminded me of an aging rock star. "Look inside," he said. "The mind, the heart, has speed. It can fly all the way to America in a single second."

CUT

People there knew about speed. There were men who spent all their free time training bulls to race, matching their quickness to TVS motorbikes. They talked about the speed, the *vekam*, of that soil. Speed there was power, force, potential that remained untapped. But speed was also haste and fervor, an inward velocity of thought and desire that had to be checked to avert the threat of ruin.

CUT

Speed kills. Driving in Los Angeles, I grew up with this slogan, sped nonetheless into accidents. "The terror of the crash, suppressed while one gathers speed, is the necessary complement to speed's thrill," Enda Duffy says.[8] Pleasure and danger, the careening weave of modern life.

CUT

"Once the cinema was able to create surprise," Paul Virilio notes, "it effectively came under the category of weapons."[9] The movie camera was bred to serve the needs of warfare. Editing can itself be violent, its "cuts" all too real. Hence the complaints about Anthony's work: "You brought this ramp cut, this jump cut. Now all these fuckers are just bombarding people like that."

CUT

The editor insists that he jumps only when needed. And it's not as though images began to leap wildly with him. "Have I told you the story of the snake and the dubbing studio?" he asks. This is the scene: There's a snake chasing the hero of a film. The hero is wearing a red shirt. A few days later, the director finds another spot he likes, wants to continue the chase. "Get the snake!" he orders. They start to shoot, but one of the assistants finally notices that the hero is wearing blue today, not red. "I'll take care of it," the director assures, and takes a close-up of the snake. Later, in the dubbing studio, the snake gets a line of his own. "You think you can just change your shirt and get away from me?" the snake calls out, as the man, now in blue, keeps running.

CUT

I'm cackling. But such devices work. Perception, attention, and experience are far more fragmentary than we think they are. Ordinary perception is built on disjointed images. Our eyes dart between objects of interest, and only later do our brains lend the perceptual world its apparent fullness and continuity. What happens in cinema is not that different, Todd Berliner and Dale Cohen suggest: "Cuts produce discontinuous fragments similar to those the brain processes all day long."[10]

CUT

It's understood. "Don't spoon-feed him too much. Make his brains work a bit," Anthony says. His back stiffens as he talks, eyes popping up and out at the action of an invisible screen. Speed of thought, speed of sensation, in and beyond the limits of the body.

CUT

There's a utopian horizon to this way of thinking. A century ago, the Futurists described a "wireless" or "telegraphic" imagination, calibrated to the lightning force of machines. Recall what F. T. Marinetti proclaimed of a poetry stripped of connective syntax: "The impetuousness of steam-emotion will blow out the pipe of the sentence, the valves of punctuation, and the adjectives that are habitually placed with regularity like bolts."[11]

CUT

Later the Futurists got into advertising, Italian fascism. We're still sold speed, this idea of rapid movement as a pleasure in itself. Cars, films, cigarettes, and more insist on the glory of such thrills. Money is made, lives are vaporized with all that exhaust.[12]

BUT

"Speed," William Connolly says, also "enables more people to come to terms with how unfinished and full of 'gaps' nature is. . . . In an up-tempo world people readily become more . . . experimental, and improvisational . . . alert to fugitive currents in themselves flowing in new directions."[13]

CUT

What happens, say, when you watch a car chase?

CUT

The closest I've come to a car chase was on a mountain road outside of Kuala Lumpur. A blue rally car painted with jagged bolts of lightning, pursued by five wailing police sedans. Vishnu Vardhan was shooting for *Billa*. "Mad, isn't it!" he kept calling out. You could hear the loud roar of the car, slowly building from a mile away. Then, there it was, suddenly, rocketing at us from around a turn, tires squealing as the rally driver slammed his brake, oversteering, the road searing as he drifted sideways, still coming, until he finally caught hold of his momentum once more, speeding through the next bend. Huddled beside the cameraman on that rocky shoulder, there was nothing to save us from those hurtling tons of steel if the driver failed to reclaim control.

CUT

Anthony has to cut a chase scene now for *Quarter Cutting*, Pushkar and Gayathri's film. A year's gone by since he was working on *Vinnaithandi Varuvaya* and *Paiyya*. On the screen, Sura is driving. The second half is twenty-five minutes too long.

CUT

Anthony works quickly. But the dialogues are out of sync. The power suddenly goes. The editor is restless. "I'm not getting any connection, brother. I'll have a smoke and come back."

CUT

"You should have seen when he used to edit drunk," Gayathri says. Once he hurled an Avid deck against the wall when it wasn't working. "Sir, that machine is like a god for us," an assistant said meekly. "Not a god but a devil," the editor retorted.

CUT

Here's the chase. Sura is driving the big red Contessa. Marthandan is next to him, Saro is in the backseat. They're racing after a pair of hit men in a yellow car who talked up Saro beside the road. Then these madcap hit men suddenly remember what they ought to be doing: chasing the red car themselves. U-turn. Guns come out. A patrol car joins the chase. The red car bursts through a traffic barricade, shakes off both pursuers.

CUT

Thomas, one of the newest assistants at Frame Works, made the rough cut. Anthony doesn't like it. The shots are long and tedious. "Right now, what you're seeing is like this, zzzzzzzz," he says, pushing his left hand toward me at a steady pace. "When I cut it, wuaaaww! Then I'll go to the opposite shot, and the car goes eyyyyy!" His right hand darts out to the side, then, leaping forward, overtakes the other hand and screeches to a halt. For the editor, film has an automotive flow.[14]

CUT

Then there's a runny nose. Anthony takes a brandy with pepper, puts off the chase. A foot-massage machine is thrumming somewhere beneath the Avid console.

CUT

 Anthony Gonsalvez
July 2, 2010 via mobile

:-(... Wish I could go from Anthony to Lewellyn ...the guy I was a few years ago ...no worries ,no tensions, happily delivering goods on my dads hercules cycle...earning 800 bucks a month...spending 5 rs for a coke after having my fav tomato rice ...and going Bk home at 5pm...wish I could...

Like · Comment   👍 37 💬 51

CUT

The editor is Anglo-Indian. His father, like his grandfather, worked for the Indian Railways, first hauling coal for steam engines, then retiring as a shunter. His father was responsible for coupling together individual railway compartments. The association is inescapable, marvelous. "In a sense, you're shunting film," I tell him. "Correct," Anthony says, laughing. "Shots also have to be pulled together, right?"

CUT

The railways of the nineteenth century gave passengers unprecedented speed but robbed them of its sensation. Thomas de Quincey favored the visceral thrills "incarnated in the . . . dilated nostril, spasmodic muscles, and thunderbeating hoofs" of the English mail coach. "Somebody *says* that we have gone fifty miles in the hour" in a steam locomotive, he wrote, but "we are far from feeling it as a personal experience."[15] Shielded from sound, wind, and vibration by suspension systems, upholstered seats, and sealed windows, passengers were "invited to relax to the soothing syncopation of muffled clickety-clacks."[16]

CUT

Anthony is also looking through a sealed window. He edits film for others who will also look into a moving world through an impermeable frame. They, like him, will end up just where they began, in the same room and seat. How will they feel the sensation of having traveled so quickly through the space of the film?

CUT

Back to the chase. "Fuck, six minutes," Anthony says, reviewing the rough cut. "Do these cars need to go so slowly?" "They're going at 89 kilometers per hour," Pushkar gamely says, but the editor is unimpressed. "My car happily goes 160, brother."

CUT

The iPod again, watching the rushes: Ozzy Osborne, Fine Young Cannibals, the Spin Doctors. Sometimes the beat of the cut from shot to shot lines up with the tempo of a song. The chords of one guitar solo drift beautifully with the yellow car weaving along the road. Then Anthony gestures quickly at the screen with his arms, pushing along the car, urging it to pass more swiftly. Does he hear what Cheryl Cole is saying on the speakers? "We've been driving so fast, we just need to slow down, and just roll. . . ."

CUT

As the tempo of the music changes, so does the tempo of the speeding cars. You can see the shadow of the crane-mounted camera rig passing over the cars with every streetlight. Whenever it seems to slow them down, the editor ramps up the velocity of the chase. He works with faith and devotion to what speed can best deliver. "In the alternating close views, in the racking focus and the edgily drifting camera," as David Bordwell observes, "the viewer is promised something significant, or at least new, at each instant."[17]

CUT

The keystrokes are too quick to keep up with. But you can see that certain things are falling away as Anthony edits, like the scaffolded backside of that banner of mustachioed demons that the Contessa tears into. The red car bursts through its orange face.

CUT

CUT

Yellow weaving on red's tail

CUT

In red, they turn, see yellow coming

CUT

Hey, go right, go right, yells someone in yellow

CUT

Shiva turns the wheel, Saro whips around to look

CUT

They're here, they're here, Marthandan wails

CUT

Saro's jaw drops, she points, they scream

CUT

The banner of smoking demons, bursting

CUT

Red cuts through the banner, glides through the air

CUT

Tires squash, suspension gives, red comes crashing down

CUT

Heads and limbs are bouncing, flailing

CUT

There goes red, there goes yellow

CUT

"Two cars racing here, sir," goes the patrol car walkie-talkie

CUT

Sirens flashing in pursuit

CUT

Lights out, they watch the sequence, cueing a track from *Tomorrow Never Dies*. "Enough. It's fast, isn't it?" Anthony says. "Nice and tight," Gayathri agrees. "Chase trim done," the editor declares. They began at 11 a.m. It's not yet 4 p.m.

CUT

There are 141 shots in 207 seconds, for an average shot length of 1.5 seconds per shot. Anthony's pace of cutting is faster than the rough cut, where the shots lasted 2.1 seconds on average. It's also much faster than the second half as a whole, with an average shot length of 2.6 seconds. Graph the length of each shot through the half, and you can see the pace of cutting build steadily into the velocity of the chase, a speed reached once again only at the film's climax.[18]

CUT

"Maybe I'm one of those characters," Anthony speculates, "one of those characters in the film. Not present on the screen, but still, in the film . . . the fourth person sitting in that car." As we talk, his hand is the car, a flat plane wheeling quickly through the space between us. Then it's a pair of scissors, cutting the momentum, cutting itself, both inside and outside the film at once. "I move along with it," Anthony says. "I know, okay, this is enough, let's go to the next one."

SNAP!

Caught up in a momentum he propels with one hand, examines with the other, the editor embodies, even personifies speed. Spending time with Anthony is both captivating and harrowing, utterly consonant with the ambiguous spirit of these times. "I think I've got to take a ride in your car sometime," I tell him, provoking more peals of laughter.

CUT

It happens a week later, on the way to the premiere of *Madrasapattinam* at Sathyam Theatres. The Spin Doctors are playing loudly from the speakers again. The car is a black Chevy Beat, a gift from Lingusamy for the runaway success of *Paiyya*. I kid you not, he actually talks speed on the way there. "You're lucky I took this car. That car, I go very fast."

CUT

In the balcony, Anthony is nervous. The audience seems subdued. At the interval, he begins to mutter something—"The reaction is not . . ."—but won't finish the sentence.

CUT

Before the film is over, the editor is already in the parking lot. He's itching to get out, but there are too many cars jammed into that blacktop pen. "After one week, it'll pick up," he promises. "It'll boom."

BOOM!

CHAPTER 17 **Wonder**

For my dissertation research in the early 2000s, I lived with a family of farmers in Tamil Nadu's rural Cumbum Valley. We were watching cable television on their small black-and-white set one night when Iswari Akka recalled something that had happened a decade earlier. A movie about the goddess Amman had come to the nearby village of Surulipatti. People thronged to see it. The theater owners tied up bunches of neem leaves around the entryway to the tin-roofed hall, as though it were a temple. They brought out ladles of smoldering frankincense for the film's climactic song, when the goddess prepared to battle the villains and avenge her loyal devotees. "My skin prickled all over," Iswari Akka told me. With the sound of ululations and temple drums, the vision of cheeks pierced by her spears, the goddess took hold of many men and women in that hall, bringing their limbs to quaver with the beat. I found this extraordinary, the idea that a film could provoke possession. But to Iswari Akka, such wonders had a place in the ordinary world, times in which to expect their eruption. Her brothers had refused at first to let her see the film, given what they heard was happening in that theater. Finally they relented, holding down her arms on either side from the beckoning of that song.

··· **H** ···

"The world is disenchanted," Max Weber declared nearly a century ago, in a 1918 lecture at Munich University. "One need no longer have recourse to magical means in order to master or implore the spirits. . . . Technical means and calculations perform the service."[1] Such claims bestow an uneasy status to what happened in that village cinema hall in south India, leaving such things as lingering relics from a more innocent and unknowing time. As Lorraine Daston and Katherine Park observe, "An odor of the popular now clings to wonders."[2]

In Western thought, the feeling of wonder has tumbled precipitously in value, from the founding passion of classical philosophy to a hallmark of the ignorant and credulous. Earnest sciences of the marvelous in the early modern era—air pumps and monstrous births, oscillating pendulums and animal ballet—have given way to an idea of enlightened inquiry as a more restrained exercise of curiosity. And yet, "deep inside," as Daston and Park also suggest, "beneath tasteful and respectable exteriors, we still crave wonders. . . . We wait for the rare and extraordinary to surprise our souls."[3]

Nowhere is this more obvious than in the dark recesses of the cinema hall. Take the abundant trick films of the earliest years of cinema, such as Georges Méliès's 1902 *A Trip to the Moon*, "a demonstration of the magical possibilities of the cinema," as Tom Gunning puts it.[4] Or consider the mythological and devotional films of modern India, new ways of manifesting the wondrous deeds and powers of divine beings.

The story of Indian cinema famously begins with Dadasaheb Phalke's encounter with a silent film, *The Life of Christ*, in 1911. "I was gripped by a strange spell," the magician and lithographic printer later marveled. "While the life of Christ was rolling fast before my eyes I was mentally visualizing the Gods, Shri Krishna, Shri Ramchandra, their Gokul and Ayodhya."[5] Seven years later, he released a film of his own called *The Birth of Shree Krishna*, which begins with the spectacle of the young Hindu deity rising up out of a river, balancing, flute in hand, within the coils of a massive serpent.[6]

Two years after Weber's Munich reflections on science in a disenchanted world, Raghupati Surya Prakash used a 35mm camera he had brought back from Europe to shoot the story of the Madurai goddess Meenakshi's wedding.[7] Many such films have been made since then in south India, most especially since the 1970s and its efflorescence of films venerating the Hindu goddesses of the region. In this cinematic genre, as Kalpana Ram argues, "a much richer and fuller confluence of sensory engagement allows . . . the spectator to experience the goddess as living flesh rather than stone."[8] These films invite, in other words, the kinds of sensuous and bodily involvement with divine powers that Iswari Akka described in her recollection.

Such immersion in the supernatural wonders of cinema, Ram notes, rankles middle-class Indian critics of popular superstition. But the line between rational conduct and irrational faith is never that easy to draw or enforce. Take *Adi Velli* [Friday in the month of Adi], the 1990 film by Rama Narayanan that provoked those episodes of possession in the village theater of Surulipatti. In the film, the goddess Amman takes physical form to protect a faithful young devotee from the villainous members of her own household. But the climax of the story turns on a fierce battle between the goddess and a computer programmer, who unleashes a monster named King Kattari—a bizarre, fire-breathing hybrid, it would seem, of Godzilla and an octopus—with a few ominous clicks on his Macintosh keyboard. Both these beings, in fact, village deity and electrogenic demon, come to life amid flashes of the same kind of lightning.[9]

"The contemporary world retains the power to enchant humans," Jane Bennett insists. "To be enchanted is to be struck and shaken by the extraordinary that lives amid the familiar and the everyday."[10] Wonder is another name for that state of being struck, and wonders are a way of describing those things in the world that strike and shake us in this fashion. This is a chapter about the making of such wonders in Tamil cinema, about those who do the work of the gods and the humble faces they put on.[11]

This building is like so many others popping up around Chennai these days, a concrete block surfaced with dark, mirrored glass. Navigate past the security desk on the lobby floor, convince someone to swipe one of the key cards required to set foot into the digital labs upstairs, and you will find yourself in a twenty-first-century edition of the European *Wunderkammer*, a contemporary cabinet of wonders packed with curious interminglings of nature and artifice.

Look closely at the banks of screens. On one monitor, Salman Khan swings an invisible sword. On another screen nearby, the dimples are disappearing from Deepika Padukone's smile. You can see the Tamil actor Jeeva here, not single or doubled but in fact quintupled, five Jeevas playing five instruments side by side. Nearby, Bugs Bunny is getting some cosmetic surgery on his ears. Technological marvels all, conjured up by computer-generated imagery, or CGI.[12]

The company is EFX, its motto "Magic in Motion." Most visual effects work in India happens in such labs, this one located on the sprawling campus of Prasad Studios. The company provides a range of digital services, from digital postproduction and color grading to stereoscopic film conversion and visual effects.

Companies like EFX are part of a global supply chain of outsourced digital effects. Scattered throughout the lab on any given day are images subcontracted from American, East Asian, and other overseas film productions. Domestic clients, meanwhile, mostly fall back on EFX for routine needs like wire removal: erasing the rigs and cables, that is, with which battling heroes like Karthi Sivakumar fly through the air.

Venki

Visual effects work falls toward the very end of the film production process, when producers are most strapped for cash yet stuck nonetheless with problems that cannot be fixed in any other way. Despite the buoyant slogans plastered on so many of the walls, not everyone is sanguine about what happens in such buildings. "Suddenly they decide they want to add some technology element to the same old story," one senior manager in the industry complained, dismissing the projects that passed through his workflow pipeline.

"We haven't done any innovative work in India. Zero."

⊢

Europe sailed into modern times in pursuit of Eastern marvels—think of Marco Polo's effusive accounts of Sumatran unicorns, India's snow-white parrots, and the levitating cups of Kublai Khan.[13] But, as we all know, the terms of this global trade in wonders have long since turned against the Orient.

"Let me be frank with you," S. T. Venki told me one morning in 2010, pausing for a while to gather his thoughts. "After *Avatar*, where are we now? James Cameron shattered the look of filmmaking. . . . I was shaken, basically."

Many spoke reverently of Venki as the father of visual effects in India. But few seemed to know that he was still here, living on a rutted lane south of Chennai, his bungalow overshadowed by the mirrored walls of a hulking IT center. On his walls were paintings copied from Matisse, van Gogh, and Picasso, along with framed certificates from the Indian Ministry of Information and Broadcasting—four consecutive national film awards for Best Special Effects in the 1990s.[14]

The awards were for his technical triumphs of the 1990s: invisible cowboys in visible clothes, snakes with human heads, women dissolving into dancing skeletons, all visual effects that depended upon new advances in digital and video technology. "It worked wonders for me," Venki recalled. "It created a trust, that this guy could do something new. People blindly believed whatever I vomited."

India's visual effects guru would often slip into melancholy reflections on the state of Indian cinema, eyes downcast with a bitter smile playing across his face. He was always asked to reproduce certain ideas of the improbable, requests he found banal and wonderless himself. "There is a certain amount of frustration, monotony," he admitted to me. "We misuse, overuse, abuse the technology."

When Venki first began to experiment with optical techniques in visual effects in the 1980s, the work was painstakingly artisanal: drawing, inking, and scratching out elements by hand, frame by individual frame. Now he hardly had a place in what visual effects had since become: a network of digital laboratory operations, companies meant only, as he once put it disdainfully, "to feed a hundred people."[15]

··········· ⊣ ···········

On one of the monitors at EFX one morning is a guy with thick arms and long stringy hair, hanging from the girders suspended over a small forest stream. "Here's the original," Sathya says, pointing at the screen. "Now here's the output." When he clicks his mouse, a bridge suddenly appears over those rickety girders and the stream begins to gush with water. "Now that we've re-created it, this is what the real bridge looks like," the demiurge explains modestly.

Sathya is a compositor, charged with layering together visual elements from different sources to create composite yet seamless images. He came to EFX three years back, with a BA in History and a certificate in visual effects from Pentamedia Graphics. "My dream is to work at ILM," he tells me with a quiet sincerity, invoking the studio—Industrial Light & Magic—founded by George Lucas in California. He talks about a film on the Aztecs that he once did for an American production: they spent thirty times as much on each shot as they typically did here.

His project manager calls out his name from across the room, and Sathya returns to report that another sequence has just arrived for the same film, *Mambattiyan*.[16] The police officer on his screen now, the one lashed to a tree atop a rocky hill: a flock of eagles must crowd the skies above him, descending one by one to peck him to death.

I watch as Sathya blends wisps of cloud into the green matte behind the tree, overlaying a circling pair of eagles into the frame. Then he adds another bird to the image, this one larger, as though approaching the man bound to the tree. The compositor gives a slight pitch to the eagle's movement, making it pinwheel downward as it comes. "Like any artist, you have to have a creative sense," Sathya says. "This one comes like this, that one comes more slowly."

There's a Tamil melody from the 1980s playing on the desktop speakers—"It's hitting me, that breeze dancing through the red screwpine flowers."—lending an incongruously pleasant texture to the policeman's hilltop rendezvous.

As Sathya loops again and again through each shot, cycling at the same time through his collection of MP3s, he has to log each completed shot onto the network's reporting system. "Note: new task cannot be started until you complete the previous task," reads a message at the top of the screen, apparently unaware of the imaginative trespass these tasks depend upon.

Two days later, the cop remains crucified on Sathya's screen, still atoning for an offense that no one in the lab can identify. The compositor is listening to the *Avatar* soundtrack now, wearing earmuffs to defend against the building's frigid cold.

Sathya sits back, letting the shots run through a window on his screen while the music plays from the speakers. As he scans through the footage, looking for more eagles to introduce into the scene, it strikes me that he's composing as much as compositing. Each fragment of material has to be judged for both its camera angle and the perspective of the shot it's intended to fill out. "Only when you comp will you know," Sathya says, "whether it works or not."

The closest record of a living eagle that the film's producers provided was an image of a bird grabbing meat from the roof of a tin shed. Sathya has to make it seem as though this animal is lunging instead for the police inspector, but there are problems that this juxtaposition poses: the eagle is grabbing with its feet instead of jabbing with its mouth, and if it were really flying in from the left, it would have to hit the trunk of the tree before reaching the man.

With this as with all else at EFX, the challenge that the compositors face is to work with what is available to them. Sathya creates a dynamic frame to extract the eagle from its original surroundings, pasting it into a shot of this hilltop. He rotates the swooping animal to make the attack seem more plausible, pausing to watch the overlap loop a few times on his monitor. "Kitchikoo, kitchikoo!" I hear him call out quietly, mimicking the raptor on the screen.

"The power of the god that the magician has earned or stolen," Lee Siegel writes in a study of Indian magic, "is essentially a cosmogonic power."[17] Listening to *Avatar*, manipulating those talons, making those calls, Sathya seems to be trespassing on the being of that eagle, working through this animal on his monitor. It's even more than that, though. There is also the sense, in the quiet work of this technician, of laying out the components of a living world.

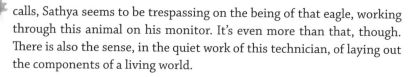

Like the Japanese animation studios described by Ian Condry in his recent book *The Soul of Anime*, the Indian visual effects lab is an environment of "collective energy" and "collaborative creativity."[18] Projects at EFX are assigned to multiple teams, and images pass back and forth among individual workstations through the company network. The currency of exchange is the shot number: "Have you done forty-two? Where's forty-four? Sundar's doing forty-seven."

The most significant division among these employees is the divide between 2D and 3D work: between those who begin with two-dimensional representations of the world outside and those who begin with abstract three-dimensional models of that world. Most 2D technicians are compositors like Sathya. On the 3D side, classifications are more detailed: there are those who specialize in modeling 3D structures, those whose task is texturing and lighting these models, and others who will be rigging them for animation by still other teams.

Praveen, for example, is introduced to me as a 3D "fur specialist," a title that he shrugs off modestly, although he later does admit that he's mostly responsible for texturing fur and cloth. He taps a keyboard to set spinning a model of a spider meant to perch on a man's shoulder. "There are four million individual hairs here," he tells me. "Only then will the density show."

Whether perceptible or imperceptible, this magnitude of detail takes time to render into complete images, especially given the physical limits of the available workstations. Praveen and his teammates pass this dead time by watching demo videos online: a ball bouncing into Jell-O, cars colliding with a rubber wall. Most of their work involves physics and dynamics, he explains, but simulating many of these effects requires hardware and software that they lack at the lab.

There is also the waiting they do for clients, for instructional meetings with the directors and producers of these films. "They forget that we're also white-collar people," one of the project managers once told me, lamenting that he's sometimes asked to ride along with the makeup men to shoots when he has two cars at home himself.

Images remain frozen on the screens, awaiting instructions, animation. Late one morning I spot one such image of the actor Dhanush on

one of the monitors, standing near the wall of a small cowshed, facing
the young woman before him. He will throw feathers, someone tells me, that will magically embed themselves as a pattern on her sari—how, no one knows just yet.

H

"The special effect should be understood against the backdrop of the religious tradition," Hent de Vries writes, "in particular, the miracle."[19] The word *miracle* itself stems from the Latin *miraculum*, something to wonder at. In the thirteenth century the Catholic theologian Thomas Aquinas drew an influential distinction between miracles and marvels: marvels, he proposed, were only effects whose natural cause still remained unknown, while miracles were more unusual events that disrupted the natural order of things.[20]

This kind of reasoning is difficult to extend to India, where the cosmos has long been taken to host supernatural beings and powers of diverse kinds. There is wonder, awe, astonishment—in Sanskrit aesthetics, *adbhuta*—in the extraordinary deeds of those who have attained a higher understanding of the universe and its elusive forces: yogis and saints, for example, or the quasi-divine protagonists of Indian devotional films.[21]

Like Dhanush, waiting with a bundle of peacock feathers in that cowshed, a character in a Tamil remake of a successful Malayalam film.[22] The makers of this film, *Seedan*, suddenly appear at EFX late one afternoon. Gathering around a monitor in one of the vacant workstation bays, the clients evaluate progress with its miraculous effects. On the screen, a framed portrait of the Tamil god Saravanan begins to glow for the woman crying beside it. The film crew wants this tweaked, as though that light was pouring from the portrait itself.

Dhanush, whose character in the film is an incarnation of the god Saravanan as a temple cook, disappears into nothing as he trots up a flight of steps. Someone suggests that he vanish into wisps of smoke rather than simply disappear, as he does now, but the EFX project manager discourages the idea: "That would look too much like a devotional film."

Then there's Dhanush again, talking to a young man on the terrace of a house. The full moon seems to be hanging too low in the sky. "Lift it a little," the director says, pointing a finger at the moon and darting it upward, as though one could shift the moon itself with something so small and casual as this finger.

The peacock feathers—tutelary symbols of the deity Saravanan, who is known to ride a peacock as his mount—are the final artifact examined by the EFX clients. Once again the director is dissatisfied with what they've done so far. "It looks artificial," he says, considering the feather motif that Praveen has applied to the young woman's sari. "There's no reality to it."

What must reality be to accommodate such wondrous deeds?

⊔

Two technicians, Senthil and Manoj, have already been working on one of the feathers that Saravanan will throw, building up a three-dimensional digital model of its structure. I watch as Manoj, a slender young man, zooms in on the plume at his workstation, manipulating the length and contours of individual stems and stalks.

As we step out to the canteen for lunch, Manoj shows me a few pages of waste paper lying on his desk, where he's been sketching anatomical drawings of muscled men in green pencil. He, like the three other EFX employees with us now, studied at the Government College of Fine Arts in Chennai. Did they ever think about pursuing art direction in cinema, I ask. The college, after all, is a pipeline for precisely this vocation.

"Language problem," Manoj says with a slight smile, and I remember that I'm conversing with four soft-spoken men from provincial towns in Tamil Nadu, all of whom speak in what Manoj ruefully describes as "butler English."

He begins to speak more earnestly, in Tamil, about his interests in archaeology, Siddha medicine, and the lost continent of Lemuria. He seems to have spiritual inclinations. "They say that cinema is magic, *maya*," I tell him, as we sit together in a sheltered courtyard on the Prasad Studio campus. "But all these things happen in your lab. What you're making now, it's a divine deed, a mysterious action. There are people who believe these things really happen, no?"

"No, sir," Manoj objects. "You must know something about physics. They study what human beings don't yet understand. Those who believe will believe, when they watch a film, the output, but each person sees it differently: as something mysterious, something beautiful, something technical, or timepass. Why bother with all this?"

I don't think he understands what I'm getting at, but my tongue seems to have slipped into a postlunch torpor. "God appears here in human form. But you're the one who makes it happen! You are that divine force that makes it fly, that makes it stick! What is that like?"

"Oh, you're asking about those feelings," he says, drawing out this English word, "feeeelings," pronouncing it with a tone that already implies that it has no place here.

"They assign us a task. 'You must complete it in this time,' they tell us. Katakatakata, I do it just like that, I'll give it by tomorrow. 'Oh, the feather is flying, oh, it's landing on the heroine,' none of those feelings are there. The work is technical, that's all."

Manoj speaks with the empiricist bent of a natural scientist rather than as a wonderstruck devotee. "If a peacock feather were truly to fly, how would it fly? We can throw one and see. To animate paper, throw a piece of paper and see. If a leaf is to fall, I look at how a leaf falls."

The lab as a disenchanted space, after all?

.... ⊢ ....

The feather goes from Manoj to Praveen, fur and cloth specialist, who will introduce the artifact into the world of the film. There it is now, positioned on a receding grid, overlaid onto the woman in the white sari. He spins the feather along a vertical axis of rotation, watching it diminish in size as it tumbles toward her. He holds out an empty hand of his own, pretending to throw something at the screen. "To visualize it," he explains. "All animators must know how to act."

The animator yawns in the darkness of the lab. I wonder if it seems sensuous at all to him, as it does to me, this grazing again and again of a young woman's body with a peacock quill, her face turning bashfully away each time. "It's a shot, that's all," he tells me. "It's all the same. A skeleton standing up, walking. A ghoul coming. There's no big feeling that comes."

Praveen is working with this material on Autodesk Maya, a software platform named after the idea of illusion popularized by Shankara, the eighth-century south Indian philosopher. Shankara's influential school of thought, Advaita Vedanta, describes worldly experience as an illusory dream, superimposed by ignorance upon the elusive and ultimate reality of *brahman*.[23] What Praveen and his teammates are doing at EFX, however, seems to have more in common with the tenets of some of Shankara's critics, such as Madhva, who insisted instead upon the reality of a world independent of Brahman, "the animator and controller of the universe."[24] I think again of the empirical truth of moving bodies pursued in small ways by Praveen and Manoj. "We know," Praveen says, "if we throw it like this, it will go like this."

At the center of Praveen's monitor desktop, in fact, is an image of the seventeenth-century Vaishnava saint Sri Raghavendra, one of Madhva's most important proponents and commentators. "He's also a god," the animator explains, when I ask him about this figure. Praveen tells me that he visits a nearby Raghavendra temple once or twice a week, but he shrugs off the significance of the desktop image, as he does with nearly everything else I ask him about.

"I put it there just like that, for no reason," he says. "Before this, there was a picture from *The Transformers*—Megatron's picture was there before."

Both of us burst out laughing. To myself, I concede defeat. So much of what is happening in the dark depths of this lab will elude my knowing.

⊢

The casting of those peacock feathers is a turning point in the film *Seedan*. Maha, a household maid and ardent devotee of the god Saravanan, despairs of ever marrying her lover. Preparations are already afoot, in fact, to wed him to someone else.

She is sulking in that cowshed when she is confronted by the cook Saravanan, an earthly incarnation of the god himself, although Maha does not realize this at the time. Failing to convince her that her hopes will yet be realized, Saravanan grasps that sheaf of feathers from a wall and throws them in her direction. She gasps as they slip through the air and glide into the very fabric of what she's wearing. "This happened, didn't it, this wonder?" the cook asks her. "Just like that, your marriage will certainly happen too."

What was made to happen in the visual effects laboratory is profoundly efficacious in the world of *Seedan*. These young men at EFX were doing the work of the gods. And yet, as we have seen, all of them disavowed the wondrous quality of their deeds. Not one of them, in fact—not Praveen, not Manoj, not Senthil—is mentioned by name in the credits that close the film. I wasn't even allowed to take a single photograph of any of them, and was given a few group photos instead by the Prasad Studios public relations office, images in which it is difficult to place any of their individual faces.

Where does that leave this chapter, or me, for that matter, the naïve and sometimes even wonderstruck observer in their midst? What we often find in contemporary anthropology, Michael Scott has recently suggested, is "a new kind of religious study of religion," a scholarly practice that defies the familiar boundary between science and religion. More than anything else, he muses, this religious quality has to do with wonder, with an interest in keeping the horizon of possibility alive even in the face of accumulating knowledge. Scott proposes a name for such endeavors, *thaumatography*, or "wonder-writing," and I can think of no better way of describing what I've been trying to do in this chapter and even throughout this book.[25]

There are, no doubt, many disenchanting and dispiriting things about the world as we have it now—in laboratories such as this visual effects studio and all such related places that value products at the expense of processes, proprietors at the expense of the countless others who bring their things into being into the first place. In the depths of those mirrored walls on the Prasad Studios campus, I found myself in the company of people robbed of the wonder of what they did, charged with producing effects whose force would be attributed to actors profoundly unlike themselves. Cinema is replete with such sleights of hand. In many ways, its wonders depend upon the illusion that they happen on their own.

In the face of such deceits, we may well be inclined to reveal and demystify, in the name of justice and critique, and rightly so. But to do no more than this is to deny the critical potential of wonder itself, that feeling that "keeps propositions provisional, open-ended, and incomplete," as Mary-Jane Rubenstein puts it. "Wonder wonders at the strangeness of the most familiar: at that which . . . still remains indeterminate, unthinkable, and impossible."[26] Wonder, in other words, is a matter of attunement, a way of attending to the tenuous life of possibility in the face of stubborn and dispiriting actuality.[27]

Were they really telling me all they felt, revealing all they did? And how exactly does this matter? I want to declare what Maha herself declares, what she says at the close of that film, when she is married just as Saravanan had promised, when he, now revealed as truly a god, calls out to her from the steps of his temple, makes himself visible to her alone and to no one else at that crowded hilltop shrine.

"I saw him!" she cries out with tears of joy to her befuddled husband. "Just me, I saw him! I saw who he really is, that Saravanan."

CHAPTER 18   **Fate**

There's a woman I know in a village west of Madurai, some-one who likes to speak in stories, songs, and riddles. One evening many years ago, she told me a tale about how things wind up the way they do. Iswaran, god, she said, makes you from a handful of earth. He takes out a palm leaf to assign your fate, reaching behind his own back with both of his arms, so that even he can't see what he's written there. Then he brings the palm leaf around to take a look. You're in luck if he's managed to write well that day. If not, what can you do but follow that line wherever it leads? Thangathai was a widow of six years when she told me this story. Two of her sons, like so many others from this valley, wound up working in Tamil cinema. I've never managed to meet them or to hear their stories. But I'm sure they must know how wildly things can pitch up and down, like those uneven lines of destiny that Iswaran scribbles with a shaky and unseen hand.

.... H ....

This theater, Amirtham, has a weirdly space-age aspect, planted onto a grimy lane in the heart of Madurai. Of course, the men at the local film distribution office, Ma-dhura Films, had already warned us to mistrust what we would see there: "That area is a little rough, a low-class area. That theater's a bit of a sham." Still, who could have expected anything like this: a broad path gently spiral-ing upward through a towering concrete silo, shafts of sunlight breaking at sharp angles through the tubular spokes and crossbeams.

Outside, blue fins like the spines of a rocket ship, doubled up in pairs along the edge of the helical struc-ture. When the cinema hall was built in the late 1970s, someone says, there was nothing in the town remotely like it. Today the double doors are thrown wide open, the air-conditioning silent. Saturday afternoon. A thou-sand twenty-four seats, almost all empty.

Why does the theater look so barren and run-down? The projectionist has a curt but entirely adequate answer: "Twenty rupees for a CD." Downstairs is another sign of the times, a warning from the theater management taped onto the wall above a popcorn machine: "Take a photo on your cell phone, and your cell phone will be handed over to the police."

People are still drifting slowly into the compound at 2:50 p.m., a total of seventy-three tickets tallied for the 2:30 matinee show. On the screen inside the cinema hall, you can see a rather similar spectacle unfolding: the image of a handful of villagers scattered sparsely across a courtyard, watching shadow puppets dance across a white fabric screen.

There, like here, an avid play of feeling, song, and expression seems to dissipate into an empty vault of darkness.

At the intermission, people begin to shuffle back into the sunlight. "The film will definitely run for a hundred days," one young man in bell-bottom slacks promises. "It's an art film, made with the stories of a long-gone time," someone else observes, unsure about the appeal of such things these days.

There are just a few women and girls, clustered around another entrance to the hall. One of them wrinkles her nose in distaste. "This film's a bore."

Saturday, one day after release. Was the film's fate still open, or already sealed?

·· └┘ ··

After all that has happened, after months and even years of dreaming, thinking, planning, working, after countless twists and turns that would no doubt make for good cinema themselves, after endless forms of careful, selective, and often misleading revelation, here at last is a film in its fullness: audible, visible, open, vulnerable to both assimilation and disdain.

This one was produced by someone you already know: *Aval Peyar Tamilarasi* [Her name is Tamilarasi], directed by Meera Kathiravan and produced by G. Dhananjayan while he was still working for Moser Baer. A story of rape and redemption, love and betrayal—an irksome and disturbing film.

There's a wealthy boy, Jyothi, who falls in love with a poor girl, Tamilarasi, well before they're old enough to understand such things. Then, as an adolescent, he rapes her in a fit of drunken rage, afraid that he might lose her. Her life falls to pieces and she disappears. He spends the next eight years looking for her, tormented by the thought of what he's done.

Will he find her? Will she forgive him? These are the questions the film invites you to pose. Although it's her name in the title and her trust that is violated, it still remains a story about him. Is this the destiny of Tamil cinema, made mostly by men, mostly for men? "It seems I had to wander like a vagrant from place to place, only to fall here," Tamilarasi tells Jyothi when he traces her at last to a brothel, late in the film. "This must be the fate written on my head."

There may come a time when women's lives and stories find a better place in Tamil cinema. For now, forgive me for lingering once more on the fate of men's deeds. This is a film about their weakness, and I too am one of them, susceptible to the tides of such tales.

··· **H** ···

Drifting in and out of the Moser Baer office over many months, I often caught glimpses of *Aval Peyar Tamilarasi*'s preparations for release: the honing of its narrative structure in the editing studio, the public launch of its songs and other promotional materials, the pitching of the film to distributors and film festival representatives.

The producer, G. Dhananjayan, appreciated its "realistic" story and its commitment to the idea that "every human being falters." I found myself moved by the stark beauty of its barren rural landscapes, carefully etched to exemplify the darkness of human nature. I became more and more curious as to how the film would do.

One December afternoon, G.D. called to say that they were about to wrap up the shooting of the film. "Come, see what we do on the last day of shoot."

They were working outside a temple in the suburbs west of Chennai that day, finishing one last song. There, as was so often the case, the edges of the set were crowded with curious and jocular eyes. Daylight was nearly gone as the crew prepared to take the final shot. "Get the pumpkin ready," one man called out, turning from the arc lights he was handling.

A pumpkin and a coconut, a lime and a silver platter piled with ash and vermilion. Small slabs of camphor were placed to light on top of each of these auspicious things. The ritual that followed, overseen by production assistants who had remained with the crew from the very first day of the film's shooting, would disperse whatever *kan drishti* the film had gathered, whatever malevolent feelings and effects that might have accumulated through the envious gaze of those who had watched it being made.[1]

"We do this with faith that the film will succeed," Karuppusamy explained. One among the set crew, he was carrying the pumpkin now.

"Where's the hero?" someone else called out. Equally important was the camera, its face and lens covered carefully with an orange cloth until it stood before the temple entrance and beside the lead actor, Jai, all of them now facing east.

In the gathering darkness, the objects lit with camphor flames were passed in circles around the faces of both actor and camera. For the first time, they turned to face the same direction: one final act that brought together those who appeared in the film with those who had always faced them from the other side of the camera.

"The film is complete," Karuppusamy told me. "After this, they will not shoot at all."

⊢

India has long been imagined by foreign observers as a land of passive and fatalistic acceptance of whatever comes. Think of karma, for example, famously characterized by the sociologist Max Weber as the foundation of India's stubborn "traditionalism."[2]

In the many years that I've spent in rural Tamil Nadu, people have often lamented the fates written into their bodies and livelihoods. But they've also told me vivid and entertaining stories of fates evaded and altered through cunning and trickery—of tigers outwitted with love potions or riches lost through slips of the tongue. What we learn from such Indian tales, Eliza Kent suggests, is that "fate can be outwitted, or that destiny may be fulfilled in surprising, ironic ways."[3]

Aval Peyar Tamilarasi is also a story about the vagaries of fate, concerning the misfortune of a feckless boy and the girl he betrays but also the folk tradition she is born into. Tamilarasi belongs to a family of itinerant leather puppeteers. Manipulating these colorful figures behind white cloth screens, they enact scenes from the *Ramayana* and other epic tales. But when a traveling circus follows them into Jyothi's village, their nightly audiences dwindle to almost nothing. Tamilarasi's grandfather is forced to walk from house to house, begging for grain.

"The world's gone upside-down," he tells Jyothi's grandfather. "Cinema, TV, that's where everyone is going. Who remembers that we were the first to tell stories on a screen?"

Many of the film's most poignant and wrenching moments involve these puppets. But if it was cinema that devastated this tradition, what can be expected from a film that lingers on its fate? Here is Jyothi as a schoolboy, less than fifteen minutes after the old puppeteer's lament, dancing inside a tin-roofed cinema hall with his friends. "Whistling loudly in the theater, we tear up all the good seats," they sing proudly under a rain of confetti, as Rajni Kanth beams beneficently down upon them.

It was this song that closed out the film's shooting in December 2009, a late addition made on the insistence of the producer's team and against the wishes of the film's director, purely with the marketing of the film in mind. "This has energy," the production controller Prabhu explained as we stood together, watching the dancers execute vigorous, aerobic moves in the theater courtyard. "When it reaches people, they'll see that some happiness is there."

Foremost on his mind were those who might distribute the film. "If they are energized, if they are convinced, we can do business—they'll take it." When it came to the tension between cinema and folk arts, the producers chose to have a cake that they could also eat—or, to use Prabhu's language, a *dosai* with *sambar*, *chutney*, and everything else on the side. To succeed, the film had to be much more than melancholy, "a mix of everything" that kept people happy despite its dark drift.

Though there was an element of deception in this planning, no one at Moser Baer seemed too perturbed. "This is the song we're going to promote continuously," G.D. announced. "It will become a college anthem."

················· H ·················

As plans for the marketing of the film continued to unfold, so did negotiations of this kind. "Please don't put anything serious there," G.D. warned Meera Kathiravan one morning at the Moser Baer office, during a discussion of the trailer. "Fully youthful, just that love, no sadness." Until the release itself, almost nothing would be known about the film, except for such brief and carefully crafted glimpses.

Even the film's publicity designer, J. A. Abdul, confessed that he didn't know the story. The director had told him only that it was a film about searching: "The hero loses a girl and comes back looking for her."

I was struck by the tone of the many posters that Abdul had already produced, their austere composition, muted colors, and abundant empty space. How did he imagine the mood of the film? "It's only sadness I can show," he replied, after some thought. "This is a certain kind of film, but for this too, there's an audience."

To reach this audience, distributors were necessary. *Aval Peyar Tamilarasi* was selected to screen at the Dubai International Film Festival in December 2009, three months after G.D. had engagingly pitched it to festival representatives as a depiction of "the plight of people when folk arts are forgotten." Though the film was welcomed in Dubai, those at Moser Baer tried to keep this news as quiet as possible. Distributors kept asking Prabhu the same question, again and again: "So, it's gone to a festival?" From their standpoint, such recognition was a problem, implying that the film lacked commercial potential among domestic audiences.

Sun Pictures had already bought the film's satellite television rights for their cable network, and G.D. hoped that they might buy the film outright, assuming the risks and rewards of its release themselves. There was also the possibility that distributors in the seven film "territories" of Tamil Nadu would come forward with "minimum guarantees" of revenue to share with the producer, in exchange for the exclusive right to distribute the film in those particular territories.[4] In the meantime, the producer developed a "plan B" alternative, plotting how they might distribute the film themselves. G.D. began to meet with distribution brokers, who could find and hold a fixed number of theaters for the film's opening weekend, in exchange for a small commission.

Two representatives from one of these brokering concerns stopped by the office late one afternoon that month. Thinking over the spate of upcoming releases, they discussed various options for *Aval Peyar Tamilarasi*. G.D. pulled out a roll of photographic poster cards, inviting the brokers to select the best advertisements for the film. One of them began to rifle quickly through the pictures, building up a small pile of images that largely featured Jyothi and Tamilarasi as smiling and mischievous youth. Later I asked what prompted these choices. "I can't say," the man replied. "Each has their own taste. There's nothing like a genius when it comes to cinema. Good decisions are based purely on luck."

Other than what was visible in these images, they too knew almost nothing about the film—most essentially, that its crucial narrative turn came when this playful young man raped the young woman sitting so happily beside him.

The censor board reminded the producer and director of precisely this five days later, at a preview theater close to the Moser Baer office—"That's the story you're telling." They cleared the film for public release without asking for any cuts, but rated it U/A instead of an unrestricted U: parental guidance required for children. "The matter is lovemaking," one board member apparently declared, soft-pedaling the story's violence.

⊢

November . . . December . . . January 15 . . . January 22 . . . February 5 . . . February 12 . . . The film was complete, cleared for release, but slots kept opening and closing fruitlessly, week after week. Twelve Tamil films were released in January 2010, and there was talk of nineteen more in the month of February.

"We're not getting the right theaters," G.D. complained. Distributors doubted whether the lead actor, Jai, could pull in a big crowd on the film's opening weekend, especially with releases confirmed for several major stars. Finally, in mid-February, G.D. wrote me once more: *Aval Peyar Tamilarasi* would open on March 5.

I was already back in Baltimore, teaching, but managed to arrange a six-day trip to India for the opening. Vishnu Vardhan's *Sarvam* was available on the Qatar Airways in-flight entertainment system, as was *Nadodigal*, starring M. Sasikumar. I had thought a lot about time with Vishnu, space with Sasi. *Sarvam* quickly proved a startling flop at the box office, while *Nadodigal* was declared a "super hit," earning much more than the cost of its production. It seemed impossible to account for such spectacular successes and failures.

That afternoon, just a few hours before my flight, I was in a classroom discussing *Sensory Biographies*, an ethnography by Robert Desjarlais. The Yolmo people of Nepal, with whom the anthropologist worked, often spoke of their fate as etched imperceptibly by the gods onto the surface of their own skulls. "Written by fate, covered by skin, how can it be seen?" goes a Nepali proverb.[5]

In Tamil Nadu too, *thalai ezhuthu*, or "the writing on the head," is often put forward as a synonym for the mysterious and often unbearable workings of fate. Could the same be said of a film, that its destiny was somehow written invisibly onto the surface of its reels, already recorded somewhere within the metal canisters in which it traveled?

Desjarlais's elderly friends tell him that what is said about the dead can also change their fate from birth to birth: "The gods listen to and heed such talk."[6] Here too, it seemed, so much would turn on the murmurs that would trail the film from one world into another.

.... ⊢ ....

It's 9 a.m. on Wednesday morning. "Welcome back to India," G.D. declares on the phone. We meet an hour later at the offices of Jaya TV, where Suhasini Maniratnam will be interviewing the film's producer, director, cameraman, and lead actress.

The producer seems buoyant. "I'm doing 360-degree marketing. Every media outlet is covered," he tells me while they wait. Then each takes a turn sitting with their host on a pair of white leather couches under large pink signs for Vivel Soaps & Shampoos.

Later, back at Moser Baer, G.D. shares some of their Internet advertising: banner images, contests, video interviews, and so on. All these articles and features, he insists, grow out of his own assiduous efforts to write about and promote Tamil cinema: "no PR, all relationships." His secretary Charu walks into the office with the latest issue of *Galatta Cinema*, and G.D. immediately begins to flip through the magazine, pointing out the many references to their film. "Everybody knows that *Aval Peyar Tamilarasi* is coming," he says.

Prabhu knocks on the door. Ninety theaters have now committed to screen the film this weekend, far more than they had anticipated. "Shall we go and see the promos?" G.D. asks, and I tag along to a small studio nearby, where a kid who looks sixteen is editing ten-second promotional clips for the film. Everything on the screen looks joyous and upbeat: Jyothi and Tamilarasi cycling together, chasing each other around a haystack, jumping enthusiastically. "I can only call this a poem," one senior director says earnestly into a mike. These clips, I learn, will be screened in rotation on multiple television channels over the next several days.

Back in the car, the phone calls continue at a dizzying pace. "See all the pressure we are keeping up?" G.D. points out. "If you don't do it, the film will come to nothing."

We head that evening to a special screening of the film for a young and prominent Tamil producer, the son of the deputy chief minister of Tamil Nadu. There, however, the reaction is muted, unnerving. "It's a little dry," the young man says curtly, before he and his entourage drive off in their black SUVs.

"We'll leave it to the audience," the producer vows. "Friday, we'll see what happens."

We stop for dinner at a Saravana Bhavan diner in the Shanthi Theater complex on Mount Road. Although there's a night show of *Asal* playing inside, the parking lot is deserted, hardly anyone in sight, only a few orphaned posters of that film's star visible in the darkness.

Asal is only the latest in a lengthy series of prominent flops. Meanwhile no one has come forward to buy *Aval Peyar Tamilarasi* or to offer any substantial guarantees of revenue for its release. The producer has no choice now but to assume these risks on his own. He admits that he's worried about who will "identify" with his film.

"Good films force you to ask questions about yourself," I respond, suddenly also nervous about its fate. "*Aval Peyar Tamilarasi* does this for me, makes me ask what it is to be a man."

"I can't afford to think about success that way," the producer retorts. "Anyhow," he adds, after some time, "I thought it would be interesting for you to see our ups and downs."

⌐

Thursday afternoon. G.D. waits for his distributors in the boardroom of the Moser Baer office. We're also looking out for their promos on a flat-screen television on the wall. This is what we see: Clear antidandruff shampoo, Pepsi's Nimbooz, Unilever's Hamam soap; two Tamil film songs, featuring Prithviraj and then Jai, followed by Rin detergent and Brooke Bond's 3 Roses tea; then come ten seconds of *Aval Peyar Tamilarasi*, followed by more advertisements for Cadbury's chocolate and another detergent, called Mr. White. The film feels lost within this clamor of things, a fleetingly earnest note in the midst of a brash cavalcade.

Here is Kamal Bora, whose company will distribute the film in Chennai and northern Tamil Nadu. One of his associates puts plastic bags of cash on the boardroom table: deposits from the theaters they've booked on a commission basis. There's something lurid about these stacked bundles of notes, but G.D. is disappointed with the modest amount they represent.

The problem, Bora explains, is that theater owners have already judged it an "art film." Even he finds it slow, the distributor admits. "Who wants award? We want reward!"

Meanwhile, downstairs, the film-processing lab has delivered the reels printed for distribution. Once again there is a ritual *puja* conducted in the office with one of these circular stacks of tin. With the passing of the camphor flame, the producer gives the first of the sweets to Ashok, whose Madhura Films will release *Aval Peyar Tamilarasi* in thirteen theaters in and around Madurai.

"Take the film and hold it," G.D. tells Ashok with an entreating smile, wishing him well. This is what he means by "hold it": convince your theater owners to keep the film running for at least two or three weeks. Giving out the film on a commission basis, theater by theater, the producer has no contractual guarantee that this will happen anywhere.

Padlocked cases of film reels are lined up along the driveway downstairs, each labeled with the name of a different theater. As they await their loading onto delivery trucks, the air feels heavy with peril, as if these were troops assembling for battle. "Go home and pray," G.D. says to each of his staff, as they take their leave for the night.

"Are you okay?" I ask him in a quiet moment.

"There's nothing okay in this," he tells me. "You're giving your film away for free. No producer can do this. Would you do this? You've invested 4 crores. We have no choice."

Later, when the actor Arya calls one of his phones, G.D. puts on a more confident tone. "Good evening, big boss! . . . I've taken a gamble, sir. There's no other choice, but we've gotten very good theaters."

What happens when a producer gambles on a film? A matter of corporate investment and personal reputation, to be sure, but there are larger stakes here as well. Think of what Don Handelman and David Shulman write about the endless games of dice that Siva plays with his consort Parvati: "If one is God, there is, finally, no other game."[7] Despite the fact that Siva always loses, these matches produce the cosmos as we know it.

If filmmakers have something to do with such gods, it is not because of what they see or know. We might think instead of the consequences of their gambles, of the vast worlds of experience formed and deformed through such play. Call this a fate to create—being bound to fashion something, to make one thing happen if not another.

⊢

Friday morning at the Udhayam theater complex in western Chennai—first day, first show. Young men, some young women throng the concrete courtyard, milling about expectantly. Most of them rush into the lobby just after 11 a.m.; they're here, as it turns out, for another film also playing here, *Vinnaithandi Varuvaya*, one of the films that Anthony was editing.

Meanwhile fans of Jai seem scarce. There are two young men, Oli and Sudhakar, pinning up vinyl banners of Jai to the bars of the compound gate. They describe themselves as managers of the actor's public welfare group. "This film will definitely succeed," they promise.

Aval Peyar Tamilarasi is playing in nine cinema halls in metropolitan Chennai. At this weathered complex serving audiences of modest means, the film will run in the Mini Udhayam, the smallest of four theaters. "Look, house full," Sudhakar says, pointing out the red placard now fixed to the ticket booth.

Immediately Oli also says, "Look!," holding out his arms for me to see his bristling hair. Standing stiffly on end, these slender filaments on his arms seem to double for the mass of excitement he expects to rise inside.[8]

⊢

Within the theater, there can't be more than two hundred seats, but all of them are indeed full. It's already hot in the air-conditioned hall. "Hey, turn a fan on or something," someone calls out crossly. As the film begins to play, the loudest cheers come for Kavya, the chubby-cheeked young girl, already popular, who plays Tamilarasi as a child.

Murmurs continue in a steady stream, difficult to pick out, but the racy and off-color lines by the comedian "Ganja" Karuppu bring loud and obvious laughs. Cupping one hand over the lit screen of my phone, I begin to exchange reactions with the producer by SMS:

> 11:58:07 AM I'm at Udayam, inside. House full! Mood is good, people lively, little girl got huge cheers
> 11:59:25 AM Happy please keep updating response
> 12:23:52 AM Nice whistles and claps for Kuju Vandi song. Laughs and claps for Nakkamukka. Audience seems focused
> 12:24:18 AM Great happy

12:26:21 AM Whistles claps for Palayankottai song

12:29:38 AM Great

12:34:12 AM Nice laughs claps for Ganja Karuppu, lines working well, last one gets a whoop!

12:35:15 AM Relieved

12:37:37 AM Blu film great!! Whistles claps laughs loud! Youve got em!

12:39:54 AM Great

Then, as the first half approaches its awful culmination, I find myself nervous and uneasy, cringing for the rape I know is coming. "Hey, Jyothi, that's enough," someone calls out, as Jyothi backs Tamilarasi into one corner of the house. At first the mood in the theater remains light and mocking. Then there is silence, as he moves to grab her.

The film breaks for the intermission, and I tag along with others shuffling down a dirty hallway toward the reek of a men's urinal. Someone tells me that the film had won an award in Dubai. At least three of the young men I speak with identify themselves as assistant directors. "Screenplay okay," one says. Another finds the performances wooden. Yet another appreciates the film's realism but complains about the selection of actors such as the young girl: too well-fed to convey the film's sorrows.

ㅐ

"Sadness," Spinoza writes, "is a man's passage from a greater to a lesser perfection."[9] I can't help but think of *Aval Peyar Tamilarasi* as a sad film in this sense proposed by the early modern philosopher. I think of the glowing bugs that float in the air like wondrous stars as Jyothi and Tamilarasi walk together as children one night, then the ashes from her burned schoolbooks that slowly drift through the air in the very same way one hot afternoon after her rape and her mother's suicide.

I think of the life that Jyothi assumes in looking for her, an entire song passing with him wandering and slumping about dolefully. I think of the brothel where they finally reconcile and clasp each other once more, eight years later: like the bugs and the ashes, two people drifting through the elements toward a state of lesser perfection.

Every film gambles with the likelihood of a sad fate. Some end well, on cinema screens. Others do well, in cinema ticket booths. But, at least in Tamil cinema, almost all films fail to do nearly as well as their makers had expected them to do.

It is this kind of passage, this movement downward from a better condition into another, somewhat worse, that Spinoza had in mind when he wrote of sadness. Films are fashioned with a unison of feeling in mind, but they splinter, for the most part, into a bedlam of discordant reactions. Joy is fleeting, evanescent.

.... ⊢ ....

By 2 p.m. on Friday, reports from various theaters around Tamil Nadu have already begun to reach the producer. Ashok of Madhura Films sends G.D. an SMS:

> Sir APT shows ur passion for making good films. CONGRATS TO U & MOSER-BAER.

Attendance in Ashok's Madurai theaters has doubled between the matinee and afternoon shows, from 60 to 120 people.

Meanwhile one of Kamal Bora's men reports fewer than a hundred attending matinee shows in the districts surrounding Chennai. At the same time, he adds, word of mouth isn't bad.

On the phone from Coimbatore, another distributor says that the first half is going well with audiences there, but the second half much less so. There is also reason for confidence, he reports, as the other two films released this weekend have already proven flops.

"The reports are good, but the revenue has to pick up," G.D. tells the film's editor, Raja Mohamed, when he calls to inquire. The producer is visibly anxious, waiting now for the first online reviews of the film. "If they say it's good, you're in trouble," he explains; because of its unconventional story, the film will need the rare three and a half to four stars out of five to create a pulse of interest and draw people to theaters—otherwise they would wait to watch it on TV. With every conversation now, he is listening for unspoken tones of ambivalence and reproach.

"The film is a hit," the director reports glibly to those who call him. But when G.D. pulls up the first reviews on his laptop a short while later, the disappointment on his face is palpable, chastening. Both Rediff and Behindwoods, two widely read websites, have given the film only two and a half stars: a good but imperfect effort. Rediff reviewers missed an emotional relation between the two lead characters. And the boldfaced "verdict" from Behindwoods reads almost as a warning: "Full on tearjerker—try if you like serious movies!"

We are in G.D.'s car now, heading to a special press screening of the film. In the theater lobby, the crew of a Zee TV show called *Nambinal Nambunga* [Believe this if you will] sets up a brief interview with the producer.

"Tell us something that scared you, something interesting," they ask. G.D. tells a story about a cremation ground he used to cycle past as a child. Then he reports something else in the manner of a confession: "When we make films, what we fear is only the audience. . . . It's a real fear. No sleep."

His secretary Charu calls from the Moser Baer office. "No, not tired," I
hear him tell her. "Worried."

——————————————————————— ⊢ ———————————————————————

There was something of mine that was also released in the months before
Aval Peyar Tamilarasi opened: a book, my first, by Duke University Press.
Whenever I shared this news with filmmakers in Chennai, where I was
pursuing this fieldwork at the time, the response was always the same:
"Congratulations. How was the opening?"

What could I say? There was no opening, nothing in the way of an immediate response, no sales or reviews to track and consider. Day after
day, week after week, just that maddeningly unchanging note on Amazon
.com: "Only 10 left in stock (more on the way)."

More on the way. There was a lot to cast with these filmmakers, after
all. Like so many of them, I would also have to wait for what they called
"late pickup," the chance that some faintly kindled interest would slowly
spread, take hold.

——————————————————————— ⊢ ———————————————————————

"We'll know by this evening. . . . We'll know by Monday. . . . We'll know in
a week." Deferrals of fate greet us at every turn on Saturday, as we tour
theaters in the city of Madurai, where *Aval Peyar Tamilarasi* is playing to
mostly empty houses.

I'm traveling here with L. Padmanabhan, the film's accountant and
cashier, and a man named Sundram, hired as a local collection agent
for Moser Baer in Madurai. People here want two songs, two fights, and
plenty of comedy, Sundram tells us. "An 'award' film, too classy," is what
they're saying about this film.

"Collection is okay, a little low," the distributor Ashok's uncle admits
at the Madhura Films office. He takes out Friday's DCR, the daily collection report, and a calculator. In twelve theaters with a combined capacity
of several thousand seats, a total of only 589 people watched the evening
show yesterday. "Nothing like the amount that we expected."

Attendance has not been climbing, show by show, and it's unclear
whether this will change today. Meanwhile fresh figures keep coming
in as we talk. There's a theater in Theni, not far from where I lived and
worked on my first book, where the first show this morning drew only
twelve people.

Over the day, we visit four theaters serving diverse neighborhoods and
social classes in Madurai. Everywhere response to the film seems equally
tepid: 55 out of 860 tickets sold at Ambika this morning, 42 out of 531 at
Tamil Jeya, 78 out of 1,024 at Amirtham, 38 out of 600 at Mappillai Vina-

yagar. At an average price of Rs. 40 per ticket, this is hardly enough for theater owners to recoup even the cost of air-conditioning these cavernous halls on a day as blistering as this one.

Waiting at each set of doors for people to step out, we manage a series of brief exchanges. Our questions mostly meet with hurried reactions and polite restraint: "It's good, yes, we will come again, we will bring our families, we will tell our friends to watch." Many praise the film's attention to folk culture and traditions. Others speculate that people these days will be looking for more thrills, and speed.

The most thoughtful response comes outside that space-age cinema hall, Amirtham, from a young man named Raj who sells *appalams* for a living. His bloodshot eyes tell of a day already spent drinking. Still, there's something lucid and intriguing about what he says.

Raj and his friends, it seems, left their seats during the film's signature love song. "They stretched it out too long," he explains, talking about the scenes that preceded the song. "We were sitting there bored. So, even though this good song came next, we still had to come out."

Raj speaks as if he were a prophet of his own experience, as though he could already see, at a given moment, the insufficiency of where it would lead him. He speaks as though he were both a filmmaker and a spectator at the same time, editing the film as he ought to have felt it even as he describes what he has just felt. Clad in a lungi and a stained polyester shirt, Raj speaks as though he has already imagined a better film, another that he is ready to see.

Padmanabhan looks on with bemusement as we talk. In his late fifties, an accountant by training and disposition, he has gladly left most of the exit interviews to me. "We can't seem to say anything about the calculations that people make," he says to a theater manager as all of us crowd into a small office piled high with ledgers later that afternoon.

"Mmm," the theater manager murmurs in assent. He remains bent over his account books, inking the failings of this latest washout into a narrow column of figures.

⊢

Astrologers in contemporary India plot individual destinies as a matter of *bhagya*, shares of wealth allotted at birth.[10] These are fortunes shaped by forces working at vastly different scales, from planetary movements to the choices made in individual lives. The complicated calculations that India's astrologers make depend upon horoscope charts as well as pocket PCs. But no device has yet been created, it seems, to identify accurately the box-office share that a film may expect when it comes into the world.

My fieldwork with Tamil filmmakers began in 2007 and continued over many trips both long and short through late 2012. The films I followed — the productions whose stories compose this book — were released as early as 2007, but most appeared in 2010 and 2011. It is difficult to say exactly what happened at the Tamil box office in those years, as trade figures for the industry remain vague and elusive. Shankar's 2010 film *Enthiran*, starring Rajni Kanth, is celebrated as one of the highest-grossing Indian films of all time. The fate of most others released in those years, however, lies somewhere between the murky projections of hearsay, the desperate hype mustered up in advertisements and fan press, and the doctored prose of Wikipedia.

Some of the films I wrote about here—*Malaikottai, Billa, Tamil Padam, Paiyya, Madraspattinam, Siruthai, Vinnaithandi Varuvaya*—were definitive hits or widely acknowledged winners at the box office. The makers of others, such as *Kandein Kadhalai, Nan Mahan Alla*, and *Yuddham Sei*, look to have recouped their investments, while *Sarvam, Drohi, Bana Kathadi, Easan, Quarter Cutting, Seedan*, and many others proved disastrous outings. Selvaraghavan's honeymoon drama was never made, and Ramesh, as far as I know, is still waiting for someone to take a chance on his tale from Thirumangalam.

What accounts for success or failure in commercial cinema? What explains the divide between fortune and misfortune, fates good and bad? The filmmakers I worked with had no choice but to worry obsessively over

ıese questions. These chapters, though, have lingered on a different con-
ırn, on what it means to *live* with the fateful play of such caprice.

··· ⊢ ···

"Dum dum dum dum dum!" *Aval Peyar Tamilarasi* ends in Tamilarasi's
voice as she concludes her own story in the manner of a fairy tale, and
a procession of puppets slowly cross the screen. "And this was how our
royal prince, crossing seven seas and mountains, defeated fate and demons and all such things, rescued our princess from the hell in which
she was imprisoned, and lived a life that everyone on earth and in the
heavens would praise."

As the film's unfortunate opening drew to a close on that weekend
in March 2010, it became clear that its makers weren't trying to defeat
fate as much as cheat it, seeking some way of salvaging the prospects of
a risky and unconventional film. By that Sunday, this seemed even less
likely. Theater attendance remained low, and reviews continued to hold
out both criticism and praise. The film appeared unlikely to recover even
its publicity and distribution costs, let alone the costs of its production.

"This is a disaster," G.D. told me. "That's the fate of the film." While I
had been in Madurai, he'd been in Delhi, discussing Moser Baer's future
in film production. His head office had decided to suspend all production
of original films in Tamil and Malayalam.

As we rode over to Devi Cinemas from the Moser Baer office for another somber theater visit, the producer spoke in a continuous stream of
reflections. It seemed that an astrologer had approached him a few weeks
before the film's release, promising fantastic success. Instead what came
was "great learning, at great cost."

G.D. felt he finally understood: "Entertainment is the key to the success of a film." He had already begun to write another column for *Galatta
Cinema* with this formula in mind.

CHAPTER 19   **An Anthropology of Creation**

On the night of December 16, 2012, in south Delhi, a
young woman was savagely raped and tortured by a
gang of men, thrown from the bus on which they attacked her, and left to die. Millions around the world
followed her struggle to remain alive. Protests and
vigils took place throughout India, condemning the
prevalence of sexual violence in the country and the ab-
ject failures of official justice.

Reporters began to call her Damini, after the heroine
of a 1993 Hindi film.[1] She and her friend were returning
that night from a screening of *The Life of Pi*. Within days
of her death, a Telugu filmmaker announced plans to
make "a typical commercial entertainer" based on the
incident.[2] Critics, meanwhile, charged Indian cinema
with complicity in the attack, calling attention to its
widespread celebration of sexual aggression.

"I live in a city where the film industry has films that
actually justify rape," Uma Vangal of the L. V. Prasad Film
and TV Academy reported in one interview, speaking of
Chennai and Tamil cinema.[3] I was halfway through a
first draft of this book at the time, and I couldn't help
but think about how so many of its films depicted rape.
*Yuddham Sei, Easan, Siruthai, Nan Mahan Alla, Drohi,
Aval Peyar Tamilarasi*—each of these films at the heart
of this book took some crucial turn after an act of
sexual violence, while several others featured jokes and
threats of rape, not to mention countless other acts of
mayhem and bloodshed.

I was writing just a couple hundred miles south of
Newtown, Connecticut, where, two days before the attack in Delhi, a young man had opened fire in a first-
grade classroom at Sandy Hook Elementary School,
killing the teacher and all but one of the students. The
incident propelled yet another tortured examination

of the national soul, as always happens with gun violence in America.
Quentin Tarantino's latest crimson poem, *Django Unchained*, awaited release. Here too cinema was widely judged an accomplice and culprit.

At home in Baltimore, our baby girl, Uma, was one week old. Our son,
Karun, described lockdown drills at his nursery school. The questions
were impossible to take lightly. Why look here, of all places, for evidence
of creation? Isn't cinema a more credible opening into the anthropology
of contemporary destruction?

CREATIVE AND DESTRUCTIVE POWERS

This problem is one that has shadowed cinema for most of its modern
existence. Consider, for example, what Siegfried Kracauer had to say
about the 1920 German Expressionist classic, *The Cabinet of Dr. Caligari*. In
the hypnotic authority of the title character, who could turn even a sleeping man into a serial killer, Kracauer found a "premonition" of Hitler.
The screenwriters "must have been driven by one of those dark impulses
which, stemming from the slowly moving foundations of a people's life,
sometimes engender true visions."[4]

Cinema was also on trial in colonial India, where Hollywood productions met with "moral panic" and "impassioned alarmism," as William
Mazzarella has noted. Films were seen to have a visceral impact on the
desires and sensations of their viewers, and India's untutored masses
seemed especially susceptible to these vicious charms. For colonial authorities and Indian elites, cinema presented new opportunities as well
as dangers: Could this treacherous medium be enlisted instead to serve
the cause of social uplift, to aid in the creation of citizens appropriate to
the spirit of the times?[5]

These contrary judgments of cinema's creative and destructive powers
still commingle closely. I think of what happened when *Aval Peyar Tamilarasi* was screened for the Central Board of Film Certification in 2009.
"The message will reach people," one woman on the censor board apparently affirmed, speaking of the narrative thread, that an act as callous
as rape can destroy an entire family. But someone else on the board was
concerned that scenes of sexual aggression would work on a more sensual level: "No matter how subtly you put it, the human mind will imagine it, no?"

We often speak of cinema bearing messages, making arguments, producing justifications. But such activity is difficult to track, given that
this is thinking entangled with the body's sensations, routed through
ephemeral currents of feeling.[6] Recall that raucous scene of *Aval Peyar*

Tamilarasi's release at the Udhayam Theatre in Chennai, and the silence that descended on that small cinema hall when Jyothi grabbed Tamilarasi at the back of the storeroom. That feeling of unease seemed to have already become something else within an hour, when Jyothi found her in a brothel in Maharashtra and closed her bedroom door to beg for forgiveness. "Hey, once more, eh?" someone called out lightly, drawing whoops of laughter from a corner of the theater.

Films can make things happen—in zeal and in boredom, with contemplation and indignation, for better and for worse. But everything turns on how we conceive of this efficacy, how we understand these effects to work both in and beyond cinematic worlds. "The film experience is meaningful *not to the side of our bodies but because of our bodies*," Vivian Sobchack emphasizes.[7] Think of the predatory dream life of *Yuddham Sei* or *Easan*'s murky space of violence and exploitation. Recall the rhythm of assault and revenge that propels *Drohi* or the way that rape is settled as a matter of fate in *Aval Peyar Tamilarasi*. These visceral modes of experience, steeped with potent yet still profoundly unpredictable forces of feeling, shape what such films can do in the world.

Do these films sanction or even encourage similar acts of violence in the world of their release? An answer to this difficult problem has far more to do with the vicissitudes of cinematic experience—with the way that a film can focus and intensify an aggressive course of thought and action, in and beyond the theater—than with the simpler question of whether a story's villain learns his lesson or gets his due.

Every film is an experiment with the thoughts and feelings of its audience, trials taken up with diverse ends in mind and precipitating, so often, starkly unanticipated ends. "Films both apply techniques to us to mobilize affect and teach us about how such techniques work outside the celluloid world," William Connolly writes.[8] Affective thought is a field of both peril and promise; these chapters too have experimented with such lessons in mind.

The modes of experience tracked in this book are modes of transformative passage, diverse ways of participating in the flux of worldly life and embodied existence. And these are the kinds of possibilities at stake in the anthropology of creation that this book has tried to put forward—less a delineation of some unique domain of human creativity, or the specificity of creative cultures here or there, than an attention to those forces and processes that make human beings other than what they are.[9]

Writing of such creation does not amount to celebrating what is made. Indeed so many of these chapters detail the making of monsters, cinema's dalliance with death as well as life.

The river was running fast and brown in the Cumbum Valley that October morning in 2001. I was out on a rise across the water when Kalyani Kumar came by, looking to cut a bundle of brushwood to sell. Hacking away at the thorny mesquite, he began to talk about some of the things he'd seen. His mother swallowing poison when he was just eight years old. His leaving school and cutting wood to survive, filling a yellow bag with whatever rice he could afford after setting aside a rupee for the bus ride home. His wandering India selling fried snacks when his father turned him out of the house.

He told me about the girl he had met in a forest near Vellore, the chasteness of their four-year courtship, his promise to come back again for her one day, and then the betrayal, his decision to marry Madhu back here at home instead. "Who knows," he said with a wan smile, "I might even sell the story of my troubles as a film script one day."

Seven months later he took his own life, drinking down a bottle of pesticide.

People blamed his wife, Madhu, a social worker, and her affair with the village postmaster. "She couldn't stand to see herself with a laborer in rags," someone told me. But everyone involved in Kalyani's death seemed tormented by such images. "He died like a dog, not a man," his brother fumed. "When someone decides to die in America, they take ten people along with them." Then there was Kalyani himself, who had sat through the night beside the inky black river, I was told, consumed by a vision of the postman and his wife.

Cinema propels both life and death. In contemporary Indian villages such as this one, there are romances kindled as echoes of cinema and lovers who destroy themselves in the shadow of the screen. Critics of cinema have long attributed such deeds to the forces of feeling that the medium can unleash, the actions it can prompt with unthinking automatism. These forces and effects are no doubt real, but there is no certainty in the nature of their mechanism.

Such was the nature of the world itself as I came to see it with those I knew in the Cumbum Valley—a landscape of profound and sometimes merciless openness, one in which, as I was often reminded, "even the temple towers turn to garbage heaps" through the sheer force of natural contingency. This was a world where the lines between humans and others, the living and the inert were confounded in ever so many ways. Plowmen struggled with thievish bulls. Women wept with desiccated plants. The earth itself, as I learned to see, was ripening—with soil and

e, perhaps even with diamonds, hopefully with a force of life borne
her by the crops that were sown.

1ese powerful yet elusive forces remained on my mind when I tracked
il cinema from the rural Cumbum Valley to its cradle in the city of
Chennai. Here were figures who appeared as veritable gods from a distance, but in their company I was often reminded of the cultivators, shep-
herds, and irrigators that I knew in Kalyani's village. In a crucial sense,
these two domains of terrestrial production—cinema and agriculture—
were fundamentally alike. Both depended upon the germinal quality of
a world at hand. And whether that world was a studio set or a wetland
field, things were ripening into fullness through the play of dreams and
desire, the travails of laboring bodies, and the vagaries of a material environment.[10]

Thinking back now to my first book, an account of moral and agrarian
cultivation in the Tamil countryside, I can see that it too could have been
composed with precisely the same horizons of feeling and experience
that animate this one: the light and the color, the hope and imagination,
the rhythm and pleasure of agrarian arts. Between this pair of disparate
worlds, what comes into focus is an ecology of creative process, less an
exercise of human agency on an inert and inactive world than a way of
working resourcefully with the active potential of diverse forces, feelings,
beings, and things.

"Who has ever mastered an action?" asks Bruno Latour. "Show me
a novelist, a painter, an architect, a cook, who has not, like God, been
surprised, overcome, ravished by what she was . . . no longer doing."[11]
Throughout this book, I've sought to think closely with the thought and
work of diverse practitioners such as these. And in so doing, I've tried
to show that creation cannot be attributed solely to the "creativity" of
these human and often quite powerful and imaginative actors.[12] In fact,
in a very real sense, some of the most crucial protagonists of these chapters are the worldly agencies that each of them has followed, impersonal
forces of change such as time, sound, desire, speed, and so on. These vec-
tors of experience, I have tried to show, undo the very distinction between subjects and objects of human action.

Onion bulbs and film reels are crops bound for regional and global
markets: realms of commercial production, stocked with things made to
sell and consume. When it comes to such market wares, especially those
likely to be claimed as intellectual or cultural property, the question of
value is typically bound up with ideas of invention and originality, the
question of who owns, so to speak, these things. In this age of ubiquitous digital piracy, will the profits of commercial production reach its

official producers, creators? And do they deserve these proceeds in the first place? Is this an original or a knock-off, the fruit of cultivation or thievery?

Although these questions consume much of the popular and critical press on Indian cinema, I have largely sidestepped them here. Instead I've been working with a different idea of creative value, anchored in the forms of experience that cinema fashions and refashions. Lives must still be led in a world become cinema, in a universe of recycled images and proliferating screens. To study creation in such a world is to focus attention on what these images do, how they reveal—or conceal—the potential for a transformative movement of life.

PROCESS, HAPPENING, EMERGENCE, BECOMING

A scene of creation: *Le Mystère Picasso*, directed by Henri-Georges Clouzot, 1956. Purple ink breaks the monotony of a flat white plain, reaching up, darting to the left. Thick strokes of green spread back and forth below; a few cerulean rounds quickly appear above. With a bent line and two elliptical curves, the prone face of a sleeping figure comes into view. The purple, her hair. One arm, then another. Brown hoops with small black crosses, maybe a pattern on her dress as she dozes on the grass. All you can see are these brushstrokes, appearing as if from nowhere onto the surface of the screen.

"Each of Picasso's strokes is a creation that leads to further creation," writes André Bazin, reflecting on the film, "not as a cause leads to an effect, but as one living thing engenders another." With the camera facing one side of an opaque canvas as Picasso paints onto the other, lines and forms assume an unpredictable existence of their own. You see a vase of flowers turn into a fish and then a rooster and then a face. A matador appears over the back of a bull. The film makes no effort to assign meanings or objectives to the artist's work. "Literally nothing happens here," Bazin observes, "nothing but the carrying out over time of the artistic process."[13]

Keep in mind that this is a film composed of a series of paintings: one creative horizon unfurling within another. There are times when the film tries to step back, to give a sense of its own creation, as when Clouzot, suddenly visible, warns Picasso that he has just five minutes of film stock left to shoot with. "Just remember, if anything at all happens, you stop, and I'll stop," you see the director tell the artist, and what follows begins to cut quickly between the painter, his canvas, the director, camera, and footage counter. The action now, however, seems staged and forced, noth-

'ng like the spontaneous appearance of the paintings themselves. Conveying their emergence so beautifully, the film fails to portray effectively the conditions of its own creation.

This book has often wrestled with precisely this limit, the point at which happenings *in* cinema stumble over the happening *of* cinema. "Creation is pure waiting and uncertainty," Bazin suggests—a reminder that films, artworks, and all such things are fashioned in circumstances that far surpass the intentions of their makers. Remember that bridge over a chasm in Badami or that auto body workshop stunt gone haywire in Kuala Lumpur. What better way of engaging creation than by tracking such things as they happen?

Another word for this, for the happening of things, is *process*. We tend, typically, to think of process in terms of its endpoints, beginning with an existing object and inferring some point of origin that must have led ineluctably to this very destination. Gilbert Simondon calls it "hylomorphism," this way of thinking, hearkening back in Western societies to the classical distinction between matter (*hyle*) and form (*morph*). "Taking the constituted individual as a given," Simondon writes, "we are then led to try to recreate the conditions that have made its existence possible."[14] Given the presence of some particular thing, in other words, we look for the causes assumed to have impressed it with its form—the intentions, for example, that must have made a film what it is.

The problem with this way of approaching the emergence of things, Simondon suggests, is that it overly simplifies the process of "ontogenesis." Projecting backward in this fashion implies that any given process does no more than to produce a known and determinate entity. But, as Simondon emphasizes, "it is equally possible to maintain that becoming exists as one of the dimensions of the being, that it corresponds to a capacity beings possess of falling out of step with themselves."[15] Process pulls forward capacities of various kinds, conserving tensions rather than resolving them fully, investing things with an intrinsic degree of openness and mutability. As the English philosopher Alfred North Whitehead put it, "*How* an actual entity *becomes* constitutes *what* that actual entity *is* . . . . Its 'being' is constituted by its 'becoming.' This is the 'principle of process.'"[16]

We make a mistake when we divide up the world into finished objects and the subjects responsible for making them, Whitehead argued in his 1929 work, *Process and Reality*. Reality is always far more fluid and supple than the representations we make of it. Things are passing continuously into and out of being. Find a way of lingering with them in this movement of becoming, and you might come to see everything—a film, to be

ad *d*

sure, but even the universe itself—in a different light, as "a creative advance into novelty."[17]

It is as an anthropologist that I have pursued these philosophical intuitions, working as an ethnographer in the midst of cinematic process.[18]
Many anthropologists now work with a sense of the unprecedented challenges that human beings face: the vicissitudes of a world in upheaval,
the surfacing of crises that call into question the very meaning of a
human life, even the possibility of collective survival. Anthropological
concepts have always been cultured in the generative matrix of experience, and these conditions will no doubt require new forms of thought
as we face the challenge, in Paul Rabinow's words, "to invent concepts to
make visible what is emerging."[19]

One of the major objectives of this book has been to convey such emergence as a matter of *method* as much as a property of contemporary conditions and concepts. Examine the creation of new horizons of experience,
draw from these processes new resources for thought, but what we learn,
ultimately, has everything to do with how we partake of their charge. Like
what happened this evening, for example:

October 27, 2009. Wow. My whole body is almost vibrating with tension.
I'm on my way back now from (director) Ameer's office, where I've just explained to his manager Mahesh that all I need at this point is to capture the
moment, once or twice, in which these two, Ameer and (composer) Yuvan,
work together on Ameer's film, *Yogi*. I shared with him the analogy or the
lesson that had hit me powerfully last night, that this was not the kind of
fieldwork in which one just stayed with people for however long; this was
more like wildlife photography, where one waited and waited for hours
on end to capture a sudden glimpse of something exotic and beautiful.
I think Mahesh understands this, and he has promised to talk with Ameer
and to help.

Meanwhile, yesterday was a nightmare in terms of all of this, as I could
hardly catch Yuvan's manager Karthik on the phone for more than a few
seconds at a time. Mahesh too was difficult to reach, and I was just home
and on the toilet in fact at 6:30 when he called and said, "You can go now,
Ameer is on his way and will be there in half an hour." So I rushed out, pack-
ing a pb sandwich and knowing full well that Sanchita would be angry,
going by auto because the driver was already on his way home, only to arrive at Kalasa Studio to find them all hanging out in the hall, discussing their
show in Dubai, and Karthik calling Ameer to find that he was in a "meeting"
and would not be coming at all. In fact, I learned from Mahesh that Ameer
did go, for half an hour or so, at around nine that night. He had been with
his editor, and that had kept going.

As Mahesh put it, trying to rationalize why he himself could not say what Ameer would do, "They themselves won't know what they will be doing." Again that open-ended time of emergence coming to bite me in the ass. Lesson learned here: emergence is great to encounter but terrible to wait for and therefore a Janus-faced thing to write about.

I didn't even know, when I typed up these field notes with a furious sense of urgency a few years ago, that Janus was a Roman god of emergence, looking through a pair of doorways to the past and the future at once. Nor am I especially attached now to this image of fieldwork as bird-watching—but then, how many of the thoughts scattered through the fields of our work manage actually to ripen into communicable ideas? To me, these notes are more compelling for their embodiment of creative process: the clamor and the tumult, the broken promises, the rushed sandwiches and abortive shittings through which a book like this might come into being.

As with the book, so with the many films at its heart. What, after all, was this moment that I was trying so desperately to witness? Nothing so dramatic as *The Creation of Cinema*. Nothing but one among a multitude of more minor events, a term in a series of instances, the consolidation of a particular form—a background score—in a field of chaotic flux.

In anthropology, we've grown accustomed to counterposing events and structures as opposing poles in an intellectual vocabulary: there is the undisciplined and eruptive chaos of worldly circumstance, then there are the frameworks and categories we impose to explain and domesticate this unruly field of events. We tend still to neglect what you might call the event *of* structure, the happening of forms, not as abstract codes that organize and confine life from without but as the very arrangements through which both empirical phenomena and conceptual knowledge take shape and evolve.[20] "Man is a mediator of things, a kind of universal catalyst," Roy Wagner observes. "But he is also able, in the most elemental sense, to make himself permeable to things, to 'become' in his thoughts, identifications, and imaginings, the things around him, to make them a part of his knowing, acting, and being."[21]

To emerge, etymologically, is to rise up out of a liquid.[22] Whitehead had a name for this kind of movement: "concrescence," the process through which a flux of many things comes together as some one thing new.[23] Perhaps wildlife photography isn't such a far-fetched image for the pursuit of such creation—ethnography as much less a matter of immersion in a fluid medium, to use the aqueous metaphor associated most often with anthropological fieldwork, than a gamble on encounters with possible forms.[24]

What does it mean to wait and watch for something happening? What does it mean to be present in the midst of such process, to discern and grasp the novelty of its circumstance? Fieldwork for this project was difficult, sometimes even torturous, because it demanded something like a spiritual retooling.[25] Dwelling in what remained formless, trying to attune myself to the germination of possible forms, opening myself to the passage of their force and the many accidents of their collapse: at first these seemed like bracing and unfamiliar habits to cultivate, but then, over time, they began to feel like the very embodiment of an anthropological sensibility.[26]

All those experiments, then, scattered throughout this book, those scenes of a writer trying to rejigger his own conditions of sensation and reflection — take these as attempts to intensify and make palpable what can always happen with ethnographic fieldwork and writing. Strange, yes, the way that a song can break open when you listen to it a thousand times over, such that you begin to hear and feel something new with every further repetition. But isn't this the kind of chance we've always courted in anthropology, returning time and again to the same tea stall bench, the same front stoop, struck by something remarkable in the ordinary?[27]

MODES OF EXPERIENCE AND EXPRESSION

Here's another scene of creation, this time a king, maybe even a god, Vishnu Purushottama, wandering through a garden looking for his beloved. Her name is Bhavana (Imagination). The king, in fact, is in love with his own imagination. Having taken the form of a young woman, she is invisible to him, but he can see her reflection on the polished face of a glossy moonstone. The image betrays the pallor of lovesickness, as she too has fallen for him. The love-struck king embraces the stone, but when Bhavana herself, still invisible, steps away from the stone, her reflection also disappears. The king plunges into a bout of madness and suddenly begins to see her everywhere, embracing every vine and creeper in the garden. Soon enough, this oddest of couples, a man and his imagination, will come together in marriage.

This moment in a Sanskrit court drama from the sixteenth century south Indian kingdom of Senji, argues David Shulman, is far from a scene of illusion or deception. What the king's imagination does here is real; the reflection of his lover, paradoxically, is far more real and forceful than the original being reflected on that rock. "The spectator is drawn into the frame of the artistic production," Shulman writes. "This frame then tends to dissolve, leaving the erstwhile spectator stranded within an imaginative world of undoubted integrity, fictive though it may be, where something novel and unexpected may begin to emerge."[28]

We see the workings here of a generative vision, one that imagines a world, even a universe of life, into being. But this is not an allegory of creation ex nihilo, Shulman emphasizes: this is not the making of something out of nothing. What surfaces always appears as a kind of enhancement or intensification of what already exists, a novel perspective on the fullness of what is already, albeit imperceptibly, present. As Purushottama himself will marvel, "The tiny has become immense, and everything looks to me like a painting."[29]

What happens when everything begins to look like a painting, or, for that matter, like a film? Shulman's reflections on the imagination in sixteenth-century south India touch on problems of far broader relevance, raising questions about the very way we take arts such as painting, poetry, drama, and indeed cinema to work.[30]

Are such endeavors best understood to *represent*—to depict, picture, or portray—some reality that lies beyond them? Certainly there are many things that purport to do just this, with varying degrees of persuasion. But throughout this book, I've been working with a rather different idea of what creative works do in relation to the reality of the world: that they *express* that reality—like Purushottama's moonstone—in a deeper or fuller fashion, that they give body, that is, to an unseen dimension of its potential.[31]

Take the world that is conjured by a work of art—the world, say, of a film. We often think of this world as bounded off from the ordinary world beyond it: as a space framed by the rectangle of the screen, a time framed by the beginning and end of a story. "In order to watch a movie," James Conant writes, "we need to be able to distinguish between what is an event that is happening in the world of the movie and what is not."[32]

This distinction may appear straightforward, but it's a line transgressed by almost everything these chapters have tried to convey. Think of Karthi's reverence for Bruce Lee's apparent acrobatics. Think of the crowds gathered around that shoot, clapping thunderously for each faux blow. Think of the anthropologist in their midst, possessed as well by the force of heroism. The frame cannot hold. Cinema spills over. The condition is pervasive, what Jean Rouch calls "film-trance," confounding reality with imagination, the world with the screen, the tangible and the elusive.[33]

How to write with such a world in mind? Again, we're most acquainted with certain habits of representation: judging from a distance, taking ourselves out of the picture, isolating an object from the chaotic field enveloping it, parsing out the difference between how it appears and what

it must really be. Here, though, I've tried to write from someplace closer
to things, allowing them, as best I can, to seep into, even contaminate the
language of description.[34] As William James wrote in 1905, "Only in so far
as they lead us, successfully or unsuccessfully, back into sensible experience again, are our abstracts and universals true or false at all."[35]

The pursuit of this kind of truth—the exercise of this kind of empirical science—has long had a place in anthropology, one of the strangest
of the academic enterprises to evolve alongside cinema in the twentieth
century.[36] "Is not every ethnographer something of a surrealist," James
Clifford asks, "a reinventor and reshuffler of realities?"[37] Take, as he does,
the West African Grebo mask that Picasso acquired in 1905 or the blue
plastic Adidas bag where a native cricketer might have stashed his betel
nuts in the Trobriand Islands. Anthropological works don't just describe
these curious worlds of unexpected possibility; they conjure them, convey the sensation of falling into them, through writing that can sometimes, as Michael Taussig suggests, "open up reality like a lever heaving
up a slab of ice at the edge of the frozen river we call life."[38]

It's an arresting image, no doubt, from an anthropologist who often
likens ethnography to cinema.[39] I don't know if you can see or imagine
that lever, that slab of ice, that frozen river as you read this page. But
the possible force of such images is something that I've sought to work
with throughout the writing of this book—to take up such images less
as illusory sensory traps that the body lays for the mind than as means
of bringing our thinking around to a more robust encounter with experience. "Obstinate and stubborn, it forces us to think, and forces us to
think what is concealed from thought," writes Deleuze: "life."[40]

Take those photographs, those snapshots fixed to the opening of each
of these chapters: I hoped they might work like cinematic frames, with
their 2.39:1 widescreen aspect ratio and the juxtapositions they assumed
with the words that followed. Or take the structure of the chapters themselves, each composed as a montage of images and episodes in which
the most significant points often come precisely in the gaps between.
"Juxtaposition of perspectives through montage is a key cinematic tool
for evoking the invisible, without reducing it to forms of visibility," Christian Suhr and Rane Willerslev suggest.[41] For me, writing this way was a
matter of intellectual value as much as aesthetic taste. I worked with the
idea that thoughts are never simply given by a text; they happen only
in the event of encounter, and there is always here the question of how.

This book too, in other words, has come together like the films it engages: as a series of wagers on the creative reach of experience. This is why
each of the chapters moves outward from a specific cinematic operation
into some mode of experience that the operation puts most concretely

into play. It has much to do with the various ventures in narrative register that these chapters undertake. It also has a lot to do with the patterns of grammatical tense into which the prose fell as it was written, such as the way that each chapter tends to begin with past events before breaking into the ongoing unfolding of something in the present tense. Take these movements as gestures to the "imaginative possibility" of thinking with the flux of sensory experience, to borrow a phrase from Vincent Crapanzano: "to hope, to the optative, to moods, like the subjunctive, borne by our grammars."[42]

The subjunctive in English concerns what might or could be, and whatever concepts or ideas that emerge from these chapters have also surfaced often in this mood: "Take this . . . suppose that . . . what if. . . ." My hope in using these tones has been to lead readers accustomed to looking chiefly for arguments back into the empirical thickets from which these arguments arise. Ethnography depends upon an enchantment with the unknown promise of worldly circumstance, with, in Ghassan Hage's words, the "minor and invisible spaces or realities that are lurking in the world around us."[43] Perhaps it's time to admit that the ideas taking form through these alchemical encounters are best understood as fables— exercises in a decidedly speculative or, better yet, mythical realism.[44]

"Since it has no interest in definite beginnings or endings, mythological thought never develops any theme to completion," Lévi-Strauss wrote in his "overture" to The Raw and the Cooked. "There is always something left unfinished." With these words, in 1964 Lévi-Strauss described his treatise on mythology as itself a myth, akin to the movement of an incomplete symphony, a form that might come together only "behind or beyond the text," that might only "become a reality in the mind of the reader."[45]

Theory as reverie, as vision of another reality—we need such visions, still.

PERSPECTIVE ON THE WORLD

One of the great myths of our time concerns the promise of a global vision, of seeing things with the power, distance, and clarity of an all-encompassing vantage point, what Donna Haraway once called "the god trick."[46] It is no surprise that the first photographs to give this kind of perspective on the Earth as a whole, taken by the astronauts of the Apollo missions of the 1960s and 1970s, were met with such wildly utopian en-
asm.

is is how the Apollo 9 astronaut Russell Schweikart put it, recall-
ow Earth looked on the long spacewalk he took in 1969: "There you

are. Hundreds of people killing each other over some imaginary line that
you're not even aware of, that you can't see. And from where you see it,
the thing is a whole, and it's so beautiful. You wish you could take a person in each hand, and say, 'Look. Look at it from this perspective. Look
at that. What's important?'"[47]

These new images of the Earth as a fragile ball sailing through the
black void of space gave tremendous impetus to the Western environ-
mental movements of that time; indeed, as the historian Robert Poole has
suggested, the Apollo 17 photograph of the Earth as a small blue marble
may well be the most widely reproduced image in human history.[48] The
redemptive potential of these images has since proved illusory, and our
world remains caught in the same impasses they were enlisted to break.
Still, though, the questions remain: What kind of perspective will human
beings need to grapple with the perils of this Anthropocene? Do we need
more of the lucid vision of daylight or the imaginative powers of some
other kind of dream? What will it take to nurture and sustain this kind
of vision?

Over the years in which this book has taken shape, I've been thinking
a lot about cinema but also about the inclinations that we bring to such
fields of vision as scholars and critics. We encounter powerful images and
we try to look behind them. We find reveries and we want to dispel them.
We meet with mythic figures and we cut them down to size. Things seem
to leap and tilt vertiginously, so we put them back in place. Irony is the
prevailing mood of the human sciences.[49] *Yes but no, not really, not quite.*

Perhaps, as public citizens, we owe it to others to point out what they
themselves fail to see, in the world at large and the circumstances of
their lives. But there is something to be said as well for another kind of
perspective on the world, neither global nor transcendental, a vantage
point more deeply implicated in the force and momentum of what we encounter and engage.

Consider this reflection by Walter Benjamin: "Just as a child learns to
grasp by stretching out his hand for the moon as it would for a ball, so
humanity, in its efforts at innervation, sets its sights as much on pres-
ently still utopian goals as on goals within reach."[50]

With this bygone term from neurophysiology, *innervation*, Benjamin
had in mind an antidote to the numbing shock of technological modernity and its sensory overload. And this kind of therapy depended upon
the workings of what he called the "mimetic" faculty: the capacity to see
correspondences between distant things, such as between a ball and the
moon—or even, perhaps, between the Earth and a marble.

What is important about this kind of vision, Miriam Hansen emphasizes, is that it brings into play an unexpected kinship between objects

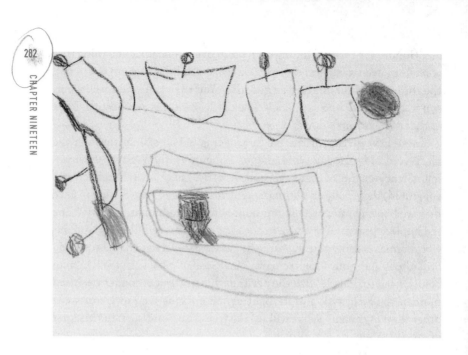

and observers; here is a way of looking out at the world "from the inside of things" rather than gazing upon them from a distance, in the manner that a child may reach out for the moon as though it were a ball already at hand.[51] For Benjamin, children see like cinema sees, an essential complicity, for hope for the future can be grasped only through the wonder of such perspective.

"The child," Benjamin observed in 1933, "plays at being not only a shopkeeper or teacher, but also a windmill and a train."[52] If he had composed these thoughts now, in the America of this writing, he would no doubt have added the figure of the pirate to this list.

There's a picture that my son, Karun, drew when he was a little more than three years old. A drawing of several ships, we thought at first, when he brought the picture home one evening from his nursery school. But then he told us that it was just one pirate ship, leaving from home, stopping along the way to do a little fishing, then finally reaching that blue-green ball of treasure in the corner. "That's the same one and the same one and the same one and the same one," he told me. "It's showing how it's going there, to the treasure."

A peculiar amalgam of movement and stillness, a moving image — when Karun explained all this to me that evening, I was possessed by the sense that the child had sketched a movie onto that sheet of white paper. There was that series of frames, so much like the nineteenth-century stop-motion chronophotography of Eadweard Muybridge and Etienne-Jules Marey. There were also those shifts in perspective as the ship rounded two bends, from a house with a chimney then along one edge to the top of the sheet. The image makes no sense unless you look *with* the ship as it moves rather than looking from some fixed point outside the scene.

Karun was born in Baltimore, a city known to the world mostly through a documentary cinema-style television show, *The Wire*. Fake pirate ships cruise the harbor and crime stories pervade the space of the city, as dystopian as many of the filmic settings in this book. These are realities that, despite our best efforts, seep into the experience of our children. There was that episode around the time that Karun drew this picture, when the road to his nursery school was blocked off one afternoon with helicopters, SWAT teams, and vivid cinematic drama for what turned out to be no more than a backpack forgotten in a parking lot. Or what is happening here now, in late April 2015, as this book goes to press: a wave of protests and civil unrest in the wake of a brutal death in police custody, with countless observers recalling *The Wire*, speculating on scenes that resemble and perhaps even owe their genesis to the looting and mayhem of a 2013 Hollywood film, and circulating more heartening images meant to dispel this sense of a fatalistic script come to life.[53]

I can't say why Karun made that kind of drawing, on that one day a few years back and no other day since. I often wonder, though, about the hope of the journey it sketches, especially when I think of the redemptive powers often granted these days to film and video. Cinematic vision is everywhere now, in this era of YouTube and Google Street View, bodycams and ubiquitous security monitors. While there is much that is troubling in this proliferation of digital eyes and ears, that utopian promise still remains: seeing and experiencing the world from the multifarious standpoint of its things, rather than from a dominating distance.

I think of how my young son plays with little cars, rocks, and plastic animals, how he bends to the ground to look from the heart of wherever those small props are in the world—just like, in fact, the many filmmakers scattered throughout this book. I once asked Karun why he does this, dropping down to play from the vantage point of such little things. "It looks like they're real," he told me. "It looks like they're one of us. It looks like they can talk to us."

In anthropology, there is a name for this kind of vision, this way of seeing everything around us—whether human or not, organic or not—as potentially a person, as having a point of view that can be occupied and made real. Eduardo Viveiros de Castro calls it "perspectivism," a "conception of the world as being composed of a multiplicity of points of view," perspectives that do something more unsettling than offer many ways of looking at the same essential reality.[54] From the standpoint of the Amerindian cosmology where Viveiros de Castro finds this idea at work, "all beings see the world in the *same* way—what changes is the *world* that they see."[55] At stake here, in other words, is something profound: the reconstitution of what is real.

With a child at play, in the mythological corpus of the Amazon, in the experience of Tamil cinema or the mode of storytelling through which this book has pursued it—wherever one may find such ideas and practices, what is crucial to grasp is the promise they bear for reconceiving the world at hand, and the possibility of working creatively with this promise.

Looking from the ground, the Earth, the lives of its beings and the potential for change their experience bears—now, more than ever, we need this kind of vision.

ACKNOWLEDGMENTS

The sun and the moon, the window's light and rustling leaves, the roots and bricks on the paths that lead to the cinder-block box in which this book was mostly written, the silence here and the coffee's buzz, the bathroom down the hall and the shower at home, the thoughts that came and went and sometimes lingered long enough to write them down, the films themselves, their sound and feeling, the images that stayed and the others that disappeared only to resurface so unexpectedly, the fuzzy gray caterpillar that suddenly fell from my desktop monitor one morning, the heaps of books and papers along which it crept, these keys under my fingers even now and the invisible circuits they press—writing is a solitary activity, they often say, but I am profoundly grateful for the creative company of all such ordinary things and more.

The people are more easily identified, though here too their multitudes will elude my grasp. In the midst of the processes and worlds that these chapters describe are the filmmakers who humored my presence, questions, and naïve impulses. I am most deeply indebted to the central figures in this book—Mysskin, G. Dhananjayan, M. Sasikumar, Rajeevan Nambiar, Selvaraghavan, Nirav Shah, Pushkar and Gayathri, Vishnu Vardhan, Karthi Sivakumar, Debi Dutta, Yuvan Shankar Raja, Sreekar Prasad, Sudha K. Prasad, Anthony Gonsalvez, and S. T. Venki—for their generosity in our countless exchanges, their perceptive reflections on these chapters, and the goodwill of their associates and assistants. Then there is that filmmaker and film thinker, almost a Tamilian himself with a foothold in colonial Ceylon—I am profoundly grateful to Walter Murch for his depth of insight and scope of imagination.

A number of institutions provided essential support for the research and writing of this book: the National Science Foundation, the American Institute of Indian Studies, the Wenner-Gren Foundation for Anthropological Research, the Hampton Fund of the University of British Columbia, and Johns Hopkins University. Nor could the book have happened without the goodwill of the production companies that allowed me to watch their projects unfold: Lone Wolf Productions, Moser Baer Entertainment, Company Productions, Studio Green Productions, Sri Lakshmi Productions, Kanagarathna Movies, Aum Films, AGS Entertainment, Y Not Studios, Ananda Picture Circuit, Ayngaran International, Sathyajyothi Films, Teamwork Production House, Indira Innovations, Frame Works, EFX, Lakshmi Shanthi Movies, and Myth Productions. Sometime in the midst of fieldwork, I began to imagine Duke University Press, analogically, as the "producer" of this particular venture, and I am grateful to Ken Wissoker and the staff at the Press for their faith and enthusiasm — and indeed for their gamble.

Although this book ultimately took the form of a few close studies, it depends throughout on lessons gleaned from the experience of hundreds of others I met on the studio floors and in the movie halls and byways of Tamil cinema. I am most indebted to the following individuals for our candid interviews and interactions: the actors Ajith, Andrea Jeremiah, Anil Menon, Arya, Dhanush, Kamal Haasan, Jiiva, Nasser, Padmapriya, Pooja Umashankar, Prabhu Ganesan, Priyamani, Raviprakash, Shiva, Sivakumar, Tamannah Bhatia, and Vishal; the art directors J. K., Milan, R. K. Naguraj, Raghavan, Rembon, Sabu Cyril, Santhanam, Selvakumar, Thotta Tharani, and Trotsky Marudu; the choreographers Baski, Bobby, and Shanthi; the cinematographers K. V. Anand, Kadhir, Ramji, P. C. Sreeram, Suresh, Vaidhi, and Velraj; the directors Ameer, C. S. Amuthan, Badri Venkatesh, Balaji Shakthivel, Balu Mahendra, Bhoopathi Pandian, Cheran, Lingusamy, Meera Kathiravan, Sasi, Siruthai Siva, Suresh, Susindran, Thankar Bachan, Vasantha Balan, A. L. Vijay, and most especially Bharathiraja; the editors Lenin, Raja Mohamed, and V. T. Vijayan; the lyricists Vairamuthu and Yugabharathi; the managers and associates Arjun, Ashok, Karthik, Mahesh, Prabhu, Swami, Udaykumar, and Viswam; the music directors G. V. Prakash, James Vasanthan, and Srikanth Deva; PRO Nikil Murugan; the producers Mano Akkineni, Alagappan, Kalaipuli Dhanu, Ramkumar Ganesan, Ajay Kumar, S. R. Prabhu, M. Saravanan, S. Sashikanth, and T. G. Thyagarajan; the singers Haricharan and Tanvi Shah; the stunt masters Ganesh and Kanal Kannan; the travel consultant N. Ramji; and the visual effects specialists Vijaya Baskar, K. Himakumar, Srinivas M. Mohan, Veera Satheesh, Milli Singhal, and Harish Vijayakumar. Many others in India provided counsel, guidance, and perspective on this work, especially Film News Anandan, Theodore Baskaran, P. Bose, V. Geetha, K. Hariharan, Kamalalayan, Rakesh Khanna, Malaichamy, Mita Kapur, Mohan Krishnan, Kamini Mahadevan, Baradwaj Rangan, R. Sivapriya, A. R. Venkatachalapathy, Su. Venkatesan, old friends of many years in the Cumbum Valley, and the inimitable M. S. S. Pandian, who did so much to set me along the path that this book takes, as with everything else I've ever tried to think through in Tamil Nadu.

A few magnanimous souls — Bill Connolly, Elizabeth Davis, Jim Gibbons, Stuart McLean, David Platzer, Hugh Raffles, David Shulman, Katie Stewart, Bernadette Wegenstein, and the students in my fall 2013 Ethnographic Writing seminar — shared incisive and invaluable reflections on a full draft of this book, as did Susan Seizer and one other reviewer for Duke University Press. My colleagues in anthropology at Johns Hopkins — Veena Das, Jane Guyer, Niloofar Haeri, Clara Han, Juan Obarrio, Debbie Poole, and especially Naveeda Khan — nurtured and sustained this project in ever so many ways, as has Chitra Venkatramani, who designed that other character ⊣ that appears throughout these pages. I am grateful to William Brown, Ashish Chadha, Venkatesh Chakravarthy, Tejaswini Ganti, Lalitha Gopalan, Steve Hughes, Anupama Kapse, David Martin-Jones, Ashish Rajadhyaksha, Jackie Stacey, Ravi Vasudevan, and Claire Wilkinson-Weber for welcoming me into cinema studies, and to friends, colleagues, and students for their reflections on the substance of these chapters — among them, Barney Bate, Jane Bennett, Dominic Boyer, Andrew Brandel, Dipesh Chakrabarty, Frank Cody, Lawrence Cohen, Vincent Crapanzano, Bob Desjarlais, Sara Dickey, Assi Doron, Bill Egginton, Adam Frank, Daniella Gandolfo, Angela Garcia, Ilana Gershon, Tobias Hecht, Ann Gold, Brian Goldstone, Stefan Helmreich, Charles Hirschkind, Laura-Zoe Humphreys, Preminda Jacob, Michael Jackson, Jake Kosek, Victor Kumar, Rajan Kurai, Adrie Kusserow, Noushin Khushrushahi, Bridget Kustin, James Laidlaw, Brian Larkin, Rochona Majumdar, Atreyee Majumder, Purnima Mankekar, Paola Marrati, William Mazzarella, Bret McCabe, Todd Meyers, Donald Moore, Tahir Naqvi, Costas Nakassis, Todd Ochoa, Stefania Pandolfo, Amit Rai, Bhavani Raman, Lucinda Ramberg, Maya Ratnam, Megha Sehdev, Bhrigu Singh, Pete Skafish, Allen Stack, Rebecca Stein, Lisa Stevenson, Mick Taussig, Brian Tilley, Boris Wiseman, Gustavo Valdivia, Selvaraj Velayutham, Marieke Wilson, Jeni Wolowic, and the students in my spring 2014 seminar Cinema and Ethnography.

Discussions of this work at the Australian National University, the Center for the Study of Developing Societies in Delhi, Columbia University, Cornell University, Harvard University, Indiana University-Bloomington, Jawaharlal Nehru University, Johns Hopkins University, the London School of Economics, Northeastern University, Rice University, the School of American Research, Syracuse University, the University of California–Berkeley, the University of California–Davis, the University of California–Irvine, the University of California–San Diego, the University of Chicago, the University of Pennsylvania, the University of Technology–Sydney, the University of Texas–Austin, Yale University, and numerous conference settings have helped tremendously in clarifying and sharpening the arguments and stakes of various chapters.

I am grateful to my parents, Lalitha and M. Ganesa Pandian, for making Tamil films an integral part of — even the soundtrack to — my

ACKNOWLEDGMENTS

American childhood, and for nourishing the curiosity with which this book unfolds. Conversations on art and aesthetics with my brother Karthik weave throughout these pages, as does what I've learned from my sister Vidhya's deep care for the everyday. It has been a privilege to talk through these films and ideas with my in-laws newly moved to Baltimore, Devika and K. B. Nair. My children, Karun and Uma, were both born in these years; they taught me how to play my way through these chapters and their trials even when I mostly wanted just to whine. And then there's Sanchita—dream, light, love, and hope, wonder in the world and so much more.

NOTES

CHAPTER 1. REEL WORLD

1. *Enga Ooru Kavalkaran* [Our village watchman], directed by T. P. Gajendran (Madras: Meenakshi Arts, 1988).

2. Benjamin, "The Work of Art in the Age of Its Technological Reproducibility," 114.

3. Reported by "Kerry," in Bull, *Sound Moves*, 46.

4. See the discussion of "Julieta" in Han, *Life in Debt*, 150–66.

5. Neal Gabler, "This Time, the Scene Was Real," *New York Times*, September 16, 2001.

6. Gold and Gold, "The 'Truman Show' Delusion."

7. *The Truman Show*, directed by Peter Weir (New York: Scott Rudin Productions, 1998).

8. As Elsaesser and Hagener observe, "The cinema seems poised to leave behind its function as a 'medium' (for the representation of reality) in order to become a 'life form' (and thus a reality in its own right)" (*Film Theory*, 12).

9. Sobchack, *The Address of the Eye*, 133. As with Sobchack's foundational work, this book attempts to engage the material and embodied experience of cinema. What follows here parts company with her approach, however, in the nature of our respective engagements with that experience. *The Address of the Eye* takes film as "an animate, conscious 'other' who visually, audibly, and kinetically intends toward the world or toward its own conscious activity in a structure of *embodied* engagement with the world and others that is similar in structure to our own" (285). I pay closer attention to forces, flows, and relations that undo the subjective integrity of film spectators and confound such attempts to put forward a parallel integrity of film as subject. *The Address of the Eye* also relies upon an understanding of "the filmmaker" as "the concrete, situated, and synoptic presence of the many persons who realized the film as concretely visible for vision" (9). My endeavor unfolds through the manifold fields of experience in which filmmakers both find and lose themselves, complicating once again the coherence of this figure and "its" experience. For a useful survey of various strands of "phenomenological" approaches to film, see del Rio, "Film."

10. Deleuze, *Cinema 1*, 59.

11. Although, in what follows, I write at times of "a" or "the" world, and at other times instead of "worlds," I seek throughout to grapple with the ways that media such as cinema transform and multiply what is real. As Nelson Goodman observes in *Ways of Worldmaking*, "the so-called possible worlds of fiction lie within actual worlds. Fiction operates in actual worlds in much the same way as nonfiction. Cervantes and Bosch and Goya, no less than Boswell and Newton and Darwin, take and unmake and remake and retake familiar worlds, recasting them in remarkable and sometimes recondite but eventually recognizable—that is *re-cognizable*—ways" (105).

12. Connolly, *A World of Becoming*, 70.

13. "A look at making media can transform our understanding of how media works," Ian Condry writes in *The Soul of Anime*, 44. For other ethnographic engagements with media production, see Mayer et al., *Production Studies*; Ginsburg et al., *Media Worlds*. As W. J. T. Mitchell affirms in *What Do Pictures Want?*, "Media are not just materials, but . . . material *practices* that involve technologies, skills, traditions, and habits" (198).

14. More recent ethnographies of American film production include Dornfeld, *Producing Public Television*; Caldwell, *Production Culture*; Ortner, *Not Hollywood*. See Ganti, *Producing Bollywood*, for an ethnographic examination of Hindi film production in Mumbai.

15. Powdermaker, *Hollywood*, 284–85.

16. Powdermaker, *Hollywood*, 306. Tellingly, this chapter is titled "Emerging from Magic."

17. "The expression and elicitation of emotion in film is a central element of the film experience," Plantinga argues in *Moving Viewers*, 5. Plantinga refers these effects to the nature of films themselves—"Films are designed to appeal to, or to 'fit' the human psyche" (222)—in a manner that appears to belie the deep indeterminacy with which they are both made and received. My approach to cinematic affect and experience has more in common with the German critical tradition discussed by Hansen in *Cinema and Experience*, which "stresses the subject's precarious mobility rather than a stable position of perception vis-à-vis an object" (xiv). Furthermore, while there have been numerous ways in which terms such as *feeling*, *affect*, and *sensation* have been distinguished from each other—see, for example, Shouse, "Feeling, Emotion, Affect"—my ethnographic findings have led me to use these terms interchangeably.

18. See Handelman and Shulman, *God Inside Out*.

19. Rarely did I encounter the "paternalism and condescension expressed toward audiences" that the anthropologist Tejaswini Ganti found among Bollywood filmmakers in the 1990s, as she reports in *Producing Bollywood* (7). Here the audience never seemed that far away, with filmmakers insisting time and again instead, "I'm the first audience for my films."

20. For another anthropologist grappling with such challenges, see Ortner, "Access."

21. Habitual attention solely to the directors and actors of well-known films, Lotte Hoek argues in *Cut-Pieces*, a recent and vivid ethnography of a Bangladeshi action film, threatens to "leave the stuntmen, projectionists, sweepers, censor board investigators, and other everyday laborers of film culture in the dusty and easily forgotten corners of film scholarship" (5–6). I too, like Hoek, had intended at one point to follow a single film from its inception to its release; as I detail in the following chapter, however, the circumstances of my field research made this aspiration impossible to fulfill. On working with actors positioned diversely in the filmmaking process, see also Mayer, *Below the Line*; Wilkinson-Weber, "The Dressman's Line."

22. James, "A World of Pure Experience," in *Essays in Radical Empiricism*, 71. See also Jackson, "Introduction."

23. In thinking with the many beings, things, forces, and relations that populate this field of contemporary practices, I owe a great deal to the work of Bruno Latour. Like his recent book, *An Inquiry into Modes of Existence* (*AIME*), the present endeavor also aspires toward "an anthropology of the Moderns," although the media-savvy moderns populating this one are not equivalent to "Whites," as is curiously the case

for Latour's *AIME* (478). More importantly, while I share with Latour a commitment to the radical empiricism of William James and others, there is a crucial shift of emphasis in deflecting this method through modes of experience rather than modes of existence. Latour encourages attention to distinctive kinds of beings, speech, and world as a way of discriminating "tonalit[ies]" of modern experience (see his "Biography of an Inquiry," 288). I take modes of experience (speed, light, rhythm, and so on) as distinctive ways of putting existence into play, as concrete paths of becoming-otherwise opened up by specific complexes of beings, speech, and world. If we seek indeed to reach, both conceptually and practically, as does Latour, those modes of "being-as-other" that have been "at once most elaborated by the other collectives and most ignored by our own" (288), the discrete forms of transformative potential lodged in such modes of experience will prove essential resources.

24. For a vivid series of anthropological case studies that situate individual creative personae in relation to the intrinsic generativity and dynamism of social and cultural circumstance, see *Creativity/Anthropology*, edited by Lavie et al.

25. I am indebted here to the philosophy of expression articulated by Deleuze in *Expressionism in Philosophy*.

26. Nietzsche, *The Will to Power*, no. 796.

27. For a critique of this position, see Ingold, *Making*.

28. McLean, "Stories and Cosmogonies," 234, 216.

29. "*Dasavatharam* in Trouble," Sify Movies, last updated May 28, 2008, http://www.sify.com/movies/boxoffice.php?id=14682530&cid=2363.

30. Central Board of Film Certification, "Annual Report 2011," 18.

31. Motion Picture Association of America, "Theatrical Market Statistics 2011." In the United States as in India, fewer films are actually released each year than are rated for release.

32. Hughes, "House Full," and "What Is Tamil about Tamil Cinema?"

33. Hughes, "What Is Tamil about Tamil Cinema?"

34. For a useful overview, see Velayutham, *Tamil Cinema*.

35. Hughes, in "What Is Tamil about Tamil Cinema?," describes new concerns for linguistic purity onscreen, critical pressures to incorporate Carnatic classical music, and close attention to the religious heritage of Tamil Saivism at the time.

36. Pandian, *The Image Trap*.

37. See Dickey, *Cinema and the Urban Poor*; Srinivas, *Megastar*.

38. See my "Cinema in the Countryside" for more on this film and related phenomena.

39. See, for example, Pradeep Sebastian, "Beyond Old Kollywood," *The Hindu*, January 13, 2008. For a close examination of one such film, see Sasikumar and Pandian, *Subramaniyapuram*.

40. Composed by the poet "Kadhal" Mani and performed to music at the launch of the Tamil film *Aravan* on July 16, 2010, at Hotel Green Park in Chennai.

41. See Jan Brouwer's study of Indian artisans in *The Makers of the World*.

42. I remain indebted to Dipesh Chakrabarty's reflections on the "originality" of India's postcolonial modernity in *Provincializing Europe*.

43. Coomaraswamy, *The Arts and Crafts of India and Ceylon*, xii. It is important to acknowledge that Coomaraswamy himself conceived of Indian craft traditions in unitary and idealized terms, lamenting their degradation by colonial modernity. As Partha Mitter observes in *Much Maligned Monsters*, "in many ways Coomaraswamy

was the last of the Neoplatonists and the image of Indian art he fashioned was essentially Idealistic" (290).

44. Tolstoy, *Hadji Murat*, 3.

45. See Seifrid, "Gazing on Life's Page." I'm grateful to Anne Eakin Moss for bringing this article to my attention.

46. Cited in Seifrid, "Gazing on Life's Page," 443.

47. For a useful survey of cinematic devices in twentieth-century American fiction, see Seed, *Cinematic Fictions*. See also McCourt, *Roll Away the Reel World*, on reflections from Joyce such as this one: "Whenever I am obliged to lie with my eyes closed I see a cinematograph going on and on and it brings back to my memory things I had almost forgotten" (9).

48. Malinowski, *Argonauts of the Western Pacific*, 4.

49. On Malinowski's Trobriands as a British colony, see Taussig, *What Color Is the Sacred?*, 106–29.

50. Although the argument has been made that Malinowski's style was more "painterly" than "cinematic" (Grimshaw, *The Ethnographer's Eye*, 56), I find the cinematic interpretation sustained by passages such as these, or reflections such as this one from his Trobriand field diaries: "Walls of rain shut out the view of the mountain and then shift and reveal it again—the damp velvety sheen of the vegetation, the marvelously deep shadows, the freshness of the stones darkened by the rain, the outline of the mountains through the curtains of rain, like shadows of reality projected on the screen of appearances" (*A Diary in the Strict Sense of the Term*, 90). While these diaries are famously rife with allusions to reading novels, it is worth noting that there was an open-air cinema beside the Port Moresby hotel where Malinowski sometimes stayed in Papua New Guinea, as reported in Young, *Malinowski*, 316.

51. Letter from Bronislaw Malinowski to Elsie Masson on October 3, 1918, in Wayne, *The Story of a Marriage*, 174. I am immensely grateful to Michael Young for this reference.

52. See my essay "The Time of Anthropology."

53. These are themes elaborated by Geertz in *The Interpretation of Cultures* and *Works and Lives*. See also Fassin, "True Life, Real Lives," for a cogent discussion of the relation between these forms of writing.

54. Such endeavors form the subject of a forthcoming volume of experimental writing in anthropology that I am coediting with Stuart McLean.

55. On this theme, see Marcus, "The Modernist Sensibility in Recent Ethnographic Writing." Unlike Marcus, I would resist taking such textual forms as evidence of anthropology's belated modernism.

56. On the "tactile and contagious quality of cinema," see Marks, *The Skin of the Film*, xii, and Barker, *The Tactile Eye*. See also Pinney, *Photos of the Gods*, on the "corpothetics" of the visual image in India, an "embodied, corporeal aesthetics" attentive to its sensory efficacy (8).

57. Taylor, "Iconophobia."

58. Deleuze, *Difference and Repetition*, 176.

59. In *The Intelligence of a Machine*, first published in 1946, Jean Epstein describes cinema as "a kind of partial mechanical brain registering visual and auditory stimuli, which it coordinates in its own way in space and time, and which it expresses in the elaborate form of often astounding combinations, out of which a plentiful philosophy

is emerging that is just as astounding" (100). On the long history of likening cinema to a thinking mind or brain, see the discussion "Cinema as Brain: Mind and Body" in Elsaesser and Hagener, *Film Theory*, 149–69.

60. Eisenstein, "A Dialectical Approach to Film Form," 47.

61. "Continuous as the process of narration might seem, the closer we inspect monographs, paragraphs, sentences, the more aware we are of internal discontinuities," Marilyn Strathern observes in *Partial Connections*. "This unity or sense of flow or movement is at the same time made up of jumps over gaps, juxtapositions, leaps— unpredictable, irregular" (xxiii).

62. Taussig, *Shamanism, Colonialism and the Wild Man*, 441.

63. "From the perspective of ordinary affects," Kathleen Stewart writes in *Ordinary Affects*, "thought is patchy and material. It does not find magical closure or even seek it, perhaps only because it's too busy just trying to imagine what's going on" (5). I am grateful to both Stewart and Michael Jackson for many illuminating exchanges on these themes.

64. "Evocation is neither presentation nor representation," Stephen Tyler writes in "Post-modern Ethnography." "It overcomes the separation of the sensible and the conceivable, of form and content, of self and other, of language and the world" (123).

65. "Anthropologists do their thinking, talking and writing in and with the world," observes Ingold in *Being Alive* (241–42). See also João Biehl, "Ethnography in the Way of Theory," for a reflection on ethnography as a "way of staying connected to open-ended, even mysterious, social processes and uncertainties—a way of counterbalancing the generation of certainties and foreclosures by other disciplines" (590).

66. Lévi-Strauss, *The Raw and the Cooked*, 31–32. See also Debaene's discussion of the French anthropological tradition as a "knowledge project that was based primarily on affective experience" (*Far Afield*, 119).

67. Foucault, "Interview with Michel Foucault," 241, 247. With these ideas of Foucault in mind, Jackson writes of anthropology as a "turbulent merger of two countervailing traditions of knowledge," both "cool inquiry and painful initiation" (*At Home in the World*, 170).

68. On the historical conjoining of experience and experimentation, see Williams, *Keywords*, 115–17, 126–29. Consider too what Roy Wagner had to say about the transformative promise of experience in anthropology: "A good artist or scientist becomes a detached part of his culture, one that grows in strange ways, and carries its ideas through transformations that others may never experience . . . this is why it is worthwhile studying other peoples, because every understanding of another culture is an experiment with our own" (*The Invention of Culture*, 12). "Experience" in Tamil is *anubavam*, a word derived from Sanskrit for the pleasures, pains, and lessons of worldly life.

69. The *Oxford English Dictionary* notes usages of this phrase as a term for a broad overview that date back to the 1930s, while usages of "big picture" to describe cinema date back to the 1910s.

70. The phrase, identified most with the work of Joseph Schumpeter, owes a great deal to the work of Karl Marx and Friedrich Engels on the character of modern capitalism.

71. Crutzen, "Geology of Mankind."

72. Chakrabarty, "The Climate of History," 211.

73. Heidegger, *The Question Concerning Technology*, 135.

74. For a cogent critique of dominant ways of presenting the Anthropocene, see Malm and Hornborg, "The Geology of Mankind?"

75. Kohn, *How Forests Think*, 223. On the relationship between this project and Kohn's call for an "anthropology beyond the human," see my "Thinking Like a Mountain."

76. Deleuze, *Cinema 1*, 81.

77. Bateson, *Steps to an Ecology of Mind*, 501.

78. This project differs most significantly from Joseph Anderson's intriguing effort, also in the name of an ecology of cinema, "to place film production and spectatorship in a natural context," insofar as I track forces and currents of mutual transformation between cinematic and worldly experience rather than graph the disjuncture between two fixed domains. "We have only the systems developed in another time, in another context, for another purpose," Anderson writes in *The Reality of Illusion* (12). "We must process the images from the glass-beaded screen and sounds from the metal speakers with the same anatomical structures and the same physiological processes through which we process scenes and sounds from the natural world" (15).

79. See also my essay for *Savage Minds*, "The Ecology of What We Write."

80. For more on the relationship between this project and the "ontological" turn in contemporary anthropology, see chapter 19 of this book.

CHAPTER 2. DREAMS

1. Munsterberg, *The Photoplay*, 61.

2. Marinelli, "Screening Wish Theories."

3. Powdermaker, *Hollywood*, 39.

4. Metz, *The Imaginary Signifier*, 8.

5. Mittermaier, *Dreams That Matter*, 11.

6. Benjamin, "The Work of Art in the Age of Its Technological Reproducibility," 118.

7. Kracauer, *Theory of Film*, 171–72.

8. Freud, *The Interpretation of Dreams*, 564.

9. Freud himself was famously averse to cinema, vehemently opposing the participation of two of his disciples in the making of *Secrets of a Soul*, a 1926 film about dream interpretation, on the grounds that pictorial representation of the unconscious was impossible (Sklarew, "Freud and Film"). "Thinking in pictures," Freud wrote, "is only a very incomplete form of becoming conscious" (*The Ego and the Id*, 14); dream images could be understood only through narratives founded on words.

10. *Yuddham Sei*, directed by Mysskin (Chennai: AGS Entertainment, 2011).

11. Contemporary Tamil directors typically write their own films. Credits are often divided into parallel acknowledgments for story, screenplay, and dialogue, but in the case of Mysskin's films, he reserves credit for *ezhuthu* and *iyakkam*, "writing" and "direction."

12. Metz, *The Imaginary Signifier*, 124.

13. Pandolfo, *Impasse of the Angels*, 175.

14. Benjamin famously wrote of cinema as a medium of "collective dream": "The ancient truth expressed by Heraclitus, that those who are awake have a world in common while each sleeper has a world of his own, has been invalidated by film" ("The Work of Art in the Age of Its Technological Reproducibility," 118). On shared dreaming

in Indian literary contexts, in which "two or more people can have the same dream, or can participate actively in the mutual shaping of a dream, exactly as if it were a waking conversation," see Shulman, *More Than Real*, 164.

15. The ten titles were these: Hesse's *Siddhartha*, Ibsen's *A Doll's House*, Mishima's *Sound of Waves*, Vishnu Sharma's *Panchatantra*, the brothers Grimm's *Fairy Tales*, Mamet's *On Directing Film*, García Márquez's *Chronicle of a Death Foretold*, Camus's *The Outsider*, Kafka's *Metamorphosis*, and M. T. Vasudevan Nair's *Vadakkan Veera Katha*.

16. Freud, "Creative Writers and Day-dreaming," 141–54.

17. *Nandalala*, directed by Mysskin (Chennai: Ayngaran International, 2010).

18. Kohn, *How Forests Think*, 188.

19. García Márquez, *Chronicle of a Death Foretold*, 97.

20. Freud, *The Interpretation of Dreams*, 346–47.

21. In *Waiting on the Weather*, Teruyo Nogami reports Kurosawa saying, the year before he died, "I don't yet have a good grasp of what cinema is, but these days, I have begun to think that the secret of cinema lies in the connection between one cut and the next" (267).

22. "The Crows," in *Akira Kurosawa's Dreams*, directed by Akira Kurosawa (Burbank, CA: Warner Home Video, 1990). For some time, the young Kurosawa himself aspired to paint.

23. Mamet, *On Directing Film*, 6.

24. Shulman, "Dreaming the Self in South India," 52, 61–62.

CHAPTER 3. HOPE

1. Crapanzano, "Reflections on Hope," 6.

2. Nehru, "Tryst with Destiny."

3. On Indian cinema and Indian nationalism, see Virdi, *The Cinematic ImagiNation*. On Indian cinema and labor migration, see Radhakrishnan, "The Gulf in the Imagination." On cinematic suicide, see the discussion of Aleyamma's attempted suicide in Chua, *In Pursuit of the Good Life*, 119–25.

4. Bloch, *The Principle of Hope*, 410.

5. *Kanden Kadhalai*, directed by Kannan (Chennai: Moser Baer Entertainment, 2009).

6. On this theme, see Pandian and Mariappan, *Ayya's Accounts*.

7. Miyazaki, *The Method of Hope*, 14.

8. As David Harvey writes in *Spaces of Hope*, "All capitalist ventures . . . are speculative. This is what it means to throw money into circulation as capital and hope to realize a profit" (204).

9. Federation of Indian Chambers of Commerce and Industry and Ernst & Young, "Indian Entertainment Down South: From Script to Screen." Cable and satellite rights amounted to 11 percent and international theatrical sales to 6 percent of total revenue. Music, home video, mobile, and Internet streams together contributed only 2 percent of revenue.

10. Baskaran, "Trade Unionism in South Indian Film Industry." These studios were operated like companies, Baskaran notes, with actors, musicians, writers, and other technicians working directly on their payroll.

11. G. Dhananjayan, "A Year of Buoyancy," *Galatta Cinema*, January 2010.

12. See Ganti, *Producing Bollywood*, 63–75, for a discussion.

13. Sreedhar Pillai, "Kollywood Goes the Corporate Way," *The Hindu*, July 9, 2007.

14. "Tamil Film Council Bans Bollywood Cine Corporations," *Times of India*, September 13, 2008.

15. Sun Pictures recommenced these operations in 2013.

16. Chua, *In Pursuit of the Good Life*, 140.

17. See especially the chapter "Inheriting Hope" in Miyazaki, *The Method of Hope*, 130–40.

18. I make this argument in further detail in "The Time of Anthropology," where I seek to work with emergent phenomena in a manner that does not, as Miyazaki argues in *The Method of Hope*, simply seek to "trace or track the world as it emerges" (138), but instead to take up such movement as precisely a means of propelling the "radical reorientation of knowledge" (139).

19. On orality in Hindi cinema, see Ganti, *Producing Bollywood*, 222–25. As a register of the dangers of exploitation and abuse associated with this verbal milieu, consider the controversy in which G. Dhananjayan was embroiled as a producer for UTV in 2012. An assistant director claimed that the film that UTV had produced and released that year, *Thandavam* (directed by A. L. Vijay), was based, without credit or acknowledgment, on a script he had submitted to Dhananjayan for consideration the previous year. The producer argued that by then, he had already *heard*, narrated to him, a very similar story from Vijay. The case was brought to the attention of the Tamil Nadu Film Directors' Association and then the Madras High Court in 2012, which ultimately dismissed the suit for inadequate evidence.

20. Take this summary, and the narration that follows below, as a faithful disguise of the original story, which still remains an unmade tale in the hands of its writer.

21. Reed, "Hope on Remand," 533.

22. Vernant, "At Man's Table," 81. I'm grateful to James Ker for calling his work to my attention.

CHAPTER 4. SPACE

1. *Easan*, directed by M. Sasikumar (Chennai: Company Productions, 2010).

2. Lefebvre, *The Production of Space*, 94.

3. See Heath, "Narrative Space"; Lefebvre, *The Production of Space*.

4. Venkatachalapathy, "Street Smart in Chennai."

5. The early development of public transportation in colonial Madras coincided with the construction of cinema halls in the most populous urban districts of the city, which drew many visiting filmgoers from beyond the city beginning in the early twentieth century, writes Hughes, "Urban Mobility and the History of Cinema-going in Chennai."

6. Ramaswamy, "The Chennai of My First Visit," 94.

7. Lefebvre, *The Production of Space*, 389.

8. Lefebvre, *The Production of Space*, 97.

9. Expressed in the contemporary cinema of Bombay, Ranjani Mazumdar argues, is an "urban delirium of the underworld," a feeling of palpable disorder conjured at the interface of rumor, reportage, and informal knowledge and experience (*Bombay Cinema*, 159).

10. Massey, *For Space*, 107.

11. I am grateful to G. Sundar and the staff of the Roja Muthiah Research Library

for their assistance in culling relevant articles of this time period from *Ananda Vika-tan*, *Bommai*, and *Cinema Express*.

12. On the significance of this interplay between the inner and the outer in Tamil cultural geographies, see Selby and Peterson, *Tamil Geographies*.

13. See Kaali, "Narrating Seduction."

14. On this theme in Bharathiraja's films, see Chakravarty, "Bharathirajavin Cinima."

15. For a further discussion of the Tamil landscape poetics of *tinai* commingling the inner and outer, *akam* and *puram*, in this manner, see my essay "Landscapes of Expression," 54–58.

16. For a discussion of caste-inflected violence in Tamil films based in the southern districts of Tamil Nadu, see Krishnan, "Imaginary Geographies."

17. *Subramaniyapuram*, directed by M. Sasikumar (Chennai: Company Productions, 2008). For a close exploration of this film and its screenplay from various angles, see Sasikumar and Pandian, *Subramaniyapuram*.

18. See Gupta and Ferguson, *Culture, Power, Place*; Forster, "Herder and the Birth of Modern Anthropology."

19. Bateson, *Steps to an Ecology of Mind*, 465.

20. On the *yantra*, or diagram, of the Brahmanical temple's space as a closed polygon, see Kramrisch, *The Hindu Temple*, 21.

21. de Certeau, *The Practice of Everyday Life*, 103.

22. The director had specifically asked his assistants to scout locations that had not yet appeared in other films, so that they would not be reminded of such existing images as they worked.

23. Lefebvre, *The Production of Space*, 191.

24. In "Precarious Boundaries," Anne Rutherford describes elements of location in Theo Angelopoulos's films as "catalysts" of "sensory awakening."

25. These are instances of "synchresis," as described by Michel Chion in *Audio-Vision*, "the spontaneous and irresistible weld produced between a particular auditory phenomenon and visual phenomenon when they occur at the same time" (63).

26. Bachelard, *The Poetics of Space*, 51.

CHAPTER 5. ART

1. Kracauer, "Calico-World," 282.

2. Dewey, *Art as Experience*, 18–19, 25.

3. Gell, *Art and Agency*, 68–69.

4. On this theme, see Bennett, *Vibrant Matter*.

5. Krauss, "The Originality of the Avant-Garde," 53.

6. See Barnwell, *Production Design*. David O. Selznick introduced the title "production designer" for *Gone With the Wind* in 1939, which in Hollywood came to stand for overall visual design, while the role of art director was restricted to supervising set construction.

7. See Mitter et al., "Decentering Modernism," and the ensuing debate in *Art Bulletin*. My thanks to Rebecca Brown for insight into these discussions.

8. Lévi-Strauss, "The Art of the Northwest Coast," 175, 181.

9. Lévi-Strauss, "The Art of the Northwest Coast," 180–81. On the aesthetics of encounter for Lévi-Strauss, see Wiseman, *Lévi-Strauss, Anthropology, and Aesthetics*.

10. Lévi-Strauss, *The Way of the Masks*, 148. See also Gell, *Art and Agency*, for a related argument concerning repetition in art: "Artists are nowadays reprimanded by critics for 'repeating themselves' since this is considered short-changing the public who demand continuous innovation. But actually all artistic practice is inevitably dependent on wholesale repetition, otherwise the concept of 'style' (which depends on some degree of resemblance between all the works in an *oeuvre*) would be impossible to apply. Without repetition, art would lose its memory" (233).

11. On the moral authority of craftsmen, see Venkatesan, "Rethinking Agency."

12. Latour, "The Migration of the Aura," 279.

13. Although, in other words, these may be diagrams of a modern process of stepwise assembly, as discussed by Ingold in *Lines*, their mode of usage has more in common with the open-ended "wayfaring" paths that Ingold counterposes to the modern line.

14. Dewey, *Art as Experience*, 157–58.

15. Kant, *Critique of the Power of Judgment*, 128–59.

16. Gell, *Art and Agency*, 94. While Gell addresses the "second-class agency which artefacts acquire once they become enmeshed in a texture of social relationships," I find this line between human and nonhuman agency unwarranted.

17. Bennett, *Vibrant Matter*, 6.

18. "The being of sensation," write Deleuze and Guattari in *What Is Philosophy?*, "is not the flesh but the compound of nonhuman forces of the cosmos, of man's nonhuman becomings" (183).

19. Deleuze, *Francis Bacon*, 48.

CHAPTER 6. LOVE

1. *Malaikottai*, directed by Boopathy Pandian (Chennai: Sri Lakshmi Productions, 2007).

2. Berlant, "Love (A Queer Feeling)," 443.

3. See Orsini, *Love in South Asia*.

4. Trawick, *Notes on Love in a Tamil Family*, 152.

5. See chapter 3 of my *Crooked Stalks* for an elaboration of these themes.

6. Gopinath, *Impossible Desires*, 101.

7. On attractions of setting and location in Bollywood film, see Dwyer and Patel, *Cinema India*.

8. Global song locations in Bollywood cinema are discussed in Gopal and Moorti, *Global Bollywood*. While some earlier Tamil films such as *Ulagam Suttrum Valiban* [The youth who circled the world, 1973] and *Ninaithale Inikkum* [The thought itself is sweet, 1979] were shot extensively in foreign locales such as Japan, Singapore, and Malaysia, the practice rose to prominence beginning in the 1990s. For a further reflection on themes of landscape and setting in relation to these materials, see my essay "Landscapes of Expression."

9. See Lefebvre, *Landscape and Film*.

10. Ahmed, "Orientations," 566.

11. "The speeds, slowness, and turns of our movements come from movements we meet about us," Alphonso Lingis writes in *Dangerous Emotions*. "The movements and intensities of our bodies take up the movements and intensities of toucans and wolves, jellyfish and whales" (29–31).

12. Grosz, "Animal Sex," 290, working with an idea proposed by Deleuze and Guattari in *Anti-Oedipus*.

13. *Nam Nadu*, directed by Suresh (Chennai: Kanagarathna Movies, 2007).

14. See Malathi Rangarajan, "Good vs. Evil—Nam Naadu," *The Hindu*, September 28, 2007.

15. I have in mind the poetic devices often at work in Tamil literary genres such as *bhakti* and *ula* and am grateful to Amanda Weidman and Blake Wentworth for their insights here.

16. Quoted in Buck and Paramasivan, *The Study of Stolen Love*, 32.

17. Quoted in Buck and Paramasivan, *The Study of Stolen Love*, 31, 33.

18. Gopalan, *Cinema of Interruptions*, 3.

CHAPTER 7. DESIRE

1. Deleuze and Guattari, *Anti-Oedipus*, 105.

2. *Gilles Deleuze from A to Z*, with Claire Parnet, directed by Pierre-André Boutang, DVD (Cambridge, MA: Semiotext(e) Foreign Agents, 2012).

3. Ali, "Anxieties of Attachment," 106.

4. Deleuze and Guattari, *Anti-Oedipus*, 1–50.

5. Eisenstein, "A Dialectical Approach to Film Form," 46.

6. Deleuze and Parnet, "Dead Psychoanalysis," 95.

7. Deleuze and Parnet, "Dead Psychoanalysis," 95.

8. Among experimental works of fiction helpful in working out the form of this chapter, I owe the greatest debt to Bohumil Hrabal's one-sentence novella originally published in Czech, *Dancing Lessons for the Advanced in Age*. I am grateful to Kylie Sharkey for the aptness of her phrase "longing for punctuation."

CHAPTER 8. LIGHT

This chapter was previously published as "In the Light of Experience: An Indian Cameraman," in *Bioscope* 4 (1): 81–92.

1. Indian philosophies of creation, Balslev argues in *A Study of Time in Indian Philosophy*, reflect a "common and steadfast adherence to the principle that being cannot come out of nothing or be reduced to nothing" (130), akin to the Greek cosmological principle of *ex nihilo nihil fit* rather than the Judeo-Christian idea of creation *ex nihilo*.

2. Merleau-Ponty, "Eye and Mind," 138.

3. *Madrasapattinam*, directed by A. L. Vijay (Chennai: AGS Entertainment, 2010).

4. On the modern city as a visual space, see Jay, *Downcast Eyes*.

5. For a discussion of this foundational theme in Western philosophy, see Blumenberg, "Light as a Metaphor for Truth."

6. This distinction is developed and explored by Zajonc, *Catching the Light*.

7. See Deleuze, *Cinema 1*, on Bergson: "This breaks with the whole philosophical tradition which placed light on the side of spirit and made consciousness a beam of light which drew things out of their native darkness. . . . Things are luminous by themselves without anything illuminating them" (60). *Parithi*, incidentally, can mean "sun" in Tamil.

8. Bille and Sorensen, "An Anthropology of Luminosity," 264.

9. Dwyer, *Filming the Gods*.

10. For a discussion of the appropriation and transformation of Zen Buddhist philosophy for contemporary Western audiences, see McMahan, "Repackaging Zen for the West."

11. For a discussion of Buddhist visual metaphor, see McMahan, *Empty Vision*, 55–82.

12. On the mystery of the f-stop as the only property of the cinematographer, see Sengupta, "Reflected Readings in Available Light."

13. I am grateful to James Laidlaw for insight into this characteristic Jain idea. See his *Riches and Renunciation* for a discussion of related themes.

14. Gibson, *The Ecological Approach to Visual Perception*, 75, 222.

15. See Alton, *Painting with Light*, for an example of this commonplace conception of cinematography. One of the most basic differences between painting and cinema, Andre Bazin wrote in *What Is Cinema?* (166), is this: paintings are "centripetal," while the cinema screen is "centrifugal." The crux of the difference, for the critic, lay in the differing function of the frame in each of the two media. The ornate and gilded frames that surround paintings turn attention inward, into the distinctive world that the picture composes. The movement of the cinema image, on the other hand, bleeds into the world that surrounds it: "What the screen shows us seems to be part of something prolonged indefinitely into the universe."

16. I am grateful to Theodore Baskaran for his insights into this theme.

17. Zajonc, *Catching the Light*, 2.

18. "Tactility is an essential aspect of light's texture," writes Cathryn Vasseleu in *Textures of Light*, "where texture refers not only to the feeling of a fabric to the touch, or the grasping of its qualities, but also to the hinges or points of contact which constitute the interweaving of the material and ideal strands of the field of vision" (12).

19. Schivelbusch, *Disenchanted Night*, 118.

20. For a discussion of German Expressionism and Indian cinematography, see Sengupta, "Reflected Readings in Available Light."

21. Baudry, "Ideological Effects of the Basic Cinematographic Apparatus," 44–45.

22. Accessed June 22, 2012, http://www.cinematography.net/read/messages?id=16 0872.

CHAPTER 9. COLOR

1. On the paucity of color words, see Wittgenstein, *Remarks on Colour*.

2. Goethe, *Theory of Colours*, 28.

3. *Va, Quarter Cutting*, directed by Pushkar and Gayathri (Chennai: Y Not Productions, 2010). The title makes use of Tamil slang for a drink or "cutting" from a quarter-bottle of alcohol. *Va* is a Tamil term for the fraction ¼, a title utilized by the film's producers to take advantage of tax concessions in Tamil Nadu for films registered with Tamil-language titles.

4. For a synthetic history of color in the modern West, see Gage, *Color and Culture*.

5. Goethe, *Theory of Colours*, 55.

6. Batchelor, *Chromophobia*, 49.

7. Taussig, *What Color Is the Sacred?*, 9.

8. Misek, *Chromatic Cinema*, 61.

9. Misek, *Chromatic Cinema*, 34.

10. Kalmus, "Color Consciousness."

11. Misek, *Chromatic Cinema*, 38.

12. Dhananjayan, *The Best of Tamil Cinema*, 148–50.

13. Cohen, "Introduction," xvi.

14. Merleau-Ponty, "Cezanne's Doubt," 68.

15. Merleau-Ponty, "Cezanne's Doubt," 67, 66.

16. On the aesthetics of chromolithographic prints in India, see Pinney, *Photos of the Gods*; Jain, *Gods in the Bazaar*, especially 183–90.

17. Fujifilm, "Eterna Vivid 500: Expanding the Expressive Range of High-Speed Film," *Exposure International* 16: 6–7.

18. Taussig, *What Color Is the Sacred?*, 146, 149.

19. For an overview, see Belton, "Painting by the Numbers."

20. Benjamin, "A Child's View of Color," 50–51.

21. As is well known, blue light burns hotter than red light.

22. Goethe, *Theory of Colours*, 25.

23. Deleuze, *Francis Bacon*, 123.

24. Deleuze, *Francis Bacon*, 31.

25. Belton, "Painting by the Numbers," has an extensive discussion of the latter, 1998 film.

26. The latter formula is most explicit in the song "Karuppu than enakku pidicha kalaru" [Black is my favorite color] with which the heroine of the Tamil film *Vetri Kodi Kattu* (directed by Cheran; Chennai: Shivashakti Movie Makers, 2000) serenades her dusky hero.

27. Goethe, *Maxims and Reflections*, 77.

CHAPTER 10. TIME

1. *Billa*, directed by Vishnu Vardhan (Chennai: Ananda Picture Circuit, 2007).

2. Bergson, *Creative Evolution*, 45. For an illuminating discussion, see Marrati, "Time, Life, Concepts."

3. Bergson, *Creative Mind*, 126.

4. Bergson, *Creative Evolution*, 371.

5. With this argument, I do not mean to counterpose an "Indian" philosophy of circular time to a putatively "Western" commitment to linear time. As Balslev writes in *A Study of Time in Indian Philosophy*, "we have to be aware of the pitfalls of such geometrical representations of time as a circle or a line. These have to be understood as theological symbolisms, whose intended spiritual significance can be grasped within their theological, conceptual structures" (150).

6. Bergson, "Memory of the Present and False Recognition," 60.

7. On this contemporaneity of present and past, see Deleuze, *Bergsonism*.

8. See Ansell-Pearson, "The Reality of the Virtual."

9. The arguments in this chapter are elaborated in further detail in my "Reel Time."

10. Charney, "In a Moment." On the influence of time horizons prevailing in the urban modernity of nineteenth- and early twentieth-century Europe on Bergson's interest in time and freedom, see Lim, *Translating Time*.

11. Ingold and Hallam, "Creativity and Cultural Improvisation," 10.

12. See Barber, "Improvisation and the Art of Making Things Stick."

13. Gottlieb, "Unknown Hitchcock," 95.

14. Deleuze, *Cinema 2*, 82. "For Deleuze," D. N. Rodowick observes in *Gilles Deleuze's Time Machine*, "the cinema of time produces an image of thought as a non-totalizable process and a sense of history as unpredictable change" (17).

15. "Each one of us . . . is nothing but an assemblage of three images, a consolidate of perception-images, action-images and affection-images," writes Deleuze (*Cinema 1*, 66), elaborating on a trinity of terms that Bergson put forward to articulate a temporal ontology of matter and image.

16. See the "situation—action—modified situation" scheme that Deleuze offers as a formula for the movement of the "action-image" in *Cinema 1*, 141–59.

17. For a useful overview of this idea, see Staiger, "Authorship Approaches."

18. Wilf, *School for Cool*, 165.

19. *Sarvam*, directed by Vishnu Vardhan (Chennai: Ayngaran International, 2009).

20. See the first chapter of Bergson's *Matter and Memory*.

21. Bergson, *Creative Evolution*, 332.

22. Bergson, *Creative Mind*, 114.

23. Rouch, *Cine-Ethnography*, 150, 151.

24. Bergson, "Memory of the Present and False Recognition," 167.

25. "Time is not the interior in us, but just the opposite, the interiority in which we are, in which we move, live and change," writes Deleuze, *Cinema 2*, 82.

26. Calvino, *If on a Winter's Night a Traveler*, 147.

CHAPTER 11. IMAGINATION

This chapter was previously published as "Imagination: Cinematic, Anthropological," in *Social Text* 30 (4): 127–41.

1. Translated in Shulman, *More Than Real*, 151.

2. *Netaji* is a common honorific for Subhas Chandra Bose, the prominent early twentieth-century Indian anticolonial militant.

3. *Siruthai*, directed by Siva (Chennai: Studio Green, 2011). The film, as discussed in chapter 5, is a remake of the Telugu film *Vikramarkudu*.

4. For an overview of ideas of imagination in Western history and philosophy, see Kearney, *The Wake of the Imagination*.

5. This account of *Siruthai*'s release is deeply indebted to a video shot and produced for me by M. K. B. Santhosh of MKB Productions, Chennai, in January 2011.

6. On this aspect of Hindu puja, see Fuller, *The Camphor Flame*.

7. On such "semiotics of kingship," see Jacob, *Celluloid Deities*.

8. As Amit Rai observes in *Untimely Bollywood*, 52, "first day, first show is a trigger for accreting potential—its seething indetermination—accompanying a film's media blitz: that is, it has caught on. This catching, however, is not simply the capture of a film's media potentiality but also its unleashing."

9. Crapanzano, *Imaginative Horizons*, 61.

10. I am grateful to G. Dhananjayan for making this possible.

11. Shulman, *More Than Real*, 261.

12. A cable television channel featuring animated and live-action programming for children, which operated in various global markets, including India, between 2004 and 2010.

13. "Focus on the inner processes of individuals effectively excludes from consider-

ation, or at least relegates to an inferior role, any external imaginary space spanning between persons, or between persons and things," argue Sneath et al. in "Technologies of the Imagination," 14.

14. Mittermaier, *Dreams That Matter*, 225.

15. Stanislavski, *Building a Character*, 65.

16. Stanislavski, *An Actor's Work*, 84.

17. Hastrup, "Playing One's Part," 28.

18. Stanislavski, *Building a Character*, 333.

19. In Indian forms of *darsan*, or devotional seeing, whether religious or cinematic, "the devotee is permitted to behold the image of the deity, and is privileged and benefited by this permission," Vasudevan writes in *The Melodramatic Public*, 114.

20. Sivakumar, *Idhu Rajapattai Alla*, 4.

21. In the guise of a mendicant, Vishnu asks the demon king for a gift of land measuring no more than three steps across. He then assumes cosmic dimensions to wrest away far more. On the Badami temples, see Ferguson and Burgess, *The Cave Temples of India*, 405–16.

CHAPTER 12. PLEASURE

1. Mulvey, "Visual Pleasure and Narrative Cinema."

2. *Bana Kathadi*, directed by Badri Venkatesh (Chennai: Sathyajyothi Films, 2010).

3. Thomas, "Indian Cinema," 119.

4. G. S. Mudur and Ananya Sengupta, "Rape Spotlight on Item Numbers," *Telegraph — Calcutta*, September 2, 2013, accessed online August 19, 2014.

5. See Nijhawan, "Excusing the Female Dancer."

6. Soneji, *Unfinished Gestures*, 110. On the incorporation of courtesan salon performance traditions into Telugu cinema, see chapter 2 of *Unfinished Gestures*.

7. Viewers of the film already know that Ramesh had borrowed money for his evening date from a friend with a weakness for prostitutes, from whose pocket he had unknowingly lifted the condom package along with a 100-rupee note.

8. Foucault, *The History of Sexuality*, 45.

9. Mulvey, "Visual Pleasure and Narrative Cinema."

10. Mulvey, "Visual Pleasure and Narrative Cinema," 344. "The satisfaction and reinforcement of the ego that represent the high point of film history hitherto must be attacked," Mulvey adds. "Not in favour of a reconstructed new pleasure, which cannot exist in the abstract, nor of intellectualized unpleasure, but to make way for a total negation of the ease and plenitude of the narrative fiction film." I argue here that the forces at work in cinematic pleasure do not necessarily involve the satisfaction of a spectatorial ego and that they do not demand, therefore, a total negation.

11. Grosz, *Time Travels*, 192–93.

12. On the tactile pleasure of haptic visuality, see the chapter "Skin" in Barker, *The Tactile Eye*, 23–68.

13. Gnoli, *The Aesthetic Experience according to Abhinavagupta*, 79–82.

14. See Gerow, "Abhinavagupta's Aesthetics as a Speculative Paradigm"; Mason, "*Rasa*, 'Rasaesthetics' and Dramatic Theory as Performance Packaging."

15. See Hahn, *Sensational Knowledge*, for a discussion of the passage of energy from teachers to students in the learning of dance.

16. Foucault, *The Use of Pleasure*, 50.

17. Ali, "Anxieties of Attachment," 112.

18. Ali, "Anxieties of Attachment," 134–39.

19. See Seizer, *Stigmas of the Tamil Stage*, on the challenges faced by Tamil women performers in handling the moral and sexual implications of public presence, and Hoek, *Cut-Pieces*, on "the oscillation between the visible and the invisible" crucial to cinematic obscenity (15).

20. As the anthropologist Katherine Frank writes, in *G-Strings and Sympathy*, of men patronizing the strip clubs of a city in the American South, "The search for pleasure required walking a fine line between safety and danger, excitement and relaxation, adventure and leisure, escape and return, desire and disgust" (227).

21. Words of praise for the courtesan Mokanamuttu, from the *Sethupathi Viralivituthuthu*, composed during the early nineteenth century by a poet in the Ramnad Court and translated in Ebeling, *Colonizing the Realm of Words*, 151.

22. See, for example, the discussion of male strip club patronage as a collaborative touristic practice in Frank, *G-Strings and Sympathy*.

23. Grosz, *Chaos, Territory, Art*, 33.

24. See Gnoli, *The Aesthetic Experience according to Abhinavagupta*: "The spectator, whose awareness of his own self . . . is lost in the events represented endowed with *camatkara*, continues, by means of his own self to see everything in this light" (113).

CHAPTER 13. SOUND

1. Chion, *Audio-Vision*, 69.

2. For a compelling cultural history of the modern gulf between sound and source, see Sterne, *The Audible Past*.

3. *Nan Mahan Alla*, directed by Susindran (Chennai: Studio Green, 2010).

4. These lines were developed on Adobe Illustrator by setting these words to follow visually the rising and falling notes of the melody predominating in the first forty bars of the song. I am grateful to Brian Tilley for identifying and notating on staff paper these notes for me. Another such inscription of a soundscape at the close of this chapter follows the melodic pitch of the final portions of the song.

5. See Sterne, *The Audible Past*, 31–51, for a fascinating discussion of a late nineteenth-century "phonoautograph" that sought to "write" sound by incorporating the physical movements of the ear, "to render an indexical, visible record of the sound waves" (38).

6. Schafer, *The Soundscape*, 7.

7. Schafer, *The Soundscape*, 216.

8. See Baskaran, *The Eye of the Serpent*, 38–61; Hughes, "Music in the Age of Mechanical Reproduction."

9. For comparative reflections on the role of the film music composer, see Beck and Grajeda, *Lowering the Boom*.

10. See Hunter, "'To Play as If from the Soul of the Composer.'" I am grateful to Michael Birenbaum Quintero for this reference.

11. Hughes, "Play It Again, Saraswathi."

12. *Yogi*, directed by Subramanya Siva (Chennai: Teamwork Production House, 2009).

13. The background score here is typically called the "re-recording," a term bor-

rowed from Hollywood and acknowledging a film's soundtrack as something recorded after its visual material and coupled later with that material.

14. Meintjes, *Sound of Africa!*, 84.

15. Meintjes, *Sound of Africa!*, 85.

16. For an exploration of the impact of these changes on the musicians of Indian (Hindi) cinema, see Booth, *Behind the Curtain*.

17. Feld, *Sound and Sentiment*, 265.

18. Patterned on the 2005 South African film *Tsotsi*, *Yogi* concerns the accidental abduction of a middle-class child by a slum-dwelling hoodlum. See also Theodor Adorno and Hanns Eisler's 1947 critique of the Hollywood convention "Birdie sings, music sings," the idea that "music must follow visual incidents and illustrate them either by directly imitating them or by using cliches that are associated with the mood and content of the picture" (*Composing for the Films*, 7). They argue instead that film music supplies "momentum, muscular energy, a sense of corporeity" to "the frozen replica of external reality" (52).

19. This is part of the conventional litany that distinguishes hearing from vision, Sterne notes in *The Audible Past*, 15.

20. Take the third and last sections of this chapter as experiments with this question.

21. She shared the 2010 Grammy Award for Best Song Written for Visual Media with A. R. Rahman and Gulzar for their work on *Slumdog Millionaire*'s "Jai Ho."

22. Eliot Bates, "What Studios Do," *Journal on the Art of Record Production* 7 (November 2012), accessed online May 2, 2013.

23. Helmreich, "An Anthropologist Underwater," 633.

24. Shulman, "The Buzz of God and the Click of Delight," 50.

25. For example, the advertisement for the film that ran in the "Chennai Times" section of the Chennai edition of *The Hindu* on Wednesday, July 21, 2010.

26. Accessed October 11, 2013, http://behindwoods.com/new-videos/videos-q1–09 /actor-actress-interview/actor-karthi.html. ThinkMusic reports that the song has been downloaded over 1.1 million times as a "ring back tone." My thanks to Pradeep Santosh for sharing this information.

CHAPTER 14. VOICE

1. Think of that scene of identification sketched by Louis Althusser in his essay on "Ideology and Ideological State Apparatuses." "Hey, you there!" a policeman calls out on the street. Someone whips his head around, fearfully presuming that the officer is hailing him. In that moment, Althusser argues, an individual becomes a subject, assumes an identity, recognizes himself as having a place in a social and political order.

2. Dolar, *A Voice and Nothing More*, 70.

3. Chion, *The Voice in Cinema*, 23.

4. One of the most famous moments in the 1952 Tamil film *Parasakthi*, which launched the career of the Tamil screen icon Sivaji Ganesan, concerns a voice erupting from unexpected quarters. The words "Hey, priest!" ring out harshly from within a shrine. Startled, that priest looks to the statue inside. "Is it the mother goddess who speaks? Parasakthi, Mother, what did you say?" he asks the dark figure, beseechingly. Then the ragged stranger played by Ganesan reveals himself behind the stone deity. "In what age did the goddess speak, you fool? It won't speak. It's stone." As

M. S. S. Pandian discusses in his essay *"Parasakthi,"* the Tamil film audiences of the 1950s couldn't hear him say that word *stone* as they watched this scene unfold; the atheist implication was too controversial, and the word was excised from the film's soundtrack. Still, the audience could see that it was there, expressed by the visible form of Ganesan's lips.

5. *Tamil Padam*, directed by C. S. Amudhan (Chennai: Y Not Studios, 2010).

6. *Karuthamma*, directed by Bharathiraja (Chennai: Vetrivel Art Creations, 1994).

7. The story is set in a village called Cinemapatti or *Cinema Village*, a place so prone to making movie heroes out of young men that the village leader, exasperated by the scourge of their celebrity, has decreed that all boy children be killed at birth.

8. Verbal feats of eloquence had much to do with the rise of Tamil cinema in the mid-twentieth century, with monologues often penned in the form of political oratory, notes Theodore Baskaran in *The Eye of the Serpent*, 62–69.

9. See Bate, *Tamil Oratory and the Dravidian Aesthetic*, 47.

10. See Doane, "The Voice in the Cinema," on sound in the space of the theater: "Sound is not 'framed' in the same way as the image. In a sense, it *envelops* the spectator" (50).

CHAPTER 15. RHYTHM

1. Lefebvre, *Rhythmanalysis*, 27. I am grateful to Katie Stewart for her insights into this work of Lefebvre's.

2. "Nothing inert in the world, no things: very diverse rhythms, slow or lively (in relation to us)," writes Lefebvre in *Rhythmanalysis*, 17.

3. Lefebvre, *Rhythmanalysis*, 21.

4. Lefebvre, *Rhythmanalysis*, 19.

5. *Drohi*, directed by Sudha K. Prasad (Chennai: Indira Innovations, 2010).

6. As attested by some of the interviews in Oldham, *First Cut*.

7. "Pace—Rhythm Within," Sreekar Prasad: Film Editor, http://www.sreekarprasad.com/pace.htm.

8. See Cowan, "The Heart Machine."

9. Deleuze and Guattari, *A Thousand Plateaus*, 313.

10. See Deleuze and Guattari, *A Thousand Plateaus*: "It is the difference that is rhythmic, not the repetition, which nevertheless produces it: productive repetition has nothing to do with reproductive meter" (314).

11. Lefebvre, *Rhythmanalysis*, 6.

12. As John Dewey writes in *Art as Experience*, "The first characteristic of the environing world that makes possible the existence of artistic form is rhythm. There is rhythm in nature before poetry, painting, architecture and music exist" (153).

13. Akkineni Sanjivi was the brother of L. V. Prasad, a leading figure in the production of Telugu and Tamil cinema in Madras, having founded Prasad Studios in 1956.

14. See Bordwell et al., "The Continuity System."

15. Ondaatje, *The Conversations*, 269.

16. On social class and affective response in another theatrical context, see Larkin, "The Materiality of Cinema Theaters in Northern Nigeria."

17. Eisenstein, "Dickens, Griffith, and the Film Today," 234.

18. Eisenstein, "Dickens, Griffith, and the Film Today," 235.

20. Freud, *Beyond the Pleasure Principle*, 10–12.

CHAPTER 16. SPEED

1. Baudrillard, *America*, 55–56. On cinematic and automotive visuality in Los Angeles, see Friedberg, "Urban Mobility and Cinematic Visuality."

2. Baudrillard, *America*, 7.

3. Duffy, *The Speed Handbook*, 1.

4. Deleuze and Guattari, *A Thousand Plateaus*, 381.

5. Murch, *In the Blink of an Eye*, 110. His 1996 Oscar for *The English Patient* was the first awarded for a digitally edited film.

6. Oliver Sacks, "Speed: Aberrations of Time and Movement," *New Yorker*, August 23, 2004, 68.

7. On the relationship between conscious thought and autonomic response in film spectatorship, see Brown, "Resisting the Psycho-Logic of Intensified Continuity."

8. Duffy, *The Speed Handbook*, 203.

9. Virilio, *War and Cinema*, 10.

10. Berliner and Cohen, "The Illusion of Continuity," 50.

11. Marinetti, "Futurist Sensibility and Wireless Imagination," 30.

12. On the toxicity of speed in contemporary machine-based gambling, see Schüll, *Addiction by Design*.

13. Connolly, *Neuropolitics*, 156–57.

14. Consider what Walter Murch (*In the Blink of an Eye*, 105) has said about editing manually on the Moviola: "The Moviola's design is almost automotive. It has pedals for forward and reverse motion and a hand brake that gives a particularly satisfying jolt when stopping the film. . . . It is a tactile, whole-body experience in the extreme."

15. De Quincey, *Joan of Arc and the English Mail-Coach*, 66, 65.

16. Schnapp, "Crash," 25.

17. Bordwell, "Intensified Continuity," 24.

18. These figures on average shot length (ASL) were generated using the Cinemetrics online movie measurement tool, at http://www.cinemetrics.lv/.

CHAPTER 17. WONDER

1. Weber, "Science as a Vocation," 139.

2. Daston and Park, *Wonders and the Order of Nature*, 367.

3. Daston and Park, *Wonders and the Order of Nature*, 368.

4. Gunning, "The Cinema of Attraction," 65.

5. Rajadhyaksha, "The Phalke Era," 48–49.

6. "The film seeks to make no intervention other than bringing that wonder cinematically alive," Rajadhyaksha writes in "The Phalke Era" (72).

7. The feature, *Meenakshi Kalyanam*, was ruined by a faulty camera, note Rajadhyaksha and Willemen (*Encyclopaedia of Indian Cinema*, 178).

8. Ram, "Bringing the Amman into Presence," 56.

9. These beings would appear to share their spirit with the "techno-animism" that Anne Allison has found in contemporary Japan, "animating contemporary tech-

nology and commodities with spirits" in a manner that is "at once playful and deadly serious" (*Millennial Monsters*, 21).

10. Bennett, *The Enchantment of Modern Life*, 4. See also Dwyer, *Filming the Gods*, who writes of an "enchanted world where gods are still present, and miracles are almost part of the everyday" (160).

11. I am grateful to Brian Goldstone for our illuminating dialogues on wonder and this chapter. See his "The Miraculous Life" for a discussion of miracles in the charismatic Christianity of Ghana, "miracle no longer a capital 'E' event . . . but rather a profusion of events . . . of seemingly commonplace encounters full to bursting with meaning" (85).

12. For historical perspective on CGI, see Pierson, "CGI Effects in Hollywood Science-Fiction Cinema."

13. Daston and Park, *Wonders and the Order of Nature*, 21–108.

14. These were awards won in 1995, 1996, 1997, and 1999 for *Gentleman* (with S. Murugesh), *Kalapani*, *Indian*, and *Jeans*, respectively. No award for special effects was given in 1998.

15. Venki had a script of his own that he had been quietly developing for more than a decade. Tragically, however, he died suddenly of a heart attack in 2012, before he could reveal his own plans for an Indian rejoinder to Cameron's *Avatar*.

16. *Mambattiyan*, directed by Thiagarajan (Chennai: Lakshmi Shanthi Movies, 2011).

17. Siegel, *Net of Magic*, 162.

18. Condry, *The Soul of Anime*, 111.

19. de Vries, "Of Miracles and Special Effects," 51.

20. Bynum, "Presidential Address."

21. See Flood, "Miracles in Hinduism."

22. *Seedan*, directed by Subramaniya Siva (Chennai: Myth Productions, 2011).

23. On the place of these ideas in Indian traditions of magic and illusory practice, see Siegel, *Net of Magic*.

24. Betty, "Dvaita, Advaita, and Visistadvaita," 217.

25. Scott, "The Anthropology of Ontology," 859, 865.

26. Rubenstein, *Strange Wonder*, 8.

27. As Bennett writes in *The Enchantment of Modern Life*, "The more aware of wonder one is—and the more one learns to cultivate it—the more one might be able to respond gracefully and generously to the painful challenges posed by our condition as finite beings in a turbulent and unjust world" (160).

CHAPTER 18. FATE

1. See Babb, "Glancing."

2. Munshi, "Max Weber on India."

3. Kent, "'What's Written on the Forehead Will Never Fail,'" 2.

4. Distributors may bid for the right to release the film throughout one of seven territories comprising the state of Tamil Nadu (Chennai City, N.S.C. [North Arcot, South Arcot, Chengalpattu], Kovai [Coimbatore], Salem, M.R. [Madurai, Ramanathapuram], T.T. [Trichy, Thanjavur], and T.K. [Tirunelveli, Kanyakumari]), as well as other states in India and F.M.S. (foreign, Malaysia, Singapore).

5. Desjarlais, *Sensory Biographies*, 75.

6. Desjarlais, *Sensory Biographies*, 297.

7. Handelman and Shulman, *God Inside Out*, 5.

8. This physiological reaction has long been invoked in Tamil literature as an embodied sign of excitement.

9. Spinoza, *A Spinoza Reader*, 188.

10. See Guenzi, "The Allotted Share."

CHAPTER 19. AN ANTHROPOLOGY OF CREATION

1. "Delhi Gang Rape Victim Gets Symbolic Name 'Damini,'" *India Today*, December 24, 2012, accessed October 24, 2013, http://indiatoday.intoday.in/story/delhi-gangrape-victim-gets-symbolic-name-damini/1/239237.html.

2. "Delhi Gang-Rape Case, and Its Filmi Aftermath," India.com, January 2, 2013, accessed October 24, 2013, http://www.bollywoodlife.com/news-gossip/delhi-gang-rape-case-and-its-filmi-aftermath/.

3. "Do Indian Films Promote Sexual Violence and Harassment?," *The World*, PRI, January 4, 2013, accessed October 24, 2013, http://www.theworld.org/2013/01/do-indian-films-promote-sexual-violence-and-harassment/.

4. Kracauer, *From Caligari to Hitler*, 72–73.

5. Mazzarella, "Making Sense of the Cinema in Late Colonial India."

6. Although more fully evident and pronounced with regard to experience such as cinema, it is arguably always the case, as recent scholarship on "embodied" cognition has emphasized. "The machinery of the mind itself is not confined to the skull," Alva Noe writes in *Out of Our Heads*. "The head is not a magical membrane. We are involved with the world around us. We are in it and of it" (82).

7. Sobchack, *Carnal Thoughts*, 60.

8. Connolly, *Neuropolitics*, 13.

9. Elizabeth Povinelli, in "Routes/Worlds," describes an "anthropology of the otherwise" as one that "locates itself within forms of life that are at odds with dominant, and dominating, modes of being." The forms of becoming-otherwise pursued in this book unfold at the interstices of these two modes, dominant and subjugated, investing the former with unanticipated kinds of transgressive potential. See also Rushton, "Deleuzian Spectatorship," on a mode of engaging cinema as "a matter of placing oneself where one is not, of becoming someone or something one is not" (51).

10. See Ingold, *Making*, for an account of making as a "process of *growth*," one that would "place the maker from the outset as a participant in amongst a world of active materials" (21).

11. Latour, *Pandora's Hope*, 283. Latour calls here for a modified "anthropology of creation" that explicitly acknowledges the implicit ways in which "modernists" actually work with things, using the word *anthropology* in a more strictly descriptive sense.

12. This is one of the central ways I have tried to part company with the abundant work on the individual "psychology" of creativity. In *The Act of Creation*, for example, Arthur Koestler acknowledges the significance of "ripe" circumstance to acts of discovery, but argues all the same that "if ripeness were all . . . the role of genius in history would be reduced from hero to midwife, who assists the inevitable birth; and the act of creation would be merely a consummation of the preordained" (109). The either-or character of this formulation depends upon a foreclosure of the creative powers of chance and milieu. Consider, as an alternative, how Bazin sought to shift attention

from the "talent of this or that film-maker" to "the genius of the system" by emphasizing "its fertility when it comes into contact with new elements" ("De la Politique des Auteurs," 27).

13. Bazin, "A Bergsonian Film," 2, 5.

14. Simondon, "The Genesis of the Individual," 297.

15. Simondon, "The Genesis of the Individual," 300.

16. Whitehead, *Process and Reality*, 23.

17. Whitehead, *Process and Reality*, 222. On Whitehead's pragmatism, see the chapter "Pulses of Emotion" in Shaviro, *Without Criteria*, 47–70. On creativity in Whitehead's thought, see the chapter "Thinking under the Constraint of Creativity," in Stengers, *Thinking with Whitehead*, 254–77.

18. For anthropological works inspired by Whitehead's sense of process, see Ingold, *Being Alive*; Leach, *Creative Land*.

19. Rabinow et al., *Designs for an Anthropology of the Contemporary*, 64.

20. This argument is further developed in my essay "In the Event of an Anthropological Thought."

21. Wagner, *The Invention of Culture*, 138.

22. As attested by the *Oxford English Dictionary*.

23. Whitehead, *Process and Reality*, 211.

24. On the idea of ethnography as immersion, see Helmreich, "An Anthropologist Underwater."

25. See Fischer, *Emergent Forms of Life and the Anthropological Voice*, for a wide-ranging reflection on ethnographic and ethical attunement to "emergent forms of life for which conventional ethical guideposts from the past are not always sufficient" (57).

26. These themes are explored in my essay "The Time of Anthropology." See also Guyer, "'The Quickening of the Unknown.'"

27. "Just as I think of the event as attached to the everyday, I think of the everyday itself as eventful," Veena Das writes in *Life and Words*, 8.

28. Shulman, *More Than Real*, 285.

29. Shulman, *More Than Real*, 264.

30. Shulman is concerned with the genesis of a new "anthropology" of the imagination in sixteenth-century south India—its "sometimes implicit, sometimes explicit redefinition of what counts as human" (*More Than Real*, 152). But as with all anthropology, the project reaches beyond this time and place. As Shulman asks with another literary protagonist, Nala, in mind, "Is he so different from ourselves?" (183).

31. "Models of mirroring or moulding—in a word, representational models—see the basic task of expression as faithfully reflecting a state of things," Massumi observes in "Like a Thought." For Deleuze and Guattari, on the contrary, "Expression is abroad in the world—where the potential is for what may become."

32. Conant, "The World of a Movie," 302.

33. Rouch, *Cine-Ethnography*, 100.

34. Potential for such passage, always at stake in ethnographic writing, is powerfully conveyed by recent ethnographic works of an experimental bent such as Bessire, *Behold the Black Caiman*; Ochoa, *Society of the Dead*; and Raffles, *Insectopedia*. As Bessire has put it most recently, "everywhere I went I heard stories so elemental and terrible that if I really got them, I risked them becoming my own" (12).

35. James, *Essays in Radical Empiricism*, 100.

36. Although I share, therefore, the desire "to question and recast our own anthropological assumptions about truth" pursued by Holbraad's *Truth in Motion* (xvii), I would query that book's repudiation of "evocation" (79) as a means of engaging in this pursuit, for in the history of evocative anthropological prose lies the kernel of a far more radical practice of truth than the faltering purchase on human nature that Holbraad describes and seeks to surpass. To take just one example, consider Tyler's characterization of the "realism" of ethnographic evocation in "Post-modern Ethnography: "It describes no objects and makes no break between describing and what is being described" (137).

37. Clifford, *The Predicament of Culture*, 147.

38. Taussig, *I Swear I Saw This*, 126.

39. See, for example, Taussig, *I Swear I Saw This*, 9, 79.

40. Deleuze, *Cinema 2*, 189. "It" here is the body, but the body as mounted with a camera.

41. Suhr and Willerslev, "Can Film Show the Invisible?," 285.

42. Crapanzano, *Imaginative Horizons*, 14.

43. Hage, "Critical Anthropological Thought," 305.

44. As Deleuze writes in *Essays Critical and Clinical*, "There is no literature without fabulation, but, as Bergson was able to see, fabulation—the fabulating function— does not consist in imagining or projecting an ego. Rather, it attains these visions, it raises itself to these becomings and powers" (3). For a helpful discussion of speculative realism, a contemporary development in continental theory and philosophy that shares an intriguing kinship with contemporary anthropology's ontological turn, see Shaviro, *The Universe of Things*.

45. Lévi-Strauss, *The Raw and the Cooked*, 6. For a lucid discussion, see Wiseman, *Lévi-Strauss, Anthropology, and Aesthetics*, who underscores that this project is better understood as a matter of aesthetic production than an idealist retreat from the world.

46. "Vision in this technological feast becomes unregulated gluttony," Haraway writes regarding the endless proliferation of cameras and sensors of all sizes and scales: "all seems not just mythically about the god trick of seeing everything from nowhere, but to have put the myth into ordinary practice" ("Situated Knowledges," 581).

47. The quotation is from his voice-over to the 1982 film *No Frames, No Boundaries*, cited in Poole, *Earthrise*, 165–66.

48. Poole, *Earthrise*, 82.

49. Hayden White argues as much in an exegesis of Foucault: "For Foucault, the human sciences of the twentieth century are characterizable precisely by the *Ironic* relationship which they sustain with their objects . . . . And his own stance . . . is post-ironic inasmuch as he desires to lose thought in myth once more" (*Tropics of Discourse*, 255).

50. Cited in Hansen, *Cinema and Experience*, 142. The following discussion is deeply indebted to her book, especially chapters 5 and 7.

51. Cited in Hansen, *Cinema and Experience*, 155.

52. Benjamin, "On the Mimetic Faculty," 720.

53. "'The Wire' References Abound on Social Media in Response to Riots," *The Baltimore Sun*, April 28, 2015, accessed April 28, 2015, http://www.baltimoresun.com /features/baltimore-insider-blog/bal-the-wire-references-abound-on-social-media -20150428-story.html/; "Baltimore Riots Compared to 'The Purge,'" *USA Today*, April 28, 2015, accessed April 28, 2015, http://www.usatoday.com/story/news/nation-now

/2015/04/28/baltimore-riots-twitter-the-purge-freddie-gray/26502459/; "Baltimore Rioting Kicked Off with Rumors of 'Purge,'" *The Baltimore Sun*, accessed April 28, 2015, http://www.baltimoresun.com/news/maryland/baltimore-riots/bs-md-ci-freddie -gray-violence-chronology-20150427-story.html/.

54. Viveiros de Castro, "Cannibal Metaphysics," 23.

55. Viveiros de Castro, *Cosmological Perspectivism in Amazonia and Elsewhere*, 107. The likeness I am drawing here complicates Viveiros de Castro's categorical distinction between a modern model of "creation-production" and a nonmodern mode of "transformation-transference." Production, in the eminently modern process of filmmaking that I have sketched here, operates through diverse relays of transformation and transference rather than through the "imposition of mental design over formless matter" (58). As Matei Candea has observed regarding the anthropomorphic thinking of behavioral ecologists, "clear-cut contrasts between us and them are constantly undermined by echoes and mirrors, copies and transformations" (130).

BIBLIOGRAPHY

Adorno, Theodor, and Hanns Eisler. *Composing for the Films*. New York: Continuum, 2007.

Ahmed, Sara. "Orientations: Toward a Queer Phenomenology." *GLQ* 12 (2006): 543–74.

Ali, Daud. "Anxieties of Attachment: The Dynamics of Courtship in Medieval India." *Modern Asian Studies* 36 (2002): 103–39.

Allison, Anne. *Millennial Monsters: Japanese Toys and the Global Imagination*. Durham, NC: Duke University Press, 2006.

Althusser, Louis. "Ideology and Ideological State Apparatuses." In *Lenin and Philosophy and Other Essays*, 127–86. New York: Monthly Review Press, 1970.

Alton, John. *Painting with Light*. Berkeley: University of California Press, 1995.

Anderson, Joseph. *The Reality of Illusion: An Ecological Approach to Cognitive Film Theory*. Carbondale: Southern Illinois University Press, 1996.

Ansell-Pearson, Keith. "The Reality of the Virtual: Bergson and Deleuze." *MLN* 120 (2005): 1112–27.

Babb, Alan. "Glancing: Visual Interaction in Hinduism." *Journal of Anthropological Research* 37 (1981): 387–401.

Bachelard, Gaston. *The Poetics of Space*. Boston: Beacon Press, 1969.

Balslev, Anindita Niyogi. *A Study of Time in Indian Philosophy*. New Delhi: Munshiram Manoharlal Publishers, 1999.

Barber, Karin. "Improvisation and the Art of Making Things Stick." In *Creativity and Cultural Improvisation*, edited by Elizabeth Hallam and Tim Ingold, 25–41. Oxford: Berg, 2007.

Barker, Jennifer. *The Tactile Eye: Touch and the Cinematic Experience*. Berkeley: University of California Press, 2009.

Barnwell, Jane. *Production Design: Architects of the Screen*. London: Wallflower Press, 2003.

Baskaran, Theodore. *The Eye of the Serpent*. Madras: EastWest Books, 1996.

Baskaran, Theodore. "Trade Unionism in South Indian Film Industry." In *History through the Lens: Perspectives on South Indian Cinema*, 87–116. Hyderabad: Orient Blackswan, 2009.

Batchelor, David. *Chromophobia*. London: Reaktion Books, 2000.

Bate, Bernard. *Tamil Oratory and the Dravidian Aesthetic*. New York: Columbia University Press, 2009.

Bateson, Gregory. *Steps to an Ecology of Mind*. Chicago: University of Chicago Press, 2000.

Baudrillard, Jean. *America*. New York: Verso, 1988.

Baudry, Jean-Louis. "Ideological Effects of the Basic Cinematographic Apparatus." *Film Quarterly* 28 (1974–75): 39–47.

Bazin, Andre. "A Bergsonian Film: The Picasso Mystery." *Journal of Aesthetic Education* 35 (2001): 1–9.

Bazin, Andre. "De la Politique des Auteurs." In *Auteurs and Authorship: A Film Reader*, edited by Barry Keith Grant, 19–28. London: Blackwell, 2008.

Bazin, Andre. *What Is Cinema?* Vol. 1. Berkeley: University of California Press, 1967.

Beck, Jay, and Tony Grajeda, eds. *Lowering the Boom: Critical Studies in Film Sound*. Urbana: University of Illinois Press, 2008.

Belton, John. "Painting by the Numbers: The Digital Intermediate." *Film Quarterly* 61 (2008): 58–65.

Benjamin, Walter. "A Child's View of Color." In *Walter Benjamin: Selected Writings*, vol. 1, *1913–1926*, edited by Marcust Bullock and Michael W. Jennings, 50–51. Cambridge, MA: Harvard University Press, 1996.

Benjamin, Walter. "On the Mimetic Faculty." In *Walter Benjamin: Selected Writings*, vol. 2, part 2, edited by Michael W. Jennings, Gary Smith, and Howard Eiland, 720–22. Cambridge, MA: Harvard University Press, 2005.

Benjamin, Walter. "The Work of Art in the Age of Its Technological Reproducibility: Second Version." In *Walter Benjamin: Selected Writings*, vol. 3, edited by Howard Eiland and Michael W. Jennings, 101–33. Cambridge, MA: Belknap Press, 2002.

Bennett, Jane. *The Enchantment of Modern Life: Attachments, Crossings, and Ethics*. Princeton, NJ: Princeton University Press, 2001.

Bennett, Jane. *Vibrant Matter: A Political Ecology of Things*. Durham, NC: Duke University Press, 2010.

Bergson, Henri. *Creative Evolution*. New York: Cosimo Classics, 2005.

Bergson, Henri. *Creative Mind*. New York: Dover, 2004.

Bergson, Henri. *Matter and Memory*. New York: Dover, 2004.

Bergson, Henri. "Memory of the Present and False Recognition." In *Mind-Energy: Lectures and Essays*, 134–85. New York: Henry Holt, 1920.

Berlant, Lauren. "Love (A Queer Feeling)." In *Psychoanalysis and Homosexuality*, edited by Tim Dean and Christopher Lane, 432–51. Chicago: University of Chicago Press, 2000.

Berliner, Todd, and Dale J. Cohen. "The Illusion of Continuity: Active Perception and the Classical Editing System." *Journal of Film and Video* 63 (2011): 44–63.

Bessire, Lucas. *Behold the Black Caiman: A Chronicle of Ayoreo Life*. Chicago: University of Chicago Press, 2014.

Betty, Stafford. "Dvaita, Advaita, and Visistadvaita: Contrasting Views of Moksa." *Asian Philosophy* 20 (2010): 215–24.

Biehl, Joao. "Ethnography in the Way of Theory." *Cultural Anthropology* 28 (2013): 573–97.

Bille, Mikkel, and Tim F. Sorensen. "An Anthropology of Luminosity." *Journal of Material Culture* 12 (2007): 264–84.

Bloch, Ernst. *The Principle of Hope*. Vol. 1. Cambridge, MA: MIT Press, 1986.

Blumenberg, Hans. "Light as a Metaphor for Truth." In *Modernity and the Hegemony of Vision*, edited by D. Levin, 30–62. Berkeley: University of California Press, 1993.

Booth, Gregory D. *Behind the Curtain: Making Music in Mumbai's Film Studios*. New Delhi: Oxford University Press, 2008.

Bordwell, David. "Intensified Continuity: Visual Style in Contemporary American Film." *Film Quarterly* 55 (2002): 16–28.

Bordwell, David, Janet Staiger, and Kristin Thompson. "The Continuity System." In *The Classical Hollywood Cinema: Film Style and Mode of Production to 1960*, 194–213. New York: Columbia University Press, 1985.

Brouwer, Jan. *The Makers of the World: Caste, Craft and Mind of South Indian Artisans.* Delhi: Oxford University Press, 1995.

Brown, William. "Resisting the Psycho-Logic of Intensified Continuity." *Projections* 5 (2011): 69–86.

Buck, Daniel C., and K. Paramasivan. *The Study of Stolen Love: A Translation of* Kalaviyal enra Iraiyanar Akapporul *with Commentary by Nakkiranar.* Atlanta: Scholars Press, 1997.

Bull, Michael. *Sound Moves: iPod Culture and Urban Experience.* New York: Routledge, 2007.

Bynum, Caroline W. "Presidential Address: Wonder." *American Historical Review* 102 (1997): 1–26.

Caldwell, John T. *Production Culture: Industrial Reflexivity and Critical Practice in Film and Television.* Durham, NC: Duke University Press, 2008.

Calvino, Italo. *If on a Winter's Night a Traveler.* New York: Harcourt Brace Jovanovich, 1982.

Candea, Matei. "Different Species, One Theory: Reflections on Anthropomorphism and Anthropological Comparison." *Cambridge Anthropology* 30 (2012): 118–35.

Central Board of Film Certification. "Annual Report 2011." Mumbai: Government of India, Ministry of Information and Broadcasting, 2012.

Chakrabarty, Dipesh. "The Climate of History: Four Theses." *Critical Inquiry* 35 (2009): 197–222.

Chakrabarty, Dipesh. *Provincializing Europe: Postcolonial Thought and Historical Difference.* Princeton, NJ: Princeton University Press, 2000.

Chakravarty, Venkatesh. "Bharathirajavin Cinima." *Ini* (October 1986).

Charney, Leo. "In a Moment: Film and the Philosophy of Modernity." In *Cinema and the Invention of Modern Life*, edited by Leo Charney and Vanessa Schwartz, 279–96. Berkeley: University of California Press, 1995.

Chion, Michel. *Audio-Vision: Sound on Screen.* New York: Columbia University Press, 1994.

Chion, Michel. *The Voice in Cinema.* New York: Columbia University Press, 1999.

Chua, Jocelyn Lim. *In Pursuit of the Good Life: Aspiration and Suicide in Globalizing South India.* Berkeley: University of California Press, 2014.

Clifford, James. *The Predicament of Culture: Twentieth-Century Ethnography, Literature, and Art.* Cambridge, MA: Harvard University Press, 1988.

Cohen, Jeffrey Jerome. "Introduction: Ecology's Rainbow." In *Prismatic Ecology: Ecotheory beyond Green*, edited by Jeffrey Jerome Cohen, xv–xxxv. Minneapolis: University of Minnesota Press, 2013.

Conant, James. "The World of a Movie." In *Making a Difference: Rethinking Humanism and the Humanities*, edited by Niklas Forsberg and Susanne Jansson, 293–324. Stockholm: Thales, 2011.

Condry, Ian. *The Soul of Anime: Collaborative Creativity and Japan's Media Success Story.* Durham, NC: Duke University Press, 2013.

Connolly, William E. *Neuropolitics: Thinking, Culture, Speed.* Minneapolis: University of Minnesota Press, 2002.

Connolly, William E. *A World of Becoming.* Durham, NC: Duke University Press, 2011.

Coomaraswamy, Ananda K. *The Arts and Crafts of India and Ceylon.* New York: Noonday Press, 1964.

Cowan, Michael. "The Heart Machine: 'Rhythm' and Body in Weimar Film and Fritz Lang's *Metropolis*." *Modernism/Modernity* 14 (2007): 225–48.

Crapanzano, Vincent. *Imaginative Horizons: An Essay in Literary-Philosophical Anthropology*. Chicago: University of Chicago Press, 2004.

Crapanzano, Vincent. "Reflections on Hope as a Category of Social and Psychological Analysis." *Cultural Anthropology* 18 (2003): 3–32.

Crutzen, Paul J. "Geology of Mankind." *Nature* 415 (2002): 23.

Das, Veena. *Life and Words: Violence and the Descent into the Ordinary*. Berkeley: University of California Press, 2007.

Daston, Lorraine, and Katherine Park. *Wonders and the Order of Nature: 1150–1750*. New York: Zone Books, 2001.

Debaene, Vincent. *Far Afield: French Anthropology between Science and Literature*. Chicago: University of Chicago Press, 2014.

de Certeau, Michel. *The Practice of Everyday Life*. Berkeley: University of California Press, 1984.

Deleuze, Gilles. *Bergsonism*. New York: Zone Books, 1991.

Deleuze, Gilles. *Cinema 1: The Movement-Image*. Minneapolis: University of Minnesota Press, 1986.

Deleuze, Gilles. *Cinema 2: The Time-Image*. Minneapolis: University of Minnesota Press, 1989.

Deleuze, Gilles. *Difference and Repetition*. London: Continuum, 2004.

Deleuze, Gilles. *Essays Critical and Clinical*. New York: Verso, 1998.

Deleuze, Gilles. *Expressionism in Philosophy: Spinoza*. New York: Zone Books, 1992.

Deleuze, Gilles. *Francis Bacon: The Logic of Sensation*. Minneapolis: University of Minnesota Press, 2003.

Deleuze, Gilles, and Félix Guattari. *Anti-Oedipus: Capitalism and Schizophrenia*. Minneapolis: University of Minnesota Press, 1983.

Deleuze, Gilles, and Félix Guattari. *A Thousand Plateaus*. Minneapolis: University of Minnesota Press, 1987.

Deleuze, Gilles, and Félix Guattari. *What Is Philosophy?* New York: Columbia University Press, 1994.

Deleuze, Gilles, and Claire Parnet. "Dead Psychoanalysis: Analyse." In *Dialogues II*, 77–123. New York: Columbia University Press, 2007.

del Rio, Elena. "Film." In *Handbook of Phenomenological Aesthetics*, edited by Hans Rainer Sepp and Lester Embree, 111–17. Dordrecht: Springer, 2010.

De Quincey, Thomas. *Joan of Arc and the English Mail-Coach*. Boston: D. C. Heath, 1907.

Desjarlais, Robert. *Sensory Biographies: Lives and Deaths among Nepal's Yolmo Buddhists*. Berkeley: University of California Press, 2003.

de Vries, Hent. "Of Miracles and Special Effects." *International Journal for Philosophy of Religion* 50 (2001): 41–56.

Dewey, John. *Art as Experience*. New York: Penguin Books, 1934.

Dhananjayan, G. *The Best of Tamil Cinema*. Vol. 1. Chennai: Galatta, 2011.

Dickey, Sara. *Cinema and the Urban Poor in South India*. Cambridge: Cambridge University Press, 1993.

Doane, Mary Ann. "The Voice in the Cinema: The Articulation of Body and Space." *Yale French Studies* 60 (1980): 33–50.

Dolar, Mladen. *A Voice and Nothing More*. Cambridge, MA: MIT Press, 2006.

Dornfeld, Barry. *Producing Public Television: Producing Public Culture*. Princeton, NJ: Princeton University Press, 1998.

Duffy, Enda. *The Speed Handbook: Velocity, Pleasure, Modernism*. Durham, NC: Duke University Press, 2009.

Dwyer, Rachel. *Filming the Gods: Religion and Indian Cinema*. London: Routledge, 2006.

Dwyer, Rachel, and Divia Patel. *Cinema India: The Visual Culture of Hindi Film*. London: Reaktion Books, 2002.

Ebeling, Sascha. *Colonizing the Realm of Words: The Transformation of Tamil Literature in Nineteenth-Century South India*. Albany: State University of New York Press, 2010.

Eisenstein, Sergei. "A Dialectical Approach to Film Form." In *Film Form: Essays in Film Theory*, 45–63. New York: Harcourt, 1977.

Eisenstein, Sergei. "Dickens, Griffith, and the Film Today." In *Film Form: Essays in Film Theory*, 195–255. New York: Harcourt, 1977.

Elsaesser, Thomas, and Malte Hagener. *Film Theory: An Introduction through the Senses*. New York: Routledge, 2010.

Epstein, Jean. *The Intelligence of a Machine*. Minneapolis: Univocal Publishing, 2014.

Fassin, Didier. "True Life, Real Lives: Revisiting the Boundaries between Ethnography and Fiction." *American Ethnologist* 41 (2014): 40–55.

Federation of Indian Chambers of Commerce and Industry and Ernst & Young. "Indian Entertainment Down South: From Script to Screen." Chennai: FICCI Frames, 2009.

Feld, Steven. *Sound and Sentiment: Birds, Weeping, Poetics and Song in Kaluli Expression*. Durham, NC: Duke University Press, 2012.

Ferguson, James, and James Burgess. *The Cave Temples of India*. London: W. H. Allen, 1880.

Fischer, Michael M. J. *Emergent Forms of Life and the Anthropological Voice*. Durham, NC: Duke University Press, 2003.

Flood, Gavin. "Miracles in Hinduism." In *The Cambridge Companion to Miracles*, edited by Graham T. Twelftree, 184–98. Cambridge: Cambridge University Press, 2011.

Forster, Michael N. "Herder and the Birth of Modern Anthropology." In *After Herder: Philosophy of Language in the German Tradition*, 199–243. Oxford: Oxford University Press, 2010.

Foucault, Michel. *The History of Sexuality, Volume 1*. New York: Vintage, 1990.

Foucault, Michel. "Interview with Michel Foucault." In *Michel Foucault: Power*, edited by James D. Faubion, 239–97. New York: New Press, 2000.

Foucault, Michel. *The Use of Pleasure*. New York: Vintage Books, 1990.

Frank, Katherine. *G-Strings and Sympathy: Strip Club Regulars and Male Desire*. Durham, NC: Duke University Press, 2002.

Freud, Sigmund. *Beyond the Pleasure Principle*. New York: W. W. Norton, 1961.

Freud, Sigmund. "Creative Writers and Day-dreaming." In *The Standard Edition of the Complete Psychological Works of Sigmund Freud*, vol. 9, edited by James Strachey, 141–54. London: Hogarth, 1959.

Freud, Sigmund. *The Ego and the Id*. New York: W. W. Norton, 1990.

Freud, Sigmund. *The Interpretation of Dreams*. New York: Avon Books, 1965.

Friedberg, Anne. "Urban Mobility and Cinematic Visuality: The Screens of Los Angeles." *Journal of Visual Culture* 1, no. 2 (2002): 183–204.

Fuller, C. J. *The Camphor Flame: Popular Hinduism and Society in India*. Princeton, NJ: Princeton University Press, 2004.

Gage, John. *Color and Culture: Practice and Meaning from Antiquity to Abstraction.* Berkeley: University of California Press, 1993.

Ganti, Tejaswini. *Producing Bollywood: Inside the Contemporary Hindi Film Industry.* Durham, NC: Duke University Press, 2012.

García Márquez, Gabriel. *Chronicle of a Death Foretold.* New York: Knopf, 1983.

Geertz, Clifford. *The Interpretation of Cultures.* New York: Basic Books, 1973.

Geertz, Clifford. *Works and Lives: The Anthropologist as Author.* Stanford, CA: Stanford University Press, 1988.

Gell, Alfred. *Art and Agency: An Anthropological Theory.* Oxford: Oxford University Press, 1998.

Gerow, Edwin. "Abhinavagupta's Aesthetics as a Speculative Paradigm." *Journal of the American Oriental Society* 114 (1994): 186–208.

Gibson, James J. *The Ecological Approach to Visual Perception.* Hillsdale, NJ: Lawrence Erlbaum, 1986.

Ginsburg, Faye, Lila Abu-Lughod, and Brian Larkin, eds. *Media Worlds: Anthropology on New Terrain.* Berkeley: University of California Press, 2002.

Gnoli, Raniero. *The Aesthetic Experience according to Abhinavagupta.* Varanasi: Chowkhamba Sanskrit Series Office, 1968.

Goethe, Johann Wolfgang. *Maxims and Reflections.* New York: Penguin Books, 1998.

Goethe, Johann Wolfgang. *Theory of Colours.* Cambridge, MA: MIT Press, 1970.

Gold, Joel, and Ian Gold. "The 'Truman Show' Delusion: Psychosis in the Global Village." *Cognitive Neuropsychiatry* 17 (2012): 455–72.

Goldstone, Brian. "The Miraculous Life." *Johannesburg Salon* 4 (2011): 81–96.

Goodman, Nelson. *Ways of Worldmaking.* Indianapolis: Hackett, 1978.

Gopal, Sangita, and Sujata Moorti, eds. *Global Bollywood: Transnational Travels of the Song-Dance Sequence.* Minneapolis: University of Minnesota Press, 2008.

Gopalan, Lalitha. *Cinema of Interruptions: Action Genres in Contemporary Indian Cinema.* London: British Film Institute, 2002.

Gopinath, Gayatri. *Impossible Desires: Queer Diasporas and South Asian Public Cultures.* Durham, NC: Duke University Press, 2005.

Gottlieb, Sidney. "Unknown Hitchcock: The Unrealized Projects." In *Hitchcock: Past and Future*, edited by Richard Allen and Sam Ishii-Gonzales, 85–106. London: Routledge, 2003.

Grimshaw, Anna. *The Ethnographer's Eye: Ways of Seeing in Modern Anthropology.* Cambridge: Cambridge University Press, 2001.

Grosz, Elizabeth. "Animal Sex: Libido as Desire and Death." In *Sexy Bodies: The Strange Carnalities of Feminism*, edited by Elizabeth Grosz and Elspeth Probyn, 278–99. London: Routledge, 1995.

Grosz, Elizabeth. *Chaos, Territory, Art: Deleuze and the Framing of the Earth.* New York: Columbia University Press, 2008.

Grosz, Elizabeth. *Time Travels: Feminism, Nature, Power.* Crows Nest, Australia: Allen and Unwin, 2005.

Guenzi, Caterina. "The Allotted Share: Managing Fortune in Astrological Counseling in Contemporary India." *Social Analysis* 56, no. 2 (2012): 39–55.

Gunning, Tom. "The Cinema of Attraction: Early Film, Its Spectator, and the Avant-Garde." *Wide Angle* 8 (1986): 63–70.

Gupta, Akhil, and James Ferguson, eds. *Culture, Power, Place: Explorations in Critical Anthropology.* Durham, NC: Duke University Press, 1997.

Guyer, Jane I. "'The Quickening of the Unknown': Epistemologies of Surprise in An- 319
thropology." *Hau: Journal of Ethnographic Theory* 3, no. 3 (2013): 283–307.

Hage, Ghassan. "Critical Anthropological Thought and the Radical Political Imaginary
Today." *Critique of Anthropology* 32 (2012): 285–308.

Hahn, Tomie. *Sensational Knowledge: Embodying Culture through Japanese Dance.*
Middletown, CT: Wesleyan University Press, 2007.

Han, Clara. *Life in Debt: Times of Care and Violence in Neoliberal Chile.* Berkeley: University of California Press, 2012.

Handelman, Don, and David Shulman. *God Inside Out: Siva's Game of Dice.* New York:
Oxford University Press, 2007.

Hansen, Miriam Bratu. *Cinema and Experience: Siegfried Kracauer, Walter Benjamin, and
Theodor W. Adorno.* Berkeley: University of California Press, 2012.

Haraway, Donna. "Situated Knowledges: The Science Question in Feminism and the
Privilege of Partial Perspective." *Feminist Studies* 14 (1988): 575–99.

Harvey, David. *Spaces of Hope.* Edinburgh: Edinburgh University Press, 2000.

Hastrup, Kirsten. "Playing One's Part: The Imaginative Framework of Agency." *Irish
Journal of Anthropology* 10 (2007): 26–34.

Heath, Stephen. "Narrative Space." In *Questions of Cinema,* 19–75. Bloomington: Indiana University Press, 1981.

Heidegger, Martin. *The Question Concerning Technology and Other Essays.* New York:
Harper and Row, 1977.

Helmreich, Stefan. "An Anthropologist Underwater: Immersive Soundscapes, Sub-
marine Cyborgs, and Transductive Ethnography." *American Ethnologist* 34 (2007):
621–41.

Hoek, Lotte. *Cut-Pieces: Celluloid Obscenity and Popular Cinema in Bangladesh.* New
York: Columbia University Press, 2013.

Holbraad, Martin. *Truth in Motion: The Recursive Anthropology of Cuban Divination.* Chicago: University of Chicago Press, 2012.

Hrabal, Bohumil. *Dancing Lessons for the Advanced in Age.* New York: Harcourt Brace,
2005.

Hughes, Stephen P. "House Full: Silent Film Genre, Exhibition and Audiences in South
India." *Indian Economic and Social History Review* 43 (2006): 31–62.

Hughes, Stephen P. "Music in the Age of Mechanical Reproduction: Drama, Gramophone, and the Beginnings of Tamil Cinema." *Journal of Asian Studies* 66 (2007):
3–34.

Hughes, Stephen P. "Play It Again, Saraswathi: Gramophone, Religion, and Devotional
Music in Colonial South India." In *More Than Bollywood: Studies in Indian Popular
Music,* edited by Gregory D. Booth and Bradley Shope, 114–41. New York: Oxford
University Press, 2013.

Hughes, Stephen P. "Urban Mobility and the History of Cinema-going in Chennai." In
Chennai Not Madras: Perspectives on the City, edited by A. R. Venkatachalapathy,
39–48. New Delhi: Marg, 2006.

Hughes, Stephen P. "What Is Tamil about Tamil Cinema?" *South Asian Popular Culture*
8 (2010): 213–29.

Hunter, Mary. "'To Play as If from the Soul of the Composer': The Idea of the Per-
former in Early Romantic Aesthetics." *Journal of the American Musicological Society*
58 (2005): 357–98.

Ingold, Tim. *Being Alive: Essays on Movement, Knowledge, and Description*. New York: Routledge, 2011.

Ingold, Tim. *Lines: A Brief History*. New York: Routledge, 2008.

Ingold, Tim. *Making: Anthropology, Archaeology, Art and Architecture*. New York: Routledge, 2013.

Ingold, Tim, and Elizabeth Hallam. "Creativity and Cultural Improvisation: An Introduction." In *Creativity and Cultural Improvisation*, edited by Elizabeth Hallam and Tim Ingold, 1–24. Oxford: Berg, 2007.

Jackson, Michael. *At Home in the World*. Durham, NC: Duke University Press, 1995.

Jackson, Michael. "Introduction: Phenomenology, Radical Empiricism, and Anthropological Critique." In *Things as They Are: New Directions in Phenomenological Anthropology*, edited by Michael Jackson, 1–50. Bloomington: Indiana University Press, 1989.

Jacob, Preminda. *Celluloid Deities: The Visual Culture of Cinema and Politics in South India*. Lanham, MD: Lexington Books, 2009.

Jain, Kajri. *Gods in the Bazaar: The Economies of Indian Calendar Art*. Durham, NC: Duke University Press, 2007.

James, William. *Essays in Radical Empiricism*. Lincoln: University of Nebraska Press, 1996.

Jay, Martin. *Downcast Eyes*. Berkeley: University of California Press, 1994.

Kaali, Sundar. "Narrating Seduction: Vicissitudes of the Sexed Subject in Tamil Nativity Film." In *Making Meaning in Indian Cinema*, edited by Ravi Vasudevan, 168–90. New Delhi: Oxford University Press, 2000.

Kalmus, Natalie. "Color Consciousness." In *Color, the Film Reader*, edited by Angela Dalle Vacche, 24–29. New York: Routledge, 2006.

Kant, Immanuel. *Critique of the Power of Judgment*. Cambridge: Cambridge University Press, 2001.

Kearney, Richard. *The Wake of the Imagination: Theories of Creativity in Western Culture*. London: Hutchinson, 1988.

Kent, Eliza. "'What's Written on the Forehead Will Never Fail': Karma, Fate, and Headwriting in Indian Folktales." *Asian Ethnology* 68 (2009): 1–26.

Koestler, Arthur. *The Act of Creation*. New York: Dell, 1964.

Kohn, Eduardo. *How Forests Think: Toward an Anthropology beyond the Human*. Berkeley: University of California Press, 2013.

Kracauer, Siegfried. "Calico-World." In *The Mass Ornament: Weimar Essays*, 281–90. Cambridge, MA: Harvard University Press, 1995.

Kracauer, Siegfried. *From Caligari to Hitler: A Psychological History of the German Film*. Princeton, NJ: Princeton University Press, 1974.

Kracauer, Siegfried. *Theory of Film: The Redemption of Physical Reality*. Princeton, NJ: Princeton University Press, 1997.

Kramrisch, Stella. *The Hindu Temple*. Vol. 1. Delhi: Motilal Banarsidass, 1976.

Krauss, Rosalind. "The Originality of the Avant-Garde: A Postmodernist Repetition." *October* 18 (1981): 47–66.

Krishnan, Rajan. "Imaginary Geographies: The Makings of 'South' in Contemporary Tamil Cinema." In *Tamil Cinema: The Cultural Politics of India's Other Film Industry*, edited by Selvaraj Velayutham, 139–53. London: Routledge, 2008.

Laidlaw, James. *Riches and Renunciation: Religion, Economy and Society among the Jains*. New York: Oxford University Press, 1995.

Larkin, Brian. "The Materiality of Cinema Theaters in Northern Nigeria." In *Media Worlds*, edited by Faye Ginsburg, Lila Abu-Lughod, and Brian Larkin, 319–36. Berkeley: University of California Press, 2002.

Latour, Bruno. "Biography of an Inquiry: On a Book About Modes of Existence." *Social Studies of Science* 43 (2013): 287–301.

Latour, Bruno. *An Inquiry into Modes of Existence.* Cambridge, MA: Harvard University Press, 2013.

Latour, Bruno. "The Migration of the Aura — or How to Explore the Original through Its Facsimiles." In *Switching Codes: Thinking through Digital Technology in the Humanities and the Arts*, edited by T. Bartscherer and R. Coover, 275–97. Chicago: University of Chicago Press, 2011.

Latour, Bruno. *Pandora's Hope: On the Reality of Science Studies.* Cambridge, MA: Harvard University Press, 1999.

Lavie, Smadar, Kirin Narayan, and Renato Rosaldo, eds. *Creativity/Anthropology.* Ithaca, NY: Cornell University Press, 1993.

Leach, James. *Creative Land: Place and Procreation on the Rai Coast of Papua New Guinea.* New York: Berghahn Books, 2003.

Lefebvre, Henri. *The Production of Space.* Oxford: Blackwell, 1991.

Lefebvre, Henri. *Rhythmanalysis.* London: Continuum, 2004.

Lefebvre, Martin, ed. *Landscape and Film.* New York: Routledge, 2006.

Lévi-Strauss, Claude. "The Art of the Northwest Coast at the American Museum of Natural History." *Gazette des Beaux-Arts* 6, no. 24 (1943): 175–88.

Lévi-Strauss, Claude. *The Raw and the Cooked.* Chicago: University of Chicago Press, 1987.

Lévi-Strauss, Claude. *The Way of the Masks.* Seattle: University of Washington Press, 1988.

Lim, Bliss Cua. *Translating Time: Cinema, the Fantastic, and Temporal Critique.* Durham, NC: Duke University Press, 2009.

Lingis, Alphonso. *Dangerous Emotions.* Berkeley: University of California Press, 2000.

Malinowski, Bronislaw. *Argonauts of the Western Pacific.* Prospect Heights, IL: Waveland Press, 1984.

Malinowski, Bronislaw. *A Diary in the Strict Sense of the Term.* Stanford, CA: Stanford University Press, 1989.

Malm, Andreas, and Alf Hornborg. "The Geology of Mankind? A Critique of the Anthropocene Narrative." *Anthropocene Review* 1 (2014): 62–69.

Mamet, David. *On Directing Film.* New York: Viking, 1991.

Marcus, George E. "The Modernist Sensibility in Recent Ethnographic Writing and the Cinematic Metaphor of Montage." *Visual Anthropology Review* 6 (1990): 2–12.

Marinelli, Lydia. "Screening Wish Theories: Dream Psychologies and Early Cinema." *Science in Context* 19 (2006): 87–110.

Marinetti, F. T. "Futurist Sensibility and Wireless Imagination." *New England Review* 17 (1995): 30–32.

Marks, Laura. *The Skin of the Film: Intercultural Cinema, Embodiment, and the Senses.* Durham, NC: Duke University Press, 2000.

Marrati, Paola. "Time, Life, Concepts: The Newness of Bergson." *MLN* 120 (2005): 1099–111.

Mason, David. "*Rasa*, 'Rasaesthetics' and Dramatic Theory as Performance Packaging." *Theatre Research International* 31 (2006): 69–83.

Massey, Doreen. *For Space*. London: Sage, 2005.

Massumi, Brian. "Like a Thought." In *A Shock to Thought: Expression after Deleuze and Guattari*, edited by Brian Massumi, xiii–xxxviii. London: Routledge, 2002.

Mayer, Vicki. *Below the Line: Producers and Production Studies in the New Television Economy*. Durham, NC: Duke University Press, 2011.

Mayer, Vicki, John Caldwell, and Miranda Banks, eds. *Production Studies: Cultural Studies of Media Industries*. New York: Routledge, 2009.

Mazumdar, Ranjani. *Bombay Cinema: An Archive of the City*. Minneapolis: University of Minnesota Press, 2007.

Mazzarella, William. "Making Sense of the Cinema in Late Colonial India." In *Censorship in South Asia: Cultural Regulation from Sedition to Seduction*, 63–86. Bloomington: Indiana University Press, 2009.

McCourt, John. *Roll Away the Reel World: James Joyce and Cinema*. Cork: Cork University Press, 2010.

McLean, Stuart. "Stories and Cosmogonies: Imagining Creativity beyond 'Nature' and 'Culture.'" *Cultural Anthropology* 24 (2009): 213–45.

McMahan, David. *Empty Vision: Metaphor and Visionary Imagery in Mahayana Buddhism*. New York: Oxford University Press, 2008.

McMahan, David. "Repackaging Zen for the West." In *Westward Dharma: Buddhism beyond Asia*, edited by C. Prebish and M. Baumann, 218–29. Berkeley: University of California Press, 2002.

Meintjes, Louise. *Sound of Africa! Making Music Zulu in a South African Studio*. Durham, NC: Duke University Press, 2003.

Merleau-Ponty, Maurice. "Cezanne's Doubt." In *The Merleau-Ponty Aesthetics Reader: Philosophy and Painting*, edited by Galen A. Johnson, 59–75. Evanston, IL: Northwestern University Press, 1993.

Merleau-Ponty, Maurice. "Eye and Mind." In *The Merleau-Ponty Aesthetics Reader: Philosophy and Painting*, edited by Galen A. Johnson, 121–50. Evanston, IL: Northwestern University Press, 1993.

Metz, Christian. *The Imaginary Signifier: Psychoanalysis and the Cinema*. Bloomington: Indiana University Press, 1982.

Misek, Richard. *Chromatic Cinema: A History of Screen Color*. New York: Wiley-Blackwell, 2010.

Mitchell, W. J. T. *What Do Pictures Want?* Chicago: University of Chicago Press, 2005.

Mitter, Partha, et al. "Decentering Modernism: Art History and Avant-Garde Art from the Periphery." *Art Bulletin* 90 (2008): 531–74.

Mittermaier, Amira. *Dreams That Matter: Egyptian Landscapes of the Imagination*. Berkeley: University of California Press, 2010.

Miyazaki, Hirokazu. *The Method of Hope: Anthropology, Philosophy, and Fijian Knowledge*. Stanford, CA: Stanford University Press, 2004.

Motion Picture Association of America. "Theatrical Market Statistics 2011." www.mpaa.org.

Mulvey, Laura. "Visual Pleasure and Narrative Cinema." In *Media and Cultural Studies: KeyWorks*, edited by Meenakshi Gigi Durham and Douglas M. Kellner, 342–52. Oxford: Blackwell, 2006.

Munshi, Surendra. "Max Weber on India: An Introductory Critique." *Contributions to Indian Sociology* 22 (1988): 1–34.

Munsterberg, Hugo. *The Photoplay: A Psychological Study*. New York: Routledge, 2002.

Murch, Walter. *In the Blink of an Eye: A Perspective on Film Editing*. Los Angeles: Silman-James Press, 2001.

Nehru, Jawaharlal. "Tryst with Destiny." In *The Essential Writings of Jawaharlal Nehru*, edited by S. Gopal and Uma Iyengar, 346–47. Delhi: Oxford University Press, 2003.

Nietzsche, Friedrich. *The Will to Power*. New York: Vintage Books, 1968.

Nijhawan, Amita. "Excusing the Female Dancer: Tradition and Transgression in Bollywood Dancing." *South Asian Popular Culture* 7 (2009): 99–112.

Noe, Alva. *Out of Our Heads: Why You Are Not Your Brain, and Other Lessons from the Biology of Consciousness*. New York: Hill and Wang, 2009.

Nogami, Teruyo. *Waiting on the Weather: Making Movies with Akira Kurosawa*. Berkeley: Stone Bridge Press, 2006.

Ochoa, Todd. *Society of the Dead: Quita Manaquita and Palo Praise in Cuba*. Berkeley: University of California Press, 2010.

Oldham, Gabriella, ed. *First Cut: Conversations with Film Editors*. Berkeley: University of California Press, 1995.

Ondaatje, Michael. *The Conversations: Walter Murch and the Art of Editing Film*. New York: Knopf, 2002.

Orsini, Francesca, ed. *Love in South Asia: A Cultural History*. Cambridge: Cambridge University Press, 2006.

Ortner, Sherry. "Access: Reflections on Studying Up in Hollywood." *Ethnography* 11 (2010): 211–33.

Ortner, Sherry. *Not Hollywood: Independent Film at the Twilight of the American Dream*. Durham, NC: Duke University Press, 2013.

Pandian, Anand. "Cinema in the Countryside: Popular Tamil Film and the Remaking of Rural Life." In *Tamil Cinema: The Cultural Politics of India's Other Film Industry*, edited by Selvaraj Velayutham. London: Routledge, 2008.

Pandian, Anand. *Crooked Stalks: Cultivating Virtue in South India*. Durham, NC: Duke University Press, 2009.

Pandian, Anand. "The Ecology of What We Write." Spring 2015 Writers' Workshop Series, edited by Carole McGranahan. *Savage Minds*, March 2, 2015. http://savageminds.org/2015/03/02/the-ecology-of-what-we-write/.

Pandian, Anand. "In the Event of an Anthropological Thought." In *Wording the World: Veena Das and Scenes of Inheritance*, edited by Roma Chatterji, 258–72. New York: Fordham University Press, 2015.

Pandian, Anand. "Landscapes of Expression: Affective Encounters in South Indian Cinema." *Cinema Journal* 51 (2011): 50–74.

Pandian, Anand. "Reel Time: Ethnography and the Historical Ontology of the Cinematic Image." *Screen* 52 (2011): 193–214.

Pandian, Anand. "Thinking Like a Mountain." *Hau: Journal of Ethnographic Theory* 4 (2014): 245–52.

Pandian, Anand. "The Time of Anthropology: Notes from a Field of Contemporary Experience." *Cultural Anthropology* 27 (2012): 547–71.

Pandian, Anand, and M. P. Mariappan. *Ayya's Accounts: A Ledger of Hope in Modern India*. Bloomington: University of Indiana Press, 2014.

Pandian, M. S. S. *The Image Trap: M. G. Ramachandran in Film and Politics*. New Delhi: Sage, 1992.

Pandian, M. S. S. "*Parasakthi*: Life and Times of a DMK Film." In *Making Meaning in Indian Cinema*, edited by Ravi Vasudevan, 65–98. New Delhi: Oxford University Press, 2000.

Pandolfo, Stefania. *Impasse of the Angels: Scenes from a Moroccan Space of Memory*. Chicago: University of Chicago Press, 1997.

Pierson, Michele. "CGI Effects in Hollywood Science-Fiction Cinema 1989–95: The Wonder Years." *Screen* 40 (1999): 158–76.

Pinney, Christopher. *Photos of the Gods: The Printed Image and Political Struggle in India*. London: Reaktion Books, 2000.

Plantinga, Carl. *Moving Viewers: American Film and the Spectator's Experience*. Berkeley: University of California Press, 2009.

Poole, Robert. *Earthrise: How Man First Saw the Earth*. New Haven, CT: Yale University Press, 2008.

Povinelli, Elizabeth. "Routes/Worlds." *e-flux journal* 27 (September 2011).

Powdermaker, Hortense. *Hollywood: The Dream Factory*. New York: Arno Press, 1950.

Rabinow, Paul, George Marcus, James Faubion, and Tobias Rees. *Designs for an Anthropology of the Contemporary*. Durham, NC: Duke University Press, 2008.

Radhakrishnan, Ratheesh. "The Gulf in the Imagination: Migration, Malayalam Cinema, and Regional Identity." *Contributions to Indian Sociology* 43 (2009): 217–45.

Raffles, Hugh. *Insectopedia*. New York: Pantheon, 2010.

Rai, Amit. *Untimely Bollywood: Globalization and India's New Media Assemblage*. Durham, NC: Duke University Press, 2009.

Rajadhyaksha, Ashish. "The Phalke Era: Conflict of Traditional Form and Modern Technology." In *Interrogating Modernity: Culture and Colonialism in India*, edited by Tejaswini Niranjana, P. Sudhir, and Vivek Dhareshwar, 47–82. Calcutta: Seagull Books, 1993.

Rajadhyaksha, Ashish, and Paul Willemen. *Encyclopaedia of Indian Cinema*. London: British Film Institute, 1999.

Ram, Kalpana. "Bringing the Amman into Presence in Tamil Cinema: Cinema Spectatorship as Sensuous Apprehension." In *Tamil Cinema: The Cultural Politics of India's Other Film Industry*, edited by Selvaraj Velayutham, 44–58. London: Routledge, 2008.

Ramaswamy, Sundara. "The Chennai of My First Visit." In *Chennai Not Madras: Perspectives on the City*, edited by A. R. Venkatachalapathy, 91–100. New Delhi: Marg, 2006.

Reed, Adam. "Hope on Remand." *Journal of the Royal Anthropological Institute* 17 (2011): 527–44.

Rodowick, D. N. *Gilles Deleuze's Time Machine*. Durham, NC: Duke University Press, 1997.

Rouch, Jean. *Cine-Ethnography: Jean Rouch*. Edited by Steven Feld. Minneapolis: University of Minnesota Press, 2003.

Rubenstein, Mary-Jane. *Strange Wonder: The Closure of Metaphysics and the Opening of Awe*. New York: Columbia University Press, 2008.

Rushton, Richard. "Deleuzian Spectatorship." *Screen* 50 (2009): 45–53.

Rutherford, Anne. "Precarious Boundaries: Affect, Mise-en-Scène and the Senses." In *Art and the Performance of Memory: Sounds and Gestures of Reconciliation*, edited by Richard Cándida Smith, 63–84. New York: Routledge, 2002.

Sasikumar, M., and Anand Pandian. *Subramaniyapuram: The Tamil Film in English Translation*. Chennai: Blaft, 2014.

Schafer, R. Murray. *The Soundscape: Our Sonic Environment and the Tuning of the World*. Rochester, VT: Destiny Books, 1994.

Schivelbusch, Wolfgang. *Disenchanted Night: The Industrialization of Light in the Nineteenth Century*. Berkeley: University of California Press, 1988.

Schnapp, Jeffrey. "Crash (Speed as Engine of Individuation)." *Modernism/Modernity* 6 (1999): 1–49.

Schull, Natasha. *Addiction by Design: Machine Gambling in Las Vegas*. Princeton, NJ: Princeton University Press, 2012.

Scott, Michael W. "The Anthropology of Ontology (Religious Science?)." *Journal of the Royal Anthropological Institute* 19 (2013): 859–72.

Seed, David. *Cinematic Fictions: The Impact of the Cinema on the American Novel up to World War II*. Liverpool: Liverpool University Press, 2009.

Seifrid, Thomas. "Gazing on Life's Page: Perspectival Vision in Tolstoy." PMLA 113 (1998): 436–48.

Seizer, Susan. *Stigmas of the Tamil Stage: An Ethnography of Special Drama Artists in South India*. Durham, NC: Duke University Press, 2005.

Selby, Martha A., and Indira V. Peterson, eds. *Tamil Geographies: Cultural Constructions of Space and Place in South India*. Albany: State University of New York Press, 2009.

Sengupta, Suddhabrata. "Reflected Readings in Available Light: Cameramen in the Shadows of Hindi Cinema." In *Bollyworld: Popular Indian Cinema through a Transnational Lens*, edited by Raminder Kaur and Ajay Sinha, 118–40. New York: Sage, 2005.

Shaviro, Steven. *The Universe of Things: On Speculative Realism*. Minneapolis: University of Minnesota Press, 2014.

Shaviro, Steven. *Without Criteria: Kant, Whitehead, Deleuze and Aesthetics*. Cambridge, MA: MIT Press, 2009.

Shouse, Eric. "Feeling, Emotion, Affect." *M/C Journal* 8 (2005). http://journal.media -culture.org.au/0512/03-shouse.php.

Shulman, David. "The Buzz of God and the Click of Delight." In *Aesthetics in Performance: Formations of Symbolic Construction and Experience*, edited by Angela Hobart and Bruce Kapferer, 43–63. New York: Berghahn Books, 2005.

Shulman, David. "Dreaming the Self in South India." In *Dream Cultures: Explorations in the Comparative History of Dreaming*, edited by David Shulman and Guy Stroumsa, 43–73. New York: Oxford University Press, 1999.

Shulman, David. *More Than Real: A History of the Imagination in South India*. Cambridge, MA: Harvard University Press, 2012.

Siegel, Lee. *Net of Magic: Wonders and Deceptions in India*. Chicago: University of Chicago Press, 1991.

Simondon, Gilbert. "The Genesis of the Individual." In *Zone 6: Incorporations*, edited by Jonathan Crary and Sanford Kwinter, 297–319. Cambridge, MA: MIT Press, 1992.

Sivakumar. *Idhu Rajapattai Alla*. Translated by Malathi Rangarajan. Chennai: Alliance, 2010.

Sklarew, Bruce. "Freud and Film: Encounters in the *Weltgeist*." *Journal of the American Psychoanalytic Association* 47 (1999): 1239–47.

Sneath, David, Martin Holbraard, and Morten Pedersen. "Technologies of the Imagination: An Introduction." *Ethnos* 74 (2009): 5–30.

Sobchack, Vivian. *The Address of the Eye: A Phenomenology of Film Experience*. Princeton, NJ: Princeton University Press, 1992.

Sobchack, Vivian. *Carnal Thoughts: Embodiment and Moving Image Culture*. Berkeley: University of California Press, 2004.

Soneji, Davesh. *Unfinished Gestures: Devadasis, Memory and Modernity*. Chicago: University of Chicago Press, 2012.

Spinoza, Benedict. *A Spinoza Reader: The "Ethics" and Other Works*. Princeton, NJ: Princeton University Press, 1994.

Srinivas, S. V. *Megastar: Chiranjeevi and Telugu Cinema after N. T. Rama Rao*. New Delhi: Oxford University Press, 2009.

Staiger, Janet. "Authorship Approaches." In *Authorship and Film*, edited by David Gerstner and Janet Staiger, 27–60. New York: Routledge, 2003.

Stanislavski, Constantin. *An Actor's Work: A Student's Diary*. London: Routledge, 2008.

Stanislavski, Constantin. *Building a Character*. London: Methuen, 1968.

Stengers, Isabelle. *Thinking with Whitehead: A Free and Wild Creation of Concepts*. Cambridge, MA: Harvard University Press, 2011.

Sterne, Jonathan. *The Audible Past: Cultural Origins of Sound Reproduction*. Durham, NC: Duke University Press, 2003.

Stewart, Kathleen. *Ordinary Affects*. Durham, NC: Duke University Press, 2007.

Strathern, Marilyn. *Partial Connections*. Walnut Creek, CA: AltaMira Press, 2004.

Suhr, Christian, and Rane Willerslev. "Can Film Show the Invisible? The Work of Montage in Ethnographic Filmmaking." *Current Anthropology* 53 (2012): 282–301.

Taussig, Michael. *I Swear I Saw This: Drawings in Fieldwork Notebooks, Namely My Own*. Chicago: University of Chicago Press, 2011.

Taussig, Michael. *Shamanism, Colonialism and the Wild Man: A Study in Terror and Healing*. Chicago: University of Chicago Press, 1987.

Taussig, Michael. *What Color Is the Sacred?* Chicago: University of Chicago Press, 2009.

Taylor, Lucien. "Iconophobia: How Anthropology Lost It at the Movies." *Transition* 69 (1996): 64–88.

Thomas, Rosie. "Indian Cinema: Pleasures and Popularity." *Screen* 26 (1985): 116–31.

Tolstoy, Leo. *Hadji Murat*. London: Hesperus Press, 2003.

Trawick, Margaret. *Notes on Love in a Tamil Family*. Berkeley: University of California Press, 1992.

Tyler, Stephen A. "Post-modern Ethnography: From Document of the Occult to Occult Document." In *Writing Culture: The Politics and Poetics of Ethnography*, edited by James Clifford and George Marcus, 122–40. Berkeley: University of California Press, 1986.

Vasseleu, Cathryn. *Textures of Light: Vision and Touch in Irigaray, Levinas, and Merleau-Ponty*. London: Routledge, 1998.

Vasudevan, Ravi. *The Melodramatic Public: Film Form and Spectatorship in Indian Cinema*. New York: Palgrave Macmillan, 2011.

Velayutham, Selvaraj, ed. *Tamil Cinema: The Cultural Politics of India's Other Film Industry*. London: Routledge, 2008.

Venkatachalapathy, A. R. "Street Smart in Chennai: The City in Popular Imagination." In *The Unhurried City: Writings on Chennai*, edited by C. S. Lakshmi, 15–26. New Delhi: Penguin Books, 2004.

Venkatesan, Soumhya. "Rethinking Agency: Persons and Things in the Heterotopia of

'Traditional Indian Craft.'" *Journal of the Royal Anthropological Institute* 15 (2009): 78–95.

Vernant, Jean-Pierre. "At Man's Table: Hesiod's Foundation Myth of Sacrifice." In *The Cuisine of Sacrifice among the Greeks*, edited by Marcel Detienne and Jean-Pierre Vernant, 23–88. Chicago: University of Chicago Press, 1989.

Virdi, Jyotika. *The Cinematic ImagiNation: Indian Popular Films as Social History*. New Brunswick, NJ: Rutgers University Press, 2003.

Virilio, Paul. *War and Cinema: The Logistics of Perception*. New York: Verso, 1989.

Viveiros de Castro, Eduardo. "Cannibal Metaphysics: Amerindian Perspectivism." *Radical Philosophy* 182 (2013): 17–28.

Viveiros de Castro, Eduardo. *Cosmological Perspectivism in Amazonia and Elsewhere*. Masterclass Series 1. Manchester, UK: Hau Network of Ethnographic Theory, 2012.

Wagner, Roy. *The Invention of Culture*. Chicago: University of Chicago Press, 1981.

Wayne, Helena, ed. *The Story of a Marriage: The Letters of Bronislaw Malinowski and Elsie Masson*, Volume 1, 1916–20. London: Routledge, 1995.

Weber, Max. "Science as a Vocation." In *From Max Weber: Essays in Sociology*, edited by H. H. Gerth and C. Wright Mills, 129–58. New York: Oxford University Press, 1946.

White, Hayden. *Tropics of Discourse: Essays in Cultural Criticism*. Baltimore: Johns Hopkins University Press, 1978.

Whitehead, Alfred North. *Process and Reality: An Essay in Cosmology*. New York: Humanities Press, 1955.

Wilf, Eitan. *School for Cool: The Academic Jazz Program and the Paradox of Institutionalized Creativity*. Chicago: University of Chicago Press, 2014.

Wilkinson-Weber, Clare. "The Dressman's Line: Transforming the Work of Costumers in Popular Hindi Film." *Anthropological Quarterly* 79 (2006): 581–608.

Williams, Raymond. *Keywords: A Vocabulary of Culture and Society*. New York: Oxford University Press, 1983.

Wiseman, Boris. *Lévi-Strauss, Anthropology, and Aesthetics*. Cambridge: Cambridge University Press, 2007.

Wittgenstein, Ludwig. *Remarks on Colour*. New York: Wiley-Blackwell, 1991.

Young, Michael W. *Malinowski: Odyssey of an Anthropologist, 1884–1920*. New Haven, CT: Yale University Press, 2004.

Zajonc, Arthur. *Catching the Light: The Entwined History of Light and Mind*. New York: Oxford University Press, 1995.

INDEX

Abdul, J. A., 255
Abhinavagupta, 171–72, 179
action, flow of, 143–44
Address of the Eye, The (Sobchack), 289n9
Adi Velli [Friday in the month of Adi], 239–40
Adorno, Theodor, 305n18
Advaita Vedanta, 247
affect and emotion: affective thought, 270; German critical tradition and, 290n17; Spinoza on sadness, 261–62; Stewart on ordinary affects, 293n63; time and affective play of feelings, 147–48. *See also* desire; hope; pleasure; wonder
Ahmed, Sara, 91
Ajith Kumar (actor), 137, 143
Akkineni Sanjivi, 212, 306n13
Alagappan, A. L., 64
Ali, Daud, 174
Allison, Anne, 307n9 (ch17)
Althusser, Louis, 305n1
Alton, John, 116
Ameer (director), 188, 275–76
Amiratham theater, Madurai, 251
Amman (deity), 239–40
Amudhan, C. S., 199–202
Anderson, Joseph, 294n78
Angelopoulos, Theo, 297n24
animators, 247–49
Annamayya, 151, 156
Anthropocene as "anthroposcene," 17
anthropology of creation. *See* creation, anthropology of
anubavam ("experience"), 293n68. *See also* experience
aphrodisia, 173–74
Apocalypse Now, xii
apprenticeship system, 27–28
Aquinas, Thomas, 245

Argonauts of the Western Pacific (Malinowski), 14
art and art direction: art director Rajeevan, 69–84; bridge construction in Badami, 74–83; creativity and, 73–76; Dewey on, 71, 80; Gell on, 72, 82, 298n13, 298n16; Lévi-Strauss on native Northwest Coast art, 75–76; *maistry* (foreman), 73–74; nature-art relationship, 79–80; originality and, 74, 78; repetition and, 75–76, 298n10; sketches, 77–79
Arya (actor), 41, 259
Asal, 225–26, 258
aspiration. *See* hope
astrology, 265
audience: box-office success and, 260–66; classification of, 215–16; open cinematic structure and, 31–32; respect for, 290n19
Autodesk Maya, 247
Aval Peyar Tamilarasi [Her name is Tamilarasi], 252–66, 267, 269–70
Avatar, 241, 243
Avid digital editing system, 205, 213, 221, 231, 232
AVM Productions, 46, 73
Ayirathil Oruvan [One in a thousand], 102, 156, 175
Azim Cine Decors, Kodambakkam, 69

Bachelard, Gaston, 67–68
Bacon, Francis, 132–33
Badami, 74–83, 164
Bali (demon), 164
Balslev, Anindita Niyogi, 299n1, 301n5
Bana Kathadi [Kite], 168–79, 265
Baskaran, Theodore, 295n10, 306n8 (ch14)
Batchelor, David, 125